Regional Institutions, Geopolitics and Economics in the Asia-Pacific

This volume discusses the relationship between economics, geopolitics, and regional institutional growth and development in the Asia-Pacific region.

How do states (re)define their relationships amid the current global power transition? How do rival actors influence the rules and formation of new institutions for their own benefit? What role will institutions take as independent actors in influencing and constraining the behavior of states? Institutional development in Asia is characterized by idiosyncratic and diverse motivations (both material and non-material), a variety of policy strategies (strategic and norm-based), and the looming question of China's future depth of involvement as its economic position becomes more stable and its confidence in foreign affairs grows. The book reflects the broadening definition of Asia by examining multiple perspectives, including Japan, China, South Korea, the United States, Australia, India, Russia, and Taiwan. In addition to state actors, the contributors address several important regional institutions in development such as the ASEAN (+3, +6, and the East Asian Summit), the Asian Infrastructure Investment Bank (AIIB), the Asian Development Bank (ADB), existing security alliances, and other bilateral institutions. Ultimately, this volume describes the unique, slow, and diverse growth of a multitude of regional institutions, the complexities of generating cooperation, membership concerns, and competition between states and with existing institutions in the context of China's increasing confidence and strength.

This book will be of much interest to students of Asian politics, regional security, international organizations, and foreign policy.

Steven B. Rothman is Associate Professor of International Relations and Peace Studies at Ritsumeikan Asia Pacific University, Japan.

Utpal Vyas is Associate Professor of International Relations and Peace Studies at Ritsumeikan Asia Pacific University, Japan.

Yoichiro Sato is Professor of International Relations and Peace Studies at Ritsumeikan Asia Pacific University, Japan.

Asian Security Studies
Series Editors: Sumit Ganguly, *Indiana University, Bloomington*, Andrew Scobell, *Research and Development (RAND) Corporation, Santa Monica* and Joseph Chinyong Liow, *Nanyang Technological University, Singapore*.

Few regions of the world are fraught with as many security questions as Asia. Within this region it is possible to study great power rivalries, irredentist conflicts, nuclear and ballistic missile proliferation, secessionist movements, ethnoreligious conflicts and inter-state wars. This book series publishes the best possible scholarship on the security issues affecting the region, and includes detailed empirical studies, theoretically oriented case studies and policy-relevant analyses as well as more general works.

The Arms Race in Asia
Trends, causes and implications
Andrew T.H. Tan

Globalization and Security Relations across the Taiwan Strait
In the shadow of China
Edited by Ming-chin Monique Chu and Scott L. Kastner

Multilateral Asian Security Architecture
Non-ASEAN stakeholders
See Seng Tan

Chinese Foreign Relations with Weak Peripheral States
Asymmetrical economic power and insecurity
Jeffrey Reeves

Democratic Transition and Security in Pakistan
Edited by Shaun Gregory

China's Use of Military Force in Foreign Affairs
The dragon strikes
Markus B. Liegl

Regional Institutions, Geopolitics and Economics in the Asia Pacific
Evolving interests and strategies
Edited by Steven B. Rothman, Utpal Vyas and Yoichiro Sato

Regional Institutions, Geopolitics and Economics in the Asia-Pacific
Evolving Interests and Strategies

Edited by Steven B. Rothman, Utpal Vyas, and Yoichiro Sato

LONDON AND NEW YORK

First published 2017
by Routledge
2 Park Square, Milton Park, Abingdon, Oxon OX14 4RN

and by Routledge
711 Third Avenue, New York, NY 10017

Routledge is an imprint of the Taylor & Francis Group, an informa business

© 2017 selection and editorial material, Steven B. Rothman, Utpal Vyas, and Yoichiro Sato; individual chapters, the contributors

The right of the editors to be identified as the authors of the editorial material, and of the authors for their individual chapters, has been asserted in accordance with sections 77 and 78 of the Copyright, Designs and Patents Act 1988.

All rights reserved. No part of this book may be reprinted or reproduced or utilized in any form or by any electronic, mechanical, or other means, now known or hereafter invented, including photocopying and recording, or in any information storage or retrieval system, without permission in writing from the publishers.

Trademark notice: Product or corporate names may be trademarks or registered trademarks, and are used only for identification and explanation without intent to infringe.

British Library Cataloguing-in-Publication Data
A catalogue record for this book is available from the British Library

Library of Congress Cataloging-in-Publication Data
Names: Rothman, Steven B., editor. | Vyas, Utpal, editor. | Sato, Yoichiro, 1966-, editor.
Title: Regional institutions, geopolitics and economics in the Asia Pacific : evolving interests and strategies / edited by Steven B. Rothman, Utpal Vyas and Yoichiro Sato.
Description: Abingdon, Oxon ; New York : Routledge, 2017. | Series: Asian security studies | Includes bibliographical references and index.
Identifiers: LCCN 2016047795 | ISBN 9781138290860 (hardback) | ISBN 9781315265902 (ebook)
Subjects: LCSH: International agencies–Asia. | International agencies–Pacific Area. | Asian cooperation. | Asia–Foreign relations. | Pacific Area–Foreign relations. | Asia–Foreign economic relations. | Pacific Area–Foreign economic relations. | Geopolitics–Asia. | Geopolitics–Pacific Area. | ASEAN
Classification: LCC JZ5333 .R43 2017 | DDC 327.5—dc23
LC record available at https://lccn.loc.gov/2016047795

ISBN: 978-1-138-29086-0 (hbk)
ISBN: 978-1-315-26590-2 (ebk)

Typeset in Times New Roman
by Swales & Willis Ltd, Exeter, Devon, UK

Contents

Acknowledgements vii
List of illustrations viii
List of contributors ix
List of abbreviations xi

1 **Introduction** 1
   STEVEN B. ROTHMAN AND UTPAL VYAS WITH YOICHIRO SATO

2 **China and IR: geopolitical implications for Northeast Asia** 11
   CHRISTOPHER R. ROBICHAUD

3 **In pursuit of Asian Infrastructure Investment Bank: the politics and geopolitics of a Chinese bank** 27
   ALICE D. BA

4 **China's financial power in Asia: strategic implications of RMB internationalization for regional relations** 46
   UTPAL VYAS

5 **From Pan-Asianism to Act East: India's evolving perspectives and roles in East Asian regional institutions** 59
   VINDU MAI CHOTANI

6 **Taiwan's inconsistent involvement in China's maritime disputes under the "One China" institution** 75
   CHING-CHANG CHEN

7 **The Japan–China gentlemen's agreement over the Senkaku Islands** 93
   YOSHINORI KASEDA

8 Effects of Japanese security considerations on ASEAN+3 and the East Asia Summit 113
CHARLY VON SOLMS

9 Realist objectives, liberal means: Japan, China, and maritime security in Southeast Asia 127
HIDETAKA YOSHIMATSU AND DENNIS D. TRINIDAD

10 The South China Sea conflict, the regional geo-economic order, and ASEAN's institutions 144
KHENG SWE LIM

11 Russia's institutional engagement with the Asia-Pacific: getting more Asian and less Pacific 156
ARTYOM LUKIN

12 The Indian Ocean matters for East Asia: emerging Indo-Pacific interests in East Asian affairs 174
MICHAEL R. PORTER

13 Conclusions: interests and strategies in Asian regional institutional development 193
STEVEN B. ROTHMAN

Bibliography 201
Index 235

Acknowledgements

The three editors would like to express their gratitude to Ritsumeikan Asia Pacific University for funding a workshop at its campus in January 2015, which formed the basis of this book. The fund was made available through the International Academic Conference Subsidy of the Ritsumeikan Center for Asia Pacific Studies.

Illustrations

Figure

5.1 India's membership in regional multilateral institutions   65

Tables

8.1 History of ASEAN+3's institutional evolution   120
8.2 History of the East Asian Summit's institutional evolution   121

Contributors

Alice D. Ba is Professor of Political Science and International Relations at the University of Delaware, USA. Her research considers ASEAN-associated regionalisms and Southeast Asia's major power relations. An associate of American University's ASEAN Studies Center, she has received US-Fulbright awards for work in Beijing and Singapore.

Ching-Chang Chen (PhD Aberystwyth) is Associate Professor in the Department of Global Studies, Ryukoku University, Japan. His recent publications focus on the relationship between threat perceptions and national identity construction, theories and practices of international relations in Confucian Asia, and Sino-Japanese territorial disputes.

Vindu Mai Chotani is a Junior Fellow at the Observer Research Foundation, New Delhi, India. Her research focuses on Japanese foreign policy, geopolitics in the Indo-Pacific, and India–Japan relations. Ms. Chotani's latest paper addresses deepening India–Japan relations in the Bay of Bengal.

Yoshinori Kaseda is Professor at Ritsumeikan Asia Pacific University, Japan. He specializes in Japanese foreign policy and Northeast Asian security. His recent works appeared in books such as *United States Engagement in the Asia Pacific* (Cambria Press, 2015) and *One Korea* (Routledge, 2016).

Kheng Swe Lim is currently a PhD student in the Department of Politics and International Studies at Cambridge University, UK. He previously worked at the S. Rajaratnam School of International Studies in Singapore, where he worked on Sino–Southeast Asian political and economic relations.

Artyom Lukin is Associate Professor at the School of Regional and International Studies, Far Eastern Federal University, Vladivostok, Russia. Lukin does research on Asia-Pacific international politics and Russia's engagement with Asia. His latest book is *Russia's Far East: New Dynamics in Asia Pacific and Beyond* (Lynne Rienner Publishers, 2015).

Michael R. Porter is a researcher with the Center for Democracy Promotion, Ritsumeikan Center for Asia Pacific Studies, and a doctoral candidate at Ritsumeikan Asia Pacific University, Japan. His research focuses on US foreign policy in East Asia and the Indian Ocean maritime region.

Christopher R. Robichaud is a PhD candidate at Ritsumeikan Asia Pacific University in Beppu, Japan, and is also currently serving as the managing editor for the *Ritsumeikan Journal of Asia Pacific Studies*. He previously worked for the U.S. Department of Commerce in Washington, DC.

Steven B. Rothman is currently Associate Professor of International Relations and Peace Studies at Ritsumeikan Asia Pacific University, Beppu, Japan. His recent publications include discussions of the soft power concept, framing and rhetoric in the Japan–Russo war, framing of the Fukushima disaster, and several pedagogical studies.

Yoichiro Sato of Ritsumeikan Asia Pacific University also taught military and diplomatic officers at the U.S. Department of Defense's Asia-Pacific Center for Security Studies. His recent works include *The U.S.–Japan Security Alliance* (Palgrave, 2011) and *United States Engagement in the Asia Pacific* (Cambria, 2015).

Dennis D. Trinidad is Associate Professor at De La Salle University, Manila. He formerly served as visiting fellow at the Japan Institute of International Affairs, Tokyo and the Institute of Developing Economies. His most recent work appeared in the second issue of the *Asian Perspective* (2016).

Charly von Solms is a doctoral student at Waseda University, Tokyo. His PhD dissertation focuses on competing regional visions in East Asian regionalism and his other research interests include Japanese foreign policy and security in East Asia. He currently teaches at Tsuda College, Tokyo.

Utpal Vyas is Associate Professor (International Relations and Political Economy) at Ritsumeikan Asia Pacific University, Japan. He is the author of *Soft Power in Japan–China Relations: State, Sub-state and Non-state Relations* (Routledge, 2010), and co-editor of *The North Korea Crisis and Regional Responses* (East-West Center, 2015).

Hidetaka Yoshimatsu is Professor of Politics and International Relations at Ritsumeikan Asia Pacific University, Japan, as well as visiting research fellow at the University of Adelaide, Australia. His recent publications include *Comparing Institution-Building in East Asia: Power Politics, Governance, and Critical Junctures* (Palgrave Macmillan, 2014).

Abbreviations

ADB	Asian Development Bank
ADIZ	Air Defense Identification Zone
ADMM+	ASEAN Defense Ministers' Meeting+
AFC	Asian financial crisis
AFTA	ASEAN Free Trade Area
AIIB	Asian Infrastructure Investment Bank
AMF	ASEAN Maritime Forum
APEC	Asia-Pacific Economic Cooperation
APT	ASEAN Plus Three
ARF	ASEAN Regional Forum
ASEAN	Association of Southeast Asian Nations
ASEM	Asia–Europe Meeting
BIMSTEC	Bengal Initiative for Multi-Sectoral Technical and Economic Cooperation
BRIC	Brazil, Russia, India, and China
BRICS	Brazil, Russia, India, China, and South Africa
CBMs	confidence-building measures
CCP	Chinese Communist Party
CEPEA	Comprehensive Economic Partnership for East Asia
CICA	Conference on Interaction and Confidence Building Measures in Asia
CMIM	Chiang Mai Initiative Multilateralization
CNOOC	China National Offshore Oil Corporation
CP	Charoen Pokphand
DAC	Development Assistance Committee
DOC	Declaration on the Conduct
EAS	East Asia Summit
EAVG	East Asian Vision Group
EBRD	European Bank for Reconstruction and Development
ECAFE	Economic Commission for Asia and the Far East
ECSPI	East China Sea Peace Initiative
EEU	Eurasian Economic Union

EEZ	exclusive economic zone
ERIA	Economic Research Institute for ASEAN and East Asia
FDI	foreign direct investment
FONOPS	Freedom of Navigation Operations
FTA	free trade agreement
GDP	gross domestic product
HA/DR	humanitarian assistance and disaster relief
IMF	International Monetary Fund
IOR-ARC	Indian Ocean Rim Association for Regional Cooperation
IR	international relations
ISC	Information Sharing Centre
ISG	Inter-Sessional Group
JCG	Japan coast guard
KMT	Kuomintang (Chinese Nationalist Party)
MDB	multilateral development bank
MECO	Manila Economic and Cultural Office
MOU	memorandum of understanding
MPAC	Master Plan on Connectivity
MSF	Marine Surveillance Force
MSR	Maritime Silk Road
NAM	Non-Aligned Movement
NATO	North Atlantic Treaty Organization
ODA	official development assistance
OECD	Organization for Economic Cooperation and Development
PBG	Pan-Beibu Gulf
PBOC	People's Bank of China
PLA	People's Liberation Army
PLAN	People's Liberation Army Navy
POA	plan of action
PRC	People's Republic of China
RCEP	Regional Comprehensive Economic Partnership
ReCAAP	Regional Cooperation Agreement on Combating Piracy and Armed Robbery against Ships in Asia
RMB	renminbi
ROC	Republic of China
SAARC	South Asian Association for Regional Cooperation
SCO	Shanghai Cooperation Organization
SCSPI	South China Sea Peace Initiative
SEATO	Southeast Asian Treaty Organization
SPT	Six-Party Talks
SREB	Silk Road Economic Belt
TAC	Treaty of Amity and Cooperation in Southeast Asia
UK	United Kingdom

UN	United Nations
UNCLOS	UN Convention on the Law of the Sea
US	United States of America
USSR	Union of the Soviet Socialist Republic
WTO	World Trade Organization
ZOPFAN	Zone of Peace, Freedom and Neutrality

1 Introduction

*Steven B. Rothman and Utpal Vyas[1] with
Yoichiro Sato*

Introduction

The Asia-Pacific region continues to be a source of economic dynamism and strategic tension in the 21st century. During and after the end of the Cold War era, the Asia-Pacific's regional institutions and alliances developed in the context of heavy US involvement in the region. However, some countries maintain an underlying current of dissatisfaction with US dominance, while China concurrently rises and Japan weakens in strength and influence in the region. Changing priorities among regional actors, and in particular increased Chinese involvement in the development and form of regional institutions, generate a number of questions about the interaction of states in the Asia-Pacific. How do states inside and outside the region (re)define their relationships with and interests in each other? How do rival actors use their varying forms of power and linkages to influence the rules and formation of new institutions as well as their place within existing institutions? What role will institutions take as independent actors in influencing and constraining the behavior of states in the region?

As the international system globalizes, the number of actors with interest in the Asia-Pacific region broadens. The book reflects this increasing interest in the Asia-Pacific, with each chapter taking on different perspectives, including Japan, China, the United States, Australia, India, Russia, and Taiwan. These chapters pay particular attention to the different interests and motivations for developing, changing, or utilizing existing institutions in further development of regional integration as well as the problems these actors face. In addition to state actors, the papers address several important regional institutions in development such as the ASEAN (+3, +6, and the East Asian Summit), the Asian Infrastructure Investment Bank (AIIB), the Asian Development Bank (ADB), existing security alliances, and other bilateral institutions.

The chapters in this volume discuss the relationship between economic interests, motivations of state action, and the interaction of states in the potential for regional institutional development in the Asia region. As a whole, these papers present a stark reality of institutional development in Asia. Institutional development in Asia is characterized by idiosyncratic and diverse motivations (both material and non-material), a variety of policy strategies (strategic and norm-based), and the looming questions of China's future depth of involvement as its economic position becomes more stable and its confidence in foreign affairs grows. Ultimately the volume describes the unique slow and diverse growth of a multitude of regional institutions, the complexities of generating cooperation, membership concerns, and competition between states and with existing institutions in the context of China's increasing confidence and strength.

The research makes both theoretical and empirical contributions to the literature on Asian institutional development and international relations. The book uses theory pragmatically, applying the relevant theories and variables depending on the actors and questions discussed. For instance, for understanding motivations and interests of states, authors rely heavily on identity, values, and institutional influences. When discussing interaction between states in bargaining and institutional development, authors rely on theories of institution building, regimes, and strategic interaction grounded in relative power concerns. Empirically, the book contributes to current scholarship by examining institution building from an interaction of actors, and the dynamics occurring, rather than each actor individually. Since actors in Asia do not operate in isolation, scholars should examine them dynamically where decisions of each both depend on and influence the future decisions of other actors.

This book offers a middle-of-the road approach between limiting the analysis narrowly to formalized institutions and addressing international relations in the region with a more open definition of "institutions." Various other studies of regional institutions have focused more on multilateral institutions (such as ASEAN and its expanded meetings, ASEAN Regional Forum (ARF), and Asia-Pacific Economic Cooperation (APEC)). While many book-length studies examined these institutions, both individually and collectively,[2] some ongoing conceptualization and proposals for new institutions warrant the need for timely paper-length discussions. This book includes some chapters that address such issues. The former group also includes books focusing on bilateral security alliances. Several book-length analyses of each bilateral alliance exist,[3] and some discuss trilateralization of US alliances.[4] These discussions usually involve broader regional international relations, but do not specifically link with further "institution building" within the region.[5]

The latter group of books[6] provide a good academic debate between liberal and neorealist varieties of institutionalism; however, ongoing developments in regional institutions and relations since the publication of these studies need to be considered in order to build upon this debate. Hence, a book-length treatment of both formal and less formal institutions with updated empirical research is called for.

Theoretical framework

In order to provide context for the book, this introduction discusses the theoretical framework based on three perspectives: defining institutions, current theories of international institutions, and strategic use of institutions where the book makes its primary contribution.

Institutions

The chapters in this book refer to a wide variety of international institutions at various stages of development in the Asia-Pacific region. At the broadest level, institutions are "systems of established and prevalent social rules that structure social interactions."[7] Beyond this most basic level of defining institutions, various scholars have conceptualized institutions for particularities of research programs by adding additional criteria. For instance, institutions may be defined by formality, functionality, or degree of internationalization. As more criteria are added, the definition of an institution narrows, adding particular values as defining elements as they take on central components of a scholarly research program.[8]

Some scholars have defined institutions in terms of formality because theory might suggest that more formalized and defined institutions have different effects on actors. Thus, scholars defined institutions based on the degree of formalization or "weakness" in terms of the degree of internalization or formal bureaucracy.[9] There have been various formulations of this distinction, and further subdivisions of each type:[10] however, for the purposes of this book, informal institutions, usually emphasized more by English School and constructivist scholars, generally consist of norms, practices, or habitual behaviors. Formal institutions tend more toward specific rules, legal frameworks, and organizations. In some instances, informal institutions evolve or formalize as treaties and organizations; it is also possible for newly created formal institutions to introduce new international norms and practices.[11] The degree of institutionalization can also be seen as a sliding scale[12] – some international norms are more entrenched (internalized), and equally some international treaties and organizations are more effective and purposeful.

Other scholars defined international treaties based on a number of criteria, including the formalization or weakness of the substantive measures in the text, as well as degree of internationalization (bilateral or multilateral), and other factors because they were of interest to the scholarly research program.[13]

Some scholars consider informal institutions as close relations to successfully internalized norms and practices.[14] The almost universally internalized norm of sovereignty, for instance, has led to an institutionalized system of international relations whereby a host of practices and behaviors morphed into an accepted institutional structure underpinning the relations between states. This is more self-evident in a region such as the Asia-Pacific, where formal institutions are weak. As can be seen from several of the chapters in this book, an institutional structure of relations exists in the Asia-Pacific, which depends on ideas and practices built up in the post Pacific War era and post Cold War era. Norms such as non-interference, a strong notion of state sovereignty, and related ideas based on an often post-colonial form of nationalism have led to a generally accepted way of conducting diplomacy and visualizing international relations in the region.

This informal institutionalization of relations has defined a base on which it has been difficult to build more formal international institutions, and yet which has enabled the reasonably smooth economic integration of the Asia-Pacific region in the post Cold War era. It is also clear from the chapters in this book that the rise of China challenges this informal institutional structure,[15] along with China's more formal institutional challenges.[16]

Theories of international institutions

The current state of research on formal international institutions suggests their importance in a variety of contexts as an independent influence on international affairs. Institutions act as agents in dispute settlement, as forums for international communication and as a repository for information, as a means to establish trust and initial frameworks for further cooperation, and as financial pools for states to generate public goods. Some of these institutions act as simple agents of the states, where the states hold all or the majority of power (e.g., the UN Security Council),[17] while other institutions act independently of the states even to the point of self-declared universal jurisdiction (e.g., the International Criminal Court).[18]

Neo-liberal institutionalist theory suggests that formal institutions arise out of need, in a functionalist sense, to provide increased information sharing, coordination, a reduction in transaction costs, and coordination of activities.[19] Formal institutions may also provide side benefits and external costs associated with their creation. Even given the anarchic system assumption adopted by both neo-liberal institutionalist theory and realism, institutions may emerge when security concerns are largely alleviated, such as under a benign hegemonic system.[20] Repeated interactions among the members and a continued desire for the institution sustain these institutions once created. In addition, institutions are long-lasting and have "staying power" or "robustness" when coupled with bureaucracies or linked to other international institutions.[21] The more a particular institution becomes linked and intertwined with other aspects of international affairs, the more likely that institution will persist.

Realist theories suggest, contrarily, that institutions are short-lived and difficult to develop and maintain because of state concern over relative power changes.[22] Despite concerns over relative power changes, the difficulty in assessing power differences, especially among many states (rather than just two), makes the concerns less important than the benefits from cooperation.[23] Institutions generally persist during times of crisis or difficulty, but deep entanglement between nations becomes disadvantageous to preserving security.[24] However, empirical studies show that institutions seem to persist beyond their original purpose and established mandate.[25]

In much of the research on international institutions, theories from Realpolitik and liberal institutionalism remain as separate entities and descriptions of how institutions operate. In particular, realist theories often point to state agents rather than emphasizing the exogenous effects on states described by liberal institutionalist theory. The debate, in a simplest form, involves whether the states are agents of change or institutions are agents of change. This debate continues to follow standard divisions between realist and liberal-institutionalist lines.

Strategic use of international institutions

One area left underexplored in this research because of the division along the lines of agency involves the ways states may use institutions as means of accomplishing their goals in international politics. Research in this realm can accept that institutions have an independent effect on states and that states have an inherent Realpolitik view of institutions to use them as a means to an end. This combination of theories resembles more closely Riker's theories on heresthetics, or working within a set of rules and constraints while also manipulating some factors that help achieve greater personal gains.[26] These manipulations involve formal agenda setting, rhetorical framing, use of amendment procedures and other rules within institutions, as well as other tactics.[27] They run the gamut of theoretical perspectives from constructivist emphasis on the importance of rhetoric and constructed understanding and identity, the institutional emphasis on institutional rules and mandates, and the realist emphasis on strategic, self-interest, and power relations.

As Riker comments, heresthetics is an art more than a science,[28] and therefore requires deep description and understanding of the political behaviors of actors and the circumstances from where they act. In international affairs, heresthetics is much more difficult to measure and research than in smaller domestic institutions or election cycles. States do not make their intentions clear, often maintain conflicting motivations, and rarely allow for additional questions or experiments after the events to determine such motivations and intentions.

Despite the difficulties, some research discusses the importance of institutions in geostrategic politics and political use of institutions to increase gains for states. The use of institutions generally flows across factors such as agenda setting,[29] framing and rhetorical communication,[30] use of institutional rules to change outcomes or votes, forum shopping,[31] and the development of new institutions to create or influence the international order.[32]

Agenda setting within institutions allows actors to use their executive power to manipulate the agenda, creating favorable outcomes based on the institutional formally specified rules. States may create institutions in order to define appropriate behavior or frame an issue, while not providing strong rules or enforcement mechanisms. Human rights agreements, for example, often define appropriate behavior and attempt to gain frame discussions without enforcing states to abide by precise rules. Forum shopping occurs most often in the European Union, where actors have the choice of institutions to utilize for their particular purpose, such as local, state, or regional courts in which to file their particular grievances that would give them the most favorable outcome. Finally, during times of heightened power in the international system, states may utilize their advantage to "lock in" particular rules and customs for the future when their power declines. This occurred dramatically after the end of World War II, as the United States and allies set up favorable institutions toward democracy and capitalist markets.

In most studies of heresthetics, actors operate within a system of formal rules and institutional constraints. In international politics, however, states can generate new institutions and rules for states, compelling other states to join enticed by benefits (or relative benefits compared to the alternative). This means that strategic influence in international affairs not only involves actions within institutions, but also the development of new institutions and rule changes within international institutions.

This study improves our understanding of the theories behind strategic development of institutions as well as the formation of new institutions and strategic interaction among states in East Asia. Through a deep examination of a number of cases where states in East Asia engage in institutional creation, change, and manipulation, we are better able to understand how states interact with institutions strategically. Not all the chapters in the book direct attention to theoretical claims or make theoretical contributions. As mentioned earlier, the book combines chapters that make empirical contributions with those that make theoretical ones, though most of the authors maintain similar assumptions of the international political system. Those assumptions amount to the importance of state policy to promote a varied self-interest and that the variables influencing state policy and international relations are numerous, including non-material factors, such as identity and discourse.

Institutional development in the Asia-Pacific

The development of institutions in the Asia-Pacific during the post-war era has been shaped by the combination of the Cold War context and the emergence of new nations and rivalries throughout the region. Cooperation was defined by nations' links to the capitalist bloc backed by the United States or by support from the Soviet Union for communist governments. A few nations purported to belong to neither bloc, but to be "non-aligned." The institutions which developed during this period were limited to establishing diplomatic channels based on a strict definition of sovereignty and nationalism, i.e., precluding any genuine cooperation based on pooling of sovereignty.

Informal institutions

In addition to international diplomacy, other informal institutions, such as trading relationships and development relationships, were formed. One important regional institutional framework was developed by Japan, the preeminent economic power in the region, which formed trade and investment links on a bilateral basis with most nations in the region after concluding peace and friendship treaties. It followed this in the 1970s with increased development aid, using its dollar trade surpluses to create close economic links between itself and its markets throughout Southeast Asia in particular. After its 1978 conclusion of a peace treaty with the People's Republic of China, that country came to be included in the development, investment, and trading regime led by Japan. These Japan-centered relationships continued to be vital to informal institutionalization in the region through to the 1990s. Important aspects of this institutional structure included the use of development partnerships between Japan and partner countries, rather than free trade agreements, and the importance of the *keiretsu* conglomerate pattern of building regional production networks across East Asia.[33] It is important to note that issues of national sovereignty were addressed by not including free trade as a goal (protection of domestic industries is prized in Japan, as in most countries in East Asia). Additionally, national security sovereignty concerns in the reason were avoided by concentrating on economic links. The result of this concentration on economic links has led to the deep economic linkages across the Asia-Pacific, based on informal institutions and bilateral agreements.[34]

In fact, the development of formal regional institutions in the field of security was also stymied by the preferred approach of the United States to its allies in the region. The United States has not generally encouraged multilateral regional organizations in East Asia (in contrast to Europe), as it has preferred to deal with each nation on a bilateral basis. This was the case in the Cold War period, and has equally been the case afterwards; after a decline in US influence in the region, George Bush's "war on terror" led to an increase in security involvement across the region on bilateral bases.

Formal institutions

Notwithstanding the US position, there have been attempts to create more formal regional institutions in the region despite the Cold War background. Security institutions such as the Southeast Asian Treaty Organization (modeled on NATO), and the nascent Association of Southeast Asian Nations were created with an eye to reducing security tensions and increasing economic links in the region. However, the overwhelming need to accommodate national security interests meant that these organizations were not able to develop very far during the Cold War era.

In the post Cold War era, the aforementioned informal institutional structure led to increased economic integration in the region. At the same time there were various attempts to initiate region-wide forums and institutions to formalize multilateral regional relationships. The Japanese-led ADB has been one of these formal institutions; it has formalized the development relationships between Japan, the United States, and other Asian countries.

However, ASEAN in particular has emerged as the initiator and driver of most regional initiatives,[35] with the tacit acceptance of Japan and the United States. With the end of the Cold War and the perceived advance of other regional blocs around the world, ASEAN shifted its focus to economic cooperation and development among its members, and the inclusion of former Communist-bloc nations Vietnam, Cambodia, and Laos. To this end, ASEAN formally expanded its membership to include these three, plus Myanmar. The ASEAN Free Trade Area (AFTA) was one result of this push, and it is still one of the most successful regional institutions, although it is difficult to describe it as truly multilateral. AFTA embodies the pattern for East Asian regional organizations of not encroaching issues of national sovereignty and of emphasizing consensus decision making. ASEAN has also been instrumental in creating space to include Japan, China, and South Korea in regional institution building, as Chapter 7 of this volume mentions.

As several of the chapters in this book mention, the particular development of informal and formal institutions in the Asia-Pacific has led to increased significance for so-called Track 2 negotiations.[36] In practice, economic institutions and cooperation forums that do not obviously impinge on perceptions of national sovereignty have often helped to coordinate diplomacy and security approaches in the region and avoid the potentially disastrous consequence of nationalist public rhetoric regarding territorial sovereignty. Perhaps more so than in Europe and other regions, these back-door negotiations have allowed nations in the Asia-Pacific to avoid conflicts in recent decades, despite the apparently increasing tensions. These institutions, which consist of seminars and policy meetings among government officials, academics, and other experts from the across the region, allow Asia-Pacific governments to assess the true security risks and opportunities which face them today.

In more recent years, it is clear that China has been the regional power which is pushing for more formal regional institutions. Traditionally rather reticent to promote regional governance, China has accelerated its initiatives after its accession to the World Trade Organization, and in particular since the beginning of Xi Jinping-led regime. Its most conspicuous project in recent times has been the AIIB, a clear attempt to challenge the incumbent ADB and development cooperation paradigms developed by Japan and the United States. In addition to this has been its Silk Road initiative, pushing through Central Asia. In the field of security, the Shanghai Six organization has attempted to coordinate responses to the perceived threat of Muslim extremism in the region. It is also actively promoting regional free trade, with the AFTA–China agreement, and the Regional Comprehensive Economic Partnership agreement.

While the territorial dispute-related tensions in the South China Sea and in the Japan Sea have prevented any effective regional security organizations forming, the proliferation of economic agreements, regional discussion forums, and cooperation in technical issues shows that there is will to create regional institutions and cooperation. It is also clear that the nations in the Asia-Pacific region are still grappling for institutions which can effectively serve the security and economic needs of the region.

Chapter overviews

The authors of the various chapters in this volume present a broad overview of recent changes in the institutional structures in the Asia-Pacific, in consideration of the points raised in this introduction.

In Chapter 2, Robichaud describes how China's changing foreign-policy stance profoundly affects the whole region and its institutional structures. In Chapter 3, Ba focuses on the case of the AIIB, a new Chinese-led institution that promises to shake up previous assumptions of how institutions work and interact in the region. Chapter 4 sees Vyas consider another facet of China's changing influence on regional institutional structures, in the case of its increasing push for financial influence with the internationalization of China's national currency, the renminbi. In Chapter 5, Chotani considers the growing role of India in institutional arrangements, whereas in Chapter 6, Chen considers the strategic situation in Asia, and how China and Taiwan's complicated and wary relationship affects tensions in the South China Sea. The focus then changes to Japan in Chapter 7, where Kaseda analyzes changes in Japan's foreign policies towards China, South Korea, and the United States. In Chapter 8, von Solms looks at the development of ASEAN-led institutions, including

Japan, China, and South Korea. Yoshimatsu and Trinidad turn to the strategic economic influence of Japan and China on institutions in Southeast Asia and the effects on the South China Sea disputes in Chapter 9. Lim in Chapter 10 considers South China Sea issues from a Southeast Asian viewpoint. Chapters 11 and 12 supply perspectives from the outer edges of the Asia-Pacific institutional structure. In Chapter 11, Lukin surveys Russia's varied strategic and economic interests in the Asia-Pacific institutional structure. In Chapter 12 Porter considers the increasing importance of the Indian Ocean and nations with interests in it. In the final chapter, Rothman presents an overview and synthesis of the book's arguments.

Notes

1 The first two authors contributed equally to the chapter, though these names are presented in alphabetical order.
2 Mark Beeson. *Institutions of the Asia-Pacific: ASEAN, APEC, and Beyond*. London: Routledge, 2009.
3 Andrew Oros. *Normalizing Japan: Politics, Identity, and the Evolution of Security Practice*. Stanford: Stanford University Press, 2009; Scott Snyder, ed. *The US–South Korea Alliance: Meeting New Security Challenges*. Boulder: Lynne Rienner, 2012; Greg Sheridan. *The Partnership: The Inside Story of the US–Australian Alliance Under Howard and Bush*. Sydney: University of New South Wales Press, 2006.
4 William Tow, Mark Thomson, Yoshinobu Yamamoto, and Satu Limaye, eds. *Asia-Pacific Security: US, Australia and Japan and the New Security Triangle*. London: Routledge, 2007; Victor Cha. *Alignment Despite Antagonism: The United States–Korea–Japan Security Triangle*. Stanford: Stanford University Press, 2000.
5 Takashi Inoguchi, G. John Ikenberry, and Yoichiro Sato, eds. *The U.S.–Japan Security Alliance: Regional Multilateralism*. New York: Palgrave Macmillan, 2011.
6 Tow et al., eds. *Asia-Pacific Security: US, Australia and Japan and the New Security Triangle*. Abingdon: Routledge, 2007; Amitav Acharya and Evelyn Goh, eds. *Reassessing Security Cooperation in the Asia-Pacific: Competition, Congruence, and Transformation*. Cambridge: MIT, 2007.
7 Geoffrey M. Hodgson. "What Are Institutions?" *Journal of Economic Issues*, XL, no. 1 (2006): 2.
8 For a discussion on conceptualization, see Gary Goertz. *Social Science Concepts: A User's Guide*. Princeton, NJ: Princeton University Press, 2005.
9 Douglass C. North. *Institutions, Institutional Change and Economic Performance* 4. Cambridge, UK: Cambridge University Press, 1990.
10 Stephen D. Krasner. *Sovereignty: Organized Hypocrisy*. Princeton, NJ: Princeton University Press, 1999; Robert O. Keohane. "International Institutions: Two Approaches." *International Studies Quarterly*, 32, no. 4 (1988): 379–96; Barry Buzan. *From International to World Society? English School Theory and the Social Structure of Globalisation*. Cambridge: Cambridge University Press, 2004.
11 Kilian Spandler. "The Political International Society: Change in Primary and Secondary Institutions." *Review of International Studies*, 41, no. 3 (2015): 601–22.
12 Krasner, *Sovereignty: Organized Hypocrisy*.
13 Ronald B. Mitchell. "International Environmental Agreements: A Survey of Their Features, Formation, and Effects." *Annual Review of Environmental Resources*, 28 (2003): 429–61.
14 Keohane, "International Institutions: Two Approaches."
15 For example, see the chapters by Robichaud, Vyas, and Kaseda in this volume.
16 See chapters by Von Solms, Ba, and Lim in this volume.

17 John J. Mearsheimer. "The False Promise of International Institutions." *International Security,* 19, no. 3, Winter (1994): 5–49.
18 Robert O. Keohane and Lisa L. Martin. "The Promise of Institutionalist Theory." *International Security,* 20, no. 1, Summer (1995): 39–51.
19 Robert O. Keohane. *After Hegemony: Cooperation and Discord in the World Political Economy.* Princeton, NJ: Princeton University Press, 1984; Robert O. Keohane. "The Demand for International Regimes." In *International Regimes,* edited by Stephen D. Krasner, x, 372. Ithaca, NY: Cornell University Press, 1983.
20 Keohane, *After Hegemony: Cooperation and Discord in the World Political Economy.*
21 Andreas Hasenclever, Peter Mayer, and Volker Rittberger. "Interests, Power, Knowledge: The Study of International Regimes." *Mershon International Studies Review,* 40, no. 2 (1996): 177–228.
22 Joseph M. Grieco. "Anarchy and the Limits of Cooperation: A Realist Critique of the Newest Liberal Institutionalism." In *Neorealism and Neoliberalism: The Contemporary Debate,* edited by David A. Baldwin. New York: Columbia University Press, 1988.
23 Duncan Snidal. "Relative Gains and the Pattern of International Cooperation." *American Political Science Review,* 85, September (1991): 701–26.
24 Jack L. Snyder. "The Security Dilemma in Alliance Politics." *World Politics,* 36, no. 4, July (1984): 461–95.
25 Hasenclever, Mayer, and Rittberger, "Interests, Power, Knowledge: The Study of International Regimes."
26 William H. Riker. *The Art of Political Manipulation.* New Haven, CT: Yale University Press, 1986.
27 Ibid.
28 Ibid.
29 Mark A. Pollack. "Delegation, Agency, and Agenda Setting in the European Community." *International Organization,* 51, no. 1 (1997): 99–134.
30 Marc A. Levy. "Is the Environment a National Security Issue?" *International Security,* 20, no. 2 (1995): 35–62.
31 Marc L. Busch. "Overlapping Institutions, Forum Shopping, and Dispute Settlement in International Trade." *International Organization,* 61, Fall (2007): 735–61.
32 G. John Ikenberry. *After Victory: Institutions, Strategic Restraint, and the Rebuilding of Order after Major Wars, Princeton Studies in International History and Politics.* Princeton, NJ: Princeton University Press, 2001.
33 Christopher M. Dent. *East Asian Regionalism.* Abingdon, Oxon: Routledge, 2008.
34 Etel Solingen. "East Asian Regional Institutions: Characteristics, Sources, Distinctiveness." In *Remapping East Asia: The Construction of a Region,* edited by T.J. Pempel, 31–53. New York: Cornell University Press, 2005; Desmond Ball. "Multilateral Security Cooperation in the Asia-Pacific Region." In *The Security Environment In The Asia-Pacific,* edited by Hung-mao and Tun-jen Cheng Tien. Armonk: ME Sharpe, 2000; Giovanni Capannelli, Jong-Wha Lee, and Peter Petri. *Developing Indicators for Regional Economic Integration and Cooperation.* Asian Development Bank, 2009. http://www.adb.org/publications/developing-indicators-regional-economic-integration-and-cooperation (accessed June 1, 2015); ADB. *Asian Economic Monitor.* Asian Development Bank. March 2013. http://www.adb.org/publications/asian-economic-integration-monitor-march-2013 (accessed June 1, 2015).
35 Ralf Emmers. *ASEAN and the Institutionalization of East Asia.* Routledge Security in Asia Pacific Series. New York: Routledge, 2012.
36 Charles E. Morrison. "Track 1/Track 2 Symbiosis in Asia-Pacific Regionalism." *Pacific Review* 17, no. 4 (2004): 547–65; Desmond Ball, Anthony Milner, and Brendan Taylor. "Track 2 Security Dialogue in the Asia-Pacific: Reflections and Future Directions." *Asian Security,* 2, no. 3 (2006): 174–88.

2 China and IR

Geopolitical implications for Northeast Asia

Christopher R. Robichaud

Introduction

In April 2014 *The Economist* published an article titled "Crowning the Dragon," proclaiming, based on newly released economic data, that China would overtake the United States' position of economic primacy by the year's end, cleverly concluding, "The American Century ends, and the Pacific Century begins."[1] Though it is unnecessary to overemphasize an article of this nature, it is important to note the context within which it was written. It is well accepted that we are in a transformative period in our history. It is almost cliché to mention the end of the Cold War and the emergence of a unipolar international system, dominated by the United States, and how that framework has been thrown into a new global makeup. The ever-evolving nature of the international order finds China, today, conveniently poised to make a regional challenge in Asia, and reassume its self-perceived role as the cultural, political, and military anchor of East Asia. The "rise of China" is the central international relations (IR) issue with which contemporary scholars of IR must contend. The distribution and redistribution of power, regionally and globally, will be decisively affected by what China's future has to offer.

The positivist nature of the quantifiable elements of IR, those that allow for decisive proclamations of an end to the "American Century," lend themselves well to the modern proclivity for all things scientific. Auguste Comte articulated this at its most basic level in his exposition of positive philosophy (conveniently the title of his three-volume work on the topic) when he wrote, "it is only by knowing the laws of phenomena, and thus being able to foresee them, that we can, in active life, set them to modify one another to our advantage."[2] The risk of over-reliance, however, on exclusively positive frames of analysis in IR research is the neglect of its constituent social complexities. The rise of China demands a proper accounting of these complexities if we are to truly understand what is occurring, and what is at stake.

To date, the wealth of China research in the field of IR has made significant inroads to this end. Recently, there has been increasing interest in explorations of a "Chinese School" of IR, as well as a more general interest in the state of IR research in China. Central to these kinds of research has been the perceptions and interpretations of Western theories of IR. As China has opened up and increasingly engaged the global community, so too have Chinese sources of foreign policy. This chapter builds on the existing research by analyzing the Chinese perception of IR and import of Western theory into a pragmatic foreign-policy program. This approach demonstrates that Chinese foreign-policy behavior, traditionally guided by the ideology of elite decision makers, adopts external theories employed as practical guides. This application of IR theory suggests China will be more engaged in fulfilling its "new" role as a great power. For Northeast Asia, this will mean less room for the settlement of territorial disputes, while at the same time stronger pushes for regional economic integration.

Historical and geopolitical context

Much of China's early history is characterized by an almost unique condition of geopolitical security and stability. The traditional buffers of Xinjiang, Tibet, the Korean Peninsula, and the eastern coast provided China's imperial dynasties with substantial insulation against foreign invaders. The eastern coast, once viewed as among China's greatest geographically strategic assets, became one of its softest weak points with the intervention of Western powers beginning in the late 18th century.

It was at this point that China began to endure its "humiliation." The source of this humiliation stemmed both from a series of unfair treaties and exploits on Chinese sovereign territory, as well as from the realization that China's political and economic traditions were not capable of competing with the modern states it then found itself confronting.[3] China was unwittingly thrust into a Westphalian state system and the educated elite realized that China had to change if it hoped to preserve anything that resembled its former glory. Thus, a distinct sense of sovereignty developed in China as a means of salvaging what little independence and domestic stability it could. Foreign intervention and ideas played a large role in the upheavals that beset China in the late 19th century, all the way up to the establishment of the People's Republic of China (PRC) on October 1, 1949. Over this nearly 100-year period, foreign political and economic ideas took hold of the educated elites, from anarchism to democracy, Marxism to capitalism. Common among these ideologies was an insistence on the preservation of territorial integrity and Chinese sovereignty. Ultimately it would be the Chinese Communist Party (CCP) that would harness and perpetuate the new "nationalism" to its domestic and foreign advantages.

History of international relations and the Chinese experience

Before I delve into a discussion of IR theory in China, a helpful distinction needs to be made between IR as practice, and IR as an academic field of study. The latter is born from and concerned with the former. IR is exclusively concerned with the state. Our modern conception of the state is itself a recent development. It wasn't until the mid 17th century, at the earliest, with the peace of Westphalia, that the state began to take shape.[4]

In China, as in the West, the systematic study of IR did not emerge until several centuries after the peace of Westphalia.[5] To assert that the origins of a systematic study of IR is a product of more modern concerns is by no means meant to downplay the importance of political thought that gave rise to IR – Hobbes' *Leviathan*, Locke's *Two Treatises of Government*, Rousseau's *The Social Contract*, or Kant's *Perpetual Peace*, among so many others.[6] In the West, a structured interest in IR was spurred on by the rapid rate at which states themselves were evolving and interacting with one another. National economies, a phenomenon that substantively emerged in the 19th century, oriented state interests toward the material. The state existed for the benefit of society. To provide for society, a state had to compete with other states. Andreas Osiander, a strong proponent of a historical understanding of the origins of IR, contends that the systematic study of IR was driven by a series of "crises of the state," set upon it by industrialization, and stimulated by increasing commercial integration and dependence among states.[7] This understanding of the emergence of IR research is supported by some of the earliest IR scholarship, which concerns itself with these very issues.[8]

The first academic department focused on IR was formally established with the Woodrow Wilson Chair of International Politics at Aberystwyth University, Wales, in 1919, soon followed by the Walsh School of Foreign Service at Georgetown that same year. In contrast to what Osiander points to as the source of the development of IR in Europe, much of what was to become IR in the United States was born from a structured consideration of the nature of the state and conceptions of sovereignty, both pursued in response to American concerns regarding European imperialism.[9] Interestingly, the fate of China unsettled American scholars the most. The first book written as an examination of world politics best elaborates this point. *World Politics at the End of the Nineteenth Century as Influenced by the Oriental Situation* was an American scholar's response to European imperialist pursuits in the Far East, and the rise of increasingly dangerous forms of nationalism fueled by what we can now understand as Osiander's "crisis of the state."[10]

The United States officially pushed back against the progression of imperialism in China through the promotion of an open-door policy. In many respects, this helped preserve some semblance of sovereignty for the transitioning, fractured, and otherwise unstable Chinese government of the time. The United Kingdom, and subsequently the other European powers with interests in China, agreed to and upheld a form of this policy until the outbreak of the Second World War.[11]

International relations in China

With an understanding of the contours of the origins of IR in the West firmly in hand, let us turn to an examination of how IR evolved in China. David Shambaugh has been a key figure in documenting how the discipline and study of IR have taken shape in China since 1949. By the mid-1980s the conservative approach to Marxist–Leninist–Maoist theory, enshrined in the personality cult of Mao Zedong, was presumably no longer the *sole* guiding light of the CCP.

This allowed for some optimism with regard to the development of IR studies. Despite this, however, the state of Chinese studies of IR remained unimpressive.[12] Though Shambaugh notes a number of other weaknesses in IR studies as he saw and experienced them during the 1980s, it was the lingering adherence to Marxism–Leninism at the exclusion of all other points of view that did the most to limit China's ability to push the boundaries of knowledge in the field.[13] This, in large part, was fueled by the pre-1978 *raison d'être* of IR studies in China. Not only was it guided by Marxism–Leninism, it was geared toward intelligence purposes, reflecting a certain amount of Soviet influences.[14] This is in sharp contrast to the IR that developed in the West, rooted in scholarly pursuits; concerned with the realm of policy, but not beholden to it.

The root of the discord between Western IR and that of communist China can be best understood through a lens of the theory of education in China during the Mao years. Lu Dingyi writes, "The educational policy of the Chinese Communist Party has always been that education should serve the politics of the working class and be combined with productive labour; and to apply this policy, education must be led by the Communist Party."[15] Mao had previously articulated this dynamic between theory and practice in the formation of knowledge, prior to the establishment of the PRC.[16] If we juxtapose this theory of education with how IR developed in the West, we can observe a deeply rooted philosophical difference in how the discipline was approached. In China, IR's dependence on practice lent itself well to ideological manipulation, leaving no room for theoretical advancement.

Higher education in general suffered a great deal between the late 1950s with the beginning of the Great Leap Forward until the late 1970s and the end of the Cultural Revolution.[17] Programs associated with the study of politics outside the party line were shut down. Programs with an international focus were especially vulnerable to accusations of harboring reactionary or imperialist sympathies. In fact, one of the core foreign-policy tenets of this period, "leaning to one side," has been cited as a driving force behind educational reforms that resulted in the radicalization of the Chinese higher education system.[18]

Although studies of international affairs and politics drew suspicion, and in most instances programs were shut down, this was not always the case. As previously mentioned, international studies had been leveraged for their important role in intelligence analysis. Thus, The College of Foreign Affairs at Renmin University was initiated in 1955, followed by programs at Peking, Fudan, and Renmin Universities in International Politics in 1964.[19] There were additional programs at other institutions, though these were more intimately tied to the direct need for intelligence. The Shanghai Institute for International Studies, for example, was established in 1960, while the Chinese Academy of Sciences, which had under its auspices the World Economic Institute and a division on world politics, established programs for international studies on Latin America, Asia, and Africa.[20] In May 1977 the Chinese Academy of Social Sciences took on the responsibility of overseeing research in the 14 departments that once made up the Department of Philosophy and Social Science.[21]

The over-dependence on, and narrow lens of, Marxist–Leninist–Mao Zedong thought, the almost exclusive interaction with other communist states, the subsequent rejection and distrust of the global community at large, and the consequences of a series of bad domestic policies, namely the Great Leap Forward and the Cultural Revolution, are all cited as reasons for the dismal state of higher education, and IR studies in particular. This kind of analysis, however, does not satisfy a need to appreciate what was happening in China at that time.

As Lu Dingyi articulated, the CCP had no intention of meeting the standards of the West. In fact, it was quite the opposite. The CCP stood in direct opposition to the West, and sought to pursue a different framework for interpreting international affairs. For this to be done, the traditional intellectual or academic institution was not the necessary vessel. The over-dependence on Marxist–Leninist–Mao Zedong thought that is cited as being detrimental to the development of IR was in fact perceived as the source of its greatest strength, and served as a platform from which China challenged convention. China was not only creating but seeking to function in an alternate reality to that of the West.

Steven Levine argues that the early years of the People's Republic were defined by a formal ideology.[22] Levine agrees the rigidity and uncompromising nature of ideology are only half the story. The tenets of Marxist–Leninist ideology, according to Chinese interpretations, freed the Chinese to think independently, define their circumstances, and pursue the best course of action for the preservation of the party.[23] Essentially, Marxist–Leninist theory was the tool with which the CCP sought to build a structure. When this formal ideology began to leave the Chinese state wanting in areas it itself defined as important in foreign policy, it was abandoned in all but the most abstract forms. This is true for the broader ideological bent of China as it developed under Deng Xiaoping. This continues to be a dynamic the PRC struggles to balance to this day, yet the consequences of a reformed and ever more open communist state have been observable. China's re-engagement with IR is a reflection of those changes.

It is important to note that the normalization of relations with the United States also played a major role in advancing Chinese understandings of IR. The normalization of relations between China and the United States translated to increased involvement of American-based philanthropic organizations in China. In particular, the Ford Foundation was exceptionally active in supporting programs geared to the development of IR. Others included the Rockefeller Foundation, Rockefeller Brothers Fund, Luce Foundation, and the MacArthur Foundation.[24] These philanthropic organizations, including the Ford Foundation, combined their efforts to support Chinese scholarship in international studies through the creation of the Committee on International Relations Studies with the People's Republic of China.[25] Progressively, Chinese scholastic isolation was remedied through study-abroad programs and the translation of a number of IR works into Mandarin. With the exception of a brief crackdown following the Tiananmen Square incident in 1989, lasting until 1992, the field of IR has continued to expand and flourish in China.

Despite external influences, there are themes in the Chinese understanding of IR that have remained constant. These constants have been termed China's "informal" ideology.[26] There are six themes in China's informal ideology that are important because they are recurring among a wide group of elites: (1) both the Chinese nation and people are "great"; (2) the modern period has been unfavorable to China, deserving correction; (3) those who harmed China in the past must offer appropriate restitution; (4) China by virtue of its "greatness" is central to world affairs and should be treated accordingly; (5) Chinese sovereignty is absolute and unconditional; (6) China engages the international community through virtue.[27]

—

China's troubled history with and late acceptance to the society of nations has meant it took a different path to an understanding of IR. Despite this, China has retained its sense of identity by adhering to an informal ideology. Next I would like to discuss in more detail the dynamic between IR and identity.

International relations as foreign

With a historical perspective on the development of IR established, I would like to begin shaping an understanding of the impact of IR theory on Chinese foreign policy. To do this, we must start with a basic premise: IR as a foreign concept. The development of IR in China is intimately tied to the development of a Chinese identity and self-perceived place in the world. In this premise, IR as foreign, we find a complexity that offers insight into the Chinese worldview.

Where the formal study of IR is a more recent advancement, the practice of foreign relations has rich roots in Chinese imperial history. That said, it is difficult to characterize the foreign relations of Imperial China as being directed by a foreign policy, in large part because external affairs were conducted more as a consequence of a perceived natural order. China would bestow culture, refinement, or civilization to those from whom the imperial court received tribute. This conceptualization rested on the idea of China as the Middle Kingdom. Geographic features that allowed China to secure its territory, whether through isolation or the projection of influence, supported this conceptualization. This system was the foundation of Chinese foreign relations until Western intervention. It was the state system itself that frustrated Imperial China, and the capitalist prevalence in the post World War II order that thwarted communist China's ideological anticipations. The trials of wars and revolutions, and the instance on ideological cohesion, meant China, until the opening up and reforms, had little experience with IR. It should be remembered that IR fed into, and was a victim of, the CCP's narrative of dangerous foreign ideas.

Today, the landscape is very different. China has a robust and vibrant community of IR intellectuals, many of whom are contributing to a global community by publishing their works in English, with some of the most prominent among them also serving the needs of government as advisors. Despite this, there remains a sense that the IR of the West cannot fully be the IR of China.[28] China's self-perceived lack of a historical stake in the development of IR, to say nothing of the philosophical foundations that make it profoundly Western, has allowed for space in Chinese IR to pursue a "Chinese School" – one that would suit the philosophical and cultural orientation of the Chinese people. This is, needless to say, questionable. The pursuit of such research may be construed as a spurious attempt of the CCP to manage the intellectual trajectory of the discipline, or, perhaps more perilously, harken from a chauvinism inspired by China's recent economic success. The sources of inspiration are hard to pinpoint, and it is undoubtedly a combination of many factors. What is clear, however, is that the debate in China inspired by this line of research has led to a fairly sharp divide among academics, practitioners of foreign policy, and an emerging hybrid, academic-practitioners. It is not essential to this chapter's argument to elaborate the intricacies of the efforts underway to establish a Chinese School of IR. It is in this debate, however, that we can observe the influence of imported IR theory.

Ancient abstractions and modern concerns in Chinese IR

Efforts to distinguish Chinese IR from the Western-rooted mainstream have found inspiration in the practices of China's imperial past. This is significantly different from the revolutionary ideology of Mao, yet highlights an interest in China today that seeks to reconnect with "great power" status. The products of this line of research are highly abstract, detached from the mainstream perspectives on IR, and largely incongruous with the traditional paradigm of Chinese foreign policy. The PRC has been reluctant to accept a leadership role in the international community, yet these ancient abstractions require it.[29]

There are three elements of Imperial Chinese foreign relations that dominate the research: Confucianism, the tribute system, and *tianxia,* or "all under heaven."[30] Confucianism offers a philosophical framework as a starting point for identifying theoretical understandings from which to build Chinese IR theories. The tribute system and *tianxia*, two concepts intimately related, offer a structural framework from which understanding can begin to take shape.

Confucianism

In contrast to a Western conception of human nature of unrestrained freedom and self-interest, the Confucian tradition is founded on the belief that human nature is predisposed toward good and community.[31] An essential element, as articulated by James C. Hsiung, is that "what determines human nature is the conditioning effects of the human environment (society), including moral education (*lijiao*)."[32] This premise of human nature bears two additional concepts: (1) that society should actively seek to remove corrupting elements; and (2) that man attains true fulfillment by actively participating in society, rather than seeking individual gain in isolation.[33] This leads to the concept of "man-in-society."[34] In a Confucian framework, society and its constituent functions are natural products of human nature. This is distinct from the Western conception of society that arises from recognition of rights and the establishment of laws.

These differences are of paramount importance to theories of governance. Where Western political philosophy holds the state's role as establishing laws to regulate human nature, and thusly the state itself is imbued with checks and balances, Confucian tradition holds a state/citizen dual responsibility as the centerpiece of its approach.[35] In this, the state works to eliminate corrupting forces and provides a nurturing environment for the moral progress of the people, in which family plays an integral role, and aid in helping people through development.[36] In this framework, politics plays a secondary role in society, with an emphasis on stability as a means of achieving harmony. Conceptions of the individual are always considered in conjunction with society in this Chinese worldview.

The attractiveness and virtues of a Confucian model rest in the requisite elements of hierarchy, balance, cooperation, and harmony in the pursuit of progress and development. This is equally attractive when abstracted out to create a paradigm of IR. The challenge, however, lies in its applicability. Where there is a fair case to be made regarding the individual being an inherent subject of society, there is no such relationship with regard to states in an international community. Additionally, the assumption of a benevolent and virtuous leader brings into question legitimate sources of power, questions that are central to IR yet unanswered by a Confucian model.

The tribute system

Confucianism had a huge impact in Asia. As such, a regional appreciation developed for order and codes of conduct that influenced foreign relations. This led to a specific imperial mode of foreign relations and the development of a tribute system as a way to manage China's foreign relations. There are three views that have come to be accepted paradigms of the tribute system: (1) the tribute system served as a mechanism of not only tribute to the Chinese imperial house, but also a means of promoting trade between China and its neighbors; (2) the tribute system was largely a bureaucratic construction designed to manage Imperial Chinese foreign relations; and (3) the tribute system was a fundamental institution within the East Asian order that served all those involved in achieving mutual ends.[37]

The practical or transactional roots of understanding in foreign affairs that developed out of the tribute system were very different from the philosophical reasoning that was applied in the West in considering concepts of legitimacy, power, and sovereign rights. China, unlike pre-Westphalian Europe, enjoyed an advancement in culture, technology, governance, commerce, and military prowess unmatched anywhere in the world. Therefore, it was unnecessary to opine the philosophical roots of foreign relations. To China these were natural consequences of their superiority. Therefore, in the West there developed a sense that foreign policy and IR, though intimately related and mutually intelligible, were distinct in form and substance; in Imperial China there was no distinction. Today, as previously discussed, the line between the two remains blurred in China.

Tianxia

An additional element underpinning the conduct of Imperial China's foreign relations was *tianxia*. *Tianxia* itself means "all under heaven" and carries with it strong chauvinistic undertones; as a concept it is linked to the idea of China as naturally superior to the rest of the world, thus occupying the "Middle Kingdom." Despite this, one can find elements that are worthy of exploration for their potential applicability to modern IR. The concept of *tianxia* adds metaphysical depth to the tribute system.

Tianxia essentially precluded territorial ambition within the practice of the tribute system and led to a lasting structure of foreign relations for thousands of years.[38] Scholars have latched on to the idea of *tianxia* as an abstract concept, not to be relegated to the rigid terms of historical definition, but rather to be interpreted in contexts appropriate to the time. In this, *tianxia* has taken on a number of attributes, whether they are geographical, political, cultural, or moral.[39] To these scholars, the *tianxia* philosophy embodies soft power in IR, all-inclusiveness, and harmonization.[40]

Though it is true that Imperial China tended not to interfere in the domestic affairs of tributary states, it is hard to attribute this too fully to *tianxia*. Again, China's superiority precluded a need for conquest. Unlike Europe, which lacked a hegemon and was at one point deeply divided by religion, China's political cohesion coupled with its cultural and military superiority lent itself to stability. Finally, the tribute system itself secured the requisite trade relations for the continued prosperity of China. Thus, it is hard to identify where *tianxia* might offer a meaningful alternative to more widely accepted IR theories that have direct relevance to a more contemporary period; theories that have some similar perspectives on IR to those articulated by proponents of *tianxia*. Most immediately this might include theories of international organization.

—

The effort to abstract from China's imperial past has not proven very fruitful. The ambiguity and obtuseness of these frameworks have limited their applicability beyond the rhetorical. To the outside observer, however, there is a wealth of important information housed in these kinds of works. One, the exploration of the Chinese School of IR itself suggests an interest in international affairs uncommon in the past. It also tells us that, to a certain extent, there is a significant community in China that is interested in exploring new constructs of an international order, or of how things should be. Finally, we gain a more developed view into the dialogue between theory and practice.

Practical treatments: realism and the importation of IR theory

By far, a realist perspective dominates contemporary Chinese IR. This is rooted in a tradition of pragmatic foreign relations born out of necessity for survival, as the CCP teetered on the edge of destruction in Yenan in the 1940s, well before any formal engagement in IR research. Modern Chinese IR, involving the CCP and later PRC, began in 1944.[41] Marxist–Leninist ideology had a distinct impact on Chinese IR rhetoric until the early 1990s, yet Chinese foreign policy in practice demonstrated a much more focused set of concerns: survival, legitimacy, and sovereignty. One can identify these same guiding concerns from the earlier discussion on the historical roots of modern Chinese foreign affairs. China's initial isolation, hesitation toward, and eventual involvement in the Korean War, the Sino-Soviet split, and ultimate Sino-American rapprochement are all cited cases of the CCP's pragmatic approach to foreign affairs. To some extent the level of pragmatism lent itself well to understanding. Furthermore, Chinese foreign-policy making was highly centralized and authoritarian, further narrowing the field of policy possibilities.[42] This was especially true during the Mao years, as discussed earlier. After the end of the Deng Xiaoping era and the consequences of reforms materialized, however, a much more sophisticated and savvy approach to international affairs analysis emerged. If we fast-forward to the present and engage with Chinese scholarship on IR, the effects of China's opening up are evident. China, through increased engagement with the international community, has sought recognition and a prominent place in the international order, while simultaneously doing so under the pretext that the international order remain external to China and not undermine "Chinese-ness."

Today, many academics and practitioners of foreign affairs have concerned themselves more with the present and the future than they have with the past. This is not to suggest that there is a lack of historical perspective. On the contrary, Chinese intellectuals seem to have a remarkably persistent historical memory. To these intellectuals, however, IR is best understood through practice – a position that has heartily been supported by the CCP.[43] To flesh this out a bit further, we find a firm belief that IR theories are founded on Western theories, and as such any Chinese understanding of IR theory must grow out of this knowledge. Men Honghua stated succinctly, "importation – critique – innovation is the inherent logic of contemporary Chinese IR theory development."[44] It is relatively unsurprising then that the theoretical tone and framework from which Chinese analysis grows are based on a distinctly realist perspective – in contrast to the historical perspective, or the Maoist–Communist ideologies of early post-war China.[45] This realism, however, has tended to be a step or two behind the trajectory of scholarly literature outside of China that has trended toward more of a multicausal analysis rather than an analysis restricted to a single theoretical framework.[46] The Chinese approach to realism has its roots in pragmatism, or what has also been identified as Chinese Realpolitik.[47] It is important to reiterate a point made earlier, that Chinese IR is most commonly understood in terms of foreign policy. In China IR has a practical application. Beyond this application, there is little interest or need.

This pragmatic bend of Chinese IR theorists has led to a dismissal of Chinese history at large, premised on the idea that imperial China lacked "international-ness."[48] To these scholars, the crutch of tradition is insufficient. It is through the importation and practice of IR theory that China will achieve the legitimacy and prestige it once enjoyed. Yet it is through this very same pragmatic approach manifest in the dominant conversation that one finds the indications of a rising power "syndrome." The literature reveals that the recent advancements in economic prosperity, military capability, and foreign engagement have uncovered a host of additional responsibilities and complexities.[49] China, as a rising power, is eager to cease upon these responsibilities and complexities. At the same time, China's self-assured sense of greatness coupled with the express acknowledgment of the need for cooperation place new limits and frustrations on its rise. It is this aspect of the contemporary international order, where the great states have the greatest responsibility to facilitate cooperation, that we find intellectual debates in China most uncomfortable. For even at its most basic formulation, the premise upon which Chinese foreign policy since 1949 was built was on a rejection of an imperialist-constructed international order and the modes with which states interacted therein. Today, the focus of IR is squarely on how China can most effectively fulfill is role as a member of the international community, while not necessarily being subject to it; to borrow constructivist terminology, how China can be the "norm-creator."

Despite this, the case for a rising China and its increased responsibility routinely amounts to little more than the logical inconsistency of increasing international engagement, while securing a Westphalian sense of sovereignty. There is nothing new to this kind of approach to Chinese foreign affairs. Chinese scholars and policy makers have yet to define China's modern IR in normative terms, opting to continue to lean on Realpolitik instead. Zhou Fanying subtly expressed frustration on this point:

> For a rising power like China, it should know that any foreign policy purely based on pragmatic purposes will not help it play a leading role in the international society. As a country expected by many to play a bigger role, China should drive home the fact that the adoption of purely pragmatic policies will not work. In the process of the evolution of the East Asian order, China should thoroughly ponder over its long-term role orientation in the regional order, and correspondingly adopt a range of concrete diplomatic policies.[50]

Chinese self-awareness of its rise is apparent. Its traditionally pragmatic approach to foreign policy is being questioned domestically. In the next section, I will give some final thoughts on what these varying perspectives on IR may mean for the geopolitics of Northeast Asia.

Conclusion and reflections on the geopolitics of Northeast Asia

Though there is some agreement on a normative approach in international affairs, whether it is from imperial abstraction or from foreign theories, the material dynamics of foreign policy nonetheless continues to factor into all considerations. This is particularly evident with regard to the geopolitics of Northeast Asia.

Historically and at present, China is geopolitically insulated from external threat. It faces no military threat from any of its contemporary rivals. The United States is perhaps the largest threat to China's maritime integrity in Northeast Asia, with its network of long-standing alliances with Japan and South Korea and relations with Taiwan. These concerns are limited, however, as the United States exhibits no cause for concern and has been a long-time proponent of free navigation. Nonetheless, China actively maintains its territorial buffers and has increased its efforts to secure the same for its eastern coast.

The geopolitics of the region is one of the most oft-discussed and analyzed topics in foreign affairs. This is especially true with regard to the structure of territorial or maritime disputes. There is something to be said, however, in light of this chapter's previous discussion. There is a distinct tendency to overlay non-Chinese perspectives on analyses of Chinese geopolitical strategy. The diagnosis born from these methods tends to favor China threat theories. Yet, the internal discourse unfolding in China suggests something different. China perceives itself as deserving a seat among the great powers, but there is also a robust debate regarding China's capacity to take on the responsibilities associated with "great power" status. Maintenance of unquestioned sovereignty remains most central to the PRC's international concerns, though this serves the dual purpose of reinforcing its ability to focus and manage domestic stability, while simultaneously securing the buffer that has protected China proper throughout history.

Northeast Asia, among one of the most economically vibrant regions of the world, is also home to some of the most hotly contested maritime disputes. If we take just one of these potential flash points and place it in this framework of formulated, orthodox realist calculations, the stakes become clearer. The Senkaku/Diaoyu Island dispute would, a priori, grow into an increasingly antagonistic confrontation, as China's risks associated with certain policy positions decrease. This does not necessitate military confrontation, and there is little suggestion that China would resort to military engagement over an area that is at best tacitly associated with its national sovereignty. The tools that could be brought to bear, political and economic, however, are significant and could provoke a range of responses. In this scenario, realist theory explains Chinese behavior well, though not because it is a representation of a universal truth of international politics, but rather that it represents how China has learned and internalized its perception of the natural order of the international system.

This same line of reasoning can be likewise applied to the construction of an airstrip in the South China Sea. This kind of assertive behavior is well beyond the normal range of conduct China exhibited in the past. What this chapter has attempted to do is outline how this kind of assertive behavior can, to an extent, be characteristic of China's perception of how a power should behave in pursuit of its interests, while simultaneously confirming the depth of Chinese historical memory and desire to reclaim what it has always asserted is Chinese sovereign territory.

Though this offers a cold and grim projection of the future, the alternative, more abstract conception of IR based on Chinese traditional thought and history, founded on principles of harmony and stability in the international system, offers little consolation. The hierarchical nature of the framework, the continued strict adherence to sovereignty, leaves little room for new creative ways of thinking about and engaging in contested issues.

China's rise is premised on economic growth that is not a foundational element of the PRC's founding paradigm, tempting speculation on its sustainability. So far, however, China has managed both stability and progress. The surest way to ensure a stable geopolitical environment in Northeast Asia would be to further engage China at a normative level, to bring a rigid conception of IR closer to the dynamic concepts characteristic of mainstream IR. It is incumbent upon those both inside and outside of China to promote China's progress toward international organization, in the hope of laying the groundwork for functional peace and stability. For as the China of today finds its place in the world, the world itself will undoubtedly need to also adjust in kind.

Notes

1 J.M.F. and L.P. "Crowning the Dragon." *The Economist*, April 30, 2014. http://www.economist.com/blogs/graphicdetail/2014/04/daily-chart-19.

2 Auguste Comte. *The Positive Philosophy of Auguste Comte*. Translated by Harriet Martineau. Vol. 1, 20–21. London: George Bell & Sons, 1896 http://archive.org/details/positivephilosop01comt.

3 Jonathan D. Spence. *The Search for Modern China*. New York: Norton, 1990; Michael Dillon. *China: A Modern History*. New paperback edition. London: I.B. Tauris, 2012.

4 It is important to note that there is a substantive debate regarding the accuracy of historically assigning the "state" too strictly to the peace of Westphalia. The modern state is better understood as something that has emerged over a long period of time, intimately tied up in a broader political discourse. Andreas Osiander. *Before the State: Systemic Political Change in the West from the Greeks to the French Revolution.* Oxford: Oxford University Press, 2007.

5 Andreas Osiander. "Rereading Early Twentieth-Century IR Theory: Idealism Revisited." *International Studies Quarterly*, 42, no. 3 (1998): 409–32; Andreas Osiander. "History and International Relations Theory." In *War, Peace, and World Orders in European History*, edited by Anja Hartmann and Beatrice Heuser. The New International Relations, 14–24. London: Routledge, 2001; Brian C. Schmidt. *The Political Discourse of Anarchy: A Disciplinary History of International Relations*. SUNY Series in Global Politics. Albany, NY: State University of New York Press, 1998.

6 Thomas Hobbes. *Leviathan*. Cambridge: Cambridge University Press, 1904. http://archive.org/details/leviathan00hobbgoog; John Locke *Two Treatises of Government.* London: Whitmore and Fenn and C. Brown, 1821. http://archive.org/details/twotreatisesofg00lockuoft; Jean-Jacques Rousseau. *The Social Contract and Discourses*. Translated by G. D. H. (George Douglas Howard) Cole. London: J.M. Dent & Sons, 1923. http://archive.org/details/therepublicofpla00rousuoft; Immanuel Kant. *Perpetual Peace: A Philosophical Essay.* Translated by Mary Campbell Smith. London: G. Allen & Unwin, 1917. http://archive.org/details/perpetualpeaceph00kantuoft.

7 Osiander, "History and International Relations Theory."

8. For an example, see Norman Angell. *The Great Illusion, 1933*. New York: G.P. Putnam's sons, 1913. http://archive.org/details/cu31924014535888.
9. Theodore Dwight Woolsey. *Introduction to the Study of International Law, Designed as an Aid in Teaching, and in Historical Studies*. New York: Charles Scribner, 1864. http://archive.org/details/introductiontos02woolgoog; Francis Lieber. *Manual of Political Ethics*, edited by Theodore Dwight Woolsey. Philadelphia, PA: J. B. Lippincott, 1911. http://archive.org/details/manualofpolitic01lieb; Stephen Leacock. *Elements of Political Science*. Boston, MA: Houghton, Mifflin, 1906. http://archive.org/details/elementspolitic00leacgoog; Raymond Garfield Gettell. *Introduction to Political Science*. Boston, MA: Ginn, 1910. http://archive.org/details/introductiontop00gett; Raymond Garfield Gettell. "Nature and Scope of Present Political Theory." *Proceedings of the American Political Science Association*, 10 (1913): 47–60. http://archive.org/details/jstor-3038416; James Bryce. "The Relations of Political Science to History and to Practice: Presidential Address, Fifth Annual Meeting of the American Political Science Association". *The American Political Science Review*, 3, no. 1 (1909): 1–19. http://archive.org/details/jstor-1945905; John Dewey. "Austin's Theory of Sovereignty." *Political Science Quarterly*, 9 (1894): 31–52. http://archive.org/details/jstor-2139902.
10. Paul Samuel Reinsch. *World Politics at the End of the Nineteenth Century as Influenced by the Oriental Situation*. New York: The Macmillan Company, 1900. http://archive.org/details/worldpoliticsate01rein.
11. Bruce A. Elleman. *International Competition in China, 1899–1991: The Rise, Fall, and Eventual Success of the Open Door Policy*. Routledge Studies in the Modern History of Asia 106. New York: Routledge, 2015.
12. David L. Shambaugh and Wang Jisi. "Research on International Studies in the People's Republic of China." *PS*, 17, no. 4 (1984): 758. doi:10.2307/418762.
13. David L. Shambaugh. "China's National Security Research Bureaucracy." *The China Quarterly*, 110 (1987): 276–304.
14. David L. Shambaugh. "International Relations Studies in China: History, Trends, and Prospects." *International Relations of the Asia-Pacific*, 11, no. 3 (September 1, 2011): 339–72, doi:10.1093/irap/lcr013.
15. Lu was the chief of the propaganda department at the establishment of the People's Republic in 1949. In 1965 he was appointed Vice-Premier and Minister of Culture. Lu Dingyi. *Education Must Be Combined with Productive Labour*), 3–4. Peking: Foreign Languages Press, 1958.
16. Mao Tse-tung. *Selected Works of Mao Tse-Tung*, vol. 1, 295–309. Beijing: Foreign Languages Press, 1965. http://archive.org/details/SelectedWorksOfMaoTse-tungVol.I.
17. Shambaugh, "International Relations Studies in China"; Song Xinning and Gerald Chan. "International Relations Theory in China." In *China's International Relations in the 21st Century Dynamics of Paradigm Shifts*, edited by Hu Weixing, Gerald Chan, and Daojiong Zha, 15–40. Lanham, MD: University Press of America, 2000; Yang Rui, Lesley Vidovich, and Jan Currie. "'Dancing in a Cage': Changing Autonomy in Chinese Higher Education." *Higher Education*, 54, no. 4 (August 28, 2007): 575–92. doi:10.1007/s10734-006-9009-5.
18. Yang Rui, Vidovich, and Currie, "'Dancing in a Cage.'"
19. Song Xinning and Chan, "International Relations Theory in China."
20. Shambaugh, "International Relations Studies in China."
21. Du Mei. "HISTORY – Chinese Academy of Social Sciences." *Chinese Academy of Social Sciences*, September 18, 2015. http://casseng.cssn.cn/about/about_history/.
22. Steven Levine. "Perception and Ideology in Chinese Foreign Policy." In *Chinese Foreign Policy: Theory and Practice*, edited by Thomas W. Robinson and David Shambaugh, 30–46. Studies on Contemporary China. Oxford: Clarendon Press, 1998.
23. Ibid.

24 Shambaugh, "International Relations Studies in China."
25 Ibid.
26 Levine, "Perception and Ideology in Chinese Foreign Policy."
27 Ibid., 43–44.
28 Lindsey Cunningham-Cross. "Narrating a Discipline: The Search for Innovation in Chinese International Relations." In *Chinese Politics and International Relations: Innovation and Invention*, edited by Nicola Horsburgh, Astrid Nordin, and Shaun Breslin. Warwick Studies in Globalisation. London: Routledge, 2014.
29 The Chinese experience in the United Nations offers a measurable example of this claim. For an indepth analysis of this topic, see Liu Wei. *China in the United Nations*. Hackensack, NJ: World Century, 2014.
30 Zheng Yongnian, ed. *China and International Relations: The Chinese View and the Contribution of Wang Gungwu*. China Policy Series. London: Routledge, 2010.
31 James C. Hsiung. "A Re-Appraisal of Abrahamic Values and Neorealist IR Theory: From a Confucian-Asian Perspective." In *China and International Relations: The Chinese View and the Contribution of Wang Gungwu*, edited by Zheng Yongnian, 17–41. China Policy Series. London: Routledge, 2010.
32 Ibid., 22.
33 Ibid., 23.
34 Ibid., 22.
35 Ibid., 23.
36 Ibid.
37 Zhang Feng. "Rethinking the 'Tribute System': Broadening the Conceptual Horizon of Historical East Asian Politics." In *China and International Relations: The Chinese View and the Contribution of Wang Gungwu*, edited by Zheng Yongnian, 75–101. China Policy Series. London: Routledge, 2010.
38 Xiao Ren. "Traditional Chinese Theory and Practice of Foreign Relations: A Reassessment." In *China and International Relations: The Chinese View and the Contribution of Wang Gungwu*, edited by Yongnian Zheng, 102–16. China Policy Series. London: Routledge, 2010.
39 Ibid.
40 Ibid.
41 James Reardon-Anderson. *Yenan and the Great Powers: The Origins of Chinese Communist Foreign Policy, 1944–1946*. Studies of the East Asian Institute, Columbia University. New York: Columbia University Press, 1980; Anastas Ivanovich Mikoyan and Zhou Enlai. "Memorandum of Conversation between Anastas Mikoyan and Zhou Enlai." February 1, 1949, APRF: F. 39, Op. 1, D. 39, Ll. 17–24. Reprinted in Andrei Ledovskii, Raisa Mirovitskaia, and Vladimir Miasnikov. *Sovetsko-Kitaiskie Otnosheniia*, Vol. 5, Book 2, 1946–February 1950. Moscow: Pamiatniki Istoricheskoi Mysli, 2005, pp. 43–48. Translated by Sergey Radchenko, History and Public Policy Program Digital Archive. http://digitalarchive.wilsoncenter.org/document/110003; Huang Hua. *Huang Hua Memoirs*. Beijing: Foreign Languages Press, 2008.
42 Lu Ning. *The Dynamics of Foreign-Policy Decisionmaking in China*, 2nd ed. Boulder, CO: Westview Press, 2000.
43 Mao Tse-tung, *Selected Works of Mao Tse-Tung*; Jiang Zemin. *Selected Works of Jiang Zemin, Vol. I*. Beijing: Foreign Languages Press, 2009. http://book.theorychina.org/upload/9912d625-487c-4b71-bc52-c514d6037af2/flipviewerxpress.html?pn=38.
44 As cited in Cunningham-Cross, "Narrating a Discipline: The Search for Innovation in Chinese International Relations," 87.
45 Lu Ning, *The Dynamics of Foreign-Policy Decisionmaking in China*.
46 Cunningham-Cross, "Narrating a Discipline: The Search for Innovation in Chinese International Relations."

47 Alastair Iain Johnston. "Cultural Realism and Strategy in Maoist China." In *The Culture of National Security: Norms and Identity in World Politics*, edited by Peter J. Katzenstein, 216–68. New York: Columbia University Press, 1996.
48 Cunningham-Cross, "Narrating a Discipline: The Search for Innovation in Chinese International Relations," 92.
49 For a recent volume on international relations, written by some of the most prominent Chinese IR scholars, see Shao Binhong, ed. *The World in 2020 According to China: Chinese Foreign Policy Elites Discuss Emerging Trends in International Politics*, vol. 2, China in the World : A Survey of Chinese Perspectives on International Politics and Economics. Leiden: Brill, 2014.
50 Zhou Fangyin. "China's Rise, the Transformation of East Asian Regional Structure, and Development Direction of the East Asian Order." In *The World in 2020 According to China: Chinese Foreign Policy Elites Discuss Emerging Trends in International Politics*, edited by Shao Binhong, vol. 2, China in the World: A Survey of Chinese Perspectives on International Politics and Economics, 179. Leiden: Brill, 2014.

3 In pursuit of Asian Infrastructure Investment Bank

The politics and geopolitics of a Chinese bank

Alice D. Ba[1]

Introduction

On October 24, 2014, China and 20 other countries[2] signed a memorandum of understanding (MOU), officially launching the Chinese-initiated Asian Infrastructure Investment Bank (AIIB). Eight months later, on June 29, 2015, over 50 states gathered for a signing ceremony at Beijing's Great Hall of the People to sign its articles of agreement. In December 2015, the AIIB officially became the newest player in the world of MDBs. Indicative of what many see to be a new era of Chinese confidence, China's successful pursuit of the AIIB has prompted both reflection and anxiety about China's place in both regional and global orders. Indeed, as much as the AIIB may mark China's entrance as a new and, for many, welcomed leading actor on the economic and financial front in East Asia, its development is also accompanied by heightened security tensions involving China, especially its activities on the maritime front.

Much about the AIIB has been playing out as a great-power drama – between China as a rising power and the United States as the long-time status quo power; however, how exactly this drama plays out will also be mitigated very much by regional powers and their relations with China. On the one hand, regional actors stand to gain and lose the most; on the other, they, as critical target audiences for China's economic initiatives, also have the ability to facilitate, obstruct, and legitimate China's interests and expanded presence. In this sense, the success of China's initiatives, as well as its legitimacy as a regionally recognized leading actor, is also very much contingent on their acceptance by regional actors. This chapter investigates that contingency as it pertains to China's pursuit of the AIIB. It does so by first giving attention to the immediate context and chronology from which the AIIB emerged – that is, the key drivers, interests, and concerns that have been associated with China's pursuit of the AIIB. It then considers and categorizes regional reactions and responses which have ranged from welcoming, to reluctant acceptance, to ambivalence, to resistance and opposition. Taken together, these different actors provide a picture of how economics and geopolitics are interacting to shape East Asia's strategic environment and China's prospective leading role in it.

The AIIB: domestic development, regional integration, and Chinese initiative

Chinese initiatives like the AIIB have sparked much discussion about the directions of Chinese foreign policy and whether we are seeing a dramatically different era. On the one hand, recent Chinese initiatives – not just the AIIB, but also the New Development Bank (the so-called "BRICS Bank") and China's "One Belt, One Road" initiatives – are all suggestive of a new and more assertive and confident Chinese foreign policy. On the other hand, the AIIB is also, in some critical respects, illustrative of some important continuities in terms of China's driving concerns and insecurities.

Perhaps the most pressing concerns have been economic and domestic. In particular, economic developments on both domestic and global fronts have raised concerns about China's ability to sustain the economic momentum and economic growth it has come to be accustomed to. For China, that ability has also become very much tied to questions of domestic regime stability and legitimacy. These concerns were also heightened by the 2008 global financial crisis (GFC), which appears to have been a defining moment. Sounding the "big alarm," China and other regional states attending regional conferences noted the region's "heavy" reliance on external, advanced markets for growth.[3] Such concerns generated much regional discussion about the need for alternative, less market-driven / "bottom-up" models of development. In particular, top-down, state-led multilateral East Asian financing and investment cooperation, including regional infrastructure projects, had been discussed well before the 2008 GFC as offering alternative ways to build and generate regional demand, as well as to attract additional private investment. For China, the regional development projects also had the attraction of offering additional drivers, outlets, and markets to which to channel and direct China's excess capacity and labor.

However, the GFC also diminished the lending capacities of existing multilateral development banks (MDBs). Most notably, with the GFC, the World Bank saw its lending capacity reduced to one-half of what it had been pre-crisis. Private lending had also plummeted to one-third of pre-crisis levels.[4] Such trends were expected to have the greatest developmental impact on China's neighboring regions, which depended on such assistance to build needed infrastructure. Even absent the crisis, for example, it was widely agreed that developing Asia would find extensive infrastructure needs would be unmet – an estimated US$8 trillion-worth in national infrastructure and another US$290 billion in regional projects, in fact.[5] By one Asian Development Bank (ADB) assessment, of that amount, existing multilateral banks collectively would have been able to cover less than 5%[6] – a situation made worse by the crisis. For China, the regional projects supported by MDB also had the attraction of offering additional drivers, outlets, and markets to which to channel and direct China's excess capacity and labor.

Such concerns may have factored into, for example, China's 2009 proposal and establishment of a US$10 billion China–ASEAN investment fund sourced by China. That fund was later supplemented by an additional US$15 billion-worth of loans in support of over 50 infrastructure projects in Southeast Asia. As early as 2010, China and other states in East Asia also began to explicitly discuss the possibility of extending China–ASEAN investment-type mechanisms to the larger East Asia. The formal initiation of ASEAN's Master Plan on Connectivity (MPAC) also appears to have provided inspiration for broader East Asian cooperation, including the possible creation of "East Asian Cooperation Funds for Infrastructure and Connectivity."

The possibility of a regional infrastructure bank became much more explicit and substantive in mid-2013 and became an official Chinese proposal in October that same year, when President Xi Jinping began peddling it just before and during the annual Asia-Pacific Economic Cooperation (APEC) meetings held in Indonesia. The year that followed was one of active Chinese diplomacy, as Chinese leaders and representatives worked to build support and potential membership for the bank. In East Asia, China especially reached out to Southeast Asian states, which, constituting one of the larger infrastructure markets within Asia,[7] would be likely recipients and beneficiaries of having an alternative source of developmental assistance. In addition to bilateral meetings with individual ASEAN states, the AIIB proposal was discussed at the ASEAN–China meetings in August 2014. In Northeast Asia, China also held bilateral consultations about the bank with South Korea and Japan. Participation and interest were also solicited from South Asia, Central Asia, and even the Middle East.

China held the first multilateral working meeting devoted to the bank in January 2014. In the months that followed, China held at least four additional multilateral working meetings devoted to the project. By October 24, China had the commitment of 20 other states, which joined China in signing an MOU on the bank. Those 20 other states included all but Indonesia[8] from ASEAN–Southeast Asia (Brunei, Cambodia, Laos, Malaysia, Myanmar, the Philippines, Singapore, Thailand, and Vietnam); India, Bangladesh, Nepal, Pakistan, and Sri Lanka from South Asia; Kazakhstan and Uzbekistan from Central Asia; and Kuwait, Oman, and Qatar from the Middle East, and also Mongolia. As reported in October 2014, the bank would begin with a starting capital account of $50 billion (later projected to $100 billion), with China anticipating a 50% stake.[9] Advanced economies – namely, the United States, Australia, and European Union – could also hold a minority stake. The AIIB officially would come into existence in December 2015, following additional negotiations over the bank's structure and administration.

The politics of the AIIB

As highlighted above, the practical need for additional sources of developmental assistance in Asia is undeniable. On the face of it, the proposed new bank had much to appeal to regional states in East Asia. In addition to the possibility of offering additional economic stimuli at a time of slowed global demand, the AIIB had the potential to support the specific national and regional integration agendas of different states. As compelling as the AIIB was practically, however, it was also met with a range of responses, including degrees of wariness and even resistance among a number of states.

That China's boldest economic initiatives to date should also coincide with its assertiveness on more conventional security issues heightened the questions about China's influence and intentions.[10] Indeed, China's efforts to promote the AIIB as a regionally-beneficial initiative sat in tension with its activities, especially in the South China Sea, which became a site of tension not just among competing claimants, but also between China and the United States, which would express the sharpest concerns about the AIIB. Officially, US concerns emphasized questions about the soundness of the would-be AIIB's lending practices – though membership from key Western economies, including the United States, would have offset some of those questions. As many noted, for example, the participation of established financial actors and Western actors, even if holding a minority stake, would help expose and encourage the bank to adopt best practices.[11] Unofficially, Washington appeared to have seen Chinese initiatives as challenges to its own place and position, a concern that has been exacerbated by the US- and European-centered GFC. Globally, for example, Washington has harbored concerns that China is pushing the AIIB as a direct challenge to the US- and European-dominated system of Bretton Woods institutions.

Regionally, the United States has viewed China's expanded influence in East Asia as coming mostly at the United States' expense. While these concerns precede the Obama administration's coming into office, the Obama administration has – through a set of military, economic, and diplomatic initiatives known as the "rebalance to Asia" – taken an especially activist approach to (re)asserting the US presence in East Asia. Indeed, according to a number of official and unofficial accounts, the "rebalance" was designed to counter the trend of expanded Chinese political and economic influence in Asia.[12]

Still, the most interesting reactions may be those from regional states. Regional reactions are also not unrelated to US concerns and its position on the AIIB. This is because US concerns about the AIIB ultimately go beyond China, extending to others in East Asia. After all, a China-led bank would be of no concern if others did not sign on. Thus, the critical question for both China and the United States as regards the AIIB is about the extent to which others in the region join and support Chinese-led initiatives. In this vein, to the extent that Washington is moved by concerns about a rival bank, it has a particular interest in seeing lower participation rates, especially from larger, middle powers. Similarly, for China, it needs a critical mass of states if the AIIB is to have practical value and enjoy normative acceptance. The discussion below gives attention to regional reactions and responses, looking at three sets of regional actors: ASEAN states; Australia and South Korea (reportedly, the two states under the most US pressure to reject the proposal); and Japan, which competes with China most directly for geopolitical influence and status as a leading actor in East Asia.

Regional reactions

ASEAN

In East Asia, ASEAN states, despite some important differences among them, represent the largest and most coherent audience for China's economic initiatives. The strongest multilateral statement made in support of the AIIB was made at the August 2014 ASEAN Post-Ministerial Meeting 10+1 session with China, just two months before the AIIB's official October 24, 2014 launch. As stated in the Chairman's statement, "The Meeting welcomed China's proposal to set up the Asian Infrastructure Investment Bank to provide financial support to regional infrastructure projects with an emphasis on supporting the implementation of the MPAC."[13] The deliberate and explicit emphasis on ASEAN's own master connectivity plan likely reflects ASEAN's concerns about controlling its own regional development agenda. On the other hand, ASEAN's own ministerial joint communiqué issued days before included no similar indication of support for the AIIB as in the 10+1 ASEAN–China Chairman's statement. As highlighted below, ASEAN states' decisions to participate in the AIIB have not been made without debate or concern; however, ASEAN states, as a whole, have generally concluded that the AIIB's promises of regional integration and development through regional infrastructure development are worth the risks.

Among ASEAN states, there were also differences worth noting. In summer months before the October 2014 MOU signing, for example, it was not clear that all ASEAN states had individually endorsed China's proposal. Of ASEAN states, only Malaysia, Cambodia, Thailand, and Singapore appeared to have expressed their official support as individual states. In this vein, it is useful to highlight some additional distinctions between ASEAN states – China's "frontier economies" (namely, Cambodia, Laos, and Myanmar); mostly dependable partners (Malaysia, Singapore, and Thailand); the most active South China Sea claimants (namely, the Philippines and Vietnam); and Indonesia.

Within ASEAN, ASEAN's frontier economies of Cambodia, Laos, and Myanmar stand to gain the most from participating in the AIIB. These states, in recent years, have benefitted much from China's economic attention already – though the AIIB would provide funds for multilateral projects beyond the bilateral and country-specific projects of their bilateral arrangements with China. Such projects would likely be more similar to the kinds of projects funded by the Greater Mekong Subregion projects under the ADB (see also discussion below). As the ADB is far from being able to meet all this subregion's significant infrastructure needs, additional funds from the AIIB would be most welcome. From a collective ASEAN standpoint, the AIIB would also help their larger objective of regional development and connectivity. Notably, these are areas of common interest between China and collective ASEAN, a point that again was emphasized by the 2014 10+1 Chairman's statement referencing MPAC.

The second ASEAN group is comprised of Malaysia, Singapore, and Thailand, which provide China with three of its more stable and predictable relationships in ASEAN. Each of these three states, for example, expressed its full support for the AIIB. Malaysia, which expressed support for the AIIB proposal in October 2013, was in fact one of the very first states not just in ASEAN but East Asia overall to publicly affirm the proposal. Thailand and Singapore both expressed their strong support in July 2014 following meetings in Beijing, though for somewhat different reasons. Thailand's Central Bank cited the failure of existing multinational development banks like the International Monetary Fund (IMF) and World Bank to adequately respond to the tremendous infrastructure needs in Asia that remained unfunded. In contrast, Singapore saw in participation an opportunity to ensure that the AIIB "stay open and inclusive, and draw upon the best practices of existing multilateral development banks in terms of governance and operations."[14]

Of ASEAN states, the responses of Vietnam and the Philippines, which comprise ASEAN's third group of states, may be the most interesting. As well detailed, Vietnam and the Philippines are the most active of ASEAN's South China Sea claimants. They have also been the states most directly affected by China's maritime actions. For example, in May 2014, at the same time that China was actively seeking regional support for the AIIB, it also made the decision to place an oil rig in waters disputed with Vietnam, an especially provocative action that complicated Vietnam's and ASEAN's efforts, at the time, to ease tensions. Two months earlier, in March, Manila, as well as Washington, also protested efforts by China's coast guards to block Filipino civilian vessels from resupplying marines located on the Second Thomas Shoal. In short, China's proactive economic diplomacy coincided with provocative maritime actions and heightened tensions. Those actions also reignited domestic pressures on both the Philippine and Vietnamese governments to take tougher approaches toward China. Hanoi, in particular, faced domestic pressure and rioting from groups which criticized it for being overly acquiescent on a host of issues *vis-à-vis* China.[15] Perhaps, not surprisingly, then, Vietnam was relatively quiet in making public statements about the bank; however, significantly, behind the scenes, there were reports of bilateral meetings between Vietnam and China about development and economic projects. Vietnam, along with the Philippines, also reportedly softened its criticisms of China at the 2014 East Asia Summit in November. At that meeting, both also emphasized cooperation and the potential of their China relations over conflict.

As for the Philippines, its response to China's proposal has been even more interesting because, more than Vietnam, the Philippines has been more vocal in criticizing China and pursuing strategic options (e.g., strengthening its alliance with the United States and taking its maritime disputes with China to the International Tribunal of the Law of the Sea). Yet, the Philippines also expressed notable public support for the AIIB through the end of 2014. In a December 2014 interview with *Nikkei Asian Review*, for example, Finance Secretary Cesar Purisima acknowledged the possibility that China might be using the AIIB to pursue Chinese hegemony or to leverage its maritime claims, but simply noted, "We will have to make sure that it will not be used for that purpose."[16] He also added that, in agreeing to be an AIIB founding member, "The Philippines gives China's regional bank the benefit of the doubt" and welcomed the economic benefits projected by the

AIIB.[17] In a November 2014 interview with China's *Xinhua* news agency, Laura Q. Del Rosario, undersecretary of the Philippine Department of Foreign Affairs, expressed even stronger support. In addition to highlighting China's greater than expected contributions to regional integration, she underscored the Philippines' tremendous infrastructure needs, especially on the maritime front, the need to "solve the congestion problem in the Port of Manila," and also the Philippines' particular geographic isolation from other states as an archipelagic state. As she put it, the Philippines, unconnected by railways or roads with the rest of the region, "can only engage in trade with its neighbours through shipping."[18] Similarly to Purisima, she concluded, "If we have shown our confidence in China's leadership, that means we know China will provide a good way for everybody to be included in infrastructure connectivity."[19]

China was also quick to respond positively to Philippine comments. This included a quick correction to a *Wall Street Journal* claim that China's "maritime silk road" initiative was "bypassing the Philippines." In its statement, the Chinese embassy in Manila affirmed that the Philippines

> is definitely part of the 21st century maritime silk road, as well as a member of the China–ASEAN maritime cooperation . . . China welcomes the Philippines to be a proactive and constructive partner of the 21st century maritime silk road, which serves the national interests of the Philippines and will contribute to the social and economic development of the Philippines.[20]

By mid-2015, however, Manila's tone had become more cautious, reflecting especially the position taken by President Benigno Aquino. At least partly, Aquino's caution appears to be moved by concerns that China's influence via the AIIB might constrain Manila's ongoing arbitration case *vis-à-vis* China as regards their competing maritime claims.[21] Domestic politics, which have plagued previous Chinese infrastructure projects in the Philippines, also likely contributed to Manila's reassessment.[22] Consequently, Manila – though still "keen" to join – decided to delay signing the June 2015 articles of agreement and to take the full time, until the end of 2015, "to prudently consider its membership."[23] On December 31, 2015, the Philippines officially committed to the AIIB and became its 57th founding member.

Last, but certainly not least, Indonesia offers yet another distinct ASEAN perspective on the AIIB. As noted above, Indonesia was the only ASEAN state not at the official MOU signing that launched the AIIB. Indonesia's absence, however, was more an issue of timing – specifically, Indonesia's ongoing presidential transition – than of special objection to the AIIB proposal. Specifically, the AIIB MOU was signed October 24, 2014, just four days after Jokowi Widodo's inauguration and before his full cabinet had been fully confirmed. Notably, Jokowi was quick to pledge support for the AIIB and two weeks later to affirm Indonesia's support at the November 9 APEC meeting in Beijing. Indonesia officially signed the AIIB MOU on November 27 and also pledged about US$416.7 million to the AIIB over five years.

Indonesia's interest in the AIIB shares some similarities with the Philippines. Like the Philippines, Indonesia has a particular interest in developing its maritime infrastructure, including deep-water ports. On this front, Indonesia has lagged behind its neighbors. As a result, Indonesia has been less able to benefit from the considerable revenues associated with extensive and growing shipping traffic through the Malacca Strait as its neighbors, Malaysia and Singapore, have. Like the Philippines, as well, Indonesia is an archipelagic country with extensive needs in the way of national integration. For Indonesia, the AIIB and the AIIB-associated Maritime Silk Road initiative are viewed as important additional resources that could serve Indonesia's interest in developing "west–east connectivity". In that infrastructure development in support of national connectivity was in fact one of Jokowi's campaign promises, Jokowi thus also has had a personal interest in working with the AIIB. Given Indonesia's financial limitations and considerable infrastructure needs, the AIIB – as one Indonesian analyst writing in the *Jakarta Post* put it – "offers a possible solution to Indonesia's infrastructure budgetary constraints."[24]

Beyond the above national integration interests, Indonesia's position on the AIIB also reflected concerns and interests that were distinctly Indonesian. Reflective of a long "free and active" foreign policy tradition, Indonesia negotiated for economic and political accommodations that would, at once, support Jakarta's long-time interest in more autonomous economic development and recognize what Jakarta saw to be its special standing in the region. Thus, Jokowi underscored the need for projects that invested in value-added refinements in Indonesia. Indonesia also pushed other interests reflective of its particular self-perception as a leading regional state, especially in ASEAN. Under Jokowi's predecessor, Susilo Bambang Yudhoyono, Indonesia actively initiated, for example, an ASEAN caucus within the AIIB framework, in which Indonesia and the other four founding ASEAN states (the "ASEAN 5") agreed to support the AIIB as a unit and to make a minimum collective contribution comparable to their contributions to the ADB.[25] Lastly, Jokowi requested that the AIIB be headquartered in Jakarta, a request he reiterated in June 2015, but was turned down.

South Korea and Australia

Of regional states, there were three other notable absences at the October 24, 2014 meeting, launching the AIIB as a regional initiative. In addition to Indonesia, whose absence again was due to its very recent electoral transition, and also Japan whose absence was expected (see discussion below), Australia and South Korea chose to stay on the sidelines, though they would reverse their decisions a year later. As close allies of the United States, both states were widely reported to have been under pressure from Washington not to participate in the AIIB.

In the case of Australia, themes of "strategic choice" – specifically between US security guarantees/relations, on the one hand, and Chinese economic benefits, on the other – featured especially large in its decision whether to join. Those tensions played out especially prominently in internal cabinet battles, with the Foreign

Ministry and National Security Council on one side, and the Treasury on the other, and Prime Minister Abbott somewhere in between. Of the two states, Australia also appears to have been under the most "intense" pressure from the Obama administration. In a "strong US regional diplomatic offensive in collaboration with Japan," the Obama administration reportedly pressured Australia via Secretary of State John Kerry, Treasury Secretary Jack Lew, and even President Obama himself.[26] According to Mark Hearn of Macquarie University, John Kerry was especially strong in impressing upon Australia the need to restrain China's ability "to rule investment and infrastructure projects in the region".[27] Reportedly, US concerns – both the official concern about financial lending standards and unofficial concern about the bank's strategic implications – were also well represented in Australia's internal debates. Prime Minister Abbott, for example, emphasized the official US line – that the AIIB was made problematic by questions about governance. As Prime Minister Abbott put it, "We would like to join, but it's got to be a multilateral institution with the kind of transparency and the kind of governance arrangements that, for argument's sake, the World Bank has."[28] Others in his cabinet – especially his foreign minister, Julie Bishop – emphasized the geopolitical ramifications of a China-dominated AIIB vis-à-vis US and Western interests in Asia.

In that internal cabinet debate, Abbott's Treasury Secretary Joe Hockey, along with his Trade Minister Andrew Robb, advocated the merits of participating in the bank at the start. To those concerned about financial lending practices, he emphasized how participation offered Australia the opportunity to shape the directions of the bank from the ground-up. To those whose concerns were more geopolitical, he noted the strategic advantages of participating in the AIIB's decision-making processes and being able to offer input on projects and priorities, including, for example, any potential projects in the nearby Pacific islands, a particular concern of Australia's.[29] Former Prime Minister Paul Keating also came out strongly in favor of the Treasury's position.[30]

In Australia, the economics of its relations with China also provided additional incentives to consider the AIIB. In 2013, for example, Australia's two-way trade with China (23.3%) was well over its trade with the United States (8.4%) and Japan (10.9%) combined (19.3%). When viewed through the lens of exports (goods and services), the contrast was even sharper, with China consuming 32.5% of Australian exports, compared to exports to the United States and Japan – 20.5%.[31] China has also been the "single largest buyer of Australian government debt."[32] At the same time, Australia's strategic questions about China have also not been insignificant. Thus, even at the same time that its economic relations with China have intensified, so too has its strategic partnership with the United States, as illustrated most prominently by Canberra's 25-year agreement to host US marines and training in Darwin in Australia's Northern Territory. The Darwin agreement, along with agreements to facilitate US surveillance activities and provide access to airstrips, as well as a possible base for US nuclear submarines near Perth, all serve to strengthen and facilitate the US presence and logistical capabilities in Southeast Asia and Oceania. In fact, Bates Gill and Tom Switzer conclude that, "Australia now figures more prominently in U.S. foreign policy than at any time since 1942–45."[33]

Given the above, it is not surprising that ongoing debates about China policy have frequently been framed in terms of Australia's economic livelihood versus its strategic and historical partnership with the United States.[34] As some put it, the choice between the US strategic relationship and the Chinese economic one had become the "classic dilemma" faced by Australia's future and the "core of Australia's apparent security dilemma."[35] In this case, Australia – despite reported Chinese promises that Australia would receive a senior role running the bank[36] – initially made the choice to side with the United States. According to the Australian press, a presentation by Foreign Minister Bishop, who "provided scenarios of how China could convert financial power via investment loans into direct military advantage in vulnerable nations close to Australia," proved especially persuasive.[37] Consequently, Australia sat out the October 2014 MOU in Beijing. This decision would be reversed in late March 2015, but notably just three days before the deadline of March 31 to file an application to join, and only after the United Kingdom, along with France, Italy, and Germany, as well as South Korea, decided to join.[38]

As for South Korea, Seoul experienced similar pressure from the United States, which expressed its "deep concern" about South Korea's potential participation in the AIIB. Seoul also shares some of the US concerns about governance and transparency. These pressures and concerns, however, sit in tension with South Korea's extensive economic relations with China. Similar to Australia, for example, South Korea's trade with China has been more than the total of its trade with the United States and Japan combined. As one indication of China's economic importance, Seoul signed a US$12.87 billion direct trade deal involving new yuan clearing and settlement arrangements with Beijing in July 2014.[39] In November 2014, on the sidelines of APEC and just after the AIIB MOU had been signed, the two governments also announced that they had finalized details on a landmark free trade agreement, which was subsequently ratified in June 2015.

Still, as important as these economic imperatives were, South Korea's more immediate and pressing concerns tended to be strategic. This is because South Korea experiences the strategic challenge and predicament in ways that are both more acute and more complex compared to some other states. It is made more acute by the more immediate (and historical) security threat from North Korea. It is made more complex by South Korea's reliance on both the United States and China to provide a measure of security or reassurance *vis-à-vis* North Korea.[40] Thus, South Korea's situation also differs fundamentally from that of Australia. Rather than an economic versus geopolitical or China versus US dilemma, as the "strategic choice" was framed in Australia, South Korea had strong strategic, as well as economic, reasons to work with China.

The importance South Korea has attached to its relationship with China is evidenced by the high-level diplomacy between Seoul and Beijing. During the period between the time that Presidents Park Geun-hye and Xi Jinping each took office in early 2013 and the AIIB's formal establishment in December 2015, the two leaders had participated in a total of six presidential summits, with three of those summits taking place before President Park's announcement that Seoul would be joining the AIIB as a founding member (an announcement made on March 26, 2014). By the end of 2014, the two leaders would meet in at least two additional face-to-face meetings (one in Seoul, the other on the sidelines of an APEC meeting). In contrast, only two summits had taken place between Washington and Seoul by the time of the October 2014 AIIB meeting, with a third following shortly afterwards at the APEC summit. As additional indications of the priority that Park and Xi each gave to their relationship, President Park chose to make China her second official Presidential state visit after the United States, as opposed to Japan, which had traditionally been the second stop of incoming South Korean presidents. President Xi reciprocated the gesture when he became the first Chinese president to visit Seoul before Pyongyang. The active diplomacy between the two states has moreover yielded benefits, including developments in their strategic relationship, an area that had been lagging behind the economic.

At the same time, other aspects of its summit diplomacy displayed Seoul's balancing act between the United States and China. In particular, President Park's much publicized decision to attend Beijing's ceremony commemorating the end of World War II on September 2, 2015, was notably preceded by a mid-August announcement that Seoul and Washington would be holding their fourth summit on October 16 – a summit that had originally been scheduled in June but postponed due to an outbreak of Middle East respiratory syndrome in South Korea. The *Korea Times* speculated that the timing of the announcement was meant to offset any perception that Seoul was prioritizing its China relations over the United States.[41]

Thus, while South Korea under President Park actively pursued, improved, and expanded relations with China, it also took steps to offset any possibility that such improvement might be at the expense of its US partnership.[42] In emphasizing a need for balance and mutual engagement of both powers such that neither relationship is harmed by the other, the question faced by South Korea is less one of "choice" between the United States and China so much as mutual strategic engagement. In a related vein, South Korean debates and discussions were more likely than those in Australia to view the AIIB debate and predicament in terms of a "G2 struggle" and "hegemony competition between the United States and China".[43] For those characterizing the AIIB in such terms, the recommendations were typically cautious, with warnings that Seoul maintain an independent stance and avoid being pressured by either the United States or China. On this point, South Korea's understood predicament and understanding of the challenge posed by United States–China differences over the AIIB and other issues shared important similarities with Southeast Asian states, which similarly feared being made casualties of great power conflict. Reportedly, South Korea, in a middle-power bid similar to Indonesia's, also probed the possibility that the AIIB might be headquartered in Seoul in exchange for its participation.

Such concerns, however, made the decision no less obvious as regards the AIIB. Indeed, South Korea was described as facing a "deep dilemma" about the AIIB for much of 2014, and as late as January 2015, Seoul was still characterized as not having made up its mind about the AIIB. Not until March 26 did Seoul agree to join the AIIB. Like Australia, the decision followed that of Western European powers. It also came just three days after a bilateral meeting between Presidents Xi and Park at the Nuclear Security Summit in The Hague.

Japan and the ADB

No doubt, the East Asian state most directly impacted by China's AIIB is Japan, which has been the leading regional power in East Asia for much of the last half-century. This is especially true in the economic realm where Japan until very recently had led other states by almost every measure. Its investment and aid activity have also played critical roles in organizing the political economies of East Asia. Politically, its status has also been institutionalized in institutions like the ADB, of which a Japanese national has served as president since the bank's founding in 1966. Geopolitically and strategically – despite constitutional constraints on its military role – Japan has also enjoyed status and importance as the anchor of the US strategic presence in East Asia. Given the recent difficulties of Japan–China relations, including maritime tensions in the East China Sea, Japan – of all the regional states – has not surprisingly been closest to the United States in its questions about China's motivations and its concern that China's expanded influence was being achieved at its expense.

Moreover, the way in which China pursued the AIIB probably did little to mitigate any suspicions that Japan may have had on this front. For example, China appears to have been late in extending or making clear a formal invitation to Japan. As noted, China had been peddling the proposal since October 2013, but not until June 30 the next year did reports highlight any potential Japanese (or US and European) involvement – though it is unclear which states had been invited to the five preparatory meetings that took place before the October 2014 launch.

In both its decision not to participate in the AIIB and also its efforts to counter China's economic initiatives with offerings of its own, Japan's response to the China-backed AIIB also tended to affirm some of the competitive dynamics associated with both states' approaches to regional institutions in East Asia. In both cases, mutual suspicions have historically complicated how each views the proposed regional initiatives from the other. Similar to the wariness with which China responded to Japan's Asian Monetary Fund, as well as early iterations of the East Asia Summit,[44] many in Japan harbored concerns about China's growing influence in the ASEAN+3 and now its pursuit of the AIIB as undermining Japan's standing and status in East Asia.[45]

For Japan, the creation of the AIIB has the most direct implications for the Japan-directed ADB. As many note, China may be justified in its dissatisfactions with existing arrangements. The ADB, along with the IMF, came to be a particular illustration of how existing arrangements had failed to keep up with changing economic realities and powers. In the case of the IMF, without reforms, China, the world's second largest economy, enjoyed only a 3.81% voting share. A 2010 agreement would have adjusted IMF voting and governing arrangements, with China standing the most to gain – but the US Senate had refused to ratify the changes, leaving reforms in limbo. It was not until nearly five years later, in late December 2015, and only just as the AIIB came into being, that the US Senate finally approved the reforms and allowed them to take effect. However, even under that agreement, China's voting share remained relatively small, increasing only 2.26 percentage points or 59% from what it had been; moreover, the G-6 economies would still control 39% to the 16.19% vote controlled by the Brazil, Russia, India, China, and South Africa (BRICS) economies plus Indonesia and South Korea. On the other hand, while the overall shift in voting power from developed economies to emergent economies has been characterized as "meager"[46] – in fact, the developing world outside the BRICS saw their voting share drop three points – the proposed changes to the IMF governing board were more significant.

The political structure of the ADB similarly gave China a smaller role than the size of its economy seemed to warrant. The United States and Japan, at the end of 2014, each controlled a 12.8% vote, contributing to an Organization for Economic Cooperation and Development total of about 58%. In contrast, China's voting power – as in the IMF and World Bank – was less than 5.5%.[47] The challenges of adjusting existing banks to better reflect changing economic realities, especially China's heightened importance, fed a sense of injustice felt not just by China but also other emerging and developing powers. The situation also provided many states with an argument for an alternative development bank.

In contrast, under the AIIB articles of agreement, signed in June 2015 and that went into effect in December that year, China enjoys 26.06% voting power, just enough to block any decision requiring a super majority constituted by three-fourths of the voting power and two-thirds of the members.[48] In response to expressed concerns about the AIIB's mandate, Chinese officials have emphasized that the AIIB would serve functions and priorities different from, and complementary to, other MDBs. China has characterized the AIIB as "focus[ing] on infrastructure construction in Asia to promote regional connectivity and economic cooperation,"[49] in contrast to the World Bank and ADB's poverty reduction priorities, for example. As ADB officials have rightly corrected, however, infrastructure projects have historically been a big part of its funding portfolio and continue to be an important area of activity for the bank, even if recent years have seen greater attention to poverty reduction consistent with UN Millennium Goals. The ADB infrastructure projects in the Mekong have been especially notable. For Japan, it has therefore been difficult not to see the AIIB, whose agenda seems to overlap so considerably with the ADB and its historical mandate and agenda, as a rival and competing institution.

Moreover, other Chinese actions may have played to those fears. For example, at the May 12, 2014 ADB meeting in Kazakhstan, China chose to pull 16 countries aside, skipping one of the scheduled, elective events, to discuss the proposed AIIB. Known states that were invited were Pakistan, South Korea, Kazakhstan, Mongolia, and Sri Lanka.[50] While China's move may have been practical – and certainly, Asia's multilateral meetings are well known for providing venues for important and substantive bilateral and other discussions between subgroups of states – the decision nevertheless seems, at a minimum, impolitic given Japan's concerns and the AIIB's overlap with the ADB.

Thus, Japan's wary response to China's AIIB proposal has not been unexpected, nor has its decision not to participate in the creation of the AIIB. In fact, in the months leading up to the October 2014 MOU, Tokyo appears to have joined the United States in trying to persuade others not to join. Those efforts, however, have been complicated by the well-known practical challenges facing both the ADB and the Asian region. As noted, infrastructure needs have been tremendous and insufficiently met by the ADB, whose infrastructure projects today also compete with ten other identified strategic priorities. (In contrast, the AIIB would focus solely on infrastructure.) Moreover, the process of approving projects in the ADB is well known to be slow and belabored – with "infrastructure projects typically fac[ing] delays of six or seven years."[51] That process has also been the subject of much complaint among recipient states eager to pursue various projects. As representatives of Thailand's central bank put it, the AIIB may be necessary, if only because "the World Bank and the ADB have not been playing their roles."[52] Thus, while Mitsuhiro Furusawa, Japan's vice finance minister, may have had good reason to be "not convinced" about the specifics of China's AIIB, it also seems a stretch to suggest, as he did in July 2014, that the ADB was without problems in representation or function.[53] In contrast, ADB President Takehiko Nakao may have been more forthright in acknowledging the potential role the AIIB could play in substantially boosting the amount of funding available to East Asia and, at the same time, forcing the ADB's red-tape-laden institution to reform. Nakao may have also offered the most honest response about the AIIB, when he said, "I understand it, but I don't welcome it."[54]

At the time of the October 2014 MOU, a comparison of the two banks would have shown the AIIB lagging behind the ADB in size, membership, and standing. In the year that followed, however, China's overtures and accommodations did much to narrow some of those gaps. For example, at the time of the October 2014 AIIB launch, the proposed AIIB, with 22 members and a projected total capital of US$50 billion, was considerably smaller in membership and capital compared to the ADB's 67 members and US$174 billion capital account. Further, the ADB was also rated AAA by Standard and Poor's compared to the AA– given to China's sovereign government.[55] However, in the subsequent months, the AIIB had gained considerably in both membership and capital. By the time states arrived in Beijing to sign the AIIB's articles of agreement in June 2015, the AIIB could boast 57 committed members, including four members of the Group of Seven – and a projected US$100 billion in capital funds.[56]

In contrast to Australia, the AIIB's expanded membership made Japan no less willing to reconsider its stance on the AIIB. And, while Jin Liqun, president of the AIIB, has said that "the door keeps open for Japan and the United States to be a member of the AIIB,"[57] Japan remains, with the United States, the key regional powers that have chosen not to participate.

Conclusion

As highlighted in the above discussion, China has had to negotiate a complex regional environment in pursuit of the AIIB. The bank responds to well-established needs in infrastructure and development, as well as some widely agreed concerns about the political biases and structural constraints of existing MDBs, especially at the global level but also the IMF. Since the signing of the AIIB's articles of agreement in June 2015, key states have experienced changes in government that have generally worked in support of, rather than against, the AIIB. Malcolm Turnbull's turn as prime minister in Australia in September 2015 appears to suggest a more pragmatic, less United States-centric, economic agenda that includes a more supportive stance towards the AIIB than that of his predecessor, Tony Abbott.[58] Perhaps most notable has been the election of Rodrigo Duterte in the Philippines in 2016. While there remain many questions about the Duterte government, statements thus far suggest that, compared to Aquino, he will be both more practical in negotiating contentious issues like the South China Sea and more open to working with China on developmental and national priorities. At a minimum, Beijing may find Duterte a welcome change given Aquino's vigilant stances on the South China Sea, prioritization of US security ties, and decision to seek international arbitration on maritime claims.

In Myanmar, as well, there have been new diplomatic openings. While the National League for Democracy's historic November 2015 victory in Myanmar's first openly contested election since 1990 initially raised questions that it would pursue policies more autonomous from China, diplomatic exchanges between the two governments over the course of 2016, including Chinese foreign minister Wang Yi's visit to Nay Pyi Taw in April and Aung San Suu Kyi's visit to Beijing in August, indicate important willingness on both sides to cooperate on the challenges that have recently complicated relations, in particular, tensions over existing Chinese projects (e.g., in the Sagaing region and Kachin state) and ethnic conflicts on the Myanmar-side of the border. In October 2016, AIIB President Jin Liqun, fulfilling a promise made in May, visited Myanmar to identify potential AIIB projects there.

Meanwhile, the AIIB has also gained additional support or, at least, acceptance from other quarters. This includes Washington, which has since expressed new support for cooperation between the AIIB and existing institutions. It is not an insignificant fact that 57 states are now members of the AIIB – a point that is not lost on Washington, which suffered considerable criticism for its initial opposition and approach, as well as its major strategic misreading of regional interests. Indeed, since the AIIB's articles of agreement officially entered into force in December 2015, 30 additional states, according to the AIIB, have now applied for or indicated interest in membership. In summer 2016, Canada under a new Liberal Party government became one of the later states to express interest. While new members will not enjoy the same status as founding states, the AIIB's growing membership nevertheless is an indication of growing acceptance of both the bank and a larger leading role for China, at least on the developmental front.

Perhaps more importantly, other multinational development banks have become more receptive about the prospect of working with the AIIB. Both the World Bank and the ADB have taken steps to work with the AIIB on joint projects.[59] In April 2016 AIIB president Jin Liqun and World Bank president Jim Yong Kim agreed to a co-financing agreement that would facilitate cooperation on nearly a dozen jointly financed projects in Central Asia, South Asia, and East Asia in water, transport, and energy. Similarly, at the ADB's annual Board of Governors' meeting in early May 2016, the AIIB and ADB signed an MOU expressing their agreement to "strengthen cooperation, including co-financing, at the strategic and technical levels on the basis of complementarity, value added, institutional strengths and comparative advantages, and mutual benefit."[60] Also in May, the AIIB signed an MOU that sets out a framework for strategic and operational cooperation with the European Bank for Reconstruction and Development.

At the same time, while there have been compelling practical and political interests motivating Asia's regional states to support China's bank, it is equally clear, as this discussion has highlighted, that those interests have also been mitigated by some considerable questions about Chinese practices and perhaps, most of all, intent. In an ideal world, "speculation about other countries' motivations" should not outweigh "estimations of what can be accomplished,"[61] but such speculation has, in fact, been the greatest obstacle faced by China in its pursuit of not just the AIIB, but more generally, legitimacy and security. No doubt, there will be frictions and continued questions as China grows into the leading position it appears to be carving for itself. While the AIIB gives greater weight to developing economies than other lending institutions, it remains the case that China enjoys disproportionate influence under the current voting and governance structure. Its decisions to give key vice presidential positions to South Korea, Indonesia, the United Kingdom, India, and Germany (whose representative also has extensive experience in the World Bank) is both political and practical, aimed at rewarding key supporters and at the same time reassuring both regional and world audiences about the bank's credibility.

Thus far, developments – including the above-mentioned co-financing and cooperative arrangements with the World Bank, ADB, and EBRD – suggest that China has been strongly motivated to create a "good" bank that can offer a meaningful and legitimate "southern alternative" to existing lending institutions and development models, but that is also, at the same time, integrated into a world lending infrastructure. Similarly, in designing the bank and in pursuit of "best practices," Beijing has actively sought the participation of established Western financial actors and the advice of former US and European financial representatives. China's choice of Jin Liqun to head the bank additionally gives credence to that motivation, as Jin's experiences working with the IMF and other financial institutions give him both the background and potential insight necessary if the AIIB is to be a "better bank." This much is clear: the nearly 60 states that are members of the AIIB have not entered that decision lightly but they are counting on China making the adjustments that support the mutually beneficial ("win–win") relationships critical to achieving the "harmonious world" that both they and China hope to enjoy.

Notes

1 The author gratefully acknowledges financial support from the Czech Science Foundation under the standard research grant no. GA16-02288S.
2 Bangladesh, Brunei Darussalam, Cambodia, India, Kazakhstan, Kuwait, Lao PDR, Malaysia, Mongolia, Myanmar, Nepal, Oman, Pakistan, Philippines, Qatar, Singapore, Sri Lanka, Thailand, Uzbekistan, and Vietnam.
3 See, for example, Network of East Asian Think Tanks. "Financing Infrastructure Connectivity in East Asia: Challenges and Solutions." Draft Report of NEAT Working Group on Connectivity Cooperation in East Asia, June 2013, Beijing, China.
4 Andrew Elek. "Welcoming China's Asian Infrastructure Investment Bank Initiative." *East Asia Forum,* September 21, 2014.
5 "An Asian Infrastructure Bank." *Economist,* October 4, 2013.
6 See comments of Indu Bhushan of the ADB quoted in Lean Alfred Santos. "ADB Open to Asia Pacific Infrastructure Development Bank." *Development Newswire.* February 21, 2014. https://www.devex.com/news/adb-open-to-asia-pacific-infrastructure-development-bank-82902.
7 See, for example, discussion in Stuart Larkin. "The Conflicted Role of the AIIB in Southeast Asia." *ISEAS Perspective,* 23, May 8 (2015).
8 Indonesia's absence was due to its recent election and the ongoing electoral transition. It committed to the bank very soon after the October 24, 2014 meeting / announcement.
9 Lean Alfred Santos. "Exclusive Details: China's Plans for a New Asian Infrastructure Investment Bank." *Development Newswire.* June 2, 2014. https://www.devex.com/news/adb-open-to-asia-pacific-infrastructure-development-bank-82902.
10 As one analyst characterizes it, there are "two mainstream conspiracy theories in the marketplace regarding China's AIIB plan. [First] many fear that the new bank is China's way of challenging the US and Japan dominated Asian Development Bank (ADB) . . . Second, China could use AIIB to legitimize its economic expansion into its neighbors' territories." See Roger Yu Du. "China Expands Asian Infrastructure Investment Bank Proposal." *Global Risk Insights.* July 13, 2014. http://globalriskinsights.com/2014/07/chinas-asian-infrastructure-investment-bank-throwing-carrots/. See also "China's $50 Billion Asia Bank Snubs Japan, India." *Bloomberg,* May 12, 2014.
11 Prior to the AIIB's establishment, some analysts had also discussed the possibility of headquartering the AIIB in a country like Singapore where the AIIB might have benefitted from an established financial community, known financial institutions, and reputable practices. The political symbolism of a China-based bank may be why China decided not to entertain proposals to base the AIIB elsewhere (see also discussions below on South Korea and Indonesia). The decision to base the bank in Beijing, not Shanghai, seems also to underscore the politics, less the economics, of the bank.
12 See, for example, Mark E. Manyin, et al. "Pivot to the Pacific? The Obama Administration's 'Rebalancing' Toward Asia." *CRS Report for Congress,* March 28, 2012.
13 Chairman's Statement on the PMC 10+1 Sessions, August 9–10, 2014. Nay Pyi Taw, Myanmar.
14 Rachel Chang. "Singapore, China Looking at Possible Third Projects." *Straits Times,* July 29, 2014.
15 See Eva Dou and Richard Paddock. "Behind Vietnam's Anti-China Riots, A Tinderbox of Wider Grievance." *The Wall Street Journal,* June 17, 2014.
16 Cliff Venzon. "Philippines Gives China's Regional Bank Benefit of the Doubt." *Nikkei Asian Review,* December 11, 2014.
17 Ibid.
18 "China has Done a Lot in Regional Economic Integration: Philippine Official." *Xinhua,* November 5, 2014.
19 "Philippines Gives Praise to China." *Xinhua,* November 7, 2014.

20 Trefor Moss. "China Says Philippines Is Part of Trade Plan." *Wall Street Journal*, November 14, 2014.
21 See Prinz Magtulis. "Phl to Participate in AIIB Crafting of By-Laws, Lending Rules." *Philippine Star*, September 7, 2015.
22 See "Why PH is Not Yet Joining the China-Led Infra Bank." *Rappler.com*, June 15, 2015.
23 Finance Secretary Cesar Purisima quoted in Minoru Satake. "Thailand, Other Holdouts Could Still Join AIIB This Year." *Nikkei Asian Review*, June 30, 2015; Chino Leyco. "PH Still Keen on AIIB—DOF." *Manila Times*, June 29, 2015.
24 Malia Roochma. "Banking on Infrastructure (Opinion)." *Jakarta Post*, December 17, 2014.
25 C.P.F. Luhilima. "Superimposition of China's 'Silk Road' and Indonesia's Maritime Fulcrum." *Jakarta Post*, December 13, 2014.
26 Paul Kelly. "Strategy Fears Sank China Deal." *Australian*, October 31, 2014.
27 Mark Hearn. "Australia Must Adjust to a Shifting Center of Gravity." *Sydney Morning Herald*, November 3, 2014.
28 Gabrielle Chan. "Australia Won't Join Asian Infrastructure Bank 'Until Rules Change'." *The Guardian*, October 31, 2014.
29 Ibid.
30 Ibid.
31 In goods alone, China consumes 36% of Australian exports, which are also heavily dominated by commodities. Australia Department of Foreign Affairs and Trade. http://dfat.gov.au/trade/resources/trade-at-a-glance/pages/html/two-way-trading-partners.aspx.
32 Bates Gill and Tom Switzer. "The New Special Relationship." *Foreign Affairs*, February 19, 2015.
33 Ibid.
34 In Australia, there have also been those who argue on strategic grounds the need to loosen Australia's relationship with the United States in order to provide China the strategic space to develop peacefully and in ways that are mutually beneficial to the region. See, in particular, the work of Hugh White. See, for example, Hugh White. "Power Shift." *Quarterly Essay*, 39 (December 2010); Hugh White. *The China Choice: Why America Should Share Power*. Colingwood: Black Inc., 2012. See also discussion in Gill and Switzer (2015).
35 Paul Kelly. "Strategy Fears Sank China Deal." *Australian*, October 31, 2014; Philippa Brant. "Australia and the AIIB: A Lost Opportunity." *Lowy Interpreter*, October 31, 2014.
36 See Phillip Coorey. "Australia Offered Top Role in China's $57b Infrastructure Bank." *Australian Financial Review*, November 3, 2014.
37 Philippa Brant. "Australia and the AIIB: A Lost Opportunity." *Lowy Interpreter*, October 31, 2014.
38 See Jane Perlez. "Australia to Join Regional Development Bank Led by China." *New York Times*, March 28, 2015.
39 "China Invites Korea to Join Asian Infrastructure Investment Bank." *Korea Herald*, July 3, 2014.
40 On China's role as a security provider as regards the Korean peninsula, see, especially, Chapter 3 in Evelyn Goh. *The Struggle for Order: Hegemony, Hierarchy, and Transition in Post-Cold War East Asia*. Oxford: Oxford University Press, 2013.
41 "After Numerous Delays, Park to Visit US in October for Talks with Obama." *Korea Times*, August 12, 2015.
42 See discussion in Jaeho Hwang. "The ROK's China policy under Park Geun-hye." Washington, DC: The Brookings Institution, August 2014.
43 Ko Chang-am (of the Korea Railway Association). "Asian Infrastructure Investment Bank and Korea's Position." *Korea Times*, August 4, 2014.

44 See, for example, Chien-Peng Chung. "China and Japan in 'ASEAN Plus' Multilateral Arrangements." *Asian Survey,* 53, no. 5 (2013): 801–24; and Jinsoo Park, "Political Rivals and Regional Leaders: Dual Identities and Sino-Japanese Relations within East Asian Cooperation." *Chinese Journal of International Politics,* 6 (2013): 85–107.
45 See Park, "Political Rivals. . ."; Christopher Dent (ed.), *China, Japan, and Regional Leadership in East Asia.* Cheltenham: Edward Elgar, 2008.
46 As Vestergaard and Wade conclude, "The headline figure of a 6.2% shift conceals the reality that the key shift from developed countries to EMDCs is only 2.6%, the rest being shifts within the category of emerging market and developing countries from 'overrepresented' EMDCs to 'underrepresented' EMDCs." See Jakob Vestergaard and Robert H. Wade. "Out of the Woods: Gridlock in the IMF, and the World Bank Puts Multilateralism at Risk." Danish Institute of International Studies (DIIS) Report 2014:06.
47 See Asian Development Bank. *Annual Report 2014.* http://www.adb.org/sites/default/files/institutional-document/158032/oi-appendix1.pdf.
48 See Scott Morris and Mamoru Higashikokubaru. "Doing the Math on AIIB Governance." Center for Global Development, last modified July 2, 2015. http://www.cgdev.org/blog/doing-math-aiib-governance.
49 Chinese Finance Minister Lou Jiwei, quoted in "China Starts Work on $50 bln Asia Infrastructure Bank." *Reuters,* March 7, 2014.
50 "China's $50 Billion Asia Bank Snubs Japan, India." *Bloomberg,* May 12, 2014.
51 Anthony Rowley. "China's Global Financing Goals Face Pushback from Development Banks." *Institutional Investor,* December 19, 2014.
52 Sarun Kijvasun and Suphanee Pootpisut. "Thailand to Help Launch Investment Bank for Asia." *The Nation (Thailand),* July 17, 2014.
53 "Japan Reluctant to Join China-led Investment Bank." *Japan Times,* July 5, 2014.
54 "Brunei to Sign on to Asian Infrastructure Investment Bank." *Brunei Times,* November 10, 2014.
55 "China's $50 Billion Asia Bank Snubs Japan, India." *Bloomberg,* May 12, 2014.
56 Seven states had to delay signing due to insufficient time to get the motion through necessary domestic ratification requirements. Details had only been finalized in late May, leaving only about five weeks for states to put the motion through any necessary domestic procedures. Denmark, Kuwait, Poland, South Africa, as well as Malaysia and Thailand, for example, had been unable to sign in June for that reason. The Philippines, as noted, chose to delay as a result of ongoing South China Sea tensions with China. The seven states were given until the end of December to sign and would all eventually do so.
57 Youkyung Lee. "AIIB Chief Says Door Open for America, Japan." *The China Post,* September 10, 2015.
58 Andrew Carr. "Will a Turnbull Government Mean a New Foreign Policy for Australia?" *East Asia Forum,* November 3, 2015.
59 Wendy Wu. "AIIB and World Bank Reach Deal on Joint Projects, as China-Led Lender Prepares to Approve US$1.2 Billion of Funds This Year." *South China Morning Post,* April 14, 2016.
60 AIIB press statement, cited in "AIIB. ADB Sign Memorandum to Co-Finance Projects." *AFP,* May 2, 2016.
61 See, for example, comments of Paolo Mauro of the Peterson Institute for International Economics. Paolo Mauro. "Why America Should Join the AIIB." *Project Syndicate* June 12, 2015.

4 China's financial power in Asia
Strategic implications of RMB internationalization for regional relations

Utpal Vyas[1]

Introduction

In recent years, the Chinese government has actively been looking to promote the usage of its national currency, the renminbi (RMB), outside its own borders. At first the RMB came to be used in regional trade, and increasingly it is now being used in China's trade with countries around the world.[2] In the post-war era, China has traditionally tightly controlled the use of its national currency in order to implement its own development strategies without external influence, for example allowing dollar accounts which cannot actually be used without converting back into RMB, in order for state-owned banks to have access to foreign exchange.[3] However, with the opening up and reform policies pursued since the 1980s, China has become increasingly reliant on the established international institutions which enable international trade and investment; this has mostly meant using the established international trading currency, the US dollar, to conduct its trade and investment. As a result of this policy, the Chinese government has accrued huge reserves of dollars as it has continually recorded trade surpluses with the United States and other major economies around the world.[4] While the use of the dollar in its international dealings allowed it to protect the RMB from direct shocks and external influence, the reliance on the dollar, and hence US fiscal and monetary policymakers, has increasingly become an irritant for Chinese leaders and businesses. The drive to internationalize the RMB has occurred in the context of US dollar dominance in the world economy and China's wish for more international financial autonomy.

The other major and interlinked background situation has been the continued striving for China and its leaders to regain its international status and prestige after the "century of humiliation" at the hands of foreigners. The Chinese Communist Party (CCP) has striven to build a national identity for China which, while trying to assert its great power status, also recalls the national history of greatness and then semi-colonization at the hand of Europeans and Japanese. The development process, including the encouragement of trade, foreign investment, and now financial internationalization, can be seen as a long-term drive to achieve the rehabilitation of China in the world. At the present time, it seems that China's preference is to achieve this within the existing international institutional framework which has been set-up in the post-war era by the United States and its partners. At a time of social instability in China, the regime needs to maintain the legitimacy of the CCP, stability in the economy, and continued economic growth[5]; the internationalization of the RMB can also be seen as part of this context.

This chapter seeks to consider these factors while asking the question: what are the reasons for and implications of RMB internationalization? It then seeks to consider in particular the strategic implications of RMB internationalization for Asian countries. The paper will firstly outline theoretical aspects of the context of RMB internationalization, including ideas of nation building, developmentalism, and national currencies. It will then consider how the RMB is being internationalized at this time, and conclude with an attempt to answer the above questions.

Theoretical perspectives

National identity, developmentalism, and global finance

Nation building and national identity construction are processes which all modern nation states have either been through to a greater or lesser extent, or are still undergoing. The initial aspects of these processes concern the securing of territorial sovereignty, building of national institutions, infrastructure, and other physical aspects of a nation state. However, instilling a sense of national identity in the minds of citizens is a longer process. Some nation states have been able to build strong national identities and culture through an organic process spanning centuries, but in the case of nation states which wish to modernize within a shorter period of time, perhaps one or two generations, a more top-down approach involving the use of national, government-controlled education systems and influence over the national discourse through national media has been evident; this is particularly the case in China. This package of processes has been termed "developmentalism," along the lines of the Japanese model of nation building.[6]

In China, the transition from feudalistic empire to a modern nation state has been traumatic, and started during a period of weakness and semi-colonization by Western powers and Japan – the so-called "century of humiliation," which is so emphasized in history education and national discourse.[7] The main goal of Chinese leaders since the collapse of the Qing Dynasty has been to unite China, and modernize its economy and society so that it may never be controlled by outsiders again. The perceived need to implement these goals as quickly as possible, and the need to legitimize the single-party rule of the CCP, has meant that a restoration of national strength and prestige has taken precedence over political and social development. National economic development has been seen as an essential ingredient of this restoration since the founding of the People's Republic of China (PRC).[8]

Deng Xiaoping's opening-up and reform measures were all implemented with this primary goal in mind. Nevertheless, his inherent pragmatism meant that he planned to achieve China's goals by joining the US-backed system of international institutions, rather than while fighting against them. His admonition for China to "stay out of the limelight and lie low" (*taoguang yanghui*)[9] implied that China should maintain a low profile internationally, until it could build enough national strength to be more assertive. The various stages of economic reform and opening up followed this dictum, until the introduction of the "go out" (*zou chuqu*) policy in 2001, which coincided with China's accession to the World Trade Organization (WTO). The first stage involved opening up trade relations with the United States and increasing trade with other capitalist nations in the 1980s. Domestic liberalization was also relatively strongly promoted in this period.[10] The second stage involved a retrenching and strengthening of national state-owned enterprises in the 1990s following the Tiananmen Square protests and the collapse of the Soviet Union, while at the same time opening up to private foreign investment. The third stage has led to encouragement from the state for Chinese companies to invest abroad and acquire foreign markets; finally, the fourth stage appears to involve the internationalization of the RMB and the strengthening of Chinese financial infrastructure. All of these stages have shown that China has been trying to achieve its goals within the established international institutional framework, by first joining the UN, the Security Council, the international aid systems, and eventually the WTO and international financial system.

The current regime under Xi Jinping is clearly comfortable with the image of China as a great power,[11] and has increasingly been making statements which advocate that the dominance of the US dollar as a global reserve currency in the international trade and financial systems should be curtailed.[12] The efforts to internationalize usage of the RMB have increased along with these statements.

Currencies and national identity

How does a national currency reflect and contribute to national identity? National currencies typically represent the credibility of a nation state to repay its debts. States therefore need to show that they can manage their finances in a trustworthy manner; if a state loses control of its debts, and eventually loses the trust that holders of its currency place in it, the value of the currency will decline and inflation in the economy will result, leading to economic and social hardship for citizens of that country.

For the CCP, this issue relates not only to national identity, but also to its own legitimacy as the sole political party to have the right to govern China.[13] One of the main planks of CCP legitimacy has traditionally been to maintain price stability[14] in order to guard against inflation and enable economic growth. There has often been a link between periods of instability for the Party and inflation in the economy.[15]

In addition to the role of the national currency as a guarantor of credibility in domestic terms, there is the international arena to consider. Currencies may be used internationally for several reasons.[16] The most fundamental reason is their credibility, as with the domestic case. In addition, companies may use an international currency to conduct trade in. For the purposes of international trade, the

US dollar has been the currency of choice in most transactions since the early 20th century[17]; this has been particularly clear in East Asia. This was due to the United States being the largest economy and trading nation after the war. Deep and highly liquid markets in the dollar meant that holding and using dollars to settle transactions was a cheaper method than using other currencies. In addition, the United States' economic dynamism meant that deciding to settle trade in dollars was a relatively safe bet for future transactions.[18] It was much easier to obtain and sell dollars in times of need, for companies and individuals.

A further use of an international currency is as a reserve currency, held by countries which see a need to guarantee the value of their own national currencies, especially in times of financial instability and debt crises. The US dollar has also been the reserve currency of choice in the post-war era. This is a consequence of its strong position over the long term, as well as an indication of other countries' trust in the United States' economic, financial, as well as security status in the world.

The US government therefore not only benefits in terms of its image from dollar hegemony, but it benefits financially from being the issuer of the world's reserve currency. US companies do not incur any foreign-exchange transaction costs when trading in dollars, and US banks and companies can benefit from low interest rates as other companies and governments are willing to buy and hold dollars, usually in the form of US treasury bills, in effect funding the US government. In addition, the cost of printing paper money, or issuing electronic money, is negligible compared to its face value, and so the issuer gains a profit from doing this (seignorage).[19]

Hence, having a strong and internationally trusted currency contributes to a country's image of credibility and economic strength, and so helps to confer a strong national identity.

Issues for RMB internationalization

Due to all of the aforementioned points, there can be advantages to issuing an internationally used currency. In order to gain some of these advantages, and based on the fact that its economy is now the largest in the world in purchasing power parity terms,[20] the Chinese government has some reason to try to internationalize the RMB. However, there are also negative aspects to having an internationally used and freely convertible currency.

Firstly, in order to create trust and credibility in a currency, the currency issuer must guarantee to convert the currency into another one when requested. This is equivalent to saying that the central bank issuer of the currency will always pay back its debts. Hence the central bank must either have sufficient reserves to do this, or have sufficient credibility in international markets or with partners to borrow money from others to repay its immediately due debts. In the case of the People's Bank of China (PBOC), as of July 2016 it had foreign exchange reserves totaling $3.2 trillion,[21] so this would not appear to be a problem. Nevertheless, in the last financial year, reserves have been declining due to capital flight and the PBOC fighting currency speculation.[22] Some economists have questioned whether the PBOC will be able to maintain adequate reserves under International Monetary Fund guidelines in the near future.[23]

Secondly, the issuer of the international currency must accept that it has to liberalize its capital account.[24] That is, money should be freely allowed to flow in and out of its economy, and users of the currency should be able to buy and sell it freely as much as they wish. If there are capital controls (e.g., restrictions on the amount of the currency that can be sent out of or brought into a country), and foreign-exchange controls (e.g., restrictions on how much currency can be bought and sold), or restrictions on who can hold the currency or how it can be used, then it is not likely to be trusted as a credible international currency.

In the case of China, although the PBOC has taken steps to liberalize the capital account, it is still not possible for companies and individuals to invest or borrow large amounts of RMB directly and freely.[25] The offshore trading which has grown in recent years was initially a result of unofficial leakage of the RMB into offshore economies, as Chinese companies agreed various deals to use RMB with foreign counterparties without specific authorization from the PBOC. On the other hand, the PBOC has not actively cracked down on the offshore RMB trading; in particular, in Hong Kong, the RMB-denominated bonds (so-called "dim sum bonds") have been issued by companies looking to use offshore RMB for investment inside and outside China. Nevertheless, it seems that the PBOC would like to maintain more control over offshore RMB trading; this is one motivation for its agreements in recent years to provide RMB credit to specific banks operating in offshore markets. The trades which are conducted through these banks must also be cleared by designated clearing banks,[26] through which it may be possible for the PBOC to monitor transactions and influence them if necessary. From the point of view of the PBOC and Chinese government, the RMB should be internationalized but they should still be able to control its value and usage as much as possible. Hence, the PBOC has been liberalizing capital controls internationally while at the same time pioneering the use of various technical and regulatory tools it has, both domestically and through its international agents, to indirectly exert control over the currency.

Thirdly, notwithstanding the above points, the issuer of the currency must accept that it may not be fully able to control the value of the currency in international markets[27] should offshore trading become significantly large. The trades and investments of large national banks and even international private banks and other corporations could affect the value of the currency if they involve sufficient volumes. Currency speculators have often been blamed for sudden movements in currency prices[28] which are designed to make them profits rather than reflecting the real economy on which the currency is based. This is the chief reason given by some countries for imposing capital controls on their currencies. The case of China is often cited as a good example of the "trilemma" which occurs in the need to juggle the conflicting goals of currency stability, interest rate control, and freedom of capital movements[29]; it is not possible for China to have a completely stable currency and complete control over interest rates while having freedom of cross-border capital movement and a freely convertible international RMB.

Traditionally, the CCP has been loath to cede any control of its economy to foreigners; there is ample evidence from other countries' efforts to manage their currencies' exchange rates, despite them being fully liberalized, that it is a difficult prospect considering the huge capital flows involved in global foreign-exchange trading. Hence, the PBOC has been attempting to liberalize gradually, in the face of opposition from domestic conservative factions who have traditionally been wary of once more ceding control of China's economy to outsiders.[30]

While there is a general consensus among Chinese scholars on the need to restore China's status,[31] there is a strong tension between those in China who wish to liberalize further, in order to fully participate in global finance and thus enhance China's standing and influence, and those factions that wish to maintain more national strength and autonomy by containing outside influences.[32] The implications of which path China takes in the future for the world and regional economies will be profound in either case.

Strategic implications for Asian countries

The growth of the Chinese economy has already had profound implications for all East Asian countries. China is now the number-one trading partner for all major economies in the region,[33] although it may not always be the main final export destination. This fact alone means that fluctuations in trade with China would have serious strategic implications for countries in the region. While China has become a member of the WTO and therefore in theory must treat all its trading partners equally, there is much scope for unilateral adjustment of trade relations for strategic reasons, for example, through the use of non-tariff barriers, nation-specific anti-trust investigations or corruption investigations, and other administrative or technical regulations.[34] The case of China's sudden restrictions on the export of rare-earth metals to Japan and other countries in 2010, which seemed to be for strategic reasons, is a clear example.[35] The Chinese government is also accelerating its pursuit of a set of regional institutions based on its own terms, which will only increase dependence on Chinese trade and capital.[36]

Apart from the strategic implications of heavy dependence on one country for trade, there are also less obvious implications that are related to which currencies are used to conduct trade in. The Chinese government, as part of its RMB liberalization program, has been encouraging its companies to conduct trade with and invest in foreign companies in RMB.[37] As soon as a company decides to conduct trade in a given currency it becomes exposed to risk in the fluctuations in value of that currency. The value of a currency can be affected in many ways, but clearly the actions of the currency-issuing country are major determinants of its value, even in the case of nominally floating value currencies. Past instances where governments have managed to change the value of their currencies are numerous; the most obvious examples have been conducted by the US government, which has at various times asked or forced its allies into adjusting the value of their currencies against the dollar for its own reasons.[38] In 1971 the United States removed gold backing for its currency, in effect forcing a dramatic devaluation of the dollar to address the balance of payments deficit and to improve export competitiveness.[39] In 1985 the United States pushed Japan and other allies to allow the yen and other currencies to appreciate strongly against the dollar (the Plaza Accord), against the background of the Cold War and Japan and others' reliance on it for security.

Even in recent years, when the United States and its partners have supposedly been adhering to a free-market system of floating exchange rates, and most major central banks are notionally independent of governments, in fact the value of currencies has been affected strongly by so-called "quantitative easing" policies which have been implemented by central banks with the cooperation of national governments. As the United States, United Kingdom, and other rich countries have printed money in order to try to keep credit flowing following the 2008 global economic crisis, the strategically rather large side-effect was to reduce the value of their currencies against developing market currencies such as the Brazilian real and South African rand, decreasing those countries' prospects for growth.[40] Japan has been printing money in order to stimulate its own moribund economy, i.e., purportedly for domestic reasons, but again the side-effect has been to reduce the value of the yen sharply against other currencies to improve prospects for its own companies which trade in dollars and report profits in yen. China has taken part in these maneuvers using a combination of monetary and fiscal stimulus in order to protect its own economy; however, the effects of this have not been felt as much around the world directly as the RMB is still not as widely used or traded as other major currencies. In 2015, the PBOC started to become increasingly worried about China's slowdown, resulting in it devaluing the RMB by around 4% in the space of two days under the cover of moving it towards a free-market rate[41]; the implications of this are being felt around the world, but in particular in Asia.[42]

Economic and financial shocks to economies have long-term impacts on their growth prospects,[43] which in turn have important strategic consequences, as less money is available for investment in security and other strategic interests. For example, the increase in the value of the Japanese yen as a result of the Plaza Accord was arguably a major factor which led to the economic bubble in Japan, its subsequent bursting, the 20-year stagnation which followed, and its current strategic weakness in the East Asia region.[44] Governments are well aware of the strategic implications of currency shocks, and the Chinese government is particularly disinclined to believe the rhetoric of free markets and free trade.

Increasing use of the RMB for trade would therefore expose developing East Asian countries in particular to such shocks which may be engineered by the Chinese government for strategic purposes, or which may result from political instability. The benefits for developing countries of accepting RMB may be too difficult to resist, however; huge pools of RMB will become available for investment in the region.[45] This in itself may present a strategic challenge; with the colossal amount of RMB which would potentially become available for investment in the region, and around the world, many potential target countries would need to be aware of the strategic implications. Most RMB would be held by Chinese investors. The form of investments which may become available in RMB can be categorized as portfolio investments, and foreign direct investments (FDI).

Portfolio investments imply that the investors are providing capital in order to receive a dividend income, or in order to realize an increase in the value of their capital, or both. Portfolio investment is also characterized by its mobility, that is to say, it is easy to invest and divest capital. Hence, huge flows of portfolio investment can lead to instability in stock markets, bubbles, and shocks. The 1997 Asian financial crisis was partly caused by a sudden outflow of portfolio investment from Southeast Asian stock markets in response to investor panic about the safety of their investments. Much of the investment had previously flowed into Southeast Asia due to Japan's economic malaise and the capital outflow which occurred in the post-bubble environment.[46] In Southeast Asia, political turmoil led to long-ruling regimes collapsing and wrenching economic and social restructuring, much of it imposed by the financially dominant nations whose investors had pulled out of Southeast Asia. A sudden influx of RMB investments could lead to financial bubbles in regional stock markets, with the subsequent financial, economic, and social pain caused by the bursting of bubbles, and the possible need for Southeast Asian countries to rely on regional financial powers for support. While nations which receive these kinds of investments need to be aware of the risks of mobile capital in any currency, the potential volume of capital flows in RMB and the unique strategic issues regarding potential Chinese financial dominance in the region mean that an internationalized RMB would need particular consideration with regard to risks.

FDI, on the other hand, is characterized as more benign investment, as it symbolizes a longer-term commitment to the investment. Typically, an FDI investor must invest in more than 10% of a company or venture, and take responsibility as a part owner.[47] It is also likely that it will be providing various resources, in the form of human capital, access to other companies' expertise, and so on. From another point of view, however, an FDI accepted by a company implies some loss of control over how the company is managed. In particular, if the foreign investor is controlled in some manner by a foreign government, control over the company is being lost to a foreign government, which may not have purely economic goals.

There have already been several cases whereby Chinese companies' investment overtures have been rejected by some governments or legislatures, due to concerns over their government connections. For example, Huawei was blocked from investing in the United States due to Congress members' concerns over its alleged connections to the People's Liberation Army, and the access they would gain to vital communications infrastructure in the United States. The China National Offshore Oil Corporation's attempt to undertake FDI was also refused for political reasons.[48]

For countries in the East Asia region, the vast pool of RMB available for investments will therefore seem like a double-edged sword in strategic terms. The investment would be welcomed for infrastructure and other capital-intensive projects for development. But, if the potential strategic issues over ceding control of strategically important companies and capital projects are considered, governments may hesitate to avail themselves. An extreme case is Myanmar; the overwhelming dominance of Chinese capital in Myanmar was an important reason in that country's decision to finally open up to the West in recent years. Considering the difficulties the Chinese government faces with regard to gaining global acceptance of the RMB as a freely convertible international currency, some experts have suggested that the main goal of the government's RMB internationalization program is to enable it to act as an Asian regional currency for the purposes of investment and regional connectivity with China in the lead.[49]

Linked to these issues is the value of the RMB itself. Since the Asian financial crisis of 1997, the PBOC has kept the Chinese RMB relatively stable, partly to increase the credibility of the currency and partly because the value of the RMB against the dollar was favorable for Chinese exporters. This has been possible because the Chinese government maintains a huge stock of foreign reserves, mostly in dollars. The strong value of the RMB has been possible partly due to the reserves, but also due to the perception of a continuing strength in the domestic economy since the Asian financial crisis. In fact, the PBOC has gradually allowed the RMB to strengthen against the dollar due to these factors, in part reflecting upward market pressure. However, there is a lingering worry over various aspects of the domestic financial system among foreign investors; in particular the amount of debt local governments and private investors actually have. Recent estimates suggest that local financial institutions have debts amounting to over 250% of gross domestic product,[50] which, while not unusual for a developed country, is rather high for a middle-income country. In fact, however, the actual amount of debt is very difficult to ascertain[51] due to lack of transparency and incentives to cover up income or investments in the domestic economy. Any Asian government which maintained a significant amount of RMB reserves would be exposed to these issues; it would be like taking a step into the dark to expose a national financial system to RMB risks, although the risks would depend greatly on the specific purpose for which the RMB was being held. Companies which maintained large holdings of RMB for investment or reserve purposes would face similar risks.

The strategic dependency on China's economic policies will only increase if another main goal of RMB liberalization is achieved – the use of RMB as a reserve currency.[52] A major reason why reserve currencies are kept by currency issuers is to allow the issuer to adjust the international value of its currency by buying or selling it using the reserve currency. Many countries maintain large foreign-currency reserves for this purpose, and in particular developing countries and countries for which exports are an important part of their economy. Foreign-currency reserves are kept as an asset based on which an issuer can maintain credibility in its own currency. The ideas of foreign currency as an asset and as being important to credibility are key to the strategic implications. If the foreign currency being held in reserve decreases or increases in value against the reserve holder's own currency substantially, the reserve holder may lose its own credibility, leading to potential economic shocks to its domestic economy, such as higher inflation domestically or reduction in international competitiveness due to higher domestic producer prices. A case in point is Japan: the central government maintains a public debt of around 250% of gross domestic product, but its currency, the yen, is not thought to be in danger in part due to its huge international reserve position, which is mainly held in dollars. A significant devaluation of the dollar could undermine Japan's financial credibility by pushing the value of Japan's public debt from being manageable into something which would lead to a loss of confidence and economic meltdown. Both Japan and China, the largest holders of US dollar reserves, have at times shown strong concern that the dollar's value was not being maintained due to quantitative easing.[53]

In sum, the risks for Asian countries of maintaining large proportions of their trade, investments, debts, and currency reserves in RMB are significant. Some countries in Southeast Asia may welcome the opportunity to reduce their dependence on the US dollar and diversify into RMB; however, the majority are likely to think about the risks carefully while at the same time showing that they are encouraging China's liberalization and reform initiatives.

Summary

This chapter has considered the issue of China's RMB internationalization program. It has argued that the program can be seen as part of a long-running process designed to enhance China's international identity and status, and follows a variation of the developmentalist model of nation building pioneered by Japan. Furthermore, the chapter suggested that, while there may be some benefits for China in liberalizing and internationalizing the RMB, there are many potentially negative aspects, such as painful domestic restructuring and a loss of control over capital flows and the value of the RMB. These issues flow from the "trilemma" problem faced by the CCP, i.e., the difficulty of maintaining stable interest rates while allowing a floating exchange rate and free cross-border movement of capital. Finally, the chapter considered the strategic implications for other Asian countries, and argued that, while many states in Asia are cautiously welcoming the Chinese initiative, they are also aware of the significant potential economic, financial, and strategic risks of diversifying their reserves and payments into RMB in the short to medium term.

Notes

1 Part of this chapter is based on a paper presented at the Institute for International Politics and Economics, Belgrade, 2014. The research for this paper was funded by a Japan Society for the Premotion of Science grant-in-aid research grant.
2 Yasuo Awai. "Chinese Yuan Coming Up in the World." *Nikkei Asian Review*, July 31, 2014. http://asia.nikkei.com/magazine/20140731-Enter-Alibaba/Markets/Chinese-yuan-coming-up-in-the-world (accessed January 15, 2015).
3 Damian Tobin. "Renminbi Internationalisation: Precedents and Implications." *Journal of Chinese Economic and Business Studies,* 11, no. 2 (2013). http://dx.doi.org/10.1080/14765284.2013.789677 (accessed April 12, 2014).

4 John Hooley. "Bringing Down the Great Wall? Global Implications of Capital Account Liberalisation in China." *Bank of England Quarterly Bulletin*, 53, no. 4 (2013). http://www.bankofengland.co.uk/publications/Documents/quarterlybulletin/2013/qb1304prereleasechina.pdf (accessed August 29, 2016).
5 Xinhua. "President Vows to Bring Benefits to People in Realizing 'Chinese Dream'." *Xinhua News*. 3 March 2013. http://news.xinhuanet.com/english/china/2013-03/17/c_132240052.htm (accessed January 8, 2015); William A. Callahan. *China Dreams: 20 Visions of the Future*. Oxford: Oxford University Press, 2013.
6 Chalmers Johnson. *MITI and the Japanese Miracle: The Growth of Industrial Policy*. Stanford, CA: Stanford University Press, 1982; Meredith Woo-Cumings, ed. *The Developmental State*. Ithaca, NY: Cornell University Press, 1999; Andrea Boltho and Maria Weber. "Did China Follow the East Asian Development Model?" *The European Journal of Comparative Economics*, 6, no. 2 (2009).
7 William A. Callahan. *China: The Pessoptimist Nation*. Oxford: Oxford University Press, 2010; Zheng Wang. "National Humiliation, History Education, and the Politics of Historical Memory: Patriotic Education Campaign in China." *International Studies Quarterly*, 52, no. 4 (2008).
8 Rex Li. *A Rising China and Security in East Asia: Identity Construction and Security Discourse*. Abingdon, Oxon: Routledge, 2009.
9 Wenchang Yang. "My Views About 'Tao Guang Yang Hui'." *Waijiao Liqi [Foreign Affairs Journal]*, 102, Winter (2011). http://cpifa.org/en/q/listQuarterlyArticle.do?articleId=214# (accessed December 18, 2014).
10 Yasheng Huang. *Capitalism with Chinese Characteristics*. New York: Cambridge University Press, 2008.
11 James Kynge and Josh Noble. "China: Turning Away From the Dollar." *Financial Times*. December 9, 2014. http://www.ft.com/cms/s/0/4ee67336-7edf-11e4-b83e-00144feabdc0.html (accessed January 7, 2015).
12 Xiaochuan Zhao. *Reform the International Monetary System*. People's Bank of China, March 23, 2009. http://www.pbc.gov.cn/publish/english/956/2009/20091229104425550619706/20091229104425550619706_.html (accessed January 15, 2015); Jean-Marc F. Blanchard. "China's Grand Strategy and Money Muscle: The Potentialities and Pratfalls of China's Sovereign Wealth Fund and Renminbi Policies." *The Chinese Journal of International Politics*, 4, no. 1 (2011).
13 Dongsheng Di. "The Renminbi's Rise and Chinese Politics." In *The Power of Currencies and the Currency of Power*, edited by Alan Wheatley. Abingdon, Oxon: Routledge/IISS, 2013.
14 Heike Holbig and Bruce Gilley. "Reclaiming Legitimacy in China." *Politics and Policy*, 38, no. 3 (2010). http://dx.doi.org/10.1111/j.1747-1346.2010.00241.x; Yang Zhong. *Political Culture and Participation in Rural China*, 50. London: Routledge, 2012.
15 Barry Naughton. *The Chinese Economy: Transitions and Growth*, 98. Cambridge, MA: MIT Press, 2007.
16 Barry J. Eichengreen. "Number One Country, Number One Currency?" *World Economy*, 36, no. 4 (2013).
17 Barry J. Eichengreen. *Exorbitant Privilege: The Rise and Fall of the Dollar and the Future of the International Monetary System*. New York: Oxford University Press, 2011.
18 Alan Wheatley. "The Origins and Use of Currency Power." In *The Power of Currencies and the Currencies of Power*, edited by Alan Wheatley. Abingdon, Oxon: Routledge/IISS, 2013.
19 Ibid.
20 Keith Fray. "China's Leap Forward: Overtaking the US as the World's Biggest Economy." *Financial Times*. 8 October 2014. http://blogs.ft.com/ftdata/2014/10/08/chinas-leap-forward-overtaking-the-us-as-worlds-biggest-economy/ (accessed January 12, 2015); World Bank. *GDP Ranking, PPP Based*. World Bank. July 1, 2015. http://data.worldbank.org/data-catalog/GDP-PPP-based-table (accessed August 21, 2015).

21 SAFE. "Official Reserve Assets." http://www.safe.gov.cn/wps/portal/english/Data (accessed September 1, 2016).
22 Gabriel Wildau and Tom Mitchell. "China Spent $470bn to Maintain Confidence in Renminbi." *Financial Times*, June 13, 2016. http://on.ft.com/1WLepiV (accessed June 13, 2016).
23 Fielding Chen and Tom Orlik. "Something in Reserve? Assessing China's FX Buffer." *Bloomberg Intelligence*, May 10, 2016. http://www.bloomberg.com/professional/blog/something-in-reserve-assessing-chinas-fx-buffer/ (accessed June 1, 2016).
24 Motomichi Ikawa. "Reform of the International Monetary System Based on Special Drawing Rights and its Implications for Asia." *Pacific Economic Review*, 14, no. 5 (2009). http://dx.doi.org/10.1111/j.1468-0106.2009.00481.x.
25 Hooley, "Bringing Down the Great Wall? Global Implications of Capital Account Liberalisation in China."
26 Bank of England. "Announcement of Renminbi Clearing Bank in London." http://www.bankofengland.co.uk/publications/Pages/news/2014/091.aspx (accessed August 6, 2014).
27 Hongfei Wang. "*Renminbi Guojihua de Xianzhuang, Yingxiangji Weilai Huobi Zhengce Quxiang* [Status Quo and Impact of RMB Internationalisation, and Orientation of the Future Monetary Policy]." *Kexue Juece (Scientific Decision Making)*, 2 (2013).
28 Michelle Chen. "Yuan Suffers Biggest Weekly Loss as PBOC Punishes Speculators." *Reuters*. February 28, 2014. http://www.reuters.com/article/2014/02/28/us-markets-china-yuan-close-idUSBREA1R0FK20140228 (accessed January 16, 2015).
29 "Beijing Faces up to its Monetary Trilemma." *Financial Times*, September 7, 2015. http://on.ft.com/1QkvIB2 (accessed May 10, 2016).
30 Willy Lam. "The Maoist Revival and the Conservative Turn in Chinese Politics." *China Perspectives* no. 2 (2012); Jennifer Pan and Yiqing Xu. *China's Ideological Spectrum*. MIT, 2015. http://papers.ssrn.com/sol3/papers.cfm?abstract_id=2593377 (accessed August 1, 2016).
31 Callahan, *China: The Pessoptimist Nation*; Dongsheng Di, Personal Interview, Beijing, August 13, 2013.
32 Ulrich Volz. "All Politics is Local: The Renminbi's Prospects as a Future Global Currency." In *Financial Statecraft of Emerging Powers*, edited by Leslie Armijo and Saori Katada. Houndmills, Basingstoke: Palgrave Macmillan, 2014.
33 WTO. "Trade Profiles." http://stat.wto.org/CountryProfile/WSDBCountryPFHome.aspx?Language=E (accessed August 1, 2015).
34 Kaoru Natsuda and John Thoburn. "Industrial Policy and the Development of the Automotive Industry in Thailand." *Journal of the Asia Pacific Economy*, 18, no. 3 (2012). http://dx.doi.org/10.1080/13547860.2012.742690 (accessed August 20, 2015).
35 Linus Hagström. "'Power Shift' in East Asia? A Critical Reappraisal of Narratives on the Diaoyu/Senkaku Islands Incident in 2010." *The Chinese Journal of International Politics*, 5, no. 3 (2012); Bin Gu. "Mineral Export Restraints and Sustainable Development—Are Rare Earths Testing the WTO's Loopholes?" *Journal of International Economic Law* (2011).
36 Yang Jiang. "Response and Responsibility: China in East Asian Financial Cooperation." *Pacific Review*, 23, no. 5 (2010); Teddy Ng. "China to Push for More Trade Pacts to Strengthen Global Economic Influence." *South China Morning Post*, December 19, 2013. http://www.scmp.com/news/china/article/1384923/china-push-regional-trade-pacts-despite-territorial-disputes-analysts (accessed December 19, 2013); see Ba's chapter in this volume.
37 Robert Cookson. "China Eases Corporate Rules on Renminbi." *Financial Times*, January 13, 2011. http://on.ft.com/1Jnd5eo (accessed June 1, 2016).
38 Arvind Subramanian. *Eclipse: Living in the Shadow of China's Economic Dominance*. Washington, DC: Peterson Institute for International Economics, 2011.
39 John S. Odell. "The US and the Emergence of Flexible Exchange Rates: An Analysis of Foreign Policy Change." *International Organization*, 33, no. 01 (1979).

40 "The Dodgiest Duo in the Suspect Six." *Economist*, November 8, 2014. http://www.economist.com/news/finance-and-economics/21631134-emerging-economies-hit-hard-times-brazil-and-russia-look-particularly-weak (accessed August 21, 2015); UNIDO. *The Global Financial Crisis and the Developing World: Transmission Channels and Fall-Outs for Industrial Development.* United Nations Industrial Development Organization. June 2009. https://www.unido.org/fileadmin/user_media/Publications/RSF_DPR/WP062009_Ebook.pdf (accessed August 21, 2015).
41 Jamil Anderlini. "Surprise China Devaluation Marks Escalation of Currency War." *Financial Times.* August 11, 2015. http://on.ft.com/1WeWi2K (accessed August 11, 2015).
42 "Asian Sell-Off Accelerates on Weak China PMI." *Financial Times.* August 21, 2015. http://www.ft.com/fastft/2015/08/21/post-379741/ (accessed August 21, 2015).
43 Davide Furceri and Annabelle Mourougane. *The Effect of Financial Crises on Potential Output: New Empirical Evidence from OECD Countries.* OECD, 2009. http://dx.doi.org/10.1787/224126122024 (accessed June 1, 2016).
44 Koichi Hamada and Yasushi Okada. "Monetary and International Factors Behind Japan's Lost Decade." *Journal of the Japanese and International Economies* 23, no. 2 (2009).
45 One estimate suggests a theoretical RMB41 trillion could become available if there is complete liberalization, although this is unlikely; see Gabriel Wildau. "China to Allow Individuals to Buy Overseas Financial Assets." *Financial Times*, May 29, 2015. http://on.ft.com/1FGUwyM (accessed June 1, 2015).
46 Michael R. King. "Who Triggered the Asian Financial Crisis?" *Review of International Political Economy,* 8, no. 3 (2001).
47 OECD. *OECD Benchmark Definition of Foreign Direct Investment (4th edition).* OECD, 2008. http://www.oecd.org/document/33/0,3343,en_2649_33763_33742497_1_1_1_1,00.html (accessed March 12, 2012).
48 Dick K. Nanto, James K. Jackson, Wayne M. Morrison, and Lawrence Kumins. *China and the CNOOC Bid for Unocal: Issues for Congress.* Congressional Research Service, 2005. http://research.policyarchive.org/2571.pdf (accessed August 1, 2016).
49 Yukon Huang. "Beijing's Drive to Make the Renminbi a Global Currency is Misguided." *Financial Times*, August 26, 2015. http://on.ft.com/1fBzYyD (accessed August 26, 2015).
50 "China's Financial System: The Coming Debt Bust." *Economist.* May 7, 2016. http://www.economist.com/news/leaders/21698240-it-question-when-not-if-real-trouble-will-hit-china-coming-debt-bust (accessed June 15, 2016); Jamil Anderlini. "China Debt Tops 250% of National Income." *Financial Times.* July 21, 2014. http://www.ft.com/intl/cms/s/0/895604ac-10d8-11e4-812b-00144feabdc0.html (accessed July 23, 2014).
51 Jack Perkowski. "China's Debt: How Serious is it?" *Forbes.* January 21, 2014. http://www.forbes.com/sites/jackperkowski/2014/01/21/chinas-debt-how-serious-is-it/ (accessed September 12, 2015).
52 Gabriel Wildau. "China Knocks on Door of Reserve Currency Club." *Financial Times* May 5, 2015. http://on.ft.com/1GZv6N4 (accessed June 1, 2015).
53 Belinda Cao and Judy Chen. "China's Premier Wen 'Worried' on Safety of Treasuries." *Bloomberg,* 2009. http://www.bloomberg.com/apps/news?pid=email_en&sid=aXW9GUdlySss (accessed June 15, 2015).

5 From Pan-Asianism to Act East

India's evolving perspectives and roles in East Asian regional institutions

Vindu Mai Chotani

Introduction

The first notions of Indian Asianism were primarily inspired by the affirmation of nationalistic feelings from India's colonial experience.[1] India's first Prime Minister after independence, Jawaharlal Nehru, envisioned a united Asia, wherein the newly emerging states would come together through community building and economic ties, rather than through the formation of military alliances. Yet, as Asia was torn apart by Cold War politics, and New Delhi, preoccupied with its domestic issues and neighbors in South Asia, looked more inward, this notion of a united Asia lost momentum.

In its quest to reintegrate itself into Asia and also establish itself as a leading power, India launched its Look East policy in 1991. This boosted a new-found Asianism in India's foreign policy, albeit one that would detour slightly from Nehruvian ideology. India looked outward, liberalized its economy, and also took the important step of winning membership in East Asian and Asia-Pacific regional institutions such as the Association of Southeast Asian Nations (ASEAN), ASEAN Regional Forum (ARF), ASEAN Maritime Forum (AMF), ASEAN Defense Ministers Meeting + (ADMM+), and East Asia Summit (EAS).

Although this last quarter-century has seen India intensify its efforts to reconnect with Asia, Asia's regional dynamic – its economic and security nexus – has moved much faster than New Delhi's readiness to adapt.[2] As a founding member of the Non-Aligned Movement (NAM), India wished to keep away from Cold War politics. The NAM, which functioned as more of a movement rather than a multilateral organization, laid out the "ten principles of Bandung."[3] This established that non-aligned countries would not enter into multilateral defense pacts or security blocs to benefit any specific interests of great powers. Thus, India on many occasions steered clear of multilateralism, unless under the auspices of the United Nations, or issues concerning economics and culture, and later on trade blocs. Instead, India preferred to prioritize and pursue its bilateral relations with East and Southeast Asian nations.

Presently as well, though there has been tremendous progress with regard to economic ties in multilateral organizations, on issues related to multilateral security cooperation, Indian policies still display great sensitivity. Prominent Indian strategic analyst C. Raja Mohan notes that, "while India is party to many regional multilateral organizations that deal with security issues overlapping the member states of ASEAN, its participation in them has been somewhat lackluster."[4] This has led to multilateral institutions, regional powers such as Japan, and many foreign scholars too calling upon India to intensify its position and approach in these regional bodies. The United States as well holds the expectation that India could play a greater role in strengthening these groupings.

More recently, the economic domination of China, its ability to tilt the balance of power in the region, as well as its increasing authority in both existing and newly formed regional institutions has influenced India's thinking. In 2006, the principles adopted at the 14th NAM summit held in Havana did not mention any adversity to collective security defense pacts, and instead stated that the promotion and defense of multilateralism and multilateral organizations were the appropriate frameworks to resolve problems affecting mankind.[5] In line with this changing position, India is intensifying its approach to regional institutions – in 2012 it elevated its ties with ASEAN to the level of a strategic partnership, while pushing hard to join key regional institutions such as Asia-Pacific Economic Cooperation (APEC). Through its Look East policy, which has now been upgraded to its Act East policy, India is lending its diplomatic voice on regional security issues and also negotiating hard for the breakthrough of the Regional Comprehensive Economic Partnership (RCEP). Further, India's growing participation in Asia-Pacific trilateral formats (India–Japan–Australia and India–United States–Japan) demonstrates its increasing interest and comfort in regional multilateralism.

However, in order to meet growing regional expectations, India needs to adapt more quickly to Asia's fast-evolving economic and security nexus. India now has to face up to the challenge of overcoming its image as a laggard in Asia's regional integration process, and also the perception that it is a reluctant regional power.[6] Against this backdrop, the first section of this paper will assess the evolution of India's perspectives on East Asian and Asia-Pacific regional institutions, and the factors that hampered, and motivated, Indian participation in these institutions over time. The second section will analyze India's roles in these multilateral institutions as India progressed from its Look East policy to its Act East policy. Finally, conclusions on India's position and roles in East Asian and Asia-Pacific regional institutions will be drawn.

The evolution of India's perspectives on regional institutions

The ideal of Asianism has always found widespread appeal in India, inspired by its association and its cultural influence with East and Southeast Asia – the spread of Buddhism to Japan in the seventh century BC, and also the presence of Indianized kingdoms such as Khmer, Sri Vijaya, Funan, to be found in Southeast Asia.[7] Indeed, as early as 1926, in his quest to revive India's widespread cultural influence in Asia, Indian intellectual Kalidas Nag started the Greater India Society, where the scholars studied and suggested that India was the cradle of Asian civilization, and Southeast Asia was an extension of India.[8]

Another view expressed contrary to this was by K. M. Panikkar, one of India's early strategists. In his book *The Future of South-East Asia, An Indian View*, written in 1943, he noted that "a sense of Asiatic solidarity was never part of the tradition of India, China or Japan." Panikkar believed that the concept of "the Asiatic" was very much brought about by Western colonization as it enabled them to distinguish themselves as a superior race.[9]

While origins on this notion of Asianism in India are subject to debate, what is clear is that India's anti-colonial movement was boosted by these discoveries of Indian civilizational influences in East and Southeast Asia, and it was the inspiration drawn from this connection that went on to facilitate the ideas of an Asian unity after the war.[10] Further enhancing India's vision of the role it could play in shaping a post World War II Asia was its significant contribution in the war. It was during this time that Panikkar argued that a stable and responsible government in India was an "essential pre-requisite" for the success of a collective security system in Southeast Asia. Without this, he believed that Southeast Asia "will remain the cockpit of colonial ambitions, incapable of defending itself, and a prey to the predatory urge of any power which is strong enough to attack it."[11]

Jawaharlal Nehru's notion of Pan-Asianism

Jawaharlal Nehru had in the 1940s been attracted to the idea of Pan-Asianism and an Asian Federation. Inspired by India's long experience with colonialism, Nehru aimed to forge unity among the newly emerging nations in Asia, many of which were still struggling to achieve independence. In his first official broadcast as vice-president of India's interim government, on September 7, 1947, Nehru stated that, "We propose as far as possible to keep away from the power politics of groups, aligned against one another, which have led in the past to two World Wars and which may again lead to disasters on an even vaster scale." [12] This philosophy of non-alignment which sought to keep states away from the United States- and USSR-led power blocs, and instead unite Asia based on shared cultural affinities and economic relations, rather than military alliances, became the cornerstone of India's foreign policy.

Showing India's solidarity to Asian nations, Nehru convened in New Delhi the Asian Relations Conference in 1947 which aimed at creating stronger economic, social, and cultural ties between the states, as well as promoting good neighborly relations. In January 1949, Nehru reacted sharply to the Dutch invasion of Indonesia and convened a special conference on Indonesia in New Delhi.[13] In line with this, India also expressed its reservations in attending the San Francisco Peace Conference in 1951 due to its concerns over the limitations it imposed upon Japanese sovereignty and national independence; India then went on to become one of the first countries to sign a peace treaty with Japan in 1952. Encouraging Asian solidarity also meant that India would have to apply this unified approach to China. Nehru at that time believed that China and India shared a philosophy of life, and in this regard he viewed China as India's partner in Asia.[14]

However, despite this current habit of romanticizing "Nehruvian" foreign policy, by the mid-1950s a loss in efficacy of Nehru's notion of Pan-Asianism was highlighted. The 1955 Bandung Conference of the non-aligned countries exposed the distrust and tensions amongst states, as well as the profound apprehensions by the smaller countries, especially the Southeast Asian states about India being a regional leader.[15] Nehru also faced a moment of humiliation when it became quite evident that many of the Southeast Asian nations were more interested in rallying around China, rather than India. By the early 1960s China had become one of India's biggest adversaries, and in 1962 India's war with China gave a huge blow to Nehru's notion of Pan-Asianism. Preoccupied with China and the ongoing Cold War, India discarded its ambitions to lead the Asian project, and began to focus less on Asia and more on Cold War politics.

During the 1950s and 60s, due to its policy of non-alignment and its opposition to a substantial American presence in Asia, India vehemently opposed the formation of Western-inspired military blocs such as Southeast Asian Treaty Organization (SEATO). Nehru was also very critical of the entry of several Asian countries into such alliances, mainly because he believed that this would introduce Cold War politics into Southeast Asia. Thus, when ASEAN was formed in 1967, India's doubtsabout the organization, because it was viewed as the rebirth of the discredited US alliance SEATO, as well as a body directed against the socialist world, prevented India from joining it.

However, as India deepened ties with the USSR, and also signed the 1971 Treaty of Peace and Friendship, its policy of non-alignment started to become synonymous with anti-Americanism.[16] This in turn led many Southeast Asian states to view these deepening Indo-Soviet ties with resentment. Other prominent East Asian countries such as Japan and South Korea which were close US allies also maintained some distance with India. Though there was an attempt by Malaysia, which served as the main arbiter to renew dialogue between India and ASEAN in 1975 and 1980, New Delhi's decision to support Vietnam's military intervention in Cambodia once again ended any possibility of *rapprochement*. Therefore Cold War politics eventually completely offset this notion of Pan-Asianism, and by the late 1980s ties between India and East Asia seemed unbridgeable.

A new Asianism under India's Look East policy

It was only after the end of the Cold War that India and East Asia were slowly able to bridge this vast gap. India, released from its Cold War ideological constraints, found itself isolated economically and strategically. The Indian economy, severely hit by the Gulf War of 1990–91, and the collapse of the Soviet Union, which was New Delhi's closest strategic partner, urged New Delhi to formulate a new multidimensional foreign policy.[17] Realizing that East and Southeast Asia offered tremendous potential for future growth, in 1991 Prime Minister P. V. Narasimha Rao advocated India's historic and groundbreaking Look East policy. This presented India with a renewed opportunity to build on a different

Asianism philosophy – one that was neither anti-Western, nor would enable them to escape Westernization – and thus began India's journey into regional institutions.

To be more easily understood the assimilation of the Look East into Indian foreign policy can be divided into three phases. The first phase (1991–2000) revolved around the sole purpose of enforcing institutional linkages and strengthening economic ties between India and ASEAN. During this time, India and the United States were also able to forge a closer economic and strategic partnership. While initially most members of ASEAN were not enthusiastic about integrating India into the organization, India's efforts eventually overrode all opposition to its entry. In 1992 India was granted the status of "sectoral dialogue partner," and in 1995 India became a full dialogue partner of ASEAN. In 1994, the ARF was launched to provide an overarching collective security framework in the region. In 1996, recognizing the role India could play in regional stability, India was granted membership of the ARF.

The second phase (2001–10) of the Look East policy focused on politico-strategic, institutional, and regional integration arrangements. India began its own annual summit meetings with ASEAN (called ASEAN Plus One).[18] In 2005, India also became a member of the EAS, and then subsequently in 2010 India was invited to join the ADMM+. Since implementing its Look East policy, India had been looking to promote foreign direct investment, and a big boost came in 2005, when India and the United States signed the civil nuclear deal. This paved the way for deeper economic ties not only with the United States, but also with Japan and South Korea, and Southeast Asia states.

The third phase (post-2010) has probably seen the biggest strides. Having consolidated its entry into key regional institutions, India became less hesitant in showing its benign military strength in the region, and began to work fairly confidently to expand its role in multilateral regional institutions across the Asia-Pacific. In 2012, India and ASEAN upgraded their relationship to the level of strategic partners; India also recorded impressive growth in trade and investments and broadened and deepened cooperation in various other sectors. Most recently, in 2014, the rechristening of the Look East policy to Prime Minister Modi's Act East policy has underscored the increasing strategic and economic importance of East Asia to India.

However, though India in its new post Cold War Asianism drive did integrate itself into these regional bodies, the degree of action and contribution on India's part is what ASEAN member states, many scholars, and countries like the United States question. While India's growing interest in regional multilateralism has achieved relative success on the economic front, on the strategic front it is often argued that India has spent much more of its energy promoting bilateralism in the region with selected strategic partners. Australian scholar Sam Bateman interestingly notes that, within Asia, India seems to have adopted its own "hub and spokes" approach to regional engagements. This places India at the center of a web of bilateral partnerships, a place where India seems to be comfortable in dealing bilaterally with both the smaller ASEAN members such as Singapore or Vietnam, and the larger, more powerful states such as the United States and Japan.[19]

Though part of this "performance deficit" has been India's responsibility, it would not be fair for India to carry the full burden of responsibility. India's domestic scenario, due to its vast diversity in interest – language, religion, politics, and location – has been nothing short of complicated. The government, which over the years was comprised of coalition partners, each focused on varying economic, strategic, and political preoccupations, has not always been able to implement seamless and expeditious decision making.[20] Further, India's immediate neighborhood in South Asia has played a big role in constraining India from being more proactive in East Asia and the Asia-Pacific. Pressing security demands on the Western front on account of instability in Pakistan; cross-border terrorism; India's border dispute with China in the northeast; and, more recently, India's renewed focus on the Bay of Bengal and the Indian Ocean region due to an increasing Chinese presence make heavy demands on India's limited strategic and economic resources, thus hampering India's policy priorities, and often acting as a barrier to regional cooperation.

While this sense of insecurity stemming from China's growing assertiveness and deepening United States–China rivalry in the region enforce ASEAN's demand on middle powers like India to do more, part of the responsibility too lies with ASEAN and the other regional organizations. Within ASEAN there is an accepted divergence on the interests and approaches of ASEAN members towards India's integration with the region, and some of these states even resisted India's entry into the EAS at the time of its formation. In an organization based on consensus diplomacy, often referred to as the "ASEAN way," deep divergences are also appearing within the organization on key regional issues. The most recent example has been the inability of ASEAN and the ARF to mention in each of their latest joint communiqués the verdict of the 2016 Permanent Court of Arbitrations ruling on the South China Sea issue.[21]

Further, in order to promote economic growth, it is imperative for India, a developing, middle-income country, to be a member of key regional economic institutions such as APEC. However, despite efforts spanning two decades to join APEC, India is still not a member. Shyam Saran, India's former Foreign Secretary, noted that "APEC is the missing link in India's Act East policy because we are already heavily engaged with APEC countries."[22] Thus, while it is important for other prominent regional actors such as India and Japan to not let the United States and China determine Asia's destiny, it is also important for East Asian and Asia-Pacific regional organizations to draw consensus and bridge this performance deficit from their part.

India's role in regional institutions

That India has been successful in becoming part of a number of regional and subregional institutions in East Asia and the Asia-Pacific (as can be seen in Figure 5.1) is not in doubt. However, in order to asses India's position, this next section will analyze India's role in four key regional institutions – ASEAN,

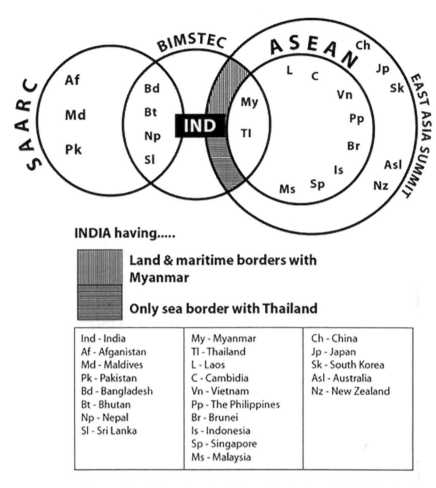

Figure 5.1 India's membership in regional multilateral institutions. SAARC, South Asian Association for Regional Cooperation; BIMSTEC, Bengal Initiative for Multi-Sectoral Technical and Economic Cooperation; ASEAN, Association of Southeast Asian Nations.[23]

ARF, ADMM+, and EAS. Further, it will also argue that in order for India to realize its "balancing role" or as that of a stabilizing power in Asia, India should be granted membership in key economic institutions such as APEC.

ASEAN

From the 1990s, relations between India and ASEAN began to grow steadily. From its inception in 1971, India has always supported ASEAN's Zone of Peace,

Freedom and Neutrality (ZOPFAN). India's economic growth, its respect for democracy and rule of law, and the fact that India shares borders with four ASEAN states, all drew upon ASEAN's interest. Further, India has always emphasized its respect for the core ASEAN principle of decision making by consensus.[24] This has been reiterated first in 1994 by then Indian Prime Minister Narasimha Rao at Singapore, and then subsequently by all Indian Prime Ministers.

Given ASEAN's growing view of India's role in the region, the tempo in India–ASEAN relations accelerated during the second phase of India's Look East policy. In 2003, at the second India–ASEAN summit held in Bali, three broad accords were signed: (1) a comprehensive economic agreement; (2) a pact aimed at combating terrorism; and (3) an agreement facilitating India's accession into ASEAN's Treaty of Amity and Cooperation, which promotes regional peace and stability. In 2004, during the third India–ASEAN summit in Laos, India and ASEAN members signed the India–ASEAN Partnership for Peace, Progress, and Shared Prosperity. Progressing from this, ASEAN and India went on to adopt two plans of action (POAs) to implement this ASEAN–India partnership established in 2004 – the first POA being adopted for 2010–15, and the second POA from 2016 to 2020. These POAs laid out measures to be undertaken by both sides to further their political-security, economic, sociocultural, as well as strategic ties. Further, as testament of India's ongoing commitment towards ASEAN, in March 2015 India established the Indian Mission to ASEAN in Jakarta.[25]

Economically speaking, since 1991, India–ASEAN relations have grown steadily. India's economic structure, being services-oriented, is largely complementary to the manufacturing-oriented economies in ASEAN.[26] ASEAN is India's fourth largest trade partner, and India is, in turn, the sixth largest trade partner for ASEAN. India and ASEAN have also signed a free trade agreement (FTA) in goods, which took effect in 2010,[27] and in 2014 both parties signed another FTA in services and investments.[28] Further, the ASEAN–India economic integration process got a fillip with the creation of the ASEAN–India Free Trade Area in July 2015. Despite this progress, the 13th India–ASEAN summit held at Kuala Lampur in 2015 did note that the trade and investment relations between India and ASEAN still remained "modest."[29] Thus much is yet to be achieved in order to boost the 2014–15 trade figures, which stand at US$76.52 billion to the 2020 goal of US$200 billion.[30]

In line with this, the RCEP agreement involving the ten ASEAN countries and six FTA partners, including India, is currently seeking to create one of the largest free trade blocs in the world. RCEP countries account for 45% of the world population and over US$21 trillion of its gross domestic product. While the RCEP has seen some breakthroughs, a 2016 conclusion of the agreement was unsuccessful. With the collapse of the Trans-Pacific Partnership, there is now a renewed push for the conclusion of RCEP by 2017. This initiative would further strengthen India–ASEAN economic ties.

While India has made considerable strides in its integration with ASEAN, on many occasions India's ASEAN partners have voiced uneasiness on slow implementation of various projects. Protests extend into the strategic domain as well.

Despite India and the ASEAN upgrading their relationship to that of a strategic partnership during the December 2012 India–ASEAN Commemorative Summit, ASEAN leaders want more, not less, security cooperation with India both at bilateral and multilateral level.[31]

India however believes its shift is real – it has been slowly expanding the scope of both its bilateral and multilateral military engagement. Moving into phase III of its Look East policy, i.e., its Act East policy, Prime Minister Modi at the 13th ASEAN–India summit in 2015 conscientiously voiced his favor for the peaceful resolution of disputes in the South China Sea in accordance with the UN Convention on the Law of the Sea. He has also emphasized the importance of projecting the right to freedom of navigation, as well as the need to abide by guidelines on the implementation of the Declaration on the Conduct of Parties in the South China Sea. Bilaterally, too, India has stepped up cooperation in the region, having signed security cooperation agreements with Singapore, Indonesia, Vietnam, Malaysia, and Thailand.

Further, reflecting India's commitment to strengthen cooperation to effectively deal with traditional and non-traditional security challenges, the 14th ASEAN–India Foreign Ministers summit declared that 2016 would see the first G-2-G ASEAN–India Cyber Dialogue. India has also offered ASEAN countries a specialized program on reducing cyber crime through knowledge exchange and capacity building and a seminar on e-governance.[32]

Currently, though, bigger problems prevail – ASEAN's ability to provide the broadest platform for Asian regionalism is being questioned. China's rise, and its ability to wean away individual members of ASEAN, underlines the dangers of the new dynamic of ASEAN. Despite ASEAN and India not openly admitting it, China has been a huge factor in their increasing cooperation.[33] However, it would be unrealistic to expect India to match China in all its moves in the Asia-Pacific region. Simultaneously, India cannot assume that repeating the slogan of ASEAN centrality is a sufficiently proactive strategy.[34]

India will need to do a lot more to ensure that ASEAN remains a strong and coherent organization. This in turn demands a more activist Indian engagement with the ASEAN states collectively and individually in political, economic, and security domains. India should continue to support the development of newer ASEAN members in terms of infrastructure, human resource development, and policy reform. Deepening its engagement with respect to connectivity projects, especially such as those in India's northeast, is also important. Further, as littoral states increasingly make the waters of Southeast Asia a matter of national security, intensifying maritime cooperation with India would be beneficial. So far, the two sides have agreed to promote maritime engagement in various spheres through the AMF, and both sides should proactively take this forward.[35]

ASEAN Regional Forum

The ARF, launched in 1994 with 13 members, came about as ASEAN's new channel of engagement of the major powers dealing in East Asian security issues, and for the promotion of mutual confidence among them. In this regard the ARF pays significant attention to areas of humanitarian assistance and disaster relief (HA/DR), and non-proliferation and disarmament. Post the 9/11 attacks, the ARF also started to show a keen interest in addressing issues related to counterterrorism and transnational crime. More recently it has also focused on maritime security and peacekeeping operations.

Given the diversity of the region and the complexity of issues, both political and security, the ARF has always adopted the idea of gradualism, i.e., confidence building and progress at a pace comfortable to all, to address these issues.[36] This idea of gradualism is deeply embodied in the ARF *Concept Paper* that was prepared in 1995.[37] This paper adopted a three-stage process, namely: (1) confidence-building measures (CBMs); (2) development of preventive diplomacy; and (3) elaboration of approaches to conflicts, to better deal with security issues.

However, over the 22 years that the ARF has been functional, its activities have primarily been devoted to stage 1, i.e., CBMs. Despite discussion on preventive diplomacy, begun in 2001 at the 8th ARF Ministerial meeting, the adoption of a work plan on preventive diplomacy was only taken ten years later at the 18th ARF Ministerial.[38] That said, more recently there has been a greater thrust to enhance its role. At Hanoi during the 17th ARF Ministerial meeting, the Hanoi POA for the implementation of the vision statement was adopted. This POA recommends that by 2020 ARF should continue its efforts on consolidating CBMs while implementing preventive diplomacy activities/measures.[39]

India's participation in the ARF has been consistent with its then Look East policy and now Act East policy, wherein India considers ASEAN as the driving force of ARF and believes that the ASEAN way of dialogue and consensus should remain ARF's guiding principle. However, regarding the three stages adopted to tackle security issues, India holds the perception that the ARF should advance from its first stage of taking CBMs to the next stage of undertaking preventive diplomacy. While this view is also held and expressed by other ARF founding members like Japan and the United States, India does not believe in forcing this view through.

Understanding the important role of ARF, India has extended full cooperation. India has organized over 20 events, including training courses, seminars, and meetings on anti-piracy, maritime security, cyber security, non-proliferation, and peacekeeping. In 2001, India co-chaired the meeting of the Inter-Sessional Group (ISG) on CBMs, and that same year it also convened a meeting of the ISG on CBMs in India. By 2009, discussion on the advancement from stage 1 to stage 2 was well on its way, and in support for promoting this advancement, India co-chaired the ARF ISG on CBMs and preventive diplomacy in the inter-sessional year 2009–10, as well as in 2015–16.[40] In 2016, the ARF ISG was held in New Delhi on April 11–12. India also actively participates in all four Inter-Sessional Meetings. Through the ARF India is also actively pursuing its contributions to anti-piracy, and relief and rescue missions in the Indian Ocean and South China Sea regions.[41] In line with these developments, it is critical for a rising global power like India to continue to participate fully and actively in advancing ARF's purposes and improve its effectiveness on a realistic basis.

ADMM+

The ADDM+ (comprising ten ASEAN countries plus eight others: Australia, China, India, Japan, South Korea, New Zealand, Russia, and the United States) is a new, ASEAN-driven security initiative, and an expanded version of the ADMM. Established in 2010, the ADMM + has since been held biannually, and unlike other regional institutions, the participants here are heads of the various defense ministries. The ADMM+ has five priority areas of cooperation: HA/DR, medicine, counterterrorism, maritime security, and peacekeeping operations.

While the ADMM+ may have had some credible achievements in such a short time, especially in the domain of non-traditional security threats, there are a number of problems. Despite having an Expert Working Group on maritime security, tangible progress in the maritime security domain has been scant.[42] Further, at its third meet in Malaysia in 2015, the grouping's failure to adopt a joint statement due to disagreements on the South China Sea has been another issue of concern.

Showing its solidarity to ASEAN, India, notwithstanding its long aversion to being part of any multilateral security alliance, decided to join the ADMM+ partly due to the fact that it was primarily ASEAN-driven, and partly because it was only a cooperative security forum that posed no threat to any great power.[43] However, in this institution as well, ASEAN has once again expressed its desire for the Indian defense establishment to be more proactive in the deliberations, propose pragmatic steps for promoting regional security, and exercise leadership.[44]

India for its part has steadily been enhancing its role. Addressing the third ADMM+ meet in 2015, Indian Defense Minister Manohar Parrikar called upon all parties to the disputes in the South China Sea region to abide by the 2002 Declaration on the Conduct of Parties.[45] In March 2016, India conducted one of the largest multinational military exercises. The field training exercise, christened Exercise Force 18, saw the participation of all members of the ADMM+ and was themed around humanitarian mine action and peacekeeping operations.[46] In May 2016 the Indian Navy in its constant endeavor to enhance maritime security in the Indo-Pacific sent Indian naval ship Airavat to participate in the ADMM+ exercise on maritime security and counterterrorism held in Brunei. Thus, despite the ADMM+ being only six years old, in consonance with its Look East and now Act East policy, India is already beginning to showcase its increasingly proactive stance to this multilateral arrangement.

East Asia Summit

The EAS was formed in 2005 and its members include ASEAN, Australia, China, India, Japan, New Zealand, Republic of Korea, the Russian Federation, and the United States. Though the EAS is not an implementing body, the 2005 Kuala Lumpur Declaration, issued by participants, laid down the future shape of the EAS – the EAS will be an annual summit that will be hosted and chaired by only

ASEAN states; ASEAN will be the driving force, working in partnership with the other members; and the EAS will make the efforts to realize an East Asia community through the ASEAN +3 process.

The 2011 Declaration of the EAS on the Principles for Mutually Beneficial Relations is another important document which further emphasized the role of the EAS as a leaders-led forum promoting not only greater regional economic integration, but also important politico-security and social issues. The EAS deals with six priority areas: environment and energy, education, finance, global health issues and pandemic diseases, natural disaster management, and ASEAN connectivity.[47]

Despite strong resistance from China, which wanted to maintain its preponderance within that framework, in 2005, Japan and most of the ASEAN states, including Singapore and Indonesia, pushed for India's membership in the EAS. Alongside balancing an increasingly assertive China, this drive to include India was also the recognition of India's fast-growing economic and strategic clout in East and Southeast Asia. Just over a decade before, India had been struggling to gain entry into ASEAN, and at the time of ARF's formation, India had not even figured in the deliberations.

India as a member of the EAS endorses regional collaboration in all six priority areas. With its broad agenda, the EAS is a good place for India to continue to earn its place in the East Asian community through exercising the right combination of activism and discretion.[48] With regard to this, India hosted an EAS–India Workshop 2012: Building Regional Framework for Earthquake Risk Management in New Delhi in November 2012. India also hosted the first Meeting of the 24×7 Points of Contact among the National Disaster Response Agencies of East Asia Summit (EAS) countries in December 2014 in New Delhi.

Over the years India has also established defense cooperation relationships with a number of EAS members. This cooperation ranges from providing training, to supply and servicing of weapons, to conducting naval exercises with almost all the EAS members. In more recent times, maritime cooperation has also emerged as a significant priority area for cooperation. At the 10th EAS in Kuala Lumpur, the Chairman's statement declared the will to explore the possibility of including maritime cooperation as a priority area of EAS cooperation.[49] India, in its drive to do more under its Act East policy, hosted the EAS Conference on Maritime Security and Cooperation in November 2015 in New Delhi. This conference called for a more cooperative and integrated future for the region through overall development of the ocean-based blue economy.

At this point it may be noted that India has also played a central role in organizing the Indian Ocean Rim Association for Regional Cooperation (IOR-ARC). IOR-ARC is the only pan-Indian ocean grouping which aims to create a platform for trade, socioeconomic, and cultural cooperation in the Indian Ocean Rim area, which constitutes a population of about two billion people.[50] This platform brings together countries from three different continents, and its members also include ASEAN states such as Singapore, Indonesia, Thailand, and Malaysia, and Japan and the United States are dialogue partners as well.

Why should India be a member of Asia-Pacific Economic Cooperation?

APEC is a forum for 21 Pacific Rim member economies that mainly concerns financial integration and that promotes free trade throughout the Asia-Pacific region. APEC accounts for 60% of the global gross domestic product, and therefore for India, participation in APEC is seen as a way to bolster New Delhi's economic integration with East Asian and Pacific Rim economies.

Since 1993, India has been attempting to join APEC, and though in 2011 it was granted "observer" membership status, till date it still has not been successful. The Modi government after launching its Act East policy has worked to deepen its ties with Pacific Rim states and East Asia. While major powers such as the United States, Japan, China, and Russia support India's membership, the mere geographic reality that India doesn't sit on the Pacific Ocean, alongside opposition of some participants who have held India's record on economic reforms and World Trade Organization engagement to be unworthy of meriting inclusion, has prohibited India's entry.[51]

However, granting India membership has a large number of merits. India's membership may act as a catalyst for trade reform among emerging economies. Further, as pointed out by member states, India's maritime strength and strong strategic relations with the region's major powers could also be used to bring strategic balance within the grouping. Daniel Twining of the German Marshall Fund had rightly argued before US Congress in 2013 that, "although India is part of Asia's security architecture, it is not part of Asia's economic architecture. This disjuncture makes little sense for a country that sits in the middle of Asia."[52] Thus, if India were to contribute effectively in shaping Asia's stable and peaceful rise, gaining full membership to a key economic regional organization would be of primary importance.

Conclusion

Amidst the United States-China rivalry playing out, Asia is struggling to find a working security architecture, as well as peace and stability that would ensure economic growth. What would be potentially damaging to the region is if the United States and China see their involvement as zero-sum competition, while other key actors, such as India, ASEAN, and Japan let China and the United States define the region's future.[53] In light of this, regional organizations like ASEAN, ARF, ADMM +, and EAS play a critical role as they enable tension to diffuse by moderating United States–China rivalry, as well as allowing for trust to build by promoting initiatives transparently. Yet, the role that rising middle powers such as India play is also critical, because ultimately the security and growth of the region are not a simple bilateral equation, but one that also depends on the involvement of regional actors.

Torn apart by Cold War politics, India primarily on the security front found it difficult to engage with multilateral institutions, and instead preferred to pursue bilateral ties. However, as can be seen from the previous section, apart from strengthening its institutional linkages and deepening its bilateral cooperation, it has becoming increasingly clear that India is now also a keen and enthusiastic supporter of multilateralism in East Asia and the Asia-Pacific. India is cooperating with regional institutions, it is contributing to multilateral security and economic forums, and it is also lending its diplomatic voice in key security issues that are affecting regional stability.

India's increasing participation in trilateral formats, as well as its increasing maritime cooperation with a number of East Asian and Asia-Pacific regional institutions, has also been impressive. India is actively engaged in counterterrorism activities, as well as in those activities dealing with HA/DR. On economic issues, India has been pushing and is continuing to push connectivity projects with ASEAN members, and its East Asian neighbors. Further, its Make in India initiative is embracing the flow of foreign direct investment from a larger number of East Asian states. At the same time India is also carefully analyzing the efficacy and implications of the RCEP and is negotiating hard for its conclusion.

Thus, despite its comfort in dealing bilaterally with states, India, which has been Acting East for only two years, is beginning to develop a more cooperative mindset, and playing a more proactive role in East Asian and Asia-Pacific regional institutions.

Notes

1 Christopher Jafferlot. "India's Look East Policy: An Asianist Strategy in Perspective." *India Review* 2, no. 2 (2003): 35–68.
2 C. Raja Mohan. "How India Can and Must Shape Asia's Future Political Order." *Observer Research Foundation*, March 2016.
3 Government of India. *History and Evolution of Non-Alignment.* New Delhi: Ministry of External Affairs, 2012.
4 C. Raja Mohan. "India and ASEAN: Toward Maritime Security Cooperation." In *Enhancing India–ASEAN Connectivity,* edited by Ted Osius and C. Raja Mohan. Centre for Strategic and International Studies (CSIS). Lanham, MD: Rowman & Littlefield, 2013.
5 *14th Summit Conference of Heads of State or Government of the Non-Aligned Movement.* Havana, Cuba. September 2006. http://cns.miis.edu/nam/documents/Official_Document/14NAMSummit-Havana-Compiled.pdf.
6 C. Raja Mohan. "Making India a Leading Power." *Live Mint.* April 6, 2016. http://www.livemint.com/Opinion/Xiw11wTk3zMHLbUw80ayWP/Making-India-a-leading-power.html.
7 Ibid., 1.
8 See Chak Mun. *India's Strategic Interests in Southeast Asia and Singapore.* New Delhi: Macmillan, 2009.
9 K. M. Panikkar. *The Future of South-East Asia, An Indian View.* New York: Macmillan, 1943.
10 Christopher Bayly and Tim Harper. *Forgotten Wars: The End of Britain's Asian Empire.* London: Allen Lane, 2007.
11 Ibid., 8.
12 Prakash Nanda. *Rediscovering Asia: Evolution of India's Look East Policy.* New Delhi: Lancer Publishers, 2003.
13 "Resolution Adopted by Conference on Indonesia Held in New Delhi." *International Organization*, 3 (1949): 389–91.

14 Ibid., 1.
15 Thongkholal Haokip. "India's Look East Policy: Its Evolution and Approach." *South Asian Survey,* 18 (2011): 239–57.
16 A. N. Ram. "India-ASEAN Relations: Evolving Convergences." In *India and South East Asia: Strategic Convergences in the Twenty First Century,* edited by T. Nirmala Devi and Adluri Subramanyam Raju. New Delhi: Manohar, 2012.
17 K. V. Kesavan. "The Role of Regional Institutions in India's Look East Policy." In *South and Southeast Asia, Responding to Changing Geo-Political and Security Challenges,* edited by K. V. Kesavan and Daljit Singh. New Delhi: K. W. Publishers, 2010.
18 G. V. C. Naidu. "India and the East Asian Summit." *Strategic Analysis,* 29, no. 4 (2005): 716.
19 Sam Bateman. "India and Regional Maritime Security." In *India's Naval Strategy and Asian Security,* edited by Anit Mukherjee and C. Raja Mohan. Abingdon, Oxon: Routledge, 2016.
20 S. D. Muni and See Chak Mun. "ASEAN–India Relations: Future Directions." *ISAS Special Reports* (2012): 1–17.
21 "Chairman's Statement of the 23rd ASEAN Regional Forum." July 2016. http://asean.org/storage/2016/07/Chairmans-Statement-of-the-23rd-ASEAN-Regional-Forum_FINAL.pdf.
22 Amanda Hodge. "Kevin Rudd Heads Push for India to Join APEC." *The Australian.* September 3, 2015. http://www.theaustralian.com.au/business/kevin-rudd-heads-push-for-india-to-join-apec/news-story/b5ba9d0f5ca93ce9f8b40590b197aa47.
23 Y. Yagama Reddy. "India and ASEAN: Towards an Integrated Regional Cooperation." In *India and South East Asia: Strategic Convergences in the Twenty First Century,* edited by T. Nirmala Devi and Adluri Subramanyam Raju. New Delhi: Manohar, 2012. Figure 12.2, p. 198. Reproduced with permission.
24 "The ASEAN Community: Unblocking the Roadblocks." *ASEAN Studies Centre.* Singapore: ISEAS Publishing, 2008.
25 Government of India. *Presentation of Credentials by H.E. Mr. Suresh K. Reddy as Ambassador of India to ASEAN.* Press release. New Delhi: Ministry of External Affairs, 2015.
26 Rahul Sen, Mukul G. Asher, and Rakishen S. Rajan. "ASEAN–India Economic Relations: Current Status and Future Prospects." *RIS Discussion Paper,* 73. New Delhi: Research and Information Systems for the Non Aligned and Other Developing Countries, 2004.
27 Pradumna B. Rana and Chia Wai-Mun. "Strengthening Economic Linkages between South Asia and East Asia: The Case for a Second Round of 'Look East' Policies." *RSIS Working Paper* 253: 2013.
28 Shruti Srivastava. "India Signs FTA in Services and Investments with ASEAN." *Indian Express.* September 9, 2014. http://indianexpress.com/article/business/business-others/india-signs-fta-in-services-investments-with-asean/.
29 "Chairman's Statement at the 13th ASEAN–India Summit." November 21, 2015. http://asean.org/chairmans-statement-of-the-13th-asean-india-summit/.
30 "Chairman's Statement at the 11th ASEAN–India Summit." October 10, 2013. http://asean.org/wp-content/uploads/images/archive/23rdASEANSummit/chairmans%20statement%20asean-india.pdf.
31 C. Raja Mohan. "India and ASEAN: Toward Maritime Security Cooperation." In *Enhancing India–ASEAN Connectivity,* edited by Ted Osius and C. Raja Mohan. Centre for Strategic and International Studies (CSIS). Lanham, MD: Rowman & Littlefield, 2013.
32 "India for Strong International Legal Regime to Deal with Terrorism-Related Cases." *Indian Express.* July 25, 2016. http://indianexpress.com/article/india/india-news-india/india-for-strong-international-legal-regime-to-deal-with-terrorism-related-cases-2935245/.
33 G. V. C. Naidu. "Whither the Look East Policy: India and Southeast Asia." *Strategic Analysis,* 28, no. 2 (2004): 331–46.

34 Benjamin Ho. "ASEAN's Centrality in Rising Asia.' *RSIS Working Paper,* 249 (2012).
35 "Vision Statement, ASEAN India Commemorative Summit." December 20, 2012. http://en.vietnamplus.vn/vision-statement-of-aseanindia-commemorative-summit/41008.vnp.
36 Ibid., 14.
37 ASEAN Regional Forum. *Concept Paper of ARF.* Jakarta: ASEAN Secretariat, 1995.
38 ASEAN Regional Forum. *Preventive Diplomacy Work Plan,* 2010. http://aseanregionalforum.asean.org/files/Archive/18th/5th%20ARF%20EEPs,%20Dili,%2027-28Jan2011/Annex%2012%20-%20ARF%20Preventive%20Diplomacy%20Work%20Plan.pdf.
39 ASEAN. "Hanoi Plan of Action to Implement the ASEAN Regional Forum Vision Statement." Hanoi: ASEAN Secretariat, 2010.
40 Government of India. *ASEAN Regional Forum (ARF).* May 2016. New Delhi: Ministry of External Affairs. https://www.mea.gov.in/Portal/ForeignRelation/ARF_May_2016.pdf.
41 S. D. Muni. "East Asia Summit and India." *Institute of South Asian Studies,* Working Paper, No. 13, 2006.
42 Anit Mukherjee. "ADMM Plus Talk Shop or Key to Asia Pacific Security." *The Diplomat.* August 22, 2013. http://thediplomat.com/2013/08/admm-plus-talk-shop-or-key-to-asia-pacific-security/1/.
43 Ibid., 14.
44 Ibid., 28.
45 "India Calls For Early Conclusion of South China Sea Code of Conduct." *Indian Express.* November 5, 2015. http://indianexpress.com/article/india/india-news-india/india-calls-for-early-conclusion-of-south-china-sea-code-of-conduct/.
46 "Exercise Force 18 Takes India's Act East Policy to the Next Level." *Rediff.* March 8, 2016. http://www.rediff.com/news/column/exercise-force-18-takes-indias-act-east-policy-to-the-next-level/20160308.htm.
47 Government of India. *About East Asia Summit.* February 2016. New Delhi: Ministry of External Affairs. http://mea.gov.in/aseanindia/about-eas.htm.
48 Rodolfo C. Severino. "East Asian regionalism and India's Possible Role in it." In *South and Southeast Asia, Responding to Changing Geo-Political and Security Challenges,* edited by K. V. Kesavan and Daljit Singh. New Delhi: K W Publishers, 2010.
49 "Chairman's Statement of the 10th East Asia Summit." ASEAN, November 22, 2015. http://asean.org/chairmans-statement-of-the-10th-east-asia-summit/.
50 Government of India. *Indian Ocean Rim Association for Regional Co-operation (IOR-ARC).* New Delhi: Ministry of External Affairs, 2012. http://mea.gov.in/in-focus-article.htm?20707/Indian+Ocean+Rim+Association+for+Regional+Cooperation+IORARC.
51 Ankit Panda. "Is India's APEC Membership on the Table at This Year's Summit?" *The Diplomat.* September 8, 2015. http://thediplomat.com/2015/09/is-indias-apec-membership-on-the-table-at-this-years-summit/.
52 Daniel Twining. "Daniel Twining's Testimony Before the House Ways and Means Committee's Trade Subcommittee About Indian Trade Protectionism." *German Marshall Fund of the United States.* March 13, 2013. http://www.gmfus.org/publications/daniel-twinings-testimony-house-ways-and-means-committee%E2%80%99s-trade-subcommittee-about.
53 Amitav Acharya. "Don't Let Superpowers Run the Show: How Regional Institutions can Stabilize Southeast Asia." Interview by Claudia K. Huber and Priya Shankar. *Global Policy Journal,* March 1, 2013.

6 Taiwan's inconsistent involvement in China's maritime disputes under the "One China" institution

Ching-Chang Chen

Maritime security issues in East Asia have been grabbing the headlines since the past decade.[1] The People's Republic of China (PRC) in particular has received much attention from the international community, both because its fast-growing capabilities have led to a popular perception of the "power shift" in East Asia and the subsequent US efforts to "rebalance" its priorities there,[2] and because it is the commonly known claimant state that has concurrent territorial and demarcation disputes in the East and South China Seas.[3] Sino-Japanese tensions began to surge in September 2010 when a Chinese trawler collided with two Japanese coast guard patrol boats in waters near the Senkaku/Diaoyu Islands. Hoping to better manage such tensions, the Japanese government moved to put the islands under its direct control in September 2012, which was seen by Beijing as an attempt to change the "status quo" and led to frequent deployment of PRC patrol vessels and aircraft into the surrounding waters and airspace. In April that same year, the standoff between a Philippine warship and two Chinese maritime surveillance vessels over the Scarborough Shoal/Huangyan Island ended up with the PRC's de facto blockade of the shoal until October 2016. The drilling work of the state-owned China National Offshore Oil Corporation's (CNOOC) oil platform near the Paracel/ Shisha Islands during summer 2014 and China's land reclamation activities in the Spratly Islands and their reported "militarization" since late 2014 were different from earlier incidents in the sense that they were Beijing's officially sanctioned initiatives rather than mere responses to other claimants' law enforcement behavior. As a result, recent developments in the South China Sea have prompted stronger reactions from the concerned parties, especially Vietnam (which lays claims on the Paracel and Spratly/Nansha Islands) and the United States (which seeks to defend perceived challenges to its freedom of navigation).[4]

The PRC is nevertheless a lone claimant state with little support from other regional stakeholders. In its territorial dispute with Tokyo, Beijing's claim has been met with a renewed US security pledge related to the Japanese-held islands. In US Secretary of State John Kerry's words, Washington's treaty commitments to Japan's security remains "iron-clad" and cover "all territories under Japan's administration, including the Senkaku Islands."[5] Although Hanoi and Manila have not been able to enlist backing from the Association of Southeast Asian Nations (ASEAN) and its member states as a whole for their respective claims, they have managed to bring in extraregional major powers, notably the United States and Japan, in the forms of arms transfer and joint military drills to counterbalance China's growing presence in the South China Sea.[6]

From Beijing's vantage point, China's continued isolation in maritime disputes is not merely detrimental to its international image. The isolation also makes China appear unreasonable, which, in turn, could lead to the further discrediting of its claims, as seen in the recent South China Sea arbitration case where China was confronted with international legal pressure.[7] Getting political support from relevant actors in maritime Asia will no doubt help mitigate (if not fully alter) negative international perceptions that a mighty, rule-breaking China is flexing its muscle and pushing its neighbors around. The question remains: getting support from whom?

Counterintuitive as it may appear, Taiwan, which was often represented by the international media as the PRC's archenemy, at least until the late 2000s, has the potential to ameliorate the latter's isolation in the ongoing maritime disputes in the East and South China Seas,[8] for three reasons. First, Beijing and Taipei make essentially the same claim that the Diaoyutai Islands were discovered, named, and used by the Chinese dating back to the Ming Dynasty (1368–1644) and they were ceded to Japan, as Taiwan's "appertaining islands," under the Treaty of Shimonoseki that concluded the Sino-Japanese War (1894–5).[9] Since Taipei's ownership claim amounts to its affirmation of the "One China" principle (there exists only one China, of which Taiwan is a part), Beijing can benefit from Taipei's involvement in the islands dispute as long as such involvement does not entail that Taiwan is a sovereign state actor. Second, the PRC's claims in the South China Sea stem from the "Location Map of South China Sea Islands" published by the ROC Ministry of the Interior between 1946 and 1948 (hereafter the 1947 map).[10] Taipei's upholding of the 1947 map is therefore crucial for Beijing to maintain its claims. Third, relations across the Taiwan Strait were expanding and intensifying on an unprecedented scale under the Ma Ying-jeou administration (2008–16) of the Kuomintang (KMT, Chinese Nationalist Party). China has been Taiwan's top trading partner and largest source of trade surplus, and Taipei and Beijing have concluded dozens of agreements to facilitate their functional cooperation in terms of freer movements of personnel, goods, services, and capital across the Strait.[11] It seems only natural for the PRC to intensify its push for some sort of cross-Strait political cooperation.[12]

By putting aside Beijing's familiar rhetoric that the Taiwan issue belongs exclusively to its domestic affairs and accepting a more flexible definition of international institutions (see Chapter 1 of this volume), this chapter will offer an empirical test of the strength of the decades-old "One China" principle as a bilateral institution. Specifically, it seeks to examine the extent to which Taipei can be said to have formed a "united front" with Beijing concerning China's territorial and demarcation disputes in the East and South China Seas under the "One China" institution. Following this introductory section, the next two sections will look at how Taiwan has responded to the Sino-Japanese row over a collision incident near the Senkaku Islands and their subsequent "nationalization" and to the rising tensions in the South China Sea since the Scarborough Shoal standoff. While Taiwan has been neutralized from the PRC–Japan island dispute following the conclusion of its fisheries agreement with Japan in April 2013, Taipei has turned down Washington's suggestion to ditch the 1947 map or redraw more realistic maritime boundaries. Having identified this apparent discrepancy between Taipei's limited cooperation with Beijing in the South China Sea and the lack thereof over the Senkakus, the fourth section will demonstrate that Taiwan's inconsistent participation in China's maritime disputes can be understood as a mixed product of its geopolitical considerations shaped by postcolonial conditions. To be sure, Taiwan's involvement in the disputes could adversely affect its relationship with Japan (East China Sea) and the United States (South China Sea) and the roles they might play in a militarized cross-Strait conflict, but this strategic imperative is mediated by Taiwan's psychological need to balance its relationship with China (the estranged self-turned-Other) and Japan (the former colonizer and a symbol of modernity); on the other hand, the island's assumed "Chineseness" enables Taipei to face its much larger Southeast Asian neighbors from an imagined higher position. After investigating the aforementioned interplay between the material and ideational factors, this chapter will conclude with brief discussions on the scholarly and policy implications of the "One China" principle as an institution.

Taiwan's responses to China's actions and statements over tensions in the East China Sea

The deterioration of Sino-Japanese relations is a relatively recent phenomenon.[13] Since the normalization of the Japan–PRC relationship, both Tokyo and Beijing have sought to keep the lid on the Senkaku Islands, which are administered by the former but also claimed by the latter, so as not to harm their overall bilateral (especially economic) relations. Nevertheless, the nationalist genie in the bottle was released by the aforementioned 2010 collision incident. On September 7, the Chinese trawler *Minjinyu* 5179 collided with two Japanese coast guard vessels, which were attempting to make the trawler leave the disputed waters. In response, Japanese coast guards boarded the Chinese trawler; the captain and his crews were arrested the following day for "obstructing the duties of public officials" and "illegal fishing."

The Chinese government swiftly reacted with a series of diplomatic protests: the Japanese ambassador to China was summoned no less than six times between September 8 and 19. Understandably, Beijing wanted to avoid the impression that Japan had the jurisdiction to indict the trawler's captain (hence possessing effective control over the Senkaku Islands and undermining China's claim under international law). Until then, the Japanese government had not applied domestic law in waters around the disputed islands, including even the landing of some Chinese "Bao-Diao" ("defending the Diaoyus") activists in 2004 who damaged Japanese property on the island.[14] Following the trawler captain's arrest, Beijing also cancelled or suspended several official and non-official bilateral exchanges, detained four Japanese nationals in Hebei Province under the charge of entering a military zone without authorization and of videotaping military targets, and allegedly halted China's export of rare-earth materials to Japan for nearly two months.[15] In the end, the *Minjinyu* 5179 and its crew were released on September 13, and the Prosecutor's Office announced the release of the trawler's captain without charges on September 24, on the grounds that further investigation would bring adverse effects "on the people of Japan and the future of Japan–China relations."[16]

Although no personnel from Taiwan was involved in the collision incident directly, two Taiwanese Bao-Diao activists were allowed to board the fishing boat *Ganen* 99 on September 13,[17] which almost reached the disputed waters the next day before being blocked by Japanese coast guard vessels. Before the *Ganen* 99's departure, Japan's representative to Taiwan Imai Tadashi was summoned by vice foreign minister Shen Lyu-shun. Shen told Imai that ROC citizens' activities in waters near the Diayutais were under the ROC's sovereign jurisdiction and their safety would be protected by the ROC government. He also asked the Japanese side not to interfere with the Bao-Diao activity and expressed his concerns over the "recent and frequent appearance of Japanese public vessels and aircraft" in the disputed area.[18] However, Shen not only repeated Taipei's claim but also reassured Imai about the importance that the Ma administration placed on the Taiwan–Japan relationship. A press release issued on the same day indicated the non-official, spontaneous nature of the *Ganen* 99's action and threatened to revoke Hong Kong and Macao activists' entry permit and prohibit them from entering Taiwan in the future should they board the boat.[19] In its press conference on September 14, the ROC foreign ministry similarly denied the connection between its summoning Imai and the PRC's diplomatic protests and any collaboration between Taiwan and China against Japan.[20]

Another round of tensions arose in 2012 after Tokyo governor Ishihara Shintaro proposed to purchase parts of the Senkaku Islands from their private landlord and develop them. Until then, the Japanese government maintained an annually renewed lease on them and forbade Japanese from landing on the islands. As Ishihara's fund-raising campaign was gaining momentum and his development plan was deemed outright provocative for China, the Noda Yoshihiko administration sought to preempt the maverick governor by purchasing the islands instead.[21] The "nationalization" move itself was nevertheless seen by Beijing as a violation of the status quo that worked to shore up Tokyo's effective control over the disputed islands.[22] This move, then, set in motion a series of violent anti-Japanese demonstrations in major Chinese cities unprecedented in Japan–PRC relations and frequent appearance of Chinese patrol vessels and surveillance aircraft in the surrounding waters and airspace. A mass boycott movement of Japanese goods and services led to a slump in Japanese exports to China and in Chinese tourists to Japan, which was estimated to lower Japan's economic growth in fiscal year 2012 by up to 0.6%.[23]

With the increasing number of aerial and maritime near misses and without hotline-like conflict prevention mechanisms between them, in January 2013,

Chinese warships were said to have pointed their fire-control radar at a Japanese helicopter and a destroyer in close distance in the East China Sea. The Sino-Japanese relationship was so tense that some media described them as being on the brink of war.[24] The PRC foreign ministry in April referred to the Diaoyus as a part of China's "core interests," a term normally associated with Xinjiang, Tibet, and Taiwan, for the first time.[25] Unabated, Beijing proceeded to include the islands into its self-declared East Sea Air Defense Identification Zone (ADIZ) in November. To make matters worse, Japanese Prime Minister Abe Shinzo's visit to the Yasukuni Shrine in December 2013 offered more munitions to the PRC government's diplomatic and media warfare that fused this territorial dispute with Japan's World War II-related "history issue," framing the latter's control of the Diaoyu Islands as "a challenge to the victorious outcome of the war against fascism and a challenge to the postwar international order."[26] The frequency of entries by Chinese public ships into the 12-nautical-mile waters around the Senkaku Islands (i.e., Japanese-defined territorial waters) eventually began to drop in October 2013 and has stayed stable since then, which might indicate Beijing's intention to signal de-escalation.[27]

Before the islands' "nationalization" took place, Bao-Diao activists from Taiwan and Hong Kong again attempted to land on the Diaoyutais. The latter managed to do so on August 15, 2012 and carried with them PRC and ROC flags upon landing. As with 2010, Taipei tolerated Bao-Diao activities as a way to extract Tokyo's recognition of the existence of a sovereignty dispute over the Senkakus, while avoiding the impression that it was teaming up with Beijing at the expense of Taiwan's relations with Japan (and, by extension, the United States). On the one hand, the ROC government asserted that the appearance of the ROC flag was consistent with its sovereignty claim to the islands and described Japan's arrest of these Hong Kong activists as "unhelpful for regional peace and security" and demanded their immediate release. On the other hand, Taipei denied its connection with Beijing and these activists (justifying Taiwanese coast guards' supply of food and water to them on "humanitarian" grounds) and downplayed the display of the PRC flag as a matter of "freedom of expression."[28]

Since August 2012, Taipei had started promoting President Ma's East China Sea Peace Initiative (ECSPI) based on the principle that "while sovereignty is indivisible, resources can be shared." The initiative called upon all parties concerned to "replace confrontation with dialogue, shelve territorial disputes through negotiations, formulate a Code of Conduct in the East China Sea and engage in joint development of resources."[29] Although the Japanese government did not henceforth change its position that "no dispute exists" over the Senkaku Islands, the non-coercive nature of the ECSPI made it possible for Tokyo to reciprocate while using policy concessions to neutralize Taipei from the bigger Sino-Japanese row. The result was the signing of the Japan–Taiwan fisheries agreement in April 2013,[30] which avoided the territorial issues in the designated waters by specifying that flag-state jurisdiction be applied. Despite its Beijing-like description of the Diaoyutais as a territory "surreptitiously occupied" (*qiezhan*) by Japan,[31] Taipei's decision to conclude a fisheries agreement that in effect discourages Taiwanese fishing boats from entering the Japanese-controlled 12-nautical-mile belt of waters surrounding the Diaoyutai Islands (hence acquiescing in Japan's effective control over them) has distanced itself from the PRC's maritime dispute with Japan.[32]

Taiwan's responses to China's actions and statements over tensions in the South China Sea

Territorial and maritime demarcation disputes have smoldered in the South China Sea for decades,[33] but tensions among the claimants themselves and with some extraregional states have turned more severe since 2011, which could lead to militarized conflicts if not properly managed. In this regard, how Taiwan responds to China's (and other concerned parties') strategic behavior in the region is not inconsequential for (de-)escalating tensions there. After all, Taiwan controls both the largest island group in the South China Sea (Tungsha/Paratas Islands) as well as the largest natural high-tide feature (Taiping/Itu Aba) in the Spratly Islands. Itu Aba hosts a renovated airstrip that can accommodate C-130 Hercules military transport aircraft and an enlarged pier that allows 3,000-tonne naval frigates and coast guard cutters to dock there; it is also the only high-tide feature with its own stable fresh-water supply, making a long-term presence possible. Moreover, Taiwanese coast guards regularly patrol the area and Taiwan's fishing industry is one of the largest in the Pacific. To borrow from Lynn Kuok's words, excluding Taiwan from South China Sea code of conduct negotiations and cooperative activities among the claimants inevitably weakens the efficacy for managing the South China Sea dispute, since an important "road user" is not included in the making of relevant rules of the road.[34]

Although such exclusion is largely attributable to the PRC's uncompromising position on Taiwan's international/legal status (and to ASEAN member states' resulting fear of offending China over the Taiwan issue), it is worthy of note that, unlike Manila and Hanoi, Taipei has *never* explicitly objected to, much less challenged, Beijing's actions in the South China Sea. On April 10, 2012, the Philippine Navy's flagship *BRP Gregorio del Pilar* was sent to inspect the activities of eight Chinese fishing boats anchored near the Scarborough Shoal. Filipino sailors claimed to find illegally harvested coral and live sharks in one vessel, and attempted to return the next day to arrest the Chinese fishermen. However, two China Marine Surveillance vessels later arrived in the area, blocking the Philippine crew from boarding to detain the fishermen.[35] Since then, China has continued to maintain its presence there and Scarborough was not reopened to Filipino vessels until October 2016.[36] In addition to various belligerent commentaries in the Chinese media,[37] Beijing in May 2012 tightened its quarantine regulations on Chinese import of Philippine fruits such as bananas – an important pillar of the Philippines' external trade – and suspended tours to the Philippines, citing safety concerns,[38] both of which could be seen as its coercive moves to alter Manila's behavior over the Scarborough Shoal.

Similar to the *Minjinyu* 5179 collision incident, Taiwan was not a party directly involved in the 2012 shoal standoff, but the way it asserted its sovereignty claim reinforced, not alleviated, an old concern among ASEAN member states that Taipei and Beijing might cooperate to defend the disputed islets/rocks against another claimant's attack or to bolster claims to the South China Sea.[39] In its press release concerning the aforementioned standoff, the ROC foreign ministry simply restated that the disputed shoal belongs to the Chungsha Islands (Macclesfield Islands), which, together with the Spratly, Paracel, and Pratas Islands and their surrounding waters, fall under the ROC's "indisputable sovereignty"; it also refuted "all claims to sovereignty over, or occupation of, these areas by other countries" and called on the parties concerned to "exercise self-restraint" and to "refrain from adopting unilateral measures that threaten the peace and stability of the region."[40] While this statement could be read as a mild criticism against both Beijing and Manila without mentioning their names, curiously, the text did not address the Scarborough Shoal as "Minzhu-jiao" ("Democracy Reef" in Chinese), the name that appeared on the ROC Ministry of Interior's 1947 map. Rather, it followed the PRC's renaming in 1983 (i.e., Huangyan-*dao*, meaning island), which added to a false impression that the object of dispute is not a few tiny rocks (each just about large enough to stand on) but a high-tide feature fitting the UN Convention on the Law of the Sea (UNCLOS) definition of an island.[41] Similarly, some Taiwanese legislators' sudden visit to Taiping Island on April 30 and proposals to expand defense capabilities there were justified on the grounds of an alleged Vietnamese shooting at Taiwanese coast guard vessels in the Taiping's vicinity on March 22,[42] but from the perspective of other concerned parties these moves worked to Beijing's overall advantage in the South China Sea.[43] Indeed, Taiwan's subsequent live fire drill on Taiping Island was perceived by the PRC positively, "conducive to the Chinese nation's common protection of sovereignty over the Nansha."[44] As an editorial of *Global Times* put it:

> [It] came at a right timing. The Taiwan authorities has always indicated that it will not directly cooperate with the mainland over territorial disputes; however, East Asian [countries'] interpretations of this drill are nuanced, and its implications are of course not that simple.[45]

In early May 2014, the CNOOC moved its oil rig *Haiyang Shiyou* 981 into disputed waters near the Paracel Islands and was about 120 nautical miles off the coast of Vietnam. The placement of the rig led to protests and demands by Hanoi that it be withdrawn, and the deployment of a Vietnamese flotilla to the area. A series of skirmishes between PRC and Vietnamese public vessels culminated in the sinking of a Vietnamese ship before the removal of the drilling platform in mid-July. Considering the still ongoing tensions in the South China Sea, China's unilateral move to introduce its oil rig into these disputed waters was qualitatively different from its previously reactive behavior and was thus more destabilizing. The placement prompted violent protests across Vietnam targeting Chinese (and other East Asian foreign-owned) business that killed one, injured hundreds, and led to property losses worth millions of dollars. Compared with the US State Department's description of Beijing's move as "provocative and unhelpful,"[46]

ROC Ministry of Foreign Affairs merely expressed its "serious concern" over "recent confrontations in the waters off the Paracel Islands" without even mentioning the PRC[47]; in fact, it only scrambled to differentiate Taiwan from China by distributing "I am Taiwanese" stickers to Taiwanese businessmen in Vietnam in the wake of the aforementioned anti-Chinese protests.

Against this backdrop, a sort of "correlation" between the PRC's demonstration of its administrative control in the South China Sea and the ROC's upgrading of its infrastructure on Itu Aba became more discernable in 2014, as seen for instance in the former's adding a school to Woody/Yongxin Island and the latter's building a new pier on Taiping Island.[48] To be sure, Taiwanese officials had repeatedly ruled out the possibility of cross-Strait cooperation over the South China Sea,[49] but their denial did little to undo the "spill-over" effect of Taipei's development work and defense buildup on Taiping Island that was seen by Beijing as strengthening *Chinese* sovereignty there.[50] With the PRC's land reclamation activities and construction of military installations gaining international attention since late 2014, it is intriguing that security discourse in Taiwan was more concerned with the growing "Vietnamese threat" to the Spratly outpost,[51] even though Taipei was clearly aware that Hanoi's reclamation and deployment on Sand Cay/Dunqian Sand Island was no match for Beijing's in the same area.[52]

Taiwan's ambivalent attitude on the South China Sea issues in relation to the PRC has prompted (former) officials and think tank researchers in the United States to call for Taiwan to abandon or clarify its expansive claim.[53] Washington's logic is that:

> if the inventors of the position [i.e., the ROC] clarify the dashed line to mean something different from what the PRC is now saying, that will ultimately undermine the PRC's claims to sovereignty or historic waters up to the dashed line.[54]

To some extent, Taipei had sought to clarify its position through the Academia Historica's "Exhibition of Historical Archives on the Southern Territories of the Republic of China," whose title indicated a focus on land rather than maritime claims. President Ma also affirmed at the opening ceremony the existence of the "land-dominates-the-sea" principle in the Law of the Sea, hence acknowledging that maritime claims begin with land.[55] However, this clarification was weakened by his mentioning of the "intertemporal law" principle, which could be seen as an attempt to buttress the legal status of the dashed line or "historic rights" to virtually everything therein on Beijing's behalf.[56] Ma later adopted a tactical argument against the charge that Taiwan's South China Sea claims were identical to that of mainland China's by pointing to the fact that the PRC was not in existence in 1947 when the ROC made the sovereignty claim; moreover, he resorted to the 1947 map for basing Taiwan's claims while addressing participants of the International Law Association and American Society of International Law Asia-Pacific Research Forum.[57]

It is therefore unsurprising that Taipei's South China Sea Peace Initiative (SCSPI),[58] which was based on the widely praised 2012 ECSPI, was given the cold shoulder by Washington. The US government was frustrated with Taipei's call on claimants to exercise restraint on the one hand and silence about Beijing's unilateral actions that could escalate tensions on the other. Worse, from Washington's viewpoint, Ma agreed to meet with President Xi Jinping in Singapore (the first summit-like meeting between leaders of Taiwan and mainland China since the end of the Chinese Civil War) at a time when the United States resumed "freedom of navigation and overflight" operations and sought to build up international pressure against the PRC over the South China Sea.[59] President Ma's sudden visit to Taiping Island in January 2016 despite prior US opposition was criticized by the State Department as a "frankly disappointing" and "unhelpful" unilateral action that "could possibly raise [tensions]."[60] Before the end of his presidency, Ma, a Harvard-trained international lawyer, waged a legal war against the Philippines that asked the Permanent Court of Arbitration to rule on some of China's claims under UNCLOS.[61] Rebutting Manila's assertion that Itu Aba is not an island but a rock, the ROC government invited domestic and foreign journalists to visit Taiping Island on March 23 and the president held a press conference personally upon their return to Taipei.[62] Although this appeared to be a desperate move by an internationally unrecognized actor to defend its sovereignty, the move provided Beijing with a potential legal cover under UNCLOS when Washington just carried out another round of freedom-of-navigation operations by sailing an aircraft carrier strike group within 12 nautical miles of artificial islands constructed by China.[63]

Making sense of Taipei's inconsistent involvement in Beijing's maritime disputes

Taken together, the previous two sections indicate that considerations of cross-Strait relations have profoundly conditioned Taiwan's territorial and maritime claims in the East and South China Seas, to the extent of clouding its otherwise cordial relationships with Japan and the United States. To be sure, Taipei's express abandonment of the Diaoyutai claim or the dashed line would lead to concerns about whether the government is moving away from the "One China" principle, which in turn could be interpreted as an act of declaring Taiwan's *de jure* independence – a *casus belli* for Beijing. In other words, it would be a strategic suicide for Taipei to do so without securing a more explicit and stronger commitment from the United States to Taiwan's defense.[64] Still, the question remains as to why the "One China" principle-affirming Ma administration adopted different approaches to the PRC's maritime disputes.

From a realist perspective, the material structure of the international system in East Asia ultimately determines Taiwan's strategic alignment behavior. Given the PRC's fast-growing capabilities and its refusal to renounce the use of force in pursuing its unification with Taiwan,[65] even the Beijing-friendly KMT government could not ignore the worst-case scenario, i.e., the loss of

Taiwan as an autonomous (albeit isolated) actor in the international arena and the ROC's last territory. On the other hand, Taiwan's limited capabilities mean that the island must cultivate relations with major powers to keep the PRC in check in peacetime and to intervene should a shooting war break out in the Taiwan Strait. In addition to Taiwan's long-standing and better-known security cooperation with the United States,[66] Japan has been the most noticeable potential security partner in the region in terms of external balancing, because of its advanced military capabilities (the navy in particular), geostrategic needs to secure its energy imports through the southern sea lanes of communication, and its own rivalry with China (especially under a "proactive pacifist" Abe administration that legalizes Japan's exercise of collective self-defense away from the Japanese homeland).[67] The possibility of Japanese participation in a US intervention in the Taiwan Strait has been further opened up, considering that US military bases in Japan would be among the primary targets of the first-wave Chinese strikes should such a cross-Strait conflict break out. Furthermore, Tokyo demonstrated necessary flexibility in the aftermath of the Senkaku Islands' "nationalization" by responding to Taipei's ECSPI positively[68]; as a result, the latter was able to conclude a fisheries agreement with Japan (which by 2012 had been negotiated for 16 rounds but to no avail) that yielded tangible gains for Taiwan's fishing industry, and Ma could declare diplomatic victory without resorting to the PRC card.

Although the Philippines should have been another potential security partner for a Taiwan facing the same systemic imperative, its lack of material capabilities means that the latter has few strategic incentives to pursue a more reconciliatory approach to South China Sea issues, which in turn adds to China's advantage. The military spending of the Philippines in 2014 ($3,292 million) was less than that of Taiwan's one-third ($10,244 million),[69] which suggests that Manila depends even more on Washington for deterring Beijing than Taipei does. Unlike Japan, moreover, the Philippines has failed to maneuver its tensions with Taiwan into a "three-wins" situation as a US ally. Following the 2013 *Guangdaxing* 28 incident where an unarmed Taiwanese fisherman was shot dead by personnel on a Philippine government vessel in the overlapping EEZs of the two countries,[70] Manila under Taipei's economic sanction eventually complied with the latter's demands, including a formal apology and compensation. Yet it took more than two and a half years for the two sides to merely conclude a damage-control-type agreement on law enforcement cooperation in the disputed EEZs.[71] By ignoring Taipei's SCSPI, Manila missed a golden opportunity to neutralize Taiwan from the Sino-Philippine territorial disputes. Rather than signing a fisheries agreement comparable to the 2013 Japan–Taiwan deal, the Philippine government asserted in its South China Sea arbitration case that no high-tide feature of the Spratly Islands (including the Taiwan-controlled Itu Aba) could meet the UNCLOS definition as an island, hence further pushing Taipei to align with Beijing.

Nevertheless, these aforementioned material capabilities and interests would not have gained their meanings and significance without being perceived by

Taiwan's policymakers and general public *as such*; their perceptions are in turn shaped by the island's fluid, postcolonial identity under the triple legacies of Japanese colonial rule, Chinese Civil War, and the US-led Cold War in Asia.[72] The separation of Taiwan from mainland China means that the former's assumed "Chineseness" is neither stable nor complete; rather, it enables Taiwanese to switch between different legacies as sources of identity formation and appropriate them selectively when facing different (real or imagined) audiences, without feeling apparent contradiction.[73] Following this postcolonial psychoanalysis, Taiwan's involvement in the PRC's maritime disputes is not an entirely irrational behavior, for its conforming to the "One China" principle represents an attempt to soothe its increasing estrangement from China against which Taiwan defines its own emerging nation-statehood. During this process of "becoming Taiwanese," "Chineseness" can take a back seat or be enlisted, depending on the ontological security need.[74]

Since the island's colonial Japanese experience has served as an important reference point to demonstrate its "non-Chineseness" in the formation of Taiwanese identity, it follows that Taipei is constantly under an imagined Japanese gaze, feeling the need to show that its relationship with Tokyo remains intimate despite the PRC–Japan row. Indeed, even when being recalled in protest of Tokyo's move to nationalize the Senkaku Islands, Taiwan's representative to Japan still described Taiwan–Japan ties as "at their best in 40 years" to legislators.[75] While identity politics has impeded Chinese identification in Taiwan concerning the East China Sea dispute, a claim of "Chineseness" has provided Taiwanese policymakers and the public with a self-empowering strategy in the face of Southeast Asian claimant states. This is to the extent that in the Taiwanese mindset it rarely occurs to them that the size of Taiwan is actually dwarfed by that of the Philippines or Vietnam in terms of landmass and population. Similar to an infamous statement by then-PRC Foreign Minister Yang Jiechi at the July 2010 ASEAN Ministers Conference that "China is a big country and other countries are small countries, and that's a fact,"[76] Taiwanese tend to assign their Southeast Asian neighbors to the "margin" of Chinese civilization and look at them through a hierarchical lens. This was the psychological basis on which the ROC government insisted on "punishing" the Philippines with high-profile economic sanctions and military exercise following the *Guangdaxing* 28 incident, despite President Benigno Aquino's dispatch of his envoy to Taipei to convey his "deep regret and apology over the unfortunate and unintended loss of life" to "the people of Taiwan."[77] What was behind the bellicose (and derogatory) rhetoric of various Taiwanese legislators and netizens was, in a nutshell, a paternalistic attitude, wanting to teach their "junior," "small," and disrespectful neighbor a lesson.[78] In the final analysis, appropriating "Chineseness" in this way has proven counterproductive, as Taipei's subsequent failure to further distance itself from the dubious U-shape line not only reinforces a region-wide perception that it has become Beijing's proxy in the South China Sea but also complicates its security cooperation with Washington.

Concluding remarks

This chapter has conducted a first-ever empirical examination of the strength of the "One China" principle as a bilateral institution in relation to the PRC's territorial and demarcation disputes in maritime Asia. Although it would require another research to investigate in detail the "One China" institution's informal (e.g., norms, practices, or habitual behaviors) and formal (e.g., rules and frameworks) aspects and its evolution since the end of the Chinese Civil War, this chapter's findings indicate that the institution in question has been internalized by Taiwan to the extent that a de facto cross-Strait "united front" over the PRC's maritime disputes (at least in the South China Sea) already took shape during President Ma's terms. Such tacit cooperation, albeit nascent and limited, is of scholarly and policy importance. Empirically, it suggests that a largely informal institution might still have independent effects on its member's strategic behavior, especially if the Ma administration's insistence that there had been no security policy coordination with Beijing can be taken at face value. However, the scope and strength of such effects should not be overestimated; as this chapter has illustrated, multiple factors (such as relative power, identity formation, and interaction of actors) can make an actor's strategic behavior inconsistent (recall Taiwan's disengagement from the Japan–PRC dispute over the Senkakus), even when the institution itself is not being weakened. Politically, this research reminds us that calls for Taipei to explicate the rationale of the 1947 map and the status of the U-shape line are unrealistic under the influence of the "One China" institution, among other factors. To provide Taipei with an exit strategy (yet not to the point of triggering Beijing's "anti-independence" war), alternative institutions should be explored and developed to socialize Taiwan (e.g., greater promotion of Taiwan's substantial participation in international institutions under a creative, "post-Westphalian" capacity)[79] under a new Tsai Ying-wen administration, which is much less interested in playing up the island's "Chineseness."

Notes

1 Regarding various disputed high-tide features in the East and South China Seas, this chapter refers to their different names interchangeably without the intention of endorsing any claimant's position. The author is grateful to the editors for their patience and Christian Wirth for his comments, without which this chapter would not have been in its current shape. Financial support from the Japan Society for the Promotion of Science, Grant-in-Aid Young Scientists (B) (16K21495), is also acknowledged.
2 Linus Hagström and Björn Jerdén. "East Asia's Power Shift: The Flaws and Hazards of the Debate and How to Avoid Them." *Asian Perspective*, 38, no. 3, (2014): 337–62; and Yoichiro Sato and See Seng Tan, eds., *United States Engagement in the Asia Pacific: Perspectives from Asia.* New York: Cambria Press, 2015.
3 Taiwan (also known as the Republic of China, ROC) is also a claimant of the Senkaku/Diaoyutai Islands (along with Japan and the PRC) and in the South China Sea (with the PRC, the Philippines, Vietnam, Malaysia, and Brunei), but this fact is often overlooked because none of these claimants diplomatically recognize the ROC on Taiwan. Yet Taiwan's lack of such recognition does not mean that it has no meaningful roles to play in these maritime disputes. See Bonnie Glaser and Jacqueline Vitello. "Taiwan's

Marginalized Role in International Security: Paying a Price." Report of the Center for Strategic and International Studies (CSIS Freeman Chair in China Studies). Washington, DC: Center for Strategic and International Studies, 2015; and Michael Mazza. "To Fix the South China Sea, Look to Taiwan." *The National Interest*, February 1, 2016.
4 Ian Storey and Cheng-Yi Lin, eds. *The South China Sea Dispute: Navigating Diplomatic and Strategic Tensions.* Singapore: ISEAS – Yusof Ishak Institute, 2016.
5 "Kerry Renews U.S. Pledge to Japan Security, Including East China Sea Islets." *Reuters*, April 27, 2015.
6 "US–Philippine War Games Begin as China Warns US." *Taipei Times*, April 5, 2016; and Prashanth Parameswaran. "Japan, Philippines to Finalize New Military Aircraft Deal for Five TC-90s." *The Diplomat*, May 4, 2016.
7 Republic of the Philippines. "Notification and Statement of Claim on West Philippine Sea." No. 13-0211. January 22, 2013. http://docslide.us/documents/notification-and-statement-of-claim-on-west-philipphil-sea.html (accessed May 7, 2016); Vietnam Ministry of Foreign Affairs. "Remarks by MOFA Spokesperson Le Hai Binh on the South China Sea Arbitration Case." December 11, 2014. http://www.vietnamembassy-seoul.org/en/vnemb.vn/tinkhac/ns141217145309 (accessed May 7, 2016); Permanent Court of Arbitration. "In the Matter of the South China Sea Arbitration Before an Arbitral Tribunal Constituted Under Annex VII to the United Nations Convention on the Law of the Sea Between the Republic of the Philippines and the People's Republic of China: Award." *PCA Case N° 2013-19*, July 12, 2016.
8 Lynn Kuok. "Tides of Change: Taiwan's Evolving Position in the South China Sea and Why Other Actors Should Take Note." *The Brookings Institution East Asia Policy Paper,* 5 (May 2015): 8–9.
9 According to this perspective, Chinese sovereignty over the islands should have been restored following the end of World War II and Japan's subsequent renunciation of all claims over Taiwan in the San Francisco Peace Treaty. People's Republic of China State Department Press Office. *"Diaoyudao shi Zhongguo de guyou lingtu* [Diaoyu Islands are China's Inherent Territory]." 2012http://www.scio.gov.cn/zfbps/ndhf/2012/Document/1225272/1225272.htm (accessed May 7, 2016); Republic of China Ministry of Foreign Affairs, *"Diaoyutai lie yu shi Zhonghua Minguo de guyou lingtu* [Diaoyutai Islands are the Republic of China's Inherent Territory]." 2012. http://www.mofa.gov.tw/News_Content.aspx?n=AA60A1A7FEC4086B&sms=66ECE8A8F0DB165D&s=26CF6ADBA824644B (accessed May 7, 2016).
10 The 1947 map contains 11 dashes that enclose much of the South China Sea and is seen as the predecessor to the controversial nine-dashed-line map, which was a product of Beijing's removal of the two dashes originally depicted inside the Gulf of Tonkin as a good-will gesture toward Hanoi during the Cold War period. U.S. Department of State, Bureau of Oceans and International Environmental and Scientific Affairs. *Limits in the Seas No. 143; China: Maritime Claims in the South China Sea.* December 5, 2014. http://www.state.gov/documents/organization/234936.pdf (accessed May 7, 2016).
11 Richard C. Bush. *Uncharted Strait: The Future of China-Taiwan Relations.* Washington, D.C.: Brookings Institution Press, 2013.
12 Bo Zhao and Xueyi Xu. "General Secretary Xi Jinping Meets with Taiwan Peaceful Reunification Groups." *Xinhuanet.* September 26, 2014.http://news.xinhuanet.com/politics/2014-09/26/c_1112641354.htm (accessed May 7, 2016).
13 Karl Gustafsson. "Routinised Recognition and Anxiety: Understanding the Deterioration in Sino-Japanese Relations." *Review of International Studies* (2016): doi:10.1017/S0260210515000546.
14 The 2004 landing incident reportedly led to a secret "confidence-building measure" agreement between Beijing and Tokyo where the former would prevent its citizens from landing on the islands and the latter would refrain from putting such individuals on trial. Paul Midford. "Sino–Japanese Conflict and Reconciliation in the East China

Sea." In *The China–Japan Border Dispute: Islands of Contention in Multidisciplinary Perspective*, edited by Tim F. Liao, Kimie Hara, and Krista Wiega, 180. Surrey: Ashgate, 2015.
15 Whether China did intend to put pressure on Japan to release the detained captain through these subsequent developments was much less clear, as demonstrated by Linus Hagström. "'Power Shift' in East Asia? A Critical Reappraisal of Narratives on the Diaoyu/Senkaku Islands Incident in 2010." *Chinese Journal of International Politics*, 5, no. 3, (2012): 267–97. Nevertheless, it was certain that such developments were widely perceived by Japanese observers as such; Beijing's actions thus had the similar *effect* of strategic coercion. See "Govt Leaders Flinch at China Intimidation." *Daily Yomiuri*, September 26, 2010.
16 "*Chugokujin sencho, shobun horyu de kaiho Naha chiken 'Nicchu kankei o koryo'* [Chinese Captain Released with Punishment Pending. Naha District Public Prosecutors Office: '[We] take Japan-China relations into account']." *Kyodo*, September 25, 2010.
17 Typically pro-unification, these activists belong to the small but vocal *Zhonghua Baodiao Xiehui* (Chinese Association for the Defense of the Diaoyus) and align themselves with their counterparts in mainland China, Hong Kong, and Macao. In my interview with a high-ranking Taiwanese diplomat (December 2012), I was told that the ROC government could not legally prohibit Bao-Diao activists from sailing to the Diaoyutais because "Taiwan is a democratic country" and "they all have fishing license."
18 Republic of China Ministry of Foreign Affairs. "*Waijiao bu yanzheng chongshen Diaoyutai wei woguo guyou lingtu* [MOFA Solemnly Reaffirms Diaoyutai Islands as Our Country's Inherent Territory]." Press release, September 13, 2010.
19 Republic of China Ministry of Foreign Affairs. "*Guanyu jinri Diaoyutai lie yu fujin haiyu dongtai, zhengfu chixu baochi gaodu guanzhu ji shiqie yinying* [Government Continues to Monitor Recent Situation in Waters near Diaoyutai Islands]." Press release, September 13, 2010. Seven activists from Hong Kong and Macao eventually did not board the *Ganen* 99 after being approached by Taiwanese immigration officers. See "*Taiwan: Gangao Bao-Diao renshi fangqi chuhai dasuan* [Taiwan: Hong Kong and Macao Bao-Diao Activists Gave up Plan to Board]." *BBC Zhongwen*, September 13, 2010. It is worthy of note that Taiwanese coastguard vessels (which outnumbered their Japanese counterpart around the Diaoyutai Islands at the time) were watching over the fishing boat but not attempting to enter the disputed waters themselves.
20 Republic of China Ministry of Foreign Affairs. "*Xinwen shuoming hui jiyao* [News Briefing Summary]." Taipei: Republic of China Ministry of Foreign Affairs, September 14, 2010.
21 Martin Fackler. "Japan Said to Have Tentative Deal to Buy 3 Disputed Islands From Private Owners." *New York Times*, September 6, 2012.
22 This observation was reaffirmed in my private conversation with two otherwise Japan-friendly Chinese officials in Jilin Province (March 2014) who complained that the Japanese "did not keep their promise."
23 "ADB Lowers Projection Over China Tensions." *Japan Times*, December 8, 2012.
24 "Dangerous Shoal." *The Economist*, January 19, 2013.
25 The PRC foreign ministry later modified the record of its press conference, broadly defining China's "core interests" as anything concerning state sovereignty, national security, and territorial integrity, and "The Diaoyu issue is related to the Chinese sovereignty." See "*Chugoku, Senkaku wa 'kakushin-teki rieki' to hajimete meigen* [The Senkakus, Referred to as China's 'Core Interests' for the First Time]." *Nihon Keizai Shimbun*, April 26, 2013.
26 Liu Jieyi, PRC ambassador to the UN, was quoted as saying in "China Says Abe No Longer Welcome after Yasukuni Visit." *Japan Times*, January 1, 2014.
27 M. Taylor Fravel and Alastair Iain Johnston. "Chinese Signaling in the East China Sea?" *Washington Post*, April 12, 2014.
28 Republic of China Ministry of Foreign Affairs. "*Xinwen shuoming hui jiyao* [News Briefing Summary]." August 16, 2012.

29 Republic of China Ministry of Foreign Affairs. "The Government of the Republic of China (Taiwan) Proposes the East China Sea Peace Initiative." August 5, 2012. http://www.mofa.gov.tw/News_Content.aspx?n=9FB1B5F1C76243EE&sms=20EB7F8877 46D351&s=4D897496805D198C (accessed May 7, 2016).
30 Hsiu-chuan Shih. "Taiwan, Japan Ink Fisheries Agreement." *Taipei Times*, April 11, 2013; and Adam Tyrsett Kuo. "Taipei–Tokyo Fishery Pact a Good Start for Further Progress: Ma." *China Post*, April 23, 2013.
31 Hsiu-chuan Shih. "Japan Stole the Diaoyutais, MOFA Says." *Taipei Times*, August 19, 2012.
32 Contrary to the aforementioned remark on the ROC government's inability to rein in Taiwanese Bao-Diao activists (see note 17), as of this writing *Zhonghua Baodiao Xiehui* has not dispatched any boats to the disputed waters since April 2013. See also Republic of China Ministry of Foreign Affairs. "*Zai Diaoyutai lieyu zhengduan, woguo bu yu Zhongguo dalu hezuo zhi lichang* [Why Our Country Does Not Cooperate with Mainland China over the Diaoyutai Islands Dispute]." February 8, 2013. http://www.mofa.gov.tw/News_Content.aspx?n=AA60A1A7FEC4086B&sms=66ECE8A8F0DB 165D&s=68C9A7761280E9E6 (accessed May 7, 2016).
33 Bill Hayton. *The South China Sea: The Struggle for Power in Asia*. New Haven, CT: Yale University Press, 2014.
34 Kuok, "Tides of Change," 21.
35 James Hookway. "Philippines Warns China in Naval Crisis." *Wall Street Journal*, April 11, 2012.
36 Jim Gomez. "Indonesia Scrambles to End ASEAN Rift Over Sea." Associated Press, July 18, 2012.
37 Hayton, *South China Sea*, 175–6.
38 "China Travel Agencies Suspend Philippine Tours." *BBC*, May 10, 2012.
39 Kuok, "Tides of Change," 20.
40 Republic of China Ministry of Foreign Affairs. "The Ministry of Foreign Affairs of the Republic of China (Taiwan) Reiterates its Position on the Huangyan Island and its Surrounding Waters." Press release, April 20, 2012.
41 Compare Permanent Court of Arbitration. "South China Sea Arbitration," 232.
42 The time lag suggests that these legislators were not concerned with the alleged Vietnamese provocation *per se*. The head of Taiwan's Coast Guard Administration later confirmed that the alleged gunshot might have been a harmless blank cartridge. Rich Chang. "Strengthen Taiping Defense: Lawmakers." *Taipei Times*, May 3, 2012.
43 The American Institute in Taiwan (AIT), the de facto US embassy in Taipei, was quick to discourage Taiwan's deployment of short-range missiles on Taiping Island. "Defense Ministry Rules Out Deploying Missiles in S. China Sea." *China Post* (Taiwan), May 4, 2012. In this regard, the fact that a senior US State Department official equivocated in a press briefing on whether Taiwan was a claimant in the South China Sea was not so much a mistake as a sign of distrust. William Lowther. "US Tries to Avoid Taiwan in S China Sea Dispute." *Taipei Times*, December 18, 2013.
44 "*Sheping: Wei Taiwan de Nansha Taiping dao jun yan guzhang* [Editorial: Applaud Taiwan's Military Drill in Nansha's Taiping Island]." *Global Times*, September 3, 2012.
45 Ibid. A deadly incident in which Philippine coastguard personnel fired upon an unarmed Taiwanese fishing boat in May 2013 in waters where the exclusive economic zones (EEZs) of Taiwan and the Philippines overlap led some scholars to propose that Taiwan and China should work together in dealing with security issues in the South China Sea. See "Scholars Call for Cross-Strait S. China Sea Cooperation." Central News Agency (Taiwan), June 20, 2013. It is also worth noting that Taiwanese marine corps carried out an unprecedented drill simulating the retaking of Itu Aba in early April 2014, which followed the Second Thomas Shoal standoff between the PRC and the Philippines; the news was disclosed by a KMT legislator *during* US President Obama's visit to the Philippines for a new bilateral security agreement. "Marines Conduct a Drill on Spratly

Islands: Lawmaker." Central News Agency, April 29, 2014; Chris Larano. "Obama Vows 'Ironclad' U.S. Defense of Philippines." *Wall Street Journal*, April 29, 2014.
46 Gerry Mullany and David Barboza. "Vietnam Squares Off With China in Disputed Seas." *New York Times*, May 7, 2014.
47 Republic of China Ministry of Foreign Affairs. "MOFA Expresses Grave Concern and Reiterates Government's Position Regarding Recent Maritime Confrontation near Shisha Islands." Press release, May 9, 2014.
48 "China Adding School to Outpost Island in Disputed Waters." *Taipei Times*, June 16, 2014; and "Taiwan Sends Equipment to Build S. China Sea Island Pier." *China Post*, June 18, 2014. Admittedly, similar constructions can also be found on features controlled by other claimants, and it is not unreasonable to argue that Taipei's decisions were in part driven by this region-wide show of sovereignty. Nevertheless, the timing of making public Itu Aba's pier construction work reinforced the impression that a tacit united front across the Taiwan Strait was taking shape.
49 Chao-kun Wang. "*Nanhai wenti Xia Liyan: Jue bu yu Dalu lianshou* [On South China Sea Issue, Hsia: Never Join Forces with the Mainland]." *Radio Taiwan International*, May 27, 2015; and Yu-chung Wang and Hui-ping Chen. "*Nanhai yiti jiaofeng: Cai pan liaojie guanfang dangan* [South China Sea Issue Confrontation: Tsai Hopes to Understand Official Archives]." *Liberty Times* (Taiwan), March 31, 2016.
50 Yann-Huei Song. "Taiwan's Development Work on Taiping Island." Asia Maritime Transparency Initiative, February 18, 2015. http://amti.csis.org/taiwans-development-work-on-taiping-island (accessed May 7, 2016); and Michael Gold. "Taiwan Considers Permanent Armed Ships for Disputed South China Sea Island." Reuters, October 16, 2014.
51 Jason Pan and Tien-pin Lo. "Threat to Spratlys Outposts 'Growing.'" *Taipei Times*, December 26, 2014; and Prashanth Parameswaran. "Vietnam a Growing Threat to Taiwan's South China Sea Claims: Report." *The Diplomat*, December 31, 2014.
52 Kuok, "Tides of Change," 10. ROC defense minister later denied that Itu Aba was under threat by Vietnam. Jason Pan."Itu Aba Military Outpost Not Under Threat by Vietnam: Defense Minister." *Taipei Times*, December 30, 2014.
53 Jeffery Bader. "The U.S. and China's Nine-Dash Line: Ending the Ambiguity," opinion, Brookings Institution, February 6, 2014; Bonnie Glaser. "A Role for Taiwan in Promoting Peace in the South China Sea." Commentary, CSIS, April 15, 2014; and William A. Stanton. "The U.S. Pivot to Asia and Taiwan's Role." World United Formosans for Independence, 2014. http://www.wufi.org.tw/the-u-s-pivot-to-asia-and-taiwans-role/ (accessed May 7, 2016).
54 Jeffrey Bader, former principal advisor to President Obama on Asia, was quoted in Kuok, "Tides of Change," 4.
55 Office of the President, Republic of China (Taiwan). "Safeguarding Sovereignty, Shelving Disputes, Pursuing Peace and Reciprocity, and Promoting Joint Exploration and Development." September 1, 2014. http://english.president.gov.tw/Default.aspx?tabid=1124&itemid=33217&rmid=3048; see also "Transcript of New York Times Interview With President Ma Ying-jeou of Taiwan." *New York Times*, October 31, 2014 (accessed May 7, 2016).
56 Under this principle, Ma indicated, "a juridical fact must be appreciated in the light of the law contemporary with it, and not of the law in force at the time when a dispute in regard to it arises or falls to be settled." Office of the President, Republic of China (Taiwan) ibid. Indeed, an *Economist* article believed that the reason for Chinese officials' presence at the exhibition opening was not so much their interest in any new empirical support for the dashed line or a claim to "historic waters" as the need to verify whether Taiwan attempted to abandon the U-shape line and, by implication, the "One China" principle. "Joining the Dashes." *The Economist*, October 4, 2014.
57 Hsiu-chuan Shih. "S China Sea Claims in Line with Law: Ma." *Taipei Times*, May 28, 2015.

58 Ying-jeou Ma. "A Plan for Peace in the South China Sea." *Wall Street Journal*, June 12, 2015.
59 Andrea Shalal and David Brunnstrom. "U.S. Navy Destroyer Nears Islands Built by China in South China Sea." Reuters, October 26, 2015.
60 Joseph Yeh. "Ma Taiping Visit Could Cause Tension: Former US Official." *China Post*, December 18, 2015; and William Lowther. "Washington 'Disappointed' with Ma's Decision." *Taipei Times*, January 29, 2016. Among the South China Sea claimants, as of this writing Ma was the only head of state to visit the region since 2008. The previous visit was made by his predecessor, Chen Shui-bian.
61 The Philippines brought the case to the Permanent Court of Arbitration in 2013 after China refused to withdraw its ships from the Scarborough Shoal. In July 2015, case hearings began with the Philippines asking the court to invalidate China's sovereignty claims. Anticipating that the ruling results would embarrass itself, the PRC government chose to boycott the case and ignore the verdict. The ROC was not invited to the tribunal and was not able to participate in the hearing process, but its Society of International Law submitted an *amicus curiae* (friend of the court) brief to the court on the legal status of Taiping Island rebutting the Philippines' claims. Taipei refused to accept the court ruling on the grounds that it was excluded from the tribunal in the first place. See "Taiwan Won't Accept Court Ruling on Islands Disputes." *China Post*, February 18, 2016. In July 2016, it was concluded that none of the high-tide features in the Spratly Islands is capable of sustaining human habitation or an economic life of their own as an island under UNCLOS. Permanent Court of Arbitration, *South China Sea Arbitration*, 254.
62 Office of the President, Republic of China (Taiwan). "President Ma's Remarks at International Press Conference Regarding Taiping Island in Nansha Islands." March 23, 2016. http://english.president.gov.tw/Default.aspx?tabid=491&itemid=36980&rmid=2355 (accessed May 7, 2016).
63 William Lowther. "US Navy Aircraft Carrier, Escorts Arrive in South China Sea for 'Show of Force.'" *Taipei Times*, March 6, 2016. Had Taiping Island been proved an island as set forth in UNCLOS (Article 121), apart from 12 nautical miles of territorial waters, the ROC would have been entitled to claim a maximum 200-nautical-mile EEZ and a continental shelf; because the ROC based its claims as the (unrecognized) representative of China, the PRC could have used Taipei's argument to justify its constructions in the Spratlys (all of which lie within 200 nautical miles of Itu Aba), regardless of the validity of its "historic rights." Jeremy Page. "Taiwan Cultivates an Argument for China's Spratlys Claim." *Wall Street Journal*, March 23, 2016.
64 Under Section 3(3) of the Taiwan Relations Act, the US President is required to inform Congress of any threat to the security of "the people on Taiwan" and any danger to the interests of the United States, but that does not amount to an unequivocal obligation to come to Taiwan's defense.
65 The PRC government has made this point clear in its White Paper on "the One-China Principle and the Taiwan Issue" and the Anti-Secession Law.
66 Shirley A. Kan. "Taiwan: Major U.S. Arms Sales since 1990." *CRS Report for Congress* RL 30957, August 29, 2014.
67 Sebastian Maslow. "A Blueprint for a Strong Japan? Abe Shinzō and Japan's Evolving Security System." *Asian Survey*, 55, no. 4, (2015): 739–65.
68 Joseph Yeh. "Tokyo's Fishery Talks Calls Show 'Good Will': Minister." *China Post*, September 15, 2012. Similar sensitivity was found in the Japanese academia. A well-connected scholar went so far as to propose that, while the US government should clearly reaffirm its treaty commitment to the defense of the territories under Japanese administration so as to deter Beijing's adventurism, Washington could also soothe Taipei's sense of being marginalized over the Senkakus by strengthening their security cooperation. See Yoichiro Sato. "The Senkaku Dispute and US–Japan Security Treaty." Pacific Forum CSIS PacNet No. 57, September 10, 2012.

69 Stockholm International Peace Research Institute. *SIPRI Yearbook 2015 Armaments, Disarmament and International Security,* 384–5. Oxford: Oxford University Press, 2015.
70 Floyd Whaley. "Charges Urged in Filipino Raid on Taiwanese Boat." *New York Times,* June 13, 2013.
71 Stacy Hsu. "Taiwan, Philippines Sign Fishing Treaty." *Taipei Times,* November 20, 2015.
72 Chih-yu Shih and Ching-Chang Chen. "How Can They Theorize? Strategic Insensitivity towards Nascent Chinese International Relations Thinking in Taiwan." In *Asian Thought on China's Changing International Relations,* edited by Niv Horesh and Emilian Kavalski, 205–9. Basingstoke: Palgrave Macmillan, 2014.
73 Chih-yu Shih. "Constituting Taiwanese Statehood: The World Timing of Un-Chinese Consciousness." *Journal of Contemporary China,* 16, no. 53 (2007): 699–716.
74 Ching-Chang Chen. "The Weakest Link? Explaining Taiwan's Response to the U.S. Rebalancing Strategy." In *United States Engagement in the Asia Pacific: Perspectives from Asia,* edited by Yoichiro Sato and See Seng Tan, 89–114. New York: Cambria Press, 2015. Compare Chih-yu Shih, ed. *Re-producing Chineseness in Southeast Asia: Scholarship and Identity in Comparative Perspectives.* London: Routledge, 2015.
75 Public Television Service (Taiwan). "*Shen Ssu-Tsun baogao Tai Ri Guanxi hanwei zhuquan* [Shen Ssu-Tsun on Taiwan-Japan Relations, Defend Sovereignty]." September 13, 2012 https://tw.news.yahoo.com/沈斯淳報告台日關係-捍衛主權-120000258.html (accessed May 8, 2016). Seen in this light, the fact that Japan's triple disasters on March 11, 2011 received the highest amount of donation from the people of Taiwan represented as much the amity between the two as the latter's anti-China performance.
76 John Pomfret. "U.S. Takes a Tougher Tone with China." *Washington Post,* July 30, 2010.
77 Michael J. Cole. "How Taiwan Bungled the Philippine Crisis." *The Diplomat,* May 21, 2013. The Philippine government has its "officially unofficial" embassy in Taiwan, i.e., Manila Economic and Cultural Office (MECO). The Ma administration refused to meet the MECO chairman (Aquino's envoy) and the Philippine's representative to Taiwan on the grounds that the apology must occur at government level and the wording "unintended loss of life" excused the act of murder, ignoring that Manila had to observe its own "One China" policy and shooting the deceased Taiwanese fisherman was not a Philippine state policy. It became understandable that Manila, humiliated, later gave Taipei the cold shoulder over the SCSPI. Michael Cole and Philip Bowring are right that Taipei failed to show magnanimity, but it is oversimplified to attribute such failure to "mundane" reasons (e.g., pressure from Ma's opponents and Taiwan's lack of diplomatic exposure) or ethnic "Han chauvinism." Cole, "How Taiwan Bungled the Philippine Crisis" and Philip Bowring. "Taiwan's Reaction to Killing of Fisherman is out of Proportion." *South China Morning Post,* May 19, 2013.
78 Jen-chun Kang. "*Qiang kaizhan! Su Ching-chuan: Feilubin zhe xiao hunhun, sadao women toushang*! [Declare War! Su Ching-chuan: The Philippines is a Little Scoundrel Riding on Us]." *NOWnews.com,* May 10, 2013.
79 One such example is "fishing entity," under which Taiwan has been able to get around with its international legal status and participate in international fisheries forums and treaties. Kuok, "Tides of Change," 17.

7 The Japan–China gentlemen's agreement over the Senkaku Islands

Yoshinori Kaseda

Introduction

Since the early 1970s, Japan has had a territorial dispute with the People's Republic of China (PRC or China) and the Republic of China (ROC or Taiwan) over the Senkaku Islands (called the Diaoyu Islands in China and the Diaoyutai Islands in Taiwan). The Senkaku Islands are composed of five major islands: Uotsuri, Kuba, Minamikojima, Kitakojima, and Taisho, in order of size. Uotsuri Island is 3.81 square kilometers, approximately four times larger than Kuba Island, and is located 410 km from Okinawa Island, 330 km from mainland China, and 170 km from Taiwan.

The territorial dispute emerged in the early 1970s as a result of two developments: (1) the 1968 discovery of potential undersea oil and gas reserves in the waters around the islands as a result of a maritime probe by the United Nations Economic Commission for Asia and the Far East (ECAFE); and (2) the Okinawa Reversion Treaty of 1971 between Japan and the United States, which transferred administrative control of the Senkaku Islands from the United States to Japan in 1972. These developments prompted China and Taiwan to assert claims of sovereignty over the islands in 1971.

Beijing has maintained that Japan's and China's leaders reached an unwritten, gentlemen's agreement to leave solving the territorial dispute over the Senkaku Islands to future generations during the bilateral talks that resulted in diplomatic normalization between the two countries in September 1972 and the Japan-PRC Treaty of Peace and Friendship in August of 1978. In contrast, Japan has denied having made such an agreement to "shelve" or "maintain the status quo" in regard to the issue of sovereignty over the Senkaku Islands. Japan's position has been that "there exists no issue of territorial sovereignty to be resolved concerning the Senkaku Islands" because "there is no doubt, in light of historical facts and based upon international law, that the Senkaku Islands are an inherent part of the territory of Japan."[1]

However, there is considerable support for the existence of such an agreement. During the normalization talks in September 1972, Prime Minister Tanaka asked Prime Minister Zou Enlai what he thought about the Senkaku issue, and Zou said that it would be better not to discuss it for the time being; Vice Prime Minister Deng Xiaoping revealed the presence of such an agreement at a press conference in Tokyo on October 25, 1978; several Japanese politicians and government officials have made remarks, supporting the existence of a gentlemen's agreement to shelve the territorial dispute[2]; Japanese mainstream media, including *Yomiuri Shimbun*, a leading daily newspaper, expressed support for the agreement; moreover, Tokyo has maintained a policy of keeping the status quo of the Senkaku Islands by refraining from building facilities on the islands and prohibiting Japanese citizens, except for authorized government officials, from landing on the islands.[3] Despite its denial of its existence, Japan has dealt with the islands in accordance with the gentlemen's agreement. In fact, China has done so as well. In practice, the agreement has served as a shared norm or regime between the two nations. As Axelrod and Keohane point out, "[One] way to facilitate cooperation is to establish an international regime."[4] In fact, Japan and China made the gentlemen's agreement to foster cooperation. And by following it they have largely succeeded in developing cooperative relationship, particularly in economic terms. However, the gentlemen's agreement was seriously eroded by Tokyo's nationalization of three Senkaku Islands in September 2012. Shortly thereafter, Beijing significantly increased the frequency of dispatch of its government vessels to the territorial waters around the Senkaku Islands. The nationalization took place in the midst of a serious deterioration in bilateral relations and public sentiments between Japan and China following the collision of a Chinese fishing vessel with two Japan Coast Guard (JCG) patrol vessels in the territorial waters around the Senkaku Islands in 2010.

Whether Japan and China can resolve the heightened bilateral tension over the Senkaku Islands is an important issue to the two nations involved and the international community. Not only are Japan's and China's economies dependent on one another, but also their status as the second and third largest economies in the world means any destabilization could significantly impact economies worldwide. As a result, there has been increasing pressure to identify a solution to the territorial dispute over the Senkaku Islands. One proposed solution has been to reinstate the original agreement to shelve the territorial dispute.[5]

This chapter assesses the plausibility of this solution by first examining the transformation of the gentlemen's agreement over the past four decades. In particular, the institutionalization of the gentlemen's agreement in the form of the Bilateral Fisheries Pact of 1997 and the impact of non-government actors on the stability of the agreement will be discussed. Following the historical examination of the agreement's transformation, the chapter will conclude with a discussion of the merits of restoring the gentlemen's agreement to shelve the territorial dispute.

Transformation of the gentlemen's agreement

This section will present a historical account of the transformation of the gentlemen's agreement to shelve the territorial dispute over the Senkaku Islands from its inception to Japan's nationalization of the three Senkaku Islands in 2012. A greater focus will be placed on the impact of Japanese actions on the agreement.

From the 1970s to the mid-1990s

China's and Taiwan's claims of sovereignty over the Senkaku Islands after the 1968 ECAFE survey and their opposition to the 1971 Okinawa Reversion Treaty led to increased nationalistic sentiments in Japan. As a result, the first landing of a Japanese citizen on the Senkaku Islands occurred immediately after the treaty became effective and their administrative control was transferred from the United States to Japan on May 15, 1972. The following day, May 16, the JCG discovered that a member of Aikoku Seinen Renmei, a rightwing group, had hoisted Japan's national flag on Uotsuri Island. This incident did not become a top story in Japan.[6] It should be noted that this incident, as well as subsequent landings by rightwing group members, was treated as a minor issue by the Japanese media. As a result, it had little impact on the normalization talks between Japan and China, which included a gentlemen's agreement to shelve their territorial dispute over the Senkaku Islands.[7] There was another landing on Uotsuri Island in November 1973, which involved several rightwing group members.

However, China was the first nation to significantly violate that agreement. On April 12, 1978, over 100 Chinese fishing vessels gathered in the waters surrounding the Senkaku Islands and remained there for nearly two weeks. Throughout the two-week period, numerous Chinese vessels repeatedly entered the territorial waters around the islands.[8] Later, it was revealed that the ships received their orders from the People's Liberation Army (PLA) and were equipped with machine guns.[9] Although in August 1978 Vice Prime Minister Deng Xiaoping promised Japan that such an incident would not happen again, memories of the incident lingered in the minds of Japanese policymakers and citizens.

Shortly thereafter, Japanese nationalists responded to the incident with a demonstration of their own. On April 28, 1978, members of a rightwing group landed on Uotsuri Island. Then, another rightwing group, the Nihon Seinen-sha, Japan's largest rightwing group, and others, formed and sent a team of rightwingers, *Senkakushotō Ryōyū Kesshitai* (Senkaku Islands Suicide Corps) to Uotsuri Island on May 11, 1978, and sent replacement teams four times over the following months in order to retain a presence on the island.[10] On August 12, 1978, one day before the signing of the Japan–PRC Peace and Friendship Treaty, the fifth team was joined by additional members of the Nihon Seinen-Sha who built a small lighthouse on the island on the following day.[11] The group clearly says that the lighthouse was built in response to the massive gathering of Chinese fishing vessels in April 1978[12] and in order to enhance Japan's effective control over the Senkaku Islands.[13] Since then, the group visited the islands at least once a year to oversee the maintenance of the lighthouse until the mid-2000s. It should be noted that Tokyo condoned such activities of rightwing groups despite its policy prohibiting Japanese citizens from landing on the Senkaku islands.

In December 1979, during the Ohira administration, the Okinawa Development Agency built a temporary helipad and conducted an environmental survey of the islands and the waters surrounding them.[14] It incited Beijing's strong protest. Consequently, Tokyo removed the helipad. In March 1982, the JCG warned members of the Nihon Seinen-sha, who were intending to land on Uotsuri Island, that they could be prosecuted for illegal sailing. However, the JCG did not pursue the prosecution and allowed the group to land.[15] In June 1988, the Nihon Seinen-sha installed a new lighthouse on Uotsuri Island to commemorate the tenth anniversary of the original lighthouse and submitted an application for official recognition of the new lighthouse to the JCG. This new installation incited strong criticism from China, Taiwan, and Hong Kong.

In response to the application, eight JCG specialists on lighthouse installation inspected the lighthouse in June 1990. Although the Nihon Seinen-sha corrected the problems identified by the JCG's inspection,[16] the JCG suspended the application. The Nihon Seinen-sha protested the suspension of the application and asked the JCG to provide the reasoning behind its decision.[17] On April 25, members of the Nihon Seinen-sha met with Transportation Minister Ohno and the head of the JCG, Tanba, and received an official written response to its protest.[18] While the response did not alter the JCG's decision to suspend the application, the group was given tacit permission during the meeting by the government to visit the Senkaku Islands to maintain the lighthouse.[19] Consequently, the group kept visiting Uotsuri Island for the maintenance.

In February 1992, China enacted the Law of People's Republic of China on the Territorial Sea and the Contiguous Zone, which asserted that the Senkaku Islands were a Chinese territory. This proclamation generated strong criticism from the Japanese government and public. While this could be considered a breach of the gentlemen's agreement, it did little to alter the reality of Japan's control over the islands.

A more significant development occurred in June 1996, when Japan and China ratified the 1994 UN Convention on the Law of the Sea (UNCLOS). As part of the ratification, Japan, in June 1996, and China, in June 1998, established their exclusive economic zones (EEZs). Both nations identified the Senkaku Islands as part of their own territory.

Following the ratification, on July 15, 1996, seven members of the Nihon Seinen-sha landed on Kitakojima Island and built a new lighthouse.[20] The group then proceeded to submit an application to the JCG for official recognition of the lighthouse. This action generated strong criticism from Beijing and Taipei. In response to the criticism, Japan's Chief Cabinet Secretary Kajiyama stated that official interference in the matter was not possible if the owner of the island permitted the construction of the lighthouse.[21]

Japan's establishment of the EEZs and construction of the lighthouse on Kitakojima Island incited protests by nationalistic citizens in Taiwan and Hong Kong. It also led to activists in Taiwan and Hong Kong attempting to enter the territorial waters around the Senkaku Islands and land, particularly on Uotsuri Island.[22] For example, in September 1996, several Chinese activists left Hong Kong and entered the territorial waters around the Senkaku Islands and jumped into the sea. However, one activist drowned before reaching land. Over the following month, 41 of the 49 ships carrying activists from Taiwan and Hong Kong entered the territorial waters of the Senkaku Islands. This resulted in four activists reaching Uotsuri Island.[23] However, the activists left the island voluntarily and

The agreement over the Senkaku Islands 97

were not captured by the Japanese authorities.[24] It should be noted that Taiwan and Hong Kong, and not mainland China, became the centers of the protest movement and remained so for a long time. This suggests that Beijing did not like such a movement to grow in China.

Following the ratification of the UNCLOS and the ensuing establishment of EEZs by the two nations, maritime probes in the overlapping zone where the Senkaku Islands are located became a politically sensitive issue. However, in September of 1996 and April of 1997, Chinese maritime probe vessels entered the territorial waters around the Senkaku Islands.[25] As these were acts of the Chinese government, not activists, they could be considered violations of the gentlemen's agreement to shelve the territorial issue.

On May 6, 1997, Nishimura Shingo, a member of Japan's House of Representatives, and three other individuals landed on Uotsuri Island. It was the first time a member of the National Assembly had landed on any of the five Senkaku Islands. This incited strong protests from Beijing and Taipei and galvanized protest movements, particularly in Taiwan and Hong Kong. Later that month, 30 ships carrying mainly Taiwanese activists approached the Senkaku Islands and three of them entered the territorial waters. Two activists jumped on to a JCG patrol ship. The JCG forced the three ships out of the territorial waters and, after deliberation by the Japanese government, returned the two activists to a protestors' ship.[26] Similar cases ensued over the next few years. In July 1997, a Taiwanese protest ship entered the territorial waters. In June 1998, six ships from Taiwan and Hong Kong approached the waters and one of them entered the waters despite the effort of the JCG to prevent it. Members of the ship attempted to land on Uotsuri Island to no avail.[27]

The Fisheries Pact of 1997

In November 1997, Tokyo and Beijing signed a Fisheries Pact, which went into effect in June 2000. The pact was a follow-up to their ratification of the UNCLOS in 1996. In the pact, the two countries agreed that their ships would be supervised by their respective government agencies and subject only to the laws of their own country in waters south of latitude 27 degrees north, where the disputed Senkaku Islands are located. This arrangement meant that the two nations were essentially shelving their territorial dispute over the islands. In fact, at a session of the Foreign Relations Committee of the House of Representatives of the 136th Diet Session held on May 14, 1996, Prime Minister Hashimoto (in office from January 1996 to July 1998) expressed his support for shelving the territorial issue in order to conclude the Fisheries Pact. Thus, the pact can be seen as a reconfirmation of the gentlemen's agreement to shelve the dispute. Moreover, the pact institutionalized the agreement. In this regard, it was a historic development. However, the existence of the Fisheries Pact and its significance have not been widely recognized in Japan, due to the minimal publicity the pact received. It is possible Tokyo has not promoted coverage of the pact because of its denial of the existence of the gentlemen's agreement.

Although the Fisheries Pact established rules for fishing in the waters around the Senkaku Islands, similar rules were not established for the territorial waters around them. As was the case before the pact, Tokyo continued to dispatch JCG patrol ships to the waters, whereas China kept refraining from doing so. It became customary for JCG patrol ships to urge Chinese fishing vessels to leave the territorial waters if they were found fishing there. The Fisheries Pact did not stop Chinese ships from entering the territorial waters around the Senkaku islands because they were rich fishing grounds.

Japan's and China's ratification of the UNCLOS in 1996 led to institutionalization of the gentlemen's agreement to shelve their territorial dispute. However, it created a new problem for Japan. After China's ratification of the UNCLOS in 1996, Chinese maritime probe ships began to enter the territorial waters around the Senkaku Islands and continued after the conclusion of the Fisheries Pact in 1997. For instance, on April 28, 1998, the JCG noticed a Chinese maritime probe vessel in the waters northwest of Uotsuri Island. The vessel conducted probe operations three times in the territorial waters, despite the JCG demanding termination of its probe and departure from the waters.[28] However, the JCG patrol ships refrained from capturing Chinese probe ships, only urging them to leave the waters.

The 2004 landing of Chinese activists

Tokyo's efforts to keep the Senkaku issue low-profile was thwarted again by the Nihon Seinen-sha in 2000. On April 20, 2000, the group built a small shrine on Uotsuri Island, called the Senkaku Jinja (Senkaku Shrine), and had a Shinto priest hold a ceremony. Since then, the group kept holding a ceremony every year, as well as continuing to maintain the lighthouses it had built until the mid-2000s.[29] The installation of the shrine incited protests from China, Taiwan, and Hong Kong and fueled their protest movements.

In April 2002, the Koizumi administration (April 2001–September 2006) signed a rental agreement with the owner of three of the five major Senkaku Islands, Uotsuri, Kitakojima, and Minimikojima,[30] "in order to keep the Senkaku Islands in peaceful and stable conditions."[31] However, the greater official control over the islands failed to quiet the protest movements in China, Taiwan, and Hong Kong.

On June 24, 2003, activists from mainland China (excluding Hong Kong) entered the territorial waters around the Senkaku Islands for the first time.[32] Similar incidents occurred on October 9, 2003, and January 15, 2004. Then, on March 24, 2004, seven Chinese activists landed on Uotsuri Island. It was the first landing by Chinese activists and the first landing by non-Japanese citizens since October 1996. The activists remained on the island for several hours until they were arrested by the police. The JCG was forced to contact the police and wait for the activists to be arrested, as the laws at the time did not extend the JCG's authority to land. This incident was the first time foreigners were arrested for landing on one of the Senkaku Islands. Beijing demanded the activists' immediate and unconditional release. In addition, at a press conference, the Chinese foreign ministry expressed the view that the landings of Japanese rightwing

The agreement over the Senkaku Islands 99

groups and their illegal constructions on the Senkaku Islands were the cause of the Chinese activists' actions.[33]

The Chinese activists were sent to the headquarters of the Okinawa Prefectural Police. Because the police officers had discovered that the small shrine located on the island had been destroyed, the activists were initially going to be sent to the prosecutor's office. However, it was eventually decided to hand the activists over to the Immigration Bureau for deportation. On March 26, the activists were deported to China. In the morning of March 25 Prime Minister Koizumi indicated that the decision to deport the activists was based on the desire to avoid disturbing the overall relationship between Japan and China.[34] It is possible that Koizumi feared further deterioration of the bilateral relations after China's recent widespread criticism of his annual visit to the controversial Yasukuni Shrine and the passage of a new history textbook written by conservative scholars through the quadrennial governmental textbook screening in April 2001. Beijing had already suspended summit meetings, which were to be held alternatively in China and Japan, following Koizumi's visit to China in October 2001.

The lighthouse nationalization of 2005

In February 2005, the Koizumi administration nationalized the lighthouse built by the Nihon Seinen-sha in 1988 apparently to stop its members from repeatedly visiting the Senkaku Islands and thereby to prevent Chinese and Taiwanese activists from landing on the islands.

Immediately after the landing of Chinese activists on Uotsuri Island in March 2004, the Nihon Seinen-sha attempted to land on the island in order to check the condition of the lighthouse. The Koizumi administration instructed the group not to go to Uotsuri Island in April 2004 and issued an official letter of instruction which banned the group from landing on the island.[35] However, the group attempted to land on the island later in the month, but failed to do so because of bad weather.[36] The Nihon Seinen-sha's disobedience is likely what prompted the Koizumi administration to nationalize the lighthouse.

According to the JCG, "Following the landing incident [of 2004], the government clearly stated its policy to ban Japanese citizens from landing on the Senkaku Islands, although it had instructed political groups and others in Japan not to land on them." "In this context, in February this year [2005] the owner (engaged in fishery) of the lighthouse on Uotsuri Island expressed his intention to abandon his ownership, and the lighthouse became a national property on the basis of a provision of the Civil Code."[37] In addition, the JCG asserted the lighthouse was installed by a Japanese political group in 1988 and then handed over to a person engaged in fishery. In February of 2005, the JCG claimed the government appointed the JCG to maintain and manage the lighthouse, because the lighthouse had contributed to fishing and safe voyage in the nearby waters and was located on an island rented by the government.[38]

However, the official story differs significantly from the one provided by the original and de facto owner of the lighthouse, the Nihon Seinen-sha. According to the group, ownership was originally transferred in 1989 to a resident of Ishigaki City, to which the Senkaku Islands belonged, after the JCG requested the name of the applicant (that is, the owner) be changed on the resubmitted application for official recognition of the lighthouse.[39] In July 2004, the Cabinet Secretariat of the Japanese government contacted the president of the Nihon Seinen-sha and expressed the intention of the government to nationalize and manage the lighthouse.[40] Then, during a meeting at the Cabinet Office on February 3, 2005, the president conveyed its decision to transfer ownership of the lighthouse to the government for free, leading to the completion of the transfer on February 9 after the de jure owner signed the relevant documents. On the following day, the Nihon Seinen-sha held a press conference in response to requests from the media, including leading daily newspapers and TV stations. However, the resultant media coverage was very limited. On March 3, 2005, at the Diet Building, the Nihon Seinen-sha gave a special lecture on its activities and its transfer of ownership of the lighthouse, which was organized by the Diet Members' Association of Acting for Protection of the Territory (*Ryōdogiren*). The nationalization of the lighthouse was satisfactory to the group because it wanted the government to give the lighthouse an official recognition. In this sense, the Koizumi administration gave the group a concession, but by doing so, it deprived the group of its primary reason to visit Uotsuri Island, that is, maintenance of the lighthouse. In fact, by making the deal, the government succeeded in stopping the group from visiting the Senkaku islands after the nationalization.[41]

However, the nationalization of the lighthouse was met with criticism from Beijing and Taipei and fueled popular protests. It also added to anti-Japanese sentiment in China, which had grown as result of Koizumi's annul visit to the Yasukuni Shrine and the renewed history textbook dispute. Then, in April 2005, large, anti-Japanese demonstrations occurred in many parts of China. These demonstrations were the largest seen since Japan–PRC normalization in 1972.

The nationalization also raises the question of the government's stance towards the Nihon Seinen-sha's lighthouse on Kitakojima Island. The author could find no official reference to, and few media reports on, the lighthouse. However, according to the Nihon Seinen-sha,[42] the lighthouse on Kitakojima Island disappeared in 1997. The members who originally installed the lighthouse believe that it was deliberately destroyed, because they learned that Prime Minister Hashimoto stated the lighthouse was no longer there while visiting China. The group attempted to bring a new lighthouse to Kitakojima Island, but was prevented from leaving Ishigaki Island by the JCG. Since then, the new lighthouse has been kept in a warehouse on Yonaguni Island in Okinawa.

It seems that the nationalization of the lighthouse on Uotsuri Island was at least partly intended to prevent Japanese activists, particularly Nihon Seinen-sha members, from landing on the Senkaku Islands.

Meanwhile, in July 2005, two Taiwanese patrol ships entered the territorial waters around the Senkaku Islands, justifying it as a proper action to protect Taiwanese fishing vessels.[43] The Japanese had focused primarily on the intrusion by Chinese ships. But there have been cases of intrusion by Taiwanese ships, including government ships. Besides, in October 2007, a ship carrying activists left Hong Kong and entered the territorial waters around the Senkaku Islands.

The Japan–Taiwan collision incident of 2008

In 2008, an incidence of great significance took place between Japan and Taiwan, although it did not attract as much attention in Japan as a similar incident between Japan and China in 2010.

At around 3:20 a.m. on June 10, 2008, a Taiwanese sport fishing ship carrying three crew members and 13 customers entered the territorial waters around the Senkaku Islands. A JCG patrol vessel noticed its incursion and approached the ship in order to identify its name and nationality. Because the Taiwanese ship fled, the JCG vessel chased it. The Taiwanese ship sailed in a zigzag manner and suddenly changed direction, consequently colliding into the patrol vessel and sinking approximately an hour after the collision. According to the JCG's report, the Taiwanese ship was responsible for the collision.[44] It was the first time a Taiwanese or any other foreign ship collided with a JCG patrol ship in the territorial waters around the Senkaku Islands and then sank.

The JCG vessel rescued the 16 Taiwanese citizens and brought them to Ishigaki in Okinawa for investigation. On the evening of June 10, a JCG vessel transferred the 13 customers who had been on board the ship to a Taiwanese coast guard vessel in international waters. However, the JCG continued to detain the three crew members, including the captain, for further investigation. On June 10, the Taiwanese coast guard ships entered territorial waters four times in order to investigate the incident. On the same day, Taiwan's foreign ministry demanded that Tokyo promptly release the crew members and conduct a probe into the incident. On June 12, the Presidential Office of Taiwan, led by President Ma Ying-jeou since May 2008, issued a statement denouncing Japan for causing the Taiwanese ship to sink in Taiwanese territorial waters and detaining its captain. The office demanded the return of the captain and compensation for the sunken ship.[45] On June 13, Japan set the captain free.[46]

On June 14, the JCG sent its report of the case to the prosecutor's office. In the report based on its investigation, the JCG concluded that the two captains were both responsible: the Japanese captain for failing to keep sufficient distance from the Taiwanese ship and the Taiwanese captain for failing to take necessary measures to avoid collision. The JCG also denied the initial account of the Japanese captain that the Taiwanese ship sailed in a zigzag fashion and made a sudden turn.[47] However, as a result of this incident, the Taiwanese government withdrew its representative (de facto ambassador) to Japan from Tokyo.

On June 15, the head of the 11th Regional Headquarters of the JCG, which patroled the waters around the Senkaku Islands, held a press conference in Naha and issued an apology for the damage the patrol ship caused to the Taiwanese ship and those on board. In addition, a high-ranking official of the Interchange Association (Japan) in Taipei (de facto Japanese embassy in Taiwan) met with the Taiwanese captain and expressed his regret for the incident. However, the anti-Japanese sentiments in Taiwan remained strong.

On June 16, a Taiwanese ship carrying activists was accompanied by nine Taiwanese coast guard vessels as it entered the Japanese territorial waters around the Senkaku Islands and sailed by JCG vessels. It was also reported that members of the Taiwanese parliament were considering dispatching a warship to the waters in order to demonstrate Taiwan's sovereignty over the islands.[48]

Later, on June 16, President Ma held a National Security Council meeting and decided to seek a peaceful resolution of the issue. On the evening of June 16, Prime Minister Fukuda (in office from September 2007 to September 2008) said, in front of media reporters:

> Japan and Taiwan have maintained a good relationship under normal circumstances. It is important for each other to restrain oneself in order not to harm the relationship and, in particular, for Taiwan to make a calm response. Then, it would be wise for Japan to make a calm response accordingly.[49]

On June 17, the Ma administration urged members of the parliament to refrain from dispatching a warship on June 18.

On June 20, the JCG made public its intention to pay compensation for the sinking of the Taiwanese ship and any injuries sustained.[50] On the same day, the Vice-Chief Representative of the Taipei Office of the Interchange Association (Japan) handed a letter from the head of the 11th Regional Headquarters of the JCG to the captain of the sunken Taiwanese ship, in which the JCG head expressed his sincere apology for the incident. In response, Taiwan's foreign ministry issued a comment that the Japanese side had done its utmost to show its sincerity and therefore the problem had been settled.[51]

According to a source within the Presidential Office, the incident was settled in this way because of direct talks between the top leaders of Japan and Taiwan, which led to the proposal from the Japanese side to offer an apology.[52] Fukuda handled the incident very effectively, minimizing the damage to the bilateral relations resulting from the incident. His administration swiftly released the captain, although the JCG judged him to be partially responsible for the collision. Also, Fukuda was shrewd, settling the confrontation by letting the regional head of the JCG make an apology and thereby avoiding an official apology by the government. It was also significant for Ma to accept this kind of settlement.

Although the case was settled, the territorial dispute between Japan and Taiwan remained. On July 4, 2008, a Taiwanese maritime probe vessel entered the territorial waters around the Senkaku Islands.

The Japan–China collision incident of 2010[53]

In late 2008, a similar incident happened between Japan and China. On December 8, two Chinese maritime probe ships entered the territorial waters around the Senkaku Islands and stayed for approximately nine hours. The Chinese action could be seen as a challenge to Japan's control over the Senkaku Islands and a violation of the gentlemen's agreement to shelve the territorial dispute over

The agreement over the Senkaku Islands 103

the islands. Not surprisingly, the action was strongly criticized by Tokyo, led by Prime Minister Aso (in office from September 2008 to September 2009). Also, it attracted greater media attention than the incident involving the Taiwanese probe vessel in July of 2008. However, the bilateral tension heightened by this irregular, temporary incident did not last very long. It was another incident, which happened in 2010 that caused very serious and lasting damage to the bilateral relations at both the governmental and popular levels.

On September 7, 2010, two JCG patrol ships found about 100 Chinese fishing vessels operating in and near the territorial waters around the Senkaku Islands. The JCG ordered the ships in territorial waters to immediately depart,[54] but one ship did not follow the order promptly. As the JCG ships prompted the Chinese ship to depart, the Chinese ship collided with the two JCG ships and fled. The JCG ships attempted to capture the Chinese ship and succeeded in doing so just outside the territorial waters. On September 8, the crew was arrested on the charge of obstruction of law enforcement. Prime Minister Kan (in office from June 2010 to September 2011) stated that his administration would handle the case solemnly in compliance with the law. The next day, the captain's case was brought to the prosecutor's office and, on September 10, the Ishigaki Summary Court allowed the office to extend the captain's detention by ten days.

Beijing was angered by the arrest and criticized Tokyo for violating the gentlemen's agreement to shelve their territorial dispute over the Senkaku Islands. On September 10, Beijing demanded the immediate release of the arrested crew. On September 1, Beijing announced its decision to postpone its talks with Tokyo in regard to concluding a treaty to jointly develop gas fields in the East China Sea. On the following day, State Councilor Dai Bingguo summoned the Japanese Ambassador to China, Niwa, and demanded that Tokyo should not misjudge the situation and make a wise, political decision. In response, on September 13, Tokyo deported the 14 crew members and returned the ship to China, but expressed its intention to have the judiciary system handle the captain's case. Then, on September 19, the summary court decided to extend the captain's detention by ten days. In response, on September 21, Prime Minister Wen Jiabao demanded the immediate and unconditional release of the captain and hinted at the possibility of additional repercussions depending on Tokyo's response.

However, Tokyo continued to refuse to release the captain. As a result, Beijing started restricting its export of rare-earth metals to Japan and captured four Japanese employees of Fujita Construction Company on the grounds that they entered a restricted military district. The rare-earth embargo[55] significantly hurt the production of high-tech equipment by Japanese firms, because over 90% of those resources had come from China. In the end, Tokyo acquiesced to Beijing's demand and released the captain on September 24. Following the release, the embargo on rare-earth metals was lifted and the Fujita employees were released.

The Chinese fishing ship incident was unprecedented. Prior to this incident, Tokyo had never captured Chinese vessels within the territorial waters around the Senkaku Islands, arrested Chinese fishermen, or attempted to put the arrested Chinese on trial. Instead, the JCG had focused solely on urging Chinese vessels to leave the territorial waters. In essence, Tokyo's decision to refrain from applying Japanese laws to Chinese ships had represented their support of the gentlemen's agreement between the two countries.

The 2010 incident resulted in a very humiliating end for Tokyo, significantly damaged Japan's relationship with China, and increased hostile feelings between the two governments and peoples. Prime Minister Kan was not seen as experienced in foreign affairs. However, he and other members of the Cabinet should have easily anticipated the possibility of a very strong backlash from Beijing if the captain was detained in an attempt to put him on trial. At the time of the incident, Maehara Seiji was the head of the Ministry of Land, Infrastructure, Transport, and Tourism, which oversees the operations of the JCG. Although he considered himself a specialist on security issues and foreign affairs, he was strongly supportive of bringing the captain's case to trial despite the risk of Beijing's strong backlash. Foreign Minister Okada, known for his doctrinarian and inflexible stances, also supported the action.

It should be noted that, reportedly, in response to the Chinese activists' landing incident in March 2004, the JCG and other relevant sections of the government compiled an internal manual to deal with future landings on the Senkaku Islands in June 2004.[56] The basic policy was not detaining the offenders after their arrest and releasing them without moving on to the criminal justice process.[57] However, if they used weapons to resist their arrest, then force could be used as self-defense and the offenders would be prosecuted following the criminal justice process.[58]

However, the way the Kan administration handled the 2010 Chinese fishing vessel collision did not follow the manual. Why? It is reported that Minister Maehara completely ignored the manual and ordered the JCG to arrest the fishing vessel crew and send them to the prosecutor's office, while Chief Cabinet Secretary Sengoku, who had just assumed the position in June 2010, had not been informed of the manual and therefore did not know of its existence.[59] There is also some suggestion that, after becoming the minister in September 2009, Maehara instructed the JCG to capture Chinese ships in the territorial waters around the Senkaku Islands if they violated the Japanese laws.[60] Maehara, who became Foreign Minister in September 2010, denied the existence of the gentlemen's agreement to shelve the territorial dispute over Senkaku Islands at a Diet session on October 21. He stated that Deng Xiaoping's reference to such an agreement in October 1978 was his one-sided opinion. Maehara's position was officially confirmed at a cabinet meeting on October 26. Some people link Maehara's handling of the Chinese captain to his strong support of the Japan–United States alliance. It is possible that Maehara and other pro-United States policymakers wanted to increase the Japanese people's security concern about China in order to make them more supportive of Tokyo's adoption of measures to restore its relations with Washington, which had been damaged by the policy of the preceding Hatoyama administration (September 2009–June 2010) because it had attempted to relocate the controversial US Marines base in Futenma out of Okinawa despite the 1996 Japan–United States agreement to relocate the

The agreement over the Senkaku Islands 105

base within Okinawa.⁶¹ It is unclear whether they had such an intention. But the collision incident and the following increase in Japanese security concern about China did result in greater public support for restoring and expanding Japan's security ties with the United States.

*Nationalization of the Senkaku Islands of 2012*⁶²

Japan's relations with China further deteriorated during the succeeding Noda administration (September 2011–December 2012) because of its purchase of three of the five Senkaku Islands, Uotsuri Island, Kitakojima Island, and Minamikojima Island, from their private owner on September 11, 2012. As mentioned above, the government had rented them from him since 2002.

The Noda administration decided to buy the islands in response to an announcement by the Governor of Tokyo, Ishihara Shintarō, a well-known right-wing politician, at the Heritage Foundation in Washington, DC on April 16, 2012. In the announcement, Ishihara stated that the Tokyo metropolitan government would purchase the three islands from their owner, who had already agreed to it. His plan received considerable support due to the anti-Chinese sentiments that became very prevalent following the Chinese fishing ship collision of 2010. It attracted donations of approximately 1.5 billion yen from all over Japan.

The government's purchase can be seen as an attempt to preclude escalation of tension between Japan and China by preventing the purchase by the Tokyo metropolitan government headed by Ishihara, who intended to build port facilities on the islands. Prime Minister Noda made public his intention to consider purchasing the islands on July 7, 2012, but refused Ishihara's demand that the government promise to build port facilities if it wanted to buy the three islands from the Tokyo metropolitan government after its purchase from their owner.⁶³

Yet, Prime Minister Noda enraged Beijing by expressing the aforementioned intention on July 7, which was the day when the Marco Polo Bridge incident had taken place in 1937, and by formally deciding to purchase the three islands immediately after his brief meeting with President Hu Jintao in Vladivostok on September 9. The decision was made at a meeting with selected cabinet members on September 10, 2012, and was implemented on the following day. The Noda administration's decision and its actual purchase humiliated Hu because during his meeting with Noda he had strongly urged Noda not to purchase the islands.⁶⁴

The Noda administration maintained that the purchase was "intended to realize peaceful and stable maintenance and management of the Senkaku Islands for a long time while carrying out measures for safe voyage in the waters around the islands."⁶⁵ The presence of this policy orientation can be seen from the handling by the Noda administration of the landing of Chinese activists from Hong Kong on Uotsuri Island on August 15, 2012. Unlike the 2010 collision incident, the Noda administration promptly deported the five activists who landed, as well as the nine others who were on board the ship.

However, the purchase triggered violent demonstrations in various parts of China, which included attacks on Japanese businesses and products. Large-scale demonstrations had occurred in 2005, but those in 2012 were even bigger and more violent. The escalation of anti-Japanese sentiments resulted in a sharp decline in sales of Japanese products in China. That was a heavy blow to many Japanese companies. In addition, after the nationalization, it became more common for Chinese government vessels to enter into the territorial waters around the Senkaku Islands. Such incidents were rare before then, even after the Chinese fishing ship collision of 2010.

It might be that Prime Minister Noda had few alternatives to nationalizing the three islands, because of Governor Ishihara's intention to purchase them. Yet, the way he implemented it was very provocative to China.[66]

In sum, both Tokyo and Beijing largely kept the gentlemen's agreement to shelve their territorial dispute over the Senkaku Islands until the maritime collision incident of 2010 and the nationalization of three islands of 2012. However, non-governmental actors, particularly the Nihon Seinen-sha, destabilized the agreement. Its construction of two lighthouses in 1988 and 1996, construction of a Shinto shrine in 2000, and frequent visits to the islands prompted protest movements in Taiwan, Hong Kong, and China and led to the first landing of Chinese activists in 2004. It is significant that Tokyo condoned the Nihon Seinen-sha's activities until 2005 and that their activities remained mostly unnoticed by the public due to limited media coverage.

However, the Japanese action most damaging to the gentlemen's agreement was Tokyo's handling of the maritime collision incident of 2010, which invited Beijing's strong response and led to the eventual purchase of the three islands by the Noda administration in 2012. Tokyo's handling of the incident in 2010 and its nationalization of the islands in 2012 weakened its control over the Senkaku Islands because it forced Tokyo to deal with the new reality of frequent incursions of Chinese governmental vessels into the territorial waters around the islands.

However, while the gentlemen's agreement was weakened through these events, the Fisheries Pact of 1997 strengthened the gentlemen's agreement by institutionalizing it *vis-à-vis* the fishing industry and limited the negative impact of the increased mutual hostility over the territorial dispute on the fishing industry.

Restoration of the informal agreement

The gentlemen's agreement was seriously eroded by the collision incident in 2010 and the nationalization of the three islands in 2012. Tokyo has various options to deal with the heightened tension with Beijing. So far, Tokyo has prioritized deterring China's aggression on the Senkaku Islands by enhancing its own military capability and strengthening its security ties with the United States and other countries. Japan's military response is understandable. However, diplomatic efforts to reduce tensions with China are needed in order to lessen the level of China's security threat to Japan. One way to achieve tension reduction is to restore the damaged gentlemen's agreement to shelve the territorial dispute over the Senkaku Islands.[67] Pursing this policy option makes sense because it is highly unlikely that either country will accept the territorial claim of the other.

The agreement over the Senkaku Islands 107

Thus, the question becomes how to restore the damaged gentlemen's agreement. Its restoration is not a formidable task, since the agreement is still alive. Despite the erosion of the agreement and the resultant deterioration of the bilateral relations, Tokyo has maintained its basic acknowledgment of the Japan–China relations as some of the most important bilateral relations for Japan. Tokyo clearly states that the stable development of the bilateral relations benefits not only the peoples of both countries, but also the region and the international community.[68] In fact, Tokyo has kept a policy of maintaining the status quo of the Senkaku Islands even after the nationalization of three of the islands in 2012, by prohibiting unauthorized Japanese citizens from visiting the islands and refraining from building new facilities. It is also notable that the nationalization has increased Tokyo's ability to prevent non-government actors, particularly rightwing groups, from constructing new facilities. China has maintained a similar stance with regard to the importance of its relationship with Japan. For instance, at the foreign ministerial talks on August 24, 2016, Chinese Foreign Minister Wang Yi expressed its desire to improve the bilateral relations and prevent contingencies from happening.

In fact, the shared perception regarding the importance of the bilateral relationship has been the foundation of the gentlemen's agreement that has promoted their bilateral cooperation in many areas, particularly in the realm of the economy. However, the perception has not been widely shared in Japan, outside of the elite, while anti-Chinese sentiments have grown stronger across the social strata due primarily to China's strong response to the collision incident of 2010 and the Senkaku nationalization of 2012. This is evident from the hostile remarks by politicians and intellectuals and from public opinion polls that show a significant increase in ill will towards China. The same can be said for China.

Growth of mutual hostility has weakened the shared perception that the bilateral relationship is of great importance, which has in turn undermined the gentlemen's agreement. In other words, the erosion of their shared perception has weakened their adherence to the gentlemen's agreement that has served as a de facto peace regime between the two nations. Therefore, it is necessary for Tokyo to revitalize the shared perception of mutual importance among the elite and the general public in Japan and China in order to prevent the erosion of the gentlemen's agreement.

An important starting point for improving Chinese perception of the importance of the bilateral relationship is for Tokyo to admit the existence of its territorial dispute with China and the gentlemen's agreement, which Beijing has urged.[69] It would be counterproductive to keep denying the presence of the dispute, when it has been widely recognized within and without Japan.[70] In order to resolve the dispute through dialogue, Tokyo has to start by admitting the existence of the dispute in the first place.[71]

Its admission might well reactivate the stalled negotiations for concluding a treaty to jointly develop gas-fields in the East China Sea and establishing a maritime and air crisis management mechanism to deal with unwanted clashes around the Senkaku Islands. The conclusion of the treaty and establishment of the mechanism can be seen as further institutionalization of the gentlemen's agreement that would improve its stability. If the joint development brings tangible economic benefits to both countries, it would deepen and widen the recognition by the elite and the public in Japan and China of the importance of cooperation by shelving the territorial issue.

Furthermore, Tokyo's admission of the existence of the territorial dispute and the gentlemen's agreement would facilitate discussions on other measures to settle the dispute, such as disregarding the Senkaku Islands in delineating the demarcation line between their EEZs and taking the dispute to the International Court of Justice.[72] In addition, Tokyo's recognition of the territorial dispute would be consistent with its demand that Seoul admit existence of its territorial dispute with Tokyo over Takeshima (*Dokdo* in Korean). Tokyo's proposal to take the Senkaku issue to the International Court of Justice would also be compatible with its corresponding proposal to Seoul *vis-à-vis* Takeshima. However, there is an important practical issue Tokyo needs to deal with if it wants to revitalize the gentlemen's agreement: the frequent incursion of Chinese government vessels into the territorial waters around the Senkaku Islands after the Senkaku nationalization in 2012. It would be ideal if Tokyo can convince Beijing to terminate their incursions, but that may be difficult to accomplish. In order to obtain concessions from Beijing on this matter, Tokyo has to provide concessions to Beijing as well. Admission of the existence of the territorial dispute and the gentlemen's agreement could be its major concession.

It is a matter of political leadership whether Tokyo can make such an admission. As mentioned above, Prime Minister Hashimoto publicly acknowledged the territorial issue and expressed his support for shelving it in order to conclude the Fisheries Pact with Beijing in 1997. If he could do so, what is preventing other prime ministers from doing so?

Notes

1 Ministry of Foreign Affairs of Japan. *Senkaku Islands Q&A*. April 13, 2016. http://www.mofa.go.jp/region/asia-paci/senkaku/qa_1010.html (accessed August 29, 2016).
2 For instance, see: William Hollingworth. "Japan, China had Agreement to Maintain Senkaku Status Quo, Suzuki-Thatcher Files Show." *The Japan Times*. December 31, 2014. http://www.japantimes.co.jp/news/2014/12/31/national/history/japan-china-agreement-maintain-senkaku-status-quo-82-suzuki-thatcher-files/#.V8jbrFuLTcs (accessed July 20, 2016).
3 For more detailed information, see: Ni Zhimin. "*Chōgyotō (Senkakushotō) ryōyūken mondai nikansuru chūnichikan no 'tanaagegōi' no shiteki keii* [Diaoyu Islands Historical Developments of the 'Shelving Agreement' between China and Japan over the Diaoyu Island (Senkaku Islands) Territorial Dispute]." *Shakaikagaku Kenkyū Nenpō [Social Science Research Yearbook]*, 43 (2012), 83–94; Kawamura Noriyuki. "*Nicchu reisen wo ikani kaihi suruka* [How to Avoid a Cold War between Japan and China]." *Diamond Online*. October 22, 2013. http://diamond.jp/articles/-/43305 (accessed August 7, 2016); "*Senkaku mondai no shinjitsu* (4/4) [The Truth of the Senkaku Issue]." *Record China*. March 6, 2015. http://www.recordchina.co.jp/a103430.html (accessed August 20, 2016).
4 Robert Axelrod and Robert O. Keohane. "Achieving Cooperation under Anarchy: Strategies and Institutions." In *Neorealism and Neoliberalism*, edited by David A. Baldwin. New York: Columbia University Press, 1993, p. 109.

5 For instance, see: Magosaki Ukeru, ed. *Kenshō Senkaku Mondai [Examination of the Senkaku Issue]*. Tokyo: Iwanami-shoten, 2012, pp. 117–50.
6 "*Uotsurijima ni jyōriku, hinomaru kakagaru* [Landing on the Uotsuri Island, Hoisting the Hinomaru]." *Asahi Shimbun*, May 18, 1972, 23.
7 "'*Senkaku' giron fukairi sezu* [Not Extensively Discussing 'the Senkaku']." *Asahi Shimbun*, October 2, 1972, 1.
8 Wakatsuki Hidekazu. "*Heiwayūkō jyōyaku teiketsu kōshō kara taichū enshakkan no kyōyo he* [From Negotiations of Conclusion of a Peace and Friendship Treaty to Provision of Yen Loans to China]." In *Nicchū Kankeishi 1972–2012, I. Seiji [History of the Japan–China Relations: 1972–2012, I. Politics]*, edited by Takahara Akio and Hattori Ryuji, 113. Tokyo: Tokyo Diagaku Shuppankai, 2012.
9 Wakatsuki, p. 113.
10 Saitō Shinji. "*Senkakushotō Tōdai Kōbō Monogatari* [A Story of the Struggle Over the Lighthouses on the Senkaku islands]." In *Wareware Nihonjin ga Senkaku wo Mamoru [We the Japanese Protect the Senkaku]*, edited by Kase Hideaki, 38–40. Tokyo: Takagi Shobou, 2012.
11 Ibid.
12 Nihon Seinen-sha. *Senkaku shotō no rekishi gaiyō [A Historical Overview of the Senkaku Islands]*. April 26, 2007. http://www.seinensya.org (accessed August 28, 2016).
13 Saitō Shinji, p. 39.
14 Nihon Seinen-sha, *Senkaku shotō no rekishi gaiyō*.
15 Ibid.
16 Nihon Seinen-sha, *Senkakushotō 25nen no ayumi [Steps Over 25 Years Regarding the Senkaku Islands]*. June 17, 2003. http://www.seinensya.org/ (accessed August 10, 2016).
17 Ibid.
18 Ibid.
19 Ibid.
20 Nihon Seinen-sha obtained a permission to do so from the owner of the island. Saitō, p. 56.
21 "'*Senkaku' ni tonai dantai ga todai* [A Political Group in Tokyo, A Lighthouse in 'Senkaku']." *Yomiuri Shimbun*, July 18, 1996, 2.
22 Kaijyō Hoanchō [Japan Coast Guard], *Heisei 9 nenban Kaijyō Hoan Hakusho [JCG White Paper 1997]*, II-1-1-1-(2). Tokyo: Ōkurashō Insatsukyoku, 1997. http://www.kaiho.mlit.go.jp/info/books/h9haku/2-1-1.htm (accessed August 20, 2016).
23 Ibid.
24 "*Nicchū ryōseifu, reiseina taiō wo kyōchō* [The Japanese and Chinese Governments Both Stress Calm Response]." *Asahi Shimbun*. March 24, 2004. http://www.asahi.com/special/senkaku/TKY200403240321.html (accessed July 25, 2016).
25 Kaijyō Hoanchō, *Heisei 9 nenban Kaijyō Hoan Hakusho*.
26 Ibid.
27 Kaijyō Hoanchō [Japan Coast Guard]. *Heisei 10 nenban Kaijyō Hoan Hakusho [JCG White Paper 1998]*, II-1-1-1-(2). Tokyo: Ōkurashō Insatsukyoku, 1998. http://www.kaiho.mlit.go.jp/info/books/h10haku/2-1.htm (accessed August 20, 2016).
28 Kaijyō Hoanchō [Japan Coast Guard]. *Heisei 11 nendoban Kaijyō Hoan Repōto [JCG White Paper 1999]*, 2-1-3. Tokyo: Ōkurashō Insatsukyoku, 1999. http://www.kaiho.mlit.go.jp/info/books/h11haku/1-1.htm (accessed August 21, 2016).
29 The last visit to the Senkaku islands reported by the group on its website took place in 2003.
30 The government had owned the five islands since January 1895, but sold four of them except for Taishojima to a private citizen in 1932.
31 Kaijyō Hoanchō [Japan Coast Guard]. *Kaijyō Hoan Repōto 2005 [JCG White Paper 2005]*. Tokyo: Kokuritsu Insatsukyoku, 1999, Tokushū 1-1-(1). http://www.kaiho.mlit.go.jp/info/books/report2005/tokushu/p018.html (accessed August 21, 2016).

32 Kaijyō Hoanchō [Japan Coast Guard]. *Kaijyō Hoan Repōto 2004 [JCG White Paper 2004]*. Tokyo: Kokuritsu Insatsukyoku, 1998. Topics 7. http://www.kaiho.mlit.go.jp/info/books/report2004/honpen/hp02010700.html (accessed August 21, 2016).
33 "'*Nicchū kankei wo sogaisenuyō taisho*' ['Responding so as not to Obstruct the Japan-China Relations']." *Asahi Shimbun.* March 25, 2004. http://www.asahi.com/special/senkaku/TKY200403250206.html (accessed August 17, 2016).
34 Ibid.
35 Nihon Seinen-sha. *Tokubetsukikaku: Nihon Seinen-sha no mokuteki to sono katsudō wo kataru zadankai (4). [Special Event: A Round-Table Talk on Nihon Seinen-sha's Objectives and Activities (4)].* n.d. http://www.seinensya.org/series/zadankai_sp/04.html (accessed August 19, 2016).
36 Ibid.
37 Kaijyō Hoanchō, *Kaijyō Hoan Repōto 2005.*
38 Ibid.
39 Nihon Seinen-sha. *Nihon Seinen-sha ga torikumu Senkakushotō jikkōshihai [Effective Control Over the Senkaku Islands Attempted by Nihon Seinen-sha].* June 17, 2003. http://www.seinensya.org/undo/ryodo/senkakushoto/030616ayumi.htm (accessed August 19, 2016)
40 Nihon Seinen-sha Sōhonbu [Nihon Seinen-sha Headquarters]. *Senkakushotō Uotsurijimatōdai Kokkaijyō madeno keii to sonogono dōkō [The Developments Leading to the Ownership Transfer of the Lighthouse on Uotsuri Island to the Government and the Developments Thereafter].* March 15, 2005. http://www.seinensya.org/ (accessed August 19, 2016); Nihon Seinen-sha suggested that Foreign Minister Machimura played a leading role in the lighthouse nationalization. Saitō, p. 64.
41 The last landing of its members on any one of the Senkaku Islands was in August 2003, according to its website. Their landing amounted to 34 times by February 2002. The number of visits was mentioned in the reply letter from Mainichi Shimbun to which Nihon Seinen-sha had sent an open inquiry letter. "*Uyoku dantai reinen yori 2kagetsu hayaku Uotsurijima jyōriku keikaku* [A Right-Wing Group Plans Landing on Uotsuri Island 2 Months Earlier than in the Past Years]." *Mainichi Shimbun*, March 6, 2002, 29; Nihon Seinen-sha, *Mainichi Shimbun-sha yori kaitō todoku! [Arrival of a Reply from the Mainichi Shimbun Corporation],* March 9, 2002. http://www.seinensya.org/topic/mein/020309mainichi.htm (accessed August 19, 2016).
42 Nihon Seinen-sha. *Tokubetsukikaku: Nihon Seinen-sha no mokuteki to sono katsudō wo kataru zadankai (4).*
43 "*Taiwan jyunshisen ga 'ryōkai shinpan'* ['Territorial Incursion' by Taiwanese Patrol Ships]." *47NEWS.* July 28, 2005. http://www.47news.jp/CN/200507/CN200507280 1002551.html (accessed April 23, 2013).
44 "*Taiwansen, jyunshisen to shōtotsu* [A Taiwanese Ship, Collision with a Patrol Ship]," *Asahi Shimbun* (evening edition), June 10, 2008, 1.
45 "*Taiwan, chinbotsu ni kōgi* [Taiwan, Protest Against Shipwreck]." *Asashi Shimbun*, June 13, 2008, 39.
46 Apparently, the other two crew members were set free before this statement, but the author could not find information to confirm this.
47 "*Jyunshisen to yūgyosen, ryōsenchō shoruisōken* [The Papers of the Captains of the Patrol Ship and the Sport Fishing Ship Sent to the Prosecutor's Office]." *Asahi Shimbun*, June 15, 2008, 37.
48 "*Taiwan, nihon he taido kōka* [Taiwan Stiffened its Attitude toward Japan]." *Asahi Shimbun*, June 16, 2008, 4.
49 "*Taiwan chūnichi daihyō ga jii* [The Taiwan Representative in Japan Intends to Resign]." *Asahi Shimbun*, June 17, 2008, 8.
50 In December 2008, the JCG and the captain reached an agreement that the former would pay about 10 million Taiwan dollars (approx. 27 million yen) to the latter.

The agreement over the Senkaku Islands 111

51 "*Taiwan no chinbotsusen senchō ni nihongawa ga shazai* [The Japanese Side Apologizes to the Captain of the Sunken Taiwanese Ship]." *Asahi Shimbun*, June 21, 2008, 11.
52 "*Ma sōtō to nihon seifu ni rūto*? [A Route Between Japan and President Ma?]" *Naruhodo za Taiwan, Narutai News*. June 23, 2008. http://www.naruhodo.com.tw/news/index.php?page_num=1302&key= (accessed August 30, 2016); *Liberty Times* (Taiwan), June 21, 2008, cited in Nagayama Hideki, "Fukuda shushō ga shazai wo mōshide? [Did PM Fukuda Offer an Apology?]." *Taiwan wa nihon no seimeisen [Taiwan is the Lifeline of Japan]* (personal blog). June 21, 2008. http://mamoretaiwan.blog100.fc2.com/blog-entry-410.html (accessed August 29, 2016).
53 A detailed account of the incident is provided by: Magosaki Ukeru. *Shōsetsu Gaimushō [A Novel: Foreign Ministry]*. Tokyo: Gendai Shokan, 2014; Kishimoto Masato. *Nihon no Gaikōryoku [Japan's Diplomatic Capability]*, 85–138. Tokyo: Mainichi Shimbunsha, 2013.
54 "*Sengoku kike! Inochigake taihogeki* [Listen, (Chief Cabinet Secretary) Sengoku, A Life-risking Arrest Operation]." *Zakzak*. November 19, 2010. http://web.archive.org/web/20101121225603/http://www.zakzak.co.jp/society/politics/news/20101119/plt1011191617006-n1.htm (accessed August 18, 2016).
55 It was not officially announced as an embargo. Baba Yōzō. "*Reaāsu mondai no seiri*" [A Summary of the Rear Earth Issue]. *Kinzoku Shigen Repōto* [Metal Resources Report], (September 2014): 71.
56 "*Senkaku taiō 'gokuhi manyuaru*' ['A Secret Manual' for Handing the Senkaku]," *AERA*, September 10, 2012, p. 10.
57 Ibid.
58 Ibid.
59 Ibid.
60 Magosaki Ukeru, *Shōsetsu Gaimushō*, p. 192.
61 Tanaka Sakai. "*Nicchū tairitsu no sainen*" [Resurfacing of the Japan–China Confrontation]." *Tanaka Sakai no kokusai nyūsu kaisetsu* [Tanaka Sakai's News Analyses]. September 17, 2010. http://www.tanakanews.com/100917senkaku.htm (accessed July 31, 2016).
62 A detailed account of this incident is provided by: Sunohara Tsuyoshi. *Antō Senkaku Kokuyūka [The Secret Strife behind the Senkaku Nationalization]*. Tokyo: Shinchōsha, 2015.
63 "*Seifu senkaku seibi niwa tadachini ōjizu* [Government, Not Promptly Agreeing to Develop the Senkaku Islands]." *NHK*. September 1, 2012. http://www3.nhk.or.jp/news/html/20120901/k10014702731000.html (accessed November 20, 2012).
64 "'*Mentsu tsubusare ikari*' ['Angered for Being Disgraced']." *Sankei News*. September 28, 2012. http://sankei.jp.msn.com/world/news/120928/chn12092801060002-n1.htm (accessed November 17, 2012).
65 Naikaku Kanbō [Cabinet Secretariat]. *Senkakushotō no shutoku ni kansuru kankei kakuryō mōshiawase [A Mutual Consent Among the Relevant Ministers on Acquisition of Senkaku Islands]*, Kaijyō Hoanchō [Japan Coast Guard], September 10, 2012. www.kaiho.mlit.go.jp/info/kouhou/h24/k20120910/k120910-2.pdf.
66 For a very insightful analysis of Beijing's interpretation of the nationalization, see: Okada Takashi. "*Kokuyūka to tanaage wa kinkō suruka*? [Will There be an Equilibrium between Nationalization and Shelving?]" *Kaikyō Ryōganron [Discussions on Both Sides of Strait]*, 33. September 20, 2012. http://www.21ccs.jp/ryougan_okada/ryougan_35.html (accessed August 29, 2016).
67 On this point, Nye and Rudd argue that "the best we can aim for is to revive the wisdom of the original Zhou-Tanaka formula." Joseph Nye and Kevin Rudd. "How to Navigate the East China Sea Dispute Between Japan and China." *The Washington Post*, April 18, 2014, https://www.washingtonpost.com/opinions/how-to-navigate-the-east-china-sea-dispute-between-japan-and-china/2014/04/18/953731a8-c67b-11e3-9f37-7ce307c56815_story.html?utm_term=.037bda7b6af4 (accessed August 30, 2016).

68 Ministry of Foreign Affairs of Japan, *Situation of the Senkaku Islands*. April 4, 2014. http://www.mofa.go.jp/a_o/c_m1/senkaku/page1we_000010.html (accessed August 29, 2016).
69 For instance, China's foreign ministry urged Japan to do so in June 2013. "*Gaikōbu: Nihon no gōiihan ga kinchō wo maneita* [Foreign Ministry: Japan's Breach of Agreement Caused Tension]." *Record China*. June 5, 2013. http://j.people.com.cn/94474/8271617.html (accessed August 30, 2016); Also, on September 25, 2012, Vice Foreign Minister Zhang Zhijun urged Tokyo to "return to the consensus and understandings reached between the two countries' leaders." "China Warns on Sovereignty at Island Talks with Japan." *BBC*. September 25, 2012. http://www.bbc.com/news/world-asia-19709355 (accessed August 29, 2016).
70 Also, taking such a position is inconsistent with its demand that Seoul should admit the existence of territorial dispute over the Takeshima Islands.
71 Such a position is taken also by Togo Kazuhiko and Sato Masaru, former diplomats, well known in Japan. Sato Masaru. "*Gaimusō wa naze yarubeki shigoto wo shinainoka* [Why Doesn't Foreign Ministry Do What It Should Do?]" *Gendai Business*. August 19, 2012. http://gendai.ismedia.jp/articles/-/33307 (accessed August 25, 2016).
72 For other options, see: Michael O'Hanlon. "A Six Point Plan to Solve the Senkaku Island Dispute." *The National Interest*. December 29, 2014. http://nationalinterest.org/feature/six-point-plan-solve-the-senkaku-island-dispute-11925 (accessed August 30, 2016); Mark E. Rosen. "Fixing the Senkaku/Diaoyu Problem Once and For All." *The Diplomat*. December 19, 2014. http://thediplomat.com/2014/12/fixing-the-senkakudiaoyu-problem-once-and-for-all/ (accessed August 30, 2016).

8 Effects of Japanese security considerations on ASEAN+3 and the East Asia Summit

Charly von Solms

A myriad of regional cooperation initiatives and frameworks have been established in East Asia[1] after the Cold War ended. Some were established under the umbrella of the Association of Southeast Asian Nations (ASEAN) and others, such as the Asia-Pacific Economic Cooperation (APEC) forum, operate outside the ASEAN framework. Most tend to extend beyond the region here defined as East Asia, often including the United States, Russia, Australia, and India. The East Asia Summit (EAS) is a prime example: its members hail from four different continents. Keeping in mind that the EAS is a product of the East Asia Vision Group (EAVG),[2] a study group established by the ASEAN+3 (the three being China, Japan, and South Korea), it appears puzzling that the membership of an East Asian regional forum established by a group of East Asian nations would not be limited to East Asia. Considering that the EAVG describes East Asian nations as sharing "geographical proximity, many common historical experiences, and similar cultural norms and values" and calls for "more deliberate regional cooperation and coordination as well as a united voice to advance the region's common interests,"[3] the membership of the United States, Russia, New Zealand, Australia, and India in the EAS appears contradictory to what the EAVG had envisioned in 2001. As of 2016, ASEAN+3 (APT) and the EAS coexist and share many similarities. While the first EAVG report still called for ASEAN+3 to evolve into the EAS, a second EAVG report published in 2012 acknowledged the complementary nature of both forums.[4] What happened to the idea of a truly East Asian Summit? How has the inclusion of Australia, New Zealand, and India in the EAS in 2005 and Russia and the United States in 2011 affected the East Asian regionalism pursued by ASEAN+3 and what were the dynamics at play in this shift?

ASEAN+3's formative years: crisis and enthusiasm

Initially an informal forum for the ASEAN member states and China, Japan, and South Korea to coordinate and prepare for the Asia–Europe Meeting (ASEM), which was first held in 1996, ASEAN+3 turned into an official regional cooperation and integration process in the wake of the 1997 Asian financial crisis (AFC). Interestingly, it was this regional crisis that kick-started East Asian regionalism. While surfacing after the government of Thailand's decision to float the Thai baht led to a sharp depreciation relative to the US dollar, to which the baht had been pegged, the roots of the AFC can be found throughout the region. Unsustainable levels of investment before the crisis added to growing current-account deficits in the region and with the currency crash came the inability to cope with external debt.[5] While Thailand, Indonesia, and South Korea were the most affected, the effects of the crisis were felt in the whole region due to trade linkages. As it became apparent that neither ASEAN nor the APEC would be of help and due to the severity of the crisis and the fear of it turning into a global one, the International Monetary Fund (IMF) stepped in to bail out the most affected economies while tying its help to a commitment of the receiving countries to structural adjustments. These policy prescriptions included high interest rates, cuts in public spending, and liberalization of the financial sector. Side-effects of implementing these policies however were sudden increases in unemployment and bankruptcies, leading to social unrest and even riots in the affected countries.[6] Japan, seeking to take the initiative against what regionally became seen as IMF mismanagement, proposed an Asian Monetary Fund (AMF), which would have been able to deliver bailout packages without requiring structural adjustments towards what was perceived to be an Anglo-American neoliberal model of capitalism.[7] This proposal was heavily criticized by both the IMF and the United States, who pressured its regional allies to step away from the idea of an Asian alternative to the Washington Consensus. Both the effects of the IMF policy prescriptions and the opposition to Japan's AMF proposal added to a mounting dissatisfaction of East Asian nations with the role of the IMF and the United States in the crisis.[8]

At this point, it became clear to East Asian leaders that the system had failed in way of both preventing the crisis and stopping it.[9] They were faced with the decision to continue under the failed system or to initiate change. A surge in nationalism directed towards the IMF and the regionally perceived need for not only mitigating the effects of future crisis but also for preventing them from recurring caused the ASEAN+3 member states to advance a new East Asian regionalism. The Joint Statement on East Asian Cooperation, finalized by ASEAN+3 leaders during a 1999 informal ASEAN summit in Manila, lists economic, monetary, and financial cooperation, social and human resources development, scientific and technical development, development cooperation, the political-security area, and transnational issues as areas of cooperation to which they would commit themselves.[10] Furthermore, the EAVG was established in 1998 and charged with the task of pondering over the future of East Asian regionalism. The EAVG submitted its final report in 2001, calling for the creation of an East Asian community and the transition from ASEAN+3 to an East Asian Summit.[11]

The one area of cooperation that clearly overcame the vision stage was East Asia's attempt at setting in place a mechanism that would prevent or at least mitigate the effects of future crises – the Chiang Mai Initiative currency swap agreements. Decided upon in 2000 after the ASEAN+3 had met in the northern Thai city of Chiang Mai, the central banks of the member states made bilateral commitments with one another to provide liquidity in times of crisis.

Effects of Japanese security considerations 115

Furthermore, the Asian Bond Markets Initiative was established by ASEAN+3 Finance Ministers in 2003 with the aim of fostering the "utilization of Asian savings for Asian investments."[12]

By 2003, Japan, China, and South Korea shared enthusiasm about the direction ASEAN+3 was headed and especially Japan had embraced the idea of an East Asian community based on ASEAN+3.[13]

Assertive China and wary Japan

Relations between Japan and China took a turn for the worse in 2004. One major issue that arose between both countries that year was a dispute about natural gas reserves under the seabed of the East China Sea. In May 2004, China started drilling for gas in the Chunxiao gas field.[14] While exploration points were outside of the median line claimed by Japan and thus understood by both parties to be within China's claimed exclusive economic zone (EEZ),[15] Japan claimed that the gas reserves stretch into Japan's EEZ and that China was therefore tapping into Japan's gas as well. The fact that Chinese drilling operations were situated just 4 kilometers from the median line added to Japanese suspicions about China's intentions.[16] Japan responded by commencing its own drilling operation in June to counter China's claim.

The dispute over the Senkaku Islands, which are administered by Japan as part of Okinawa prefecture and claimed by both China and Taiwan under the name Diaoyu and Tiaoyutai respectively, also flared up in 2004. In January that year, a Japanese coast guard ship fired its water cannon at two Chinese ships carrying mainland activists inside Japanese territorial waters surrounding the islands.[17] Just two months later, seven Chinese activists landed on one of the islands and were subsequently arrested by Okinawa prefectural police forces, who had flown in by helicopter.[18]

A reflection of the downturn in relations between the two countries could also be observed among the general public. China hosted a regional soccer tournament, the Asian Cup, in July and August 2004 and the final match saw China and Japan playing for the title. The stadium was mostly filled by Chinese spectators and Japanese fans were vastly outnumbered. While Japan was winning the game, some of the Chinese spectators started shouting "Kill! Kill! Kill!," directing their chants towards Japanese fans and the Japanese team. Others wore t-shirts printed with the slogan "Protect the Diaoyu Islands!" Security personnel tasked with protecting the Japanese team and Japanese fans, as well as keeping Chinese spectators from starting a riot, numbered around 10,000.[19] The televised nature of such a big event led to scrutiny by the Japanese media and Japanese public opinion of China fell to its lowest point since 1996 in 2004, with 71.2% of respondents to a survey conducted by *The Yomiuri Shimbun*, Japan's biggest newspaper in terms of circulation, stating that they did not trust China.[20] *The Yomiuri Shimbun* speculated that Chinese attitude towards Japan at the Asia Cup and the intrusion of a Chinese submarine into Japanese waters in November that year were major factors in influencing Japanese public perception of China for the worse.

The Chinese submarine incident was special in a way, as it expanded the dimension of the mounting conflict between both countries to the military level. The Han Class nuclear submarine entered Japanese territorial waters near the Sakishima Islands in Okinawa prefecture on November 10, being tracked by a Japanese Self Defense Forces helicopter for the two hours it sailed in Japanese waters. The crew of the submarine did not initiate identification routines. Since the submarine was cruising at shallow depth and the Han Class submarines are said to be relatively noisy, the Japanese Defense Agency (now Ministry of Defense) saw the intrusion as "highly provocative."[21] While China officially apologized for the intrusion, citing technical errors as a reason, concerns over why a Chinese nuclear submarine was cruising around that area could not be alleviated.[22] The intrusion may have indeed been a deliberate action aimed at testing the response of Japanese Marine Self Defense Forces, constituting an example of Chinese salami tactics.[23]

Relations did not improve with the turn of the year. Several issues sparked widespread anti-Japanese protests in China in March and April, 2005. One such issue was the approval of a revisionist history textbook by Japanese authorities. Another issue was Japan granting oil exploration rights to two Japanese companies in disputed territory in the East China Sea. Japan's bid for a permanent seat on the United Nations Security Council, which was officially opposed by Chinese Premier Wen Jiabao on April 13, 2005, may have added fuel to the fire as well, being perceived as a Japanese plot to return to its past militarism.

Inception of the East Asia Summit: expanding the region

While relations between China and Japan soured in 2004 and 2005, attempts at regional community building did not stop. At the 2004 ASEAN summit in Vientiane, Laos, ASEAN members decided to host the first EAS in 2005 in Malaysia. This was further discussed at the accompanying ASEAN+3 summit, where Japan proposed that the ASEAN+3 foreign ministers meet again in 2005 in order to work out the details concerning the EAS. The foreign ministers met in July 2005 in Laos, where it was decided that Australia, India, and New Zealand would be invited to the EAS as full members under the condition that they would sign the Treaty of Amity and Cooperation in Southeast Asia (TAC), a de facto non-aggression pact governing the relations both among ASEAN members and between ASEAN and non-ASEAN states. India had already signed the TAC in 2003, whereas New Zealand and Australia adopted the instrument in 2005. Australia, which had previously been opposed to signing TAC, attributed its initial reluctance to sign as one of the reasons why it even was invited to the EAS, implying that Australia needed to pay a price for joining and signing the TAC turned out to be that price.[24]

The interesting question here is why the EAS became an ASEAN+3+3 forum. The 2004 outbreak of Sino-Japanese tensions appears to have had a major influence on this. Up to that point, relations between the two countries were slowly improving after the 1998 Japan–China Joint Declaration, which established annual leader visits and a direct hotline.[25]

Effects of Japanese security considerations 117

In regard to regional cooperation, the enthusiasm of the early ASEAN+3 years started to dissipate when it became apparent that China's rise meant that China would be more assertive in pushing through its interests and in defending its claims – and Chinese interests were not the same as Japanese interests, as exemplified in the maritime disputes between the two countries. This can be observed by looking at the change in tone on the Japanese side. Both Japanese Foreign Minister Taro Aso and Democratic Party of Japan President Seiji Maehara called China a threat in 2005.[26] The rather sudden decision of ASEAN to establish the EAS therefore opened up the opportunity for Japan to counter rising Chinese power and influence over the direction East Asian regionalism was going to take by advocating the inclusion of Australia, India, and New Zealand, three democracies likely to side with Japan in security-related issues.[27] Japan started pursuing realist goals through liberal means, i.e., containing China by expanding the scope of regional cooperation. Security became an area of concern for Japan in its regional cooperation policy.

At the 2005 ASEAN+3 Foreign Ministers Meeting, Japanese Senior Vice Minister for Foreign Affairs Ichiro Aisawa made it clear that Japan's stance on the EAS was that it should follow the principle of "open regional cooperation", focusing on a "(i) functional approach; (ii) respect for and observation of universal values, including freedom, democracy and human rights, and global rules; (iii) promotion of people-to-people and intellectual exchanges with a view to deepening a sense of commonality" and that "security cooperation should be mainly pursued in non-traditional areas for the time being."[28] While stressing the importance of "open regionalism" and "universal values" such as democracy and human rights may not necessarily have been a direct jab at China, the Chinese media were clearly under the impression that Japan's stance toward the EAS was marked by the goal of suppressing Chinese influence. An opinion piece in the *People's Daily* quoted "ASEAN diplomats" as saying that Japan was trying to include non-regional states such as India and Australia into the region in order to counterbalance China.[29] Furthermore, it was predicted that Japan would use human rights issues to gain the high ground at the first EAS and that Japan would try to "attempt to crumble away cooperative forces and weaken Chinese influence in East Asia" by playing on the different levels of economic development and different political systems between the different countries.[30]

Another point of contention between Japan and China in the negotiations leading up to the EAS was about who would be in the agenda-setting driver seat. A main feature of all ASEAN-related forums and dialogues is that of ASEAN centrality, meaning that ASEAN gets to set the pace and objectives of regional cooperation, while the "ASEAN way" of non-interference and consensus is maintained. China however pushed for the EAS to have ASEAN+3 at its center, effectively giving China (as well as Japan and South Korea) more influence in not only setting the agenda but also in deciding on what issues to avoid. Furthermore, putting ASEAN+3 in the center would have created a conveniently layered EAS, with the newcomers Australia, New Zealand, and India finding themselves in the outer layer and possibly less involved in East Asian regionalism. While supporting ASEAN centrality, Japan nevertheless wanted to introduce a co-chairmanship system under which the summits could be held outside of ASEAN countries every other year, partially siding with China.[31]

ASEAN centrality and chairmanship were seen as non-negotiable by some ASEAN members however. Especially Indonesia was wary of diminishing ASEAN's role in the new framework and strongly opposed the EAS for this reason.[32] Thailand was also reserved about any possibilities of ASEAN vacating the driver's seat.[33] Overall, ASEAN members were in favor of keeping ASEAN centrality and did not support a tiered system that would discriminate between ASEAN+3 members and new members inside the EAS.[34] In the end, ASEAN centrality prevailed due to fears of increasing Chinese, Japanese, and Korean influence.[35]

The first East Asia Summit was held on December 14, 2005 in Kuala Lumpur, Malaysia, back-to-back with ASEAN and ASEAN+3 summits. The result of this first meeting, the Kuala Lumpur Declaration on the East Asia Summit, is a testament to the compromises that had to be made in order to accommodate the different ideas about the direction the EAS should take in the future. In this declaration, the EAS member states "[share] the view that the East Asia Summit could play a significant role in community building in this region."[36] The ambiguity over the EAS's role in community building not only reflects the lack of consensus among member states, but also shows that concerns over how the EAS would be differentiated from ASEAN+3 were valid.

In order to accommodate Japan's idea of taking the EAS as the base for community building without upsetting the Chinese[37] idea of taking ASEAN+3 as the foundation for an East Asian community, a middle ground had to be found. The consensus-based nature of the EAS therefore only left two possible choices in regard to the declaration. One was to include the ambiguous wording that ultimately found its way into the declaration and another was to not produce a declaration at all, which would have severely damaged the summit's chances of further development.

With the commitment of ASEAN and other participating nations, China realized that the EAS was there to stay. A *People's Daily* opinion piece expected the EAS to become a bridge between East Asian and Asia-Pacific cooperation, citing the inclusion of Australia and New Zealand as factor that would hopefully relax the opposing attitude taken by the United States toward East Asian cooperation.[38] The concept of open regionalism as a pillar of the EAS was not seen by China as allowing for an expansion of the East Asian region to include new states, but as a new type of regional cooperation connecting East Asia with states on its periphery that are linked to the region through mostly economic interests. In addition, it was assumed that the political significance of the EAS was greater than the importance of the topics the EAS would deal with.[39]

The East Asia Summit gains traction

The EAS already set its sights on membership expansion during the first meeting, where Russian President Vladimir Putin, as a special guest of the Malaysian government, addressed the 16 EAS leaders and made his case for Russia's role in East Asia. Russia was denied its wish to join the EAS until 2011, when it became a member. Victor Sumsky argues that the rationale for inviting Russia was the need for a member that was supportive of ASEAN while keeping a geopolitical middle ground in an environment that was increasingly affected by United States–China competition.[40]

Since trying to steer the direction of the EAS into one's own preferred direction meant devoting resources to it, the EAS became more prominent over time. China's increasing involvement, which originated in its former quasi-opposition to the summit, may have been just what Japan wanted. It was Japan's goal to base an East Asian community on the EAS, rather than the ASEAN+3, after all, and this would not be possible without active Chinese participation and involvement.

While it is unclear how exactly an East Asian community would be realized and what the benchmark for this would be, the EAS over the years expanded the breadth of issue areas it was dealing with. While one of the first specific issues the EAS was dealing with was the outbreak of avian influenza in the region, Japan was keen on developing the economic cooperation aspect of the forum. Alongside the ASEAN+3 and EAS summits in Cebu, Philippines in January 2007, Japan proposed the creation of an Economic Research Institute for ASEAN and East Asia (ERIA). The inauguration of ERIA was approved by the 16 EAS member nations at the third EAS in Singapore in November, 2007 and it was formally inaugurated and recognized as an international organization in 2008. The institute is tasked with policy analysis and with delivering policy recommendations to leaders at the ASEAN and EAS summits in order to facilitate economic community building, the narrowing of developmental gaps, and general economic integration under ASEAN leadership. The Japanese proposal to establish ERIA was accompanied with a proposal for free trade agreement among the 16 EAS member nations, the Comprehensive Economic Partnership for East Asia (CEPEA), and ERIA was to take a role in working out the details how to enact such a framework. CEPEA took off after Australia, India, and New Zealand had concluded free trade agreements with ASEAN and the proposed framework was taken over by the Regional Comprehensive Economic Partnership (RCEP) mechanism in 2011. Formal RCEP negotiations were announced in 2012 and started in 2013 when officials of the 16 member nations met in Brunei Darussalam. Even though Russia and the United States became members of the EAS in 2011, they are not parties to RCEP, as both countries do not have free trade agreements with ASEAN as a whole.

By basing the future of an East Asian economic community on ASEAN centrality and on the original 16-member EAS, rather than just the 13 geographically East Asian members of ASEAN+3, Japan was able to further solidify the open regionalism approach employed by the EAS. Furthermore, RCEP offers China the opportunity to participate in a region-wide free trade agreement without committing itself to the Trans-Pacific Partnership agreement, which has become a critical endeavor of the US government under President Barack Obama. RCEP shows just how complex the economic–security nexus in the region has become. Notwithstanding serious security issues among RCEP members, progress in economic cooperation is made. In 2016 alone, six RCEP negotiations and ministerial meetings were scheduled.

While both ASEAN+3 and EAS expanded their portfolio of issue areas (Tables 8.1 and 8.2), their respective main focus areas, if measured by degree of accomplishment and scope of ambition, are financial stability for ASEAN+3 and economic cooperation for the 16-member EAS. In the case of ASEAN+3, the Chiang Mai Initiative, its multilateralization, the Asian Bonds Market Initiative, and the establishment of the ASEAN+3 Macroeconomic Research Office have become the most prominent achievements. ERIA and the development of CEPEA and RCEP strengthened the economic aspect of EAS.

Table 8.1 History of ASEAN+3's institutional evolution

1997	Established
1998	East Asian Vision Group I
1999	Joint Declaration for Cooperation in East Asia
2000	Chiang Mai Initiative
2001	ASEAN Ministerial Meeting on Agriculture and Forestry + 3 established
2002	
2003	Asian Bond Markets Initiative established
2004	Decision to establish East Asia Summit
	APT Research Group established
	APT Ministerial Meeting on Energy established
	APT Ministerial Meeting on Transnational Crime established
2005	APT Senior Officials Meeting on Transnational Crime established
	APT Senior Officials Meeting on Social Welfare and Development established
2006	APT Labor Ministers Meeting established
2007	APT Cooperation Work Plan (07-12)
	APT Ministers Responsible for Culture and Arts Meeting established
2008	APT Cooperation Fund established
	APT Senior Officials Meeting on Youth established
2009	Chiang Mai Initiative Multilateralization (CMIM) agreement
	APT Civilian Nuclear Energy Meeting established
	APT Ministers Responsible for Information Meeting established
2010	APT Youth Caucus established
	APT Ministerial Meeting on Youth established
	APT Ministerial Meeting on Social Welfare and Development established
	APT Conference on Civil Service Matters established
2011	ASEAN+3 Macroeconomic Research Office established
	East Asia Vision Group II
2012	APT Youth Environment Meeting established
	CMIM expansion agreement from $120 billion to $240 billion
	APT Education Ministers Meeting established
2013	APT Rectors' Conference established
	APT Cooperation Work Plan (13–17)

Source: ASEAN, Association of Southeast Asian Nations; APT, ASEAN+3.

Effects of Japanese security considerations 121

Table 8.2 History of the East Asia Summit's institutional evolution

2005	First East Asia Summit (EAS)
2006	Comprehensive Economic Partnership for East Asia (CEPEA) discussed and later turned into Regional Comprehensive Economic Partnership (RCEP)
2007	EAS Energy Ministers Meeting established
2008	Economic Research Institute for ASEAN and East Asia (ERIA) established EAS Environment Ministers Meeting established
2009	Support for revival of Nalanda University in India
2010	
2011	United States and Russia become members EAS Foreign Ministers Meeting established
2012	EAS Education Ministers Meeting established Phnom Penh Declaration on the EAS Development Initiative
2013	EAS Economic Ministers Meeting established
2014	Plan of action to implement the Phnom Penh Declaration on EAS Development Initiative (2014–15)
2015	Plan of action to implement the Phnom Penh Declaration on EAS Development Initiative (2015–17)

2010 and onwards: renewed friction

Relations between China and Japan relatively improved after 2007, at least in comparison to the preceding years. Chinese President Hu Jintao followed up an invitation by the Japanese government to visit Japan in May 2008 and Japanese Prime Minister Aso Taro visited China in October the same year in order to commemorate the 30th anniversary of the signing of the Treaty of Peace and Friendship between Japan and the People's Republic of China, the formal peace treaty between the two nations. In addition, while China, Japan, and Korea had been holding trilateral leader summits alongside ASEAN+3 summits, they started to hold separate leader summits in the three countries, starting in 2008, when Prime Minister Aso hosted Chinese Premier Wen Jiabao and Korean President Lee Myung-bak in his home town of Fukuoka. The issues that had led to the deterioration of relations in 2004 and 2005 however had not magically disappeared. The Senkaku Islands dispute flared up again in 2010, when in September that year a Chinese fishing vessel collided with a Japan coast guard patrol boat in the vicinity of the islands. The arrest of the Chinese captain of the fishing ship led to a diplomatic row between both countries which in turn caused both anti-Japanese protests in China and some anti-Chinese protests in Japan. This incident led to accusations by Japan that China had put an export stop on rare-earth metals, on which Japanese high-tech firms are highly dependent, in response to the collision. China however denied this. Relations further deteriorated in 2012, when the Japanese government assumed legal ownership of three of the islands by purchasing them from their previous private Japanese owner. While this was done in order to keep the Tokyo municipal government under leadership of far-right Governor Shintaro Ishihara from buying the islands and using them to further provoke China, the perceived unilateral change of the status quo evoked previously unseen strong reactions by the Chinese government and especially by the Chinese public. Widespread anti-Japanese protests and riots were seen through 2012 and had a significant economic impact on Japanese businesses operating in China.

The rift between the two countries, especially in regard to the Senkaku Islands dispute, had an indirect effect on the EAS. With the ascension of the United States to full member status in 2011, territorial disputes and thus traditional security issues became part of the discussions at the EAS.[41] This was wrapped around the topic of maritime security, especially in the South China Sea, where China has territorial disputes over islands and maritime boundaries with all ASEAN members except for Thailand, Laos, and Myanmar. Sixteen out of the 18 EAS members addressed maritime security at the leaders' retreat during the sixth EAS in Bali, Indonesia, with the South China Sea mentioned as the most prominent maritime security issue.[42] While Chinese Premier Wen Jiabao responded to other leaders in a timid manner,[43] the reaction expressed by the Chinese media was sharp. An opinion piece published in the English-language *China Daily* and redistributed by the *People's Daily* mentioned that "Chinese leaders and people" thought that bringing the unrelated issue of the South China Sea to the table served the American agenda goal of driving a wedge between China and Southeast Asian states as well as reducing regional Chinese influence.[44] A year later, after the conclusion of the seventh EAS in Phnom Penh, Cambodia, the United States was accused by Chinese media of having encouraged Vietnam and the Philippines to "harass" the EAS by raising the issue of territorial disputes over islands in the South China Sea again.[45] This shows again how EAS members that share territorial disputes with China were pursuing realist goals through liberal means. The EAS gave them a forum to marginalize Chinese maritime and territorial claims, which encroached on the security of the affected states.

China feared that the discussion of territorial disputes at the EAS would multilateralize the issues. So far, China preferred a bilateral approach when dealing with the countries involved. As China's relative bargaining power is very strong when facing just one Southeast Asian nation, rather than ten or a grouping including the United States, China may be afraid that it will not be able to continue expanding its territorial claim asserting operations in the disputed areas at the same pace. Furthermore, bringing these issues to the table may have seemed to instill at least some sort of atmosphere receptive to leaders grouping up against China. This partially led to a change in the Chinese approach to dealing with maritime security issues, as Chinese Premier Li Keqiang outlined a "dual-track approach" at the ninth East Asian Summit in 2014 in Naypyidaw, Myanmar. Under this approach, the respective territorial issues would still be dealt with on a bilateral level, but a code of conduct concerning the South China Sea, as well as efforts for peace and stability, would fall under the China–ASEAN framework.[46] The reason for this appears to lie in the Chinese desire to exclude the United States, Japan, Australia, and other not directly involved EAS members from South China Sea issues in order to minimize any hypothetical concessions made.

The fragility of ASEAN in terms of the South China Sea dispute however became further apparent after China's rejection of the award published by the arbitral tribunal set up in the Philippines *v.* China case regarding their disputes in the South China Sea. The tribunal concluded that China's claim to historic rights inside the boundaries of the "nine-dash line" became invalid with China's accession to the United Nations Convention on the Law of the Sea. ASEAN failed to address the tribunal's ruling in any of the joint statements released during the 2016 summit in Laos, mainly due to opposition by Cambodia, which had just been promised an aid package by China a week before the summit.[47]

Conclusion

Overall, East Asian regionalism in the 21st century has been strongly influenced by power dynamics between China and Japan, as well as an American refocus on East Asia. The incidental timing of the establishment of the EAS overlapping with the rapid deterioration of Sino-Japanese relations in 2004 and 2005 had the effect of changing the nature of the EAS from the start. Rather than becoming a new ASEAN+3, the EAS quickly redefined East Asian regionalism to be more open and less exclusive by accepting the participation of Australia, India, and New Zealand. It is unclear whether the EAS would have taken the same direction had Sino-Japanese relations been better at that time. The early ASEAN+3 years may have given Japan the impression that China would be controllable through multilateral regional socialization, forfeiting the need to involve like-minded nations from outside the region, but the years 2004 and 2005 shattered this illusion and instilled upon Japanese policymakers that China's rise constitutes a threat to Japanese security. Japanese foreign policy on regional cooperation therefore increasingly started to favor an inclusive approach to East Asian regionalism.

China, on the other hand, while favoring the exclusive nature of ASEAN+3, had to get involved in the EAS in order to ensure that Japan would not be able to freely design the future of regional cooperation in such a manner that Chinese influence over the region would be brought down to a minimum level. Sino-Japanese competition certainly made the EAS a more important framework than it may have ended up being under less confrontational circumstances. Furthermore, the inclusion of the United States in 2011 introduced traditional security issues into the summit, pushing China into a more defensive stance.

Today, East Asian regionalism operates on three tracks: ASEAN+3, ASEAN+6 (RCEP), and ASEAN+8 (EAS). The different countries involved have different ideas about which of these three frameworks will constitute the foundation of a future East Asian community, but it is safe to say that RCEP at the very minimum has the capacity to provide an economic pillar for such a community. As long as ASEAN centrality remains unchallenged, the possibility of forsaking East Asia for the Asia-Pacific remains slim. Unless ASEAN itself becomes a stronger community that is less based on lowest-common-denominator consensus, ASEAN lacks the capability to effectively guide and unite anything larger than the current EAS. It is unclear whether the United States even wants to be part of an

East Asian community protecting East Asian interests and highly unlikely that the United States would be willing to fully subordinate itself to ASEAN in the region. Participation in East Asian regionalism should ultimately be seen as part of US "hedging" and engagement strategy towards China, rather than a new-found East Asian identity.

The past decade has shown that bilateral disputes and multilateral cooperation efforts in East Asia are linked. Interim measures, such as shelving disputes, and keeping a fragile and ambiguous status quo are detrimental to community building, since escalation often is not done at the hand of the leaders but caused by uncontrollable and incidental circumstances.

Notes

1 The author defines East Asia as the sum of both the Northeast and Southeast Asian subregions, i.e., China, Japan, the two Koreas, Taiwan, plus the ASEAN member states.
2 Note that the EAVG report calls for an East *Asian* Summit, whereas the actual established forum is called East *Asia* Summit. One could argue about the nuances of East Asian versus East Asia and it might as well be that there was a deliberate shift from one to the other in order to show that it would be a summit in East Asia, but not necessarily a purely East Asian one. Since such an argument would however be based purely on speculation, it will not be considered here.
3 East Asia Vision Group. *Towards an East Asian Community: Region of Peace, Prosperity and Stability.* Ministry of Foreign Affairs of Japan. 2001. http://www.mofa.go.jp/region/asia-paci/report2001.pdf.
4 East Asia Vision Group. *Report of the East Asia Vision Group II.* Ministry of Foreign Affairs of the Kingdom of Thailand. 2013. http://www.mfa.go.th/asean/contents/files/asean-media-center-20130312-112418-758604.pdf.
5 Yiping Huang. "From Crisis to Crisis: Changing Capital Flows and Foreign Exchange Reserves in Asia." In *Asian Regionalism in the World Economy: Engine for Dynamism and Stability*, 281, edited by Masahiro Kawai, Jong-Wha Lee, and Peter A. Petri. Cheltenham, UK: Edward Elgar, 2010.
6 Richard Higgott. "The Asian Economic Crisis: A Study in the Politics of Resentment." *New Political Economy*, 3, no. 3 (1998): 338.
7 Ibid., 333.
8 Richard Stubbs. "ASEAN Plus Three: Emerging East Asian Regionalism?" *Asian Survey*, 42, no. 3 (2002): 449.
9 Higgott, 340, 349, 351.
10 "Joint Statement on East Asia Cooperation 28 November 1999." *Association of Southeast Asian Nations*, 8 November 1999. http://www.asean.org/news/item/joint-statement-on-east-asia-cooperation-28-november-1999.
11 East Asia Vision Group, 2001, 17.
12 "Chairman's Press Release on the Asian Bond Markets Initiative." *Ministry of Finance Japan.* August 7, 2003. http://www.mof.go.jp/english/international_policy/convention/asean_plus_3/20030807_02.htm.
13 Takashi Terada, "Constructing an 'East Asian' Concept and Growing Regional Identity: From EAEC to ASEAN+3." *The Pacific Review,* 16, no. 2 (2003): 269, 273.
14 Japan calls this gas field Shirakaba.
15 Note that China claims that its EEZ starts at the end of its submerged continental shelf, rather than at its shore. China's actually claimed EEZ therefore extends much further than 200 nautical miles from its coast.
16 Kent E. Calder. "China and Japan's Simmering Rivalry." *Foreign Affairs,* 85, no. 2 (2006): 130.

Effects of Japanese security considerations   125

17 "Japan, China Clash over Senkaku." *BBC News*, January 16, 2004. http://news.bbc.co.uk/2/hi/asia-pacific/3402077.stm.
18 "Chinese Activists Reach Senkaku." *BBC News*, March 24, 2004. http://news.bbc.co.uk/2/hi/asia-pacific/3563777.stm.
19 Jim Yardley. "In Soccer Loss, a Glimpse of China's Rising Ire at Japan." *The New York Times*. August 9, 2004. http://www.nytimes.com/2004/08/09/international/asia/09china.html.
20 *"Nichibei kyoudou yoron chousa"* ["Japan–U.S. Joint Survey of Public Opinions"]. *Yomiuri Shimbun*. December 16, 2004. Tokyo ed.
21 Nao Shimoyachi. "Chinese Submarine Intrusion Considered an Act of Provocation." *The Japan Times*. November 13, 2004. http://www.japantimes.co.jp/news/2004/11/13/national/chinese-submarine-intrusion-considered-an-act-of-provocation.
22 Reiji Yoshida. "Beijing Says Tech Glitch Led to Sub Intrusion." *The Japan Times*. November 17, 2004. http://www.japantimes.co.jp/news/2004/11/17/national/beijing-says-tech-glitch-led-to-sub-intrusion.
23 For a detailed explanation of *salami tactics* or *salami slicing* in regard to Chinese foreign policy, see Robert Haddick. "Salami Slicing in the South China Sea." *Foreign Policy*, August 3, 2012.
24 As expressed by Australian Minister for Foreign Affairs Alexander Downer on radio. "Australia to Sign Southeast Asian Non Aggression Pact." *AM*, ABC Local Radio. Sydney, NSW:2BL, December 10, 2005.
25 "Japan–China Joint Declaration on Building a Partnership of Friendship and Cooperation for Peace and Development." *Ministry of Foreign Affairs of Japan*. November 26, 1998. http://www.mofa.go.jp/region/asia-paci/china/visit98/joint.html.
26 FM Aso's statement that China was "on the course to constitute a considerable threat" came as a response to a question regarding his views on Maehara's earlier classification of China as a threat. See "Press Conference by Foreign Minister Taro Aso." *Ministry of Foreign Affairs of Japan*. December 22, 2005. http://www.mofa.go.jp/announce/fm_press/2011/3/0304_01.html.
27 While it was ASEAN that decided on establishing the EAS, the initiative came from Malaysia and South Korea.
28 "ASEAN+3 Foreign Ministers Meeting (Summary)." *Ministry of Foreign Affairs of Japan*. July 28, 2005. http://www.mofa.go.jp/region/asia-paci/asean/conference/asean3/summary0507.html.
29 "East Asia Summit: In the Shadow of Sharp Divisions." *People's Daily Online*. December 7, 2005. http://en.people.cn/200512/07/eng20051207_226350.html.
30 Ibid.
31 MOFA, July 28, 2005.
32 "ASEAN Fails to Agree on East Asian Summit Plan." *Japan Economic Newswire*, November 27, 2004. LexisNexis.
33 "Indonesia Raises Questions About Planned East Asia Summit." *Deutsche Presse Agentur*, November 30, 2004. LexisNexis.
34 Eric Teo Chu Cheow. "E. Asia Summit's Birthing Pains." *Straits Times*, February 22, 2005. LexisNexis.
35 *"Higashi ajia samitto, 12 gatsu 14 nichi, 16 kakoku de – ASEAN+3, gaishoukaigi de goui."* *Nihon Keizai Shimbun*, July 28, 2005, 9.
36 "Kuala Lumpur Declaration on the East Asia Summit." *Ministry of Foreign Affairs of Japan*. December 14, 2005. http://www.mofa.go.jp/region/asia-paci/eas/joint0512.html.
37 It should be noted that this point of contention was, of course, not only relevant to China and Japan. Both sides had their respective backers, with Malaysia favoring the Chinese approach of a less inclusive regional community.
38 Jianren Lu. "East Asia Summit: In the Shadow of Sharp Divisions." *People's Daily Online*. December 14, 2005. http://en.people.cn/200512/07/eng20051207_226350.html.

39 Ibid.
40 Victor Sumsky. "The Enlargement of the East Asia Summit: The Reasons and Implications of Bringing Russia in." In *ASEAN-Russia: Foundations and Future Prospects*, edited by Victor Sumsky, Mark Hong, and Amy Lugg, 77. Singapore: ISEAS Publications, 2012.
41 These issues were not included on the official agenda however, for obvious reasons.
42 Myanmar and Cambodia were the only countries not to mention maritime security, while Singapore, the Philippines, Vietnam, and Malaysia were early in raising this issue. "Background Briefing on Obama Meetings at ASEAN, East Asia Summit." *U.S. Department of State*. November 19, 2011. http://iipdigital.usembassy.gov/st/english/texttrans/2011/11/20111119142035su0.1164907.html#axzz3OAEEsk5k.
43 Ibid.
44 Litai Xue. "The Role That US Plays in Asia." *China Daily*. November 24, 2011. http://www.chinadaily.com.cn/cndy/2011-11/24/content_14151382.htm.
45 Liming Wu. "Commentary: Harassing East Asia Summit with Islands Disputes Was Unwise." *Xinhua*. November 21, 2012. http://news.xinhuanet.com/english/indepth/2012-11/21/c_131989588.htm.
46 "Chinese Premier Advocates Peace, Economic Integration at East Asia Summit." *People's Daily Online*. November 14, 2014. http://en.people.cn/n/2014/1114/c90883-8808772.html.
47 Tan Hui Yee. " South China Sea Dispute: Asean Voice Drowned Out as Big Powers Pipe Up." *The Straits Times*. July 29, 2016. http://www.straitstimes.com/asia/se-asia/asean-voice-drowned-out-as-big-powers-pipe-up.

9 Realist objectives, liberal means

Japan, China, and maritime security in Southeast Asia

Hidetaka Yoshimatsu and Dennis D. Trinidad

Introduction

The use of economic tools to advance security objectives has become a common strategy in the conduct of foreign affairs in East Asia. This is evident in the way China and Japan have pursued their interests on the issue of maritime territorial dispute in the South China Sea. Both countries have used a mix of economic measures such as foreign aid, trade and investment, and multilateral institutions in order to establish linkage with Southeast Asian countries. One plausible explanation regarding the use of such strategy is the realization among policy-makers that the region's economies have become more interdependent, which can be exploited to their nation's advantage. Indeed, in the past two decades or so regional economic interdependence has deepened, as evidenced by overall increase in intraregional trade and investments while, at the same time, territorial disputes have beset the region.

One such dispute that has increasingly called the attention of scholars is the South China Sea issue. Quite a few scholars have examined the geopolitical nature of the dispute, the motivations, involvements, and influences of other great powers such as the United States, India, and Japan.[1] Others have examined underpinning geopolitical factors and motivations pertinent to China's assertive diplomatic postures towards the South China Sea dispute.[2] Broadly, Goldstein and Mansfield's edited volume explored the interaction of interdependence and conflict in East Asian regional affairs but focused mainly on Sino–United States relations and set aside Japan's role.[3]

The past studies' strong interest in geopolitical aspects in the South China Sea dispute is understandable given that the core of the dispute lies in the question of sovereignty, seeking to gain exclusive jurisdictional rights over the surrounding waters and seabed,[4] as well as the South China Sea's importance for the states' national interests as sea lines of communications. However, the South China Sea dispute has developed in the milieu where the parties involved have forged mutually dependent relationships through growing economic interdependence and the development of formal institutions. These environments should have significant impacts on relevant parties' positions and actions, as well as the overall development of the dispute.

This chapter has two primary objectives. First is to examine China's and Japan's policies towards Southeast Asia in the context of maritime security, which constitutes one of the most crucial security concerns in East Asia today. Second is to analyze the implications of these rival policies on the formation of regional institutions for maritime security. China as a direct party has a crucial stake in the conflict and has undertaken political, economic, and even military interactions with rival claimants in Southeast Asia. Though not a direct party in the dispute, Japan has a similar maritime dispute with China in the East China Sea and thereby the dispute in the South China Sea has an implication of a quasi-dispute for Japan.

This paper argues that both China and Japan have utilized economic means and formal institutions either as tools of coercion or attraction or both[5] to prop up their positions in maritime security issues in Southeast Asia. China's strong preference and improved ability to deploy economic resources for strategic benefits,[6] proliferation of regional economic institutions, and increased economic interdependence between nations in the region are some of the factors why these liberal toolkits are preferred. At the same time the region is beset by disputes over territories and maritime rights[7] and security challenges from China's rise as a regional power. As shown in the succeeding sections, Japan's use of both toolkits in pursuit of its strategic goals has become more straightforward under the Abe cabinet while China showed more willingness in exploiting the asymmetrical dependence of target countries in order to influence their positions on the South China Sea issue.

Liberal toolkits to attain realist objectives

Formal institutions and economic measures are two of the most common tools that nations employ to advance their national interests in the modern age. They are liberal toolkits in a sense because of their crucial roles in the Kantian tripod for perpetual peace.[8] Ideally, economic resources like foreign aid contribute to interdependence by consolidating economic and trade linkages and in creating stable political relations between donors and recipient-countries. The resulting increased commercial transactions make private actors and government officials recognize that their own wealth and prosperity rely on economic linkages with partners and that military conflict would impose significant costs on their economic benefits and overall wellbeing.[9]

However, as realists point out, interdependence is not a matter of mutual and symmetrical exchanges among states, and the power relation inherent in asymmetrical economic relationships does matter for the states concerned.[10] Asymmetrical economic interdependence enables states to utilize it for achieving their strategic and security policy objectives. States employ economic means as toolkits of "statecraft"[11] to enhance overall strategic and security advantages *vis-à-vis* other specific states or in the international system.[12] States use positive and negative economic statecraft in order to alter specific external or internal policies of the target state.[13] As a foreign-policy instrument, economic measures like foreign aid have the ability not just to coerce but also to attract target states. States can realize certain policy utility by using aid to establish commitment and dependency.[14] Aid dependency occurs when the cost of terminating aid relations with donors is very high. More often aid allotments are influenced by donor countries' political and strategic considerations than by any other incentives.[15]

Liberals see three ways by which formal multilateral institutions may contribute to peace and stability: First, they create mutual gains among participating states and thereby make states find vested interests in cooperation. Once planning and decision-making processes for institution building begin, some distribution of labor in the expertise and planning capacity is formed with the expectation of continuity of commitment. Such situations can raise the costs of breaking connecting links and may dissuade a state from adopting policy changes in isolation.[16] Second, the membership of institutions restrains and socializes state behavior. In particular, increased joint membership in institutions reduces the propensity for outright conflict among the members.[17] Third, multilateral institutions play functional roles in rectifying various problems inherent in the anarchical, self-help system by providing legal liability that establishes stable and mutual expectation about others' patterns of behavior; by offering relatively symmetrical information to the members, thereby reducing levels of uncertainty and the risks of making agreements; and by reducing the transaction costs of legitimate bargains and increasing them for illegitimate ones.[18]

This view, nonetheless, tends to downplay or ignore the motives of states in creating and joining formal institutions. It is reasonably accepted that certain kinds of institutions will produce increased cooperation, and states find interest in creating and joining such institutions when they want this outcome.[19] Important is that institutions are "the product of the same factors – states' interests and the constraints imposed by the system – that influence whether states should cooperate," and thereby institutions do not have much explanatory power of their own but are regarded as part of what is being explained.[20] This implies that the creation and design of institutions are heavily dependent on the interests of the states, and some states create institution as an instrument of statecraft to maintain and increase influence among members that belong to the institution.

The dual effects of these toolkits – improving bilateral relations and creating dependency, simultaneously– make their usage irresistibly tempting for Japan and China particularly in a region where economics and security issues are inextricably linked.

Japan's relations with Southeast Asia in light of maritime security

Japan's interest in maritime security in Southeast Asia

The South China Sea is strategically important to Japan for two reasons. One, the area is a crucial sea line of communication in Southeast Asia. Ninety-six percent of Japan's energy resources, mainly from the Middle East, pass through the South China Sea and Malacca Straits. According to one estimate, in the case of moderate tensions in the South China Sea, the average insurance cost for a commercial ship will increase by some 10 million yen per day when going through the area.[21] Japan's response to the dispute is, in a sense, intended to protect maritime trade.[22]

Two, the dispute in the South China Sea has inextricable linkages with Japan's own maritime dispute with China over the Senkaku/Diaoyu Islands in the East China Sea.[23] If China is able to persuade or coerce other Asian countries into accepting its claimed historic rights in the South China Sea, not only would it undermine international legal norms but it also would have serious negative impacts on territorial disputes in the East China Sea.[24] This is acknowledged by Defense Minister Onodera during a visit to Manila in June 2013, when he noted that the East China Sea of Japan and the South China Sea face a very similar situation.[25]

Thus, it is in Japan's interest to maintain the stability and freedom of navigation in the South China Sea. To do so, it must strengthen its alliance with the United States and defense ties with Southeast Asian states that are parties to the dispute. In line with this, Japan has revised its security policy, ended its self-imposed arms export, and attempted to orient its official development assistance (ODA) to strategic uses under Abe's administration.

Japan's ODA in a changing regional security environment

For a long time, Japan has held a predominant status as provider of ODA in Southeast Asia. The emergence of new aid providers, particularly China, at the onset of the new millennium would challenge this position. Between 2010 and 2012 the Chinese government claimed that it allotted 14.41 billion US dollars to its global aid programs.[26] It increasingly became clear that China has become a major source of foreign aid and has provided economic and technical assistance to low-income Association of Southeast Asian Nations (ASEAN) member countries since 2003.[27] As a result, China enjoys a much more favorable image, especially within mainland Southeast Asia. In response to the new aid landscape and security challenges and in seeking to contribute more proactively to peace, the Abe cabinet adopted a new ODA charter in February 2015.[28]

Prior to this, Japanese aid was mainly used for infrastructural development of recipients. Financial support was provided for developing maritime infrastructure in Southeast Asia, including development of land and sea corridors, port development, and ASEAN-wide soft infrastructure. Assistance was extended for the formation of roll-on/roll-off vessels, which was one of the 15 priority projects envisioned in the ASEAN Connectivity Master Plan. This support aimed to strengthen logistic networks in Southeast Asia and transfer Japan's superior shipbuilding technologies and know-how for sea operation.

As the 2003 ODA charter explicitly prohibits the use of aid for military purposes, security-related acquisitions and projects funded through ODA were justified as part of Japan's support for maritime infrastructure, safety, and counter-piracy measures. For instance, the grant aid worth 1.92 billion yen provided by the Japanese government to Indonesia in 2006 for the project Construction of

Realist objectives, liberal means 131

Patrol Vessels for the Prevention of Piracy, Maritime Terrorism and Proliferation of Weapons was justified as an exception to the Three Principles on Arms Export that virtually prohibit exports of all weapons and related technologies, as they were provided without arms and to a non-military force[29] and thus did not violate the use of ODA as stipulated in the charter.

Recently, however, the use of aid to pursue strategic aims has become more straightforward. There are now implicit efforts to utilize ODA to finance dual-purpose equipment, such as communications systems, patrol boats, radars, and the likes, for Southeast Asian recipients. The provision of patrol boats to littoral states was part of the new initiatives to promote regional peace that was confirmed in the Japan–US Security Consultative Committee (2+2) in April 2012. Moreover, in line with his Proactive Contribution to Peace policy, Abe ended Japan's self-imposed ban on selling weapons in April 2014[30] and sought to revise the ODA charter, which, an observer noted, could potentially allow the government to use it indirectly to assist foreign militaries.[31] While the new Development Cooperation Charter continues to uphold the ODA's "non-military use" principle, it "extended" the scope of cooperation and allowed a "case-by-case" approach to circumstances in which armed forces of recipient countries can be involved.

Japan's more straightforward posture on defense and regional security is clearly evident in the case of its relations with the Philippines. In December 2013, foreign ministers of Japan and the Philippines signed the exchange of notes on the provision of patrol vessels to the Philippine coast guard. This provision of yen loans worth 18.7 billion yen was used to purchase ten patrol vessels for coast guard and maritime communication systems. The transfer of the patrol vessels was expected to boost the Philippines' maritime domain awareness and advance Japan's strategic overtures in Southeast Asia.[32] On top of this, the two countries also signed a security agreement in January 2015, where joint naval exercises are planned to be conducted.[33] Tokyo also plans to finance infrastructure improvements around a Philippine military base in Palawan Island.[34]

Aside from the Philippines, Japan sought to use ODA funds to provide patrol boats to Vietnam. However, the ODA use for patrol boats in Vietnam was problematic because the Vietnam marine police (coast guard) was organizationally under the Vietnamese People's Army. Accordingly, the Japanese government suggested that Vietnam separate coast guard administration from its military.[35] The Vietnamese government implemented administrative reforms to make its marine police an independent administrative body. When Foreign Minister Fumio Kishida made a formal visit to Hanoi in August 2014, he and Vietnam's Minister for Planning and Investment, Bui Quang Vinh, signed an exchange of notes concerning Japan's provision of six used vessels, lifeboats, and radar worth 500 million yen (4.86 million US dollars).

Advancing formal institutions for maritime security

Japan's commitment to multilateral institutions for maritime security has also become more straightforward and increasingly defense-related, especially under the Abe cabinet. Since the mid-2000s, Japan has actively promoted the institutionalization of maritime cooperation in East Asia. In accordance with its pacifist orientation, early proposals for maritime cooperation, such as the Regional Cooperation Agreement on Combating Piracy and Armed Robbery against Ships in Asia (ReCAAP), were related to ensuring safety of commercial ships in the South China Sea. Another is the Information Sharing Centre (ISC), established in Singapore in November 2006 to facilitate informal exchange and the sharing of best practices and operational cooperation. Japan has been the second-largest contributor of funding for the ISC (after Singapore) and the inaugural executive director and his successor have both been Japanese nationals.[36] Importantly, the 14 founding members were all Asian countries, including China and India, and this membership composition reflected Japan's interests in resolving purely maritime safety problems by gaining support from Asian countries.[37]

After maritime security affairs became major issues in East Asia, Japan sought to develop the East Asia Summit (EAS) into a substantial forum to discuss political and security affairs. Japan made efforts to raise maritime security as a theme of discussion during the sixth EAS in November 2011.[38] At the eighth EAS in October 2013, Prime Minister Abe opened his remarks by stressing that the EAS is a significant forum where leaders frankly exchange views centered on political and security areas and expressed his desire to further bolster the development of the forum.[39] The 2013 Chairman's statement contained an independent section on 'Maritime Security and Cooperation' in which the term, South China Sea, was used for the first time in the Chairman's statement.[40]

Moreover, Japan took a lead in launching a new institution to discuss maritime security affairs among EAS members. At the EAS in November 2011, Prime Minister Yoshihiko Noda proposed holding a dialogue to discuss the promotion of maritime cooperation. ASEAN leaders formally agreed to hold the Expanded ASEAN Maritime Forum in April 2012, and its first meeting was held in Manila in October 2012. The forum, comprised of governmental and non-governmental delegates from EAS members, became a key venue to discuss maritime cooperation and maritime security in East Asia. The forum was institutionalized, and the second and third meetings were held in October 2013 and August 2014.

Japan also sought to form close institutional linkages with Southeast Asian countries. In this respect, bilateral dialogue on maritime and oceanic affairs with several Southeast Asian countries was initiated. The first Japan–Philippines Dialogue on Maritime and Oceanic Affairs was held in September 2011.[41] Japan confirmed its support for capacity building of the Philippine coast guard and further strength in cooperation between defense authorities. Two months later, a similar dialogue was held with Singapore, discussing a wide range of issues, from safe navigation in vital shipping lanes such as the Straits of Malacca and Singapore, counter-piracy measures, the ReCAAP, to maritime security efforts in ASEAN, and both sides confirmed that maritime security affairs should be settled with basic rules of maritime affairs and international laws. When then Indonesian President Joko Widodo made a formal visit to Tokyo in March 2015,

Widodo and Abe agreed to establish the Japan–Indonesia Maritime Forum to strengthen cooperation in maritime safety and security and the promotion of maritime industries.

Equally important is the formation of institutional linkages with ASEAN in the defense field. The first Japan–ASEAN Defense Vice-Ministerial Meeting was held in March 2009. For the first four meetings, a seminar on common security challenges dealt with broader regional security affairs, including regional architectures for security cooperation, climate change, and the role of armed forces, resource problems, and so on. The relative position of maritime security increased during the holding of the meetings. For instance, two sessions at the sixth meeting in October 2014 were held "to promote maritime defence cooperation" and "possible maritime cooperation from perspective of equipment and technology cooperation and capacity building."[42]

During the Japan–ASEAN Commemorative Summit in December 2013, Abe proposed to hold the Japan–ASEAN Defense Ministerial Roundtable Meeting. This proposal came to light in November 2014, when Defense Minister Akinori Eto and the Defense Ministers from all ten ASEAN member countries held the first Japan–ASEAN Ministerial Roundtable Meeting in Myanmar. In this meeting, Eto reiterated Japan's commitment to contribute to regional peace and security under the banner of "proactive contribution to peace based on the principle of international cooperation." This was acknowledged and welcomed by all members in the Chairman's statement on the occasion of the 17th ASEAN–Japan Summit that was held also in Myanmar.[43] In this summit, Prime Minister Abe announced that Japan would continue to cooperate on Japan–ASEAN joint exercises, human resources development, and safety of navigation. He also mentioned that he wanted to further deepen cooperation between the defense authorities of Japan and ASEAN.[44]

The Abe government is also more straightforward in forging bilateral ties that are undoubtedly defense-related. In January 2015, the Secretary of National Defense of the Philippines, Voltaire T. Gazmin, visited Tokyo and signed with Japan's Minister of Defense Gen Nakatani a Memorandum on Defense Cooperation and Exchanges.[45] The agreement was the outcome of negotiations between the two sides, since a statement of intent was signed in 2012 by Secretary Gazmin and then Defense Minister Satoshi Morimoto.

China's relations with Southeast Asia in light of maritime security

China's position in maritime security in Southeast Asia

China is a direct party of the South China Sea dispute, and repeated diplomatic and military interactions have occurred in the Paracel and Spratly Islands with Vietnam, the Philippines, and others in Southeast Asia. For instance, military battles with Vietnam in the Johnson Reef in the Paracels in 1988 led to the casualty of some 80 Vietnamese soldiers. In 1995, the Chinese navy occupied Mischief Reef in the Spratly, claimed by the Philippines. After this incident, China increasingly resorted to a "charm offensive" using soft power to project a good image[46] and participated in multilateral cooperation with neighboring Southeast Asian countries. In 1997, then President Jiang Zemin and ASEAN leaders issued the Joint Statement on Good Neighborliness.[47] During the fourth China–ASEAN Summit, Premier Zhu Rongji reiterated China's support and increase of Chinese assistance to Southeast Asia.[48]

At the China–ASEAN summit in 2002, the two parties issued the Declaration on the Conduct (DOC) of Parties in the South China Sea. Under the DOC, the two parties agreed on peaceful dispute resolution without resorting to threat or use of force in accordance with universally recognized principles of international law. Since the DOC was just a political statement without legally binding power, ASEAN members sought to change it into a legally binding code of conduct in the South China Sea. However, negotiations on the code of conduct reached a stalemate, largely because of China's strong preferences for bilateral means of conflict management and ASEAN's inability to reach internal consensus.[49]

Territorial disputes in the South China Sea, however, would eventually gain more attention from 2011. In the first half of that year, patrol ships of the Chinese Marine Surveillance Force (MSF) disrupted seismic surveys conducted by Vietnam and the Philippines within their claimed exclusive economic zones. In March, two MSF vessels expelled a vessel that was conducting a seismic survey in a Philippines exploration block in the northwestern portion of the Spratly Islands. Additionally, in late May 2011, an MSF vessel severed the exploration cables of a Vietnamese oil survey ship searching for oil and gas deposits 120 nautical miles off the coast of central Vietnam.[50]

In April 2012, a Philippine navy ship attempted to arrest Chinese fishermen with an accusation of illegally harvesting coral and poaching sharks in the waters surrounding Scarborough Shoal (called Huangyan Island in Chinese). However, two Chinese MSF vessels blocked such an attempt. The standoff continued until mid-June, when China assumed substantial control on the shoal and adjacent waters. After this incident, Manila sought to strengthen military cooperation under its alliance with Washington. Tension between Beijing and Manila escalated after the Philippines appealed to the United Nations for clarified interpretation of the UN Convention on the Law of the Sea. On January 22, 2013, the Philippines officially filed arbitral proceedings against China in the Permanent Court of Arbitration.[51]

Dealing with maritime tension through economic means

China has regarded the South China Sea as a crucial part of its "vital interest." At the same time, the maintenance of stable and friendly relationships with its southern neighbors has been an important diplomatic objective for China. Accordingly, China has adopted a mix of economic means in dealing with maritime tensions with other claimants while at the same time ensuring that its economic development is sustained. Sutter aptly points out that China's priority is domestic economic development, political stability, and avoiding major confrontation or controversy in foreign affairs.[52] These factors explain China's posture in the dispute and the use of economic means to achieve diplomatic and strategic objectives.

One economic instrument that China has increasingly employed of late in advancing its national interests is foreign aid.[53] With about 7.1 billion US dollars total aid allotments in 2013,[54] China is now a major source of aid. The Chinese government makes its aid "attractive" by emphasizing non-interference, equality, independent national development, and mutual benefit in its aid relations with recipient-countries. This explains why Chinese aid does not come with policy conditions that are usually associated with aid from Development Assistance Committee of the Organization for Economic Cooperation and Development (DAC/OECD) members. A huge volume of its aid program is also allotted to infrastructure projects which are often tied to Chinese businesses. During the period 2010–2012, 44.8% of Chinese aid was allotted for economic infrastructure.[55] Moreover, China claims that its aid is a form of South–South cooperation, which is intended to solidify affinity with developing countries.[56]

In Southeast Asia, the Mekong countries of Myanmar, Cambodia, and Laos have traditionally received the largest share of Chinese foreign aid, mainly because of China's long historical and diplomatic ties with them.[57] While the volume of Chinese foreign aid to these countries is not as large as those from other states such as Japan and the United States, taken together with trade and investment, China's economic cooperation has constituted a trifecta of exchange that translated into its dominant influence on these states.[58] "China is now Cambodia's largest foreign investor, a major donor of aid and an increasingly important trading partner."[59] In 2014, China accounted for 24.4% of Cambodia's total investment, including domestic sources, and was the largest source of imported goods, constituting 32.6% of Cambodia's total imports (the United States was second, with 12.2% import share).[60]

Crucially important is the fact that Chinese aid in Cambodia and Myanmar was used for infrastructure projects while Japanese/Western aid allotments, mainly in the form of ODA grants, tended to be used for basic human needs and social services, which are less attractive for national leaders who seek political legitimacy. Japan, for instance, offered concessional loans for the construction of bridges and improvement in roads, but disbursed more grants and technical assistance in Cambodia. China is the only major donor in Cambodia that provides concessional loans directly to the government for public works, infrastructure, and hydropower projects.[61] Preference is given to Chinese aid because of its no-condition and non-interference aid policies.[62]

During the 2000s China pledged a large volume of aid to countries that are parties to the South China Sea dispute, most notably the Philippines and Vietnam. Nonetheless, China's "charm offensive" in the Philippines did not work effectively because of controversies that eventually arose from Chinese-assisted projects.[63] Moreover, unlike Cambodia, the Philippines is not heavily dependent on China's economic assistance. In 2014, the Philippines' top aid donor was the World Bank, which provided nearly 40% of the country's total aid portfolio, followed by Japan (28.25%) and Asian Development Bank (providing 19.96%). Chinese loans constituted 1.03% of foreign aid to the Philippines for the calendar year 2014.[64]

Consequently, China is more successful in scoring diplomatic successes in Cambodia and Myanmar than in the Philippines. In March 2012, Chinese President Hu Jintao made a formal visit to Phnom Penh. Hu promised to Prime Minister Hun Sen that China would provide economic assistance of 450 million yuan, including a grant of 250 million yuan. The two leaders also reached an agreement to expand the value of bilateral trade to 5 billion US dollars by 2017. In exchange for such commitments, Hun Sen reconfirmed that his government would try to resolve the South China Sea problem within the framework of ASEAN and China and that "Cambodia shared China's belief that the issue should not be internationalized."[65] Furthermore, China's growing influence on Cambodia became evident at the ASEAN Ministerial Meeting in July 2012. The Philippines and Vietnam asserted the inclusion of disputes of Scarborough Reef and "respect for the exclusive economic zone (EEZ)," respectively, into the joint statement at the conclusion of the meeting. However, Cambodia, the chair and host country for that year, showed a cautious stance, on the grounds that the inclusion of these issues would raise tension with China. Eventually, ASEAN foreign ministers failed to issue a joint statement for the first time in the ASEAN Ministerial Meeting's 45-year history.

In the case of Myanmar, when its President Thein Sein made a formal visit to Beijing in May 2011, Thein Sein pledged to his Chinese counterpart Hu Jintao that his new government maintained support for the "One China" policy and backed China regarding the South China Sea problem. This pledge was provided in return for China's support for Myanmar's taking ASEAN's chairmanship in 2014 and financial support for a number of development projects.[66]

Unlike its aid relation, the Philippines' trade relation with China is more asymmetrical. After the Scarborough Shoal incident, Chinese quarantine authorities reportedly blocked hundreds of container vans of Philippine bananas from entering Chinese ports, claiming that the fruit contained pests. This measure to quarantine the bananas delivered a telling blow to the Philippines that exported more than 30% of total bananas to China. In March 2012, China accounted for 14.9% of Philippine exports, with 642 million US dollars in shipments, up 27.8% from the same month in 2011.[67] By 2013, China was already the Philippines' second largest market for its export products after Japan and its largest source of imports.[68]

The above cases reveal that interdependence in the areas of trade and aid can be exploited to achieve strategic aims and that China is willing to exploit asymmetrical trade dependence. Unlike Cambodia and Myanmar, the Philippines was less dependent on Chinese assistance. However, Vietnam's trade dependence was higher than the Philippines, as China's share in Vietnam's total trade increased from 13.2% in 2005 to 19.0% in 2013 and Vietnam's industrial growth was heavily dependent on intermediate goods imported from China.[69] On the other hand, China's share in the Philippines' overall trade as of the first semester of 2015 was 13.1%.[70]

Realist objectives, liberal means 137

Strengthening China's commitments to institutional linkages with ASEAN

Apart from fostering trustworthy relationships, the development of China's western region is a primary objective of its economic cooperation with ASEAN.[71] Maritime infrastructure in littoral Mekong countries would therefore benefit China's four land-locked western provinces of Yunnan, Guangxi, Sichuan, and Guizhou. In this light, the Chinese government initiated two institutions for maritime cooperation with ASEAN. The first is Pan-Beibu Gulf (PBG) economic cooperation, which was proposed when the first forum on PBG economic cooperation was held in Nanning in July 2006. The PBG cooperation involves not only China and Vietnam but also other maritime ASEAN members, such as Malaysia, Indonesia, Brunei, Singapore, and the Philippines. The members of the PBG cooperation have organized an annual forum to confirm the progress of various projects. The PBG cooperation prioritizes the development of a transportation hub by water, targeting Fangcheng Port, Qinzhou Port, and Beihai Port in the coastal area of Guangxi, as well as Hai Phong Port and Gailing Port on the northern coast of Vietnam, in order to expand trade in southwest and mid-west China and the north of the Indochina peninsula.[72]

The second is the establishment of a permanent fund for maritime cooperation. When the 14th ASEAN–China summit was held in Bali in November 2011, Premier Wen proposed the establishment of the ASEAN–China Maritime Cooperation Fund with 3 billion yuan (484 million US dollars). The fund aims to promote practical cooperation in the areas of maritime connectivity, marine research, and environmental protection, and navigation safety between China and ASEAN members. Wen's announcement was followed by a Workshop on the Regional Oceanography of the South China Sea, which was held in Qingdao, China, in 2011.[73] Moreover, a Workshop on China–ASEAN Maritime Cooperation in the South China Sea was held in June 2012.[74] When the 4th ASEAN–China Senior Officials' Meeting on the implementation of the DOC was held in Beijing in January 2012, both sides agreed to take advantage of the established maritime cooperation fund and organize seminars and workshops to promote practical maritime cooperation between China and ASEAN members.[75]

China's commitment to institution building for maritime cooperation with ASEAN became more intensive at the onset of the Xi-Li regime in March 2013. A key idea is the 21st-century Maritime Silk Road (MSR). This idea was revealed in Xi Jinping's speech at the Indonesian Parliament in October 2013. Xi stated that:

> Southeast Asia has since ancient times been an important hub along the ancient Maritime Silk Road. China will strengthen maritime cooperation with ASEAN countries to make good use of the China–ASEAN Maritime Cooperation Fund set up by the Chinese government and vigorously develop maritime partnership in a joint effort to build the Maritime Silk Road of the 21st century.[76]

Comprising the "One Belt, One Road" project in parallel to the Silk Road Economic Belt, the MSR aims to develop economic-oriented practical cooperation and foster trustworthy relationships by relying on the distinctive values and ideas of the ancient Silk Road. Indeed, the MSR covers broad areas, including Indian Ocean countries such as Sri Lanka, and the Maldives, Southeast Asia, as the first stop on the MSR outside China was very crucial for the project. In fact, the main theme of the 2014 China–ASEAN Expo was "jointly building the 21st Century Maritime Silk Road."[77]

The MSR is a symbolic concept to promote cooperation on maritime connectivity, port and harbor development, and maritime commerce. Concrete institutions are necessary to realize the concept. One of them was launched by President Xi during a meeting with Asian leaders in November 2014. Xi made a pledge to establish the Silk Road Fund with 40 billion US dollars. China had announced the establishment of the Asian Infrastructure Investment Bank (AIIB) in October 2013.[78] The fund has an open and flexible nature and constitutes a fine alternative to the ADB in financing infrastructure constructions in Asian countries.[79]

China's MSR initiative gained positive feedback from the ASEAN side. For instance, a former director of ASEAN Community Affairs Development stated that the creation of the new MSR is a very good concept and will bring new opportunities for China and ASEAN to cooperate in many sectors, such as trade, infrastructure, and cultural exchange.[80] However, the possibility that the initiatives in advancing multilateral institutions will have spill-over effects on security relations depend on the extent to which such initiatives enhance political mutual trust. Namely, as long as aggressive actions in the South China Sea contribute to enhancing political mistrust, diplomatic efforts in forging closer institutional linkages do not yield expected outcomes.

Conclusion

In this chapter, we examined China's and Japan's policies towards Southeast Asia in the context of maritime dispute and analyzed the impacts of these rival policies on the formation of institutions for maritime security. In so doing, the essay considered economic and institutional elements, examining how the two great powers have employed liberal toolkits in pursuit of their maritime interests in the South China Sea.

Japan has consistently employed economic measures, particularly foreign aid, to attract ASEAN to its side, occasionally influenced its agenda, and succeeded in extending the scope of its cooperation with ASEAN or its member countries on security affairs. While China too utilized economic resources to attract Cambodia and Myanmar in order to gain their support for its position in the South China Sea, it exploited asymmetrical dependence as a means of exerting pressure on a rival claimant.

Both states have utilized existing institutions and, on various occasions, initiated the formation of new institutions to pursue political-security objectives in relation to maritime disputes in the South China Sea. Japan previously aimed

Realist objectives, liberal means 139

at resolving purely maritime safety problems but gradually intensified maritime security objectives in forming bilateral and multilateral institutions. China has sought to strengthen institutional cooperation with ASEAN by expanding the base of cooperation to broader maritime issues, which would be conducive to practical economic benefits. Thus, Japan has found the value in formal institutions as a means of statecraft while China has strategically utilized the institutions as the base of cooperation and trust building.

Notes

1 See, for instance, Michael McDevitt. "The South China Sea and U.S. Policy Options." *American Foreign Policy Interests*, 35 (2013): 175–87; David Scott. "India's Role in the South China Sea: Geopolitics and Geoeconomics in Play." *India Review*, 12, no. 2 (2013): 51–69; Ian Storey. "Japan's Maritime Security Interests in Southeast Asia and the South China Sea Dispute." *Political Science*, 65, no. 2 (2013): 135–56; and Hong Zhao. "The South China Sea Dispute and China–ASEAN Relations." *Asian Affairs*, 44, no. 1 (2013): 27–43.
2 Jingdong Yuan. "Emerging Maritime Rivalry in the South China Sea: Territorial Disputes, Sea-lane Security, and the Pursuit of Power." Paper prepared for the International Security Research and Outreach Programme, International Security and Intelligence Bureau, September 12, 2012; Michael Yahuda. "China's New Assertiveness in the South China Sea." *Journal of Contemporary China*, 22, no. 81 (2013): 446–59.
3 Avery Goldstein and Edward D. Mansfield (eds.). *The Nexus of Economics, Security, and International Relations in East Asia*. Stanford, CA: Stanford University Press, 2012.
4 Ralf Emmers. "ASEAN's Search for Neutrality in the South China Sea." *Asian Journal of Peacebuilding*, 2, no. 1 (2014): 61–77.
5 The use of attraction or co-optation in foreign policy and international politics literature is often associated with Joseph Nye's notion of soft power, which is defined as the ability to affect others to obtain the outcomes one wants through attraction rather than coercion or payment. In this chapter, we view foreign aid and use of formal institutions as diplomatic toolkits that can be used to co-opt and/or to coerce target states. See Joseph S. Nye, Jr. *Soft Power: The Means to Success in World Politics*. New York: Public Affairs, 2004.
6 James Reilly. "China's Economic Statecraft: Turning Wealth into Power." *Analysis*. Sydney: Lowy Institute for International Policy, November 2013.
7 For a brief summary of these disputes, see Tuosheng Zhang. "Disputes over Territories and Maritime Rights and Interests: Their Political Economic Implications." In *The Nexus of Economics, Security, and International Relations in East Asia*, edited by A. Goldstein and E. D. Mansfield, 120–43. Stanford, CA: Stanford University Press, 2012.
8 The Kantian tripod for peace includes democracy, interdependence, and membership in international organizations.
9 Peter Cain. "Capitalism, War and Internationalism in the Thought of Richard Cobden." *British Journal of International Studies*, 5, no. 3 (1979): 229–47; Arthur R. Stein. "Governments, Economic Interdependence, and International Cooperation." In *Behavior, Society and International Conflict, vol. 3*, edited by P. Tetlock, et al., 241–324. New York: Oxford University Press, 1993.
10 Susan M. McMillan. "Interdependence and Conflict." *Mershon International Studies Review*, 41, no. 1 (1997): 33–58.
11 The statecraft is defined as "the use of policy instruments to satisfy the core objectives of nation-states in the international system." See Michael Mastanduno. "Economics and Security in Statecraft and Scholarship." *International Organization*, 52, no. 4 (1998): 826.

12 Albert O. Hirschman. *National Power and the Structure of Foreign Trade.* Berkeley, CA: University of California Press, 1980; David A. Baldwin. *Economic Statecraft.* Princeton, NJ: Princeton University Press, 1985.
13 Michael Mastanduno. "Economics Statecraft." In *Foreign Policy: Theories, Actors, Cases,* edited by S. Smith, A. Hadfield, and T. Dunne. Oxford: Oxford University Press, 2008.
14 Robert D. McKinlay and R. Little. "A Foreign Policy Model of U.S. Bilateral Aid Allocation." *World Politics,* 30, no. 1 (1977): 62–4.
15 Alberto Alesina and David Dollar. "Who Gives Foreign Aid to Whom and Why?" *Journal of Economic Growth,* 5, no. 1 (2000): 33–63.
16 G. John Ikenberry. *After Victory: Institutions, Strategic Restraint, and the Rebuilding of Order after Major Wars,* 67. Princeton, NJ: Princeton University Press, 2001.
17 Stephan Haggard. "Liberal Pessimism: International Relations Theory and the Emerging Powers." *Asia and Pacific Policy Studies,* 1, no. 1 (2014): 1–17.
18 Robert O. Keohane. *After Hegemony: Cooperation and Discord in the World Political Economy.* Princeton, NJ: Princeton University Press, 1984.
19 Robert Jervis. "Realism, Neoliberalism, and Cooperation: Understanding the Debate." In *Progress in International Relations Theory: Appraising the Field,* edited by C. Elman and M. F. Elman, 296. Cambridge, MA: MIT Press, 2003.
20 Charles L. Glaser. "Realists as Optimists: Cooperation as Self-help." *International Security,* 19, no. 3 (1994/95): 85.
21 Hung Son Nguyen. "ASEAN–Japan Strategic Partnership in Southeast Asia: Maritime Security and Cooperation." Tokyo: Japan Center for International Exchange, 2013, 220. http://www.jcie.org/japan/j/pdf/pub/publst/1451/12_nguyen.pdf.
22 Ian Storey. "Japan Steps Up to the South China Sea Plate: Tokyo is Confronting Beijing and Increasing Defence Ties with ASEAN Members to Protect Maritime Trade." *Wall Street Journal.* July 9, 2012. http://www.wsj.com/articles/SB10001424052702303567704577516252626896574.
23 Min Gyo Koo. *Island Disputes and Maritime Regime Building in East Asia: Between a Rock and a Hard Place.* Dordrecht: Springer, 2009.
24 Storey. "Japan's Maritime Security Interests in Southeast Asia and the South China Sea Dispute," 2013.
25 William Depasupil. "Japan to Defend PH from China." *The Manila Times.* June 27, 2013. http://www.manilatimes.net/japan-to-defend-ph-from-china/13666/.
26 Information Office of the State Council of the People's Republic of China (PRC). *China's Foreign Aid.* Beijing, PRC: State Council, 2014. http://english.gov.cn/archive/white_paper/2014/08/23/content_281474982986592.htm.
27 Ibid.
28 "Cabinet Decision on the Development Cooperation Charter." February 10, 2015. http://www.mofa.go.jp/files/000067701.pdf.
29 Ministry of Foreign Affairs (MOFA). *Japan's Official Development Assistance White Paper 2006.* Tokyo: MOFA, 2006. http://www.mofa.go.jp/policy/oda/white/2006/ODA2006/html/honpen/index.htm.
30 Martin Fackler. "Japan Ends Decades-long Ban on Export of Weapons." *The New York Times.* April 1, 2014. http://www.nytimes.com/2014/04/02/world/asia/japan-ends-half-century-ban-on-weapons-exports.html?_r=1.
31 Atsushi Hiroshima. "Abe Administration Seeks to Revise ODA Charter to Assist Militaries." *The Asahi Shimbun.* April 1, 2014. Available from: http://ajw.asahi.com/article/behind_news/politics/AJ201404010044.
32 Julius Cesar I. Trajano. "Japan–Philippine Relations: New Dynamics in Strategic Partnership." *RSIS Commentaries,* 037 (2013). February 28, 2013. https://dr.ntu.edu.sg/bitstream/handle/10220/13333/RSIS0372013.pdf?sequence=1.

Realist objectives, liberal means 141

33 The first joint naval exercise between Japan and the Philippines was held on July 13, 2015 off Manila bay. The drill was focused on combating piracy and armed robbery at sea.
34 Tim Kelly and Nobuhiro Kubo. "Testing Beijing, Japan Eyes Growing Role in South China Sea Security." *Reuters*. March 10, 2015. http://www.reuters.com/article/ 2015/03/11/us-japan-southchinasea-idUSKBN0M62B920150311.
35 National Institute for Defence Studies (NIDS). *East Asian Strategic Review 2014*, 144–5. Tokyo: NIDS, 2014.
36 Storey, 2013, 141.
37 Australia and the United States became the 19th and 20th parties in August 2013 and in September 2014, respectively.
38 Kimihiro Ishikane. "After the Closing of ASEAN Plus Three and East Asia Summit. A Report at the 48th Policy Plenary Meeting." December 19. Tokyo: The Council on East Asia Community, 2011.
39 "The Eighth East Asia Summit." http://www.mofa.go.jp/mofaj/area/page3_000488. html.
40 "Chairman's Statement of the 8th East Asia Summit." October 10, 2013. http://www. asean.org/storage/images/archive/23rdASEANSummit/chairmans%20statement%20 -%208th%20east%20asia%20summit%20-%20final.pdf.
41 "The Holding of the First Japan–Philippines Dialogue on Maritime and Oceanic Affairs." September 9, 2011. http://www.mofa.go.jp/mofaj/press/release/23/9/0909_09.html.
42 "The Sixth Japan–ASEAN Defence Vice-Ministerial Meeting." http://www.mod. go.jp/j/approach/exchange/dialogue/asia_tokyoseminar/06a.html.
43 "Chairman's Statement of the 17th ASEAN–Japan Summit. November 12, 2014, Nay Pyi Taw, Myanmar," 2. http://www.mofa.go.jp/files/000059372.pdf.
44 "17th Japan–ASEAN Summit Meeting, MOFA." http://www.mofa.go.jp/a_o/rp/ page3e_000260.html.
45 Department of National Defense (DND). "Philippines and Japan Ink Defence Cooperation Agreement." Manila: DND, 2015. http://www.dndph.org/2015-updates/ philippines-and-japan-ink-defense-cooperation-agreement.
46 Joshua Kurlantzick. *Charm Offensive: How China's Soft Power is Transforming the World*. New Haven, CT: Yale University Press, 2007.
47 The Joint Statement on Good Neighbourliness was contained in ASEAN– China Cooperation in the 21st century statement in Kuala Lumpur, Malaysia on December 1997. A copy of the statement is available from: http://asean. org/?static_post=joint-statement-of-the-meeting-of-heads-of-stategovernment-of-the-member-states-of-asean-and-the-president-of-the-people-s-republic-of-china-kuala-lumpur-malaysia-16-december-1997.
48 China's pledge to increase assistance to ASEAN was contained in the speech of former Chinese premier Zhu Rongji on the occasion of Fourth ASEAN–China Summit in Singapore in November 2000. A copy of the speech is available from: http://www. fmprc.gov.cn/zdjn/eng/zywj/t270549.htm.
49 Evelyn Goh. *The Struggle for Order: Hegemony, Hierarchy, and Transition in Post-Cold War East Asia*, 105–6. Oxford: Oxford University Press, 2013.
50 M. Taylor Fravel. "China's Strategy in the South China Sea." *Contemporary Southeast Asia*, 33, no. 3 (2011): 306.
51 On July 12, 2016, the Permanent Court of Arbitration, based in The Hague, issued its decision in favor of the Philippines, which effectively invalidated China's "nine-dash line" and historic claim on nearly the entire South China Sea.
52 Robert Sutter. "China's Regional Strategy and Why it May Not Be Good for America." In *Power Shift: China and Asia's New Dynamics*, edited by David Shambaugh, 290. Berkeley, CA: University of California Press, 2006.
53 China's foreign aid does not meet the Development Assistance Committee of the Organization for Economic Cooperation and Development's (DAC/OECD) definition

of ODA, nor conform to its standards. For a brief overview of characteristics of Chinese aid, see Deborah Brautigam. "Aid with Chinese Characteristics: Chinese Foreign Aid and Development Finance meet the OECD-DAC Aid Regime." *Journal of International Development*, 23, no. 5 (2011): 752–64. The authors used foreign aid or economic assistance instead of ODA to refer to Chinese aid in this paper.
54 Naohiro Kitano and Yukinori Harada. "Estimating China's Foreign Aid 2001–2013." *Working Paper* No. 78. Tokyo: Japan International Cooperation Agency Research Institute (JICA RI), 2014.
55 Information Office of the State Council of the PRC. *China's Foreign Aid*. 2014.
56 Dennis D. Trinidad. *China and Japan's Economic Cooperation with the Southeast Asian Region: The Foreign Aid of a Rising and a Mature Asian Power*, 6. Tokyo: The Japan Institute of International Affairs (JIIA), 2013.
57 Ibid.
58 Jeffrey Reeves. "China's Unraveling Engagement Strategy." *Washington Quarterly*, 36, no. 4 (2013): 143.
59 Peakdey Heng. "Chinese Investment and Aid in Cambodia: A Controversial Affair." *East Asia Forum*. July 16, 2013. http://www.eastasiaforum.org/2013/07/16/chinese-investment-and-aid-in-cambodia-a-controversial-affair/.
60 The Council for the Development of Cambodia "Investment Trend." 2016. http://www.cambodiainvestment.gov.kh/investment-enviroment/investment-trend.html; World Trade Organization (WTO). "Trade Profiles: Cambodia." 2014. http://stat.wto.org/CountryProfile/WSDBCountryPFView.aspx?Language=E&Country=KH.
61 Chanboreth Ek and Hach Sok. "Aid Effectiveness in Cambodia." *Working Paper* 7. Washington, DC: Wolfensohn Centre for Development, 2008; Council for the Development of Cambodia (CDC). *The Cambodia Aid Effectiveness Report 2010*, 33–6. Phnom Penh: The Cambodian Rehabilitation and Development Board of the CDC, Royal Government of Cambodia, 2010. http://www.cdc-crdb.gov.kh/cdc/third_cdcf/aer_2010_en.pdf.
62 Heng, "Chinese Investment and Aid in Cambodia," 2013.
63 For an overview of these controversies, see *The PCIJ Blog*. "U.P. Study Finds North Rail Contract Illegal, Disadvantageous to Government." 2005. http://pcij.org/blog/2005/09/29/up-study-finds-north-rail-contract-illegal-diadvantageous-to-government.
64 National Economic and Development Authority (NEDA). *ODA Portfolio Review 2014*, 9. Pasig City, Philippines: Monitoring and Evaluation Staff, 2015.
65 Prak Chan Thul. "Hu Wants Cambodia Help on China Sea Dispute, Pledges Aid." *Reuters*. April 1, 2012. http://www.reuters.com/article/us-cambodia-china-idUSBRE82U04Y20120331.
66 Irrawaddy. "Burma–China Strategic Alliance Threatens ASEAN Unity." May 30, 2011. http://www2.irrawaddy.org/article.php?art_id=21390.
67 "The China–Philippine Banana War." *Asia Sentinel*. June 6, 2012. http://www.asiasentinel.com/society/the-china-philippine-banana-war/.
68 Philippine Statistics Authority (PSA). *Foreign Trade*. Manila: PSA, 2014. http://www.nscb.gov.ph/secstat/d_trade.asp.
69 Daisuke Hosokawa. "*Betonamu no keizai to anzenhosho* [Vietnam's Economy and Security]." *Kokusai Mondai*, 634 (2014): 27–9.
70 Philippine Statistics Authority (PSA). *Philippine Major Trading Partners: First Semester 2015*. 2016. https://psa.gov.ph/sites/default/files/attachments/itsd/special release/TABLE%204%20%20Philippine%20Major%20Trading%20Partners%20%20 First%20Semester%202015.pdf.
71 Truong Giang Bui. "ASEAN and China Relations: Seeking for Economic Cooperation." In *Making New Partnership: A Rising China and Its Neighbors*, edited by Zhang Yunling. UK: Paths International and Beijing: Social Sciences Academic Press, 2011.

72 Xiaosong Gu and Mingjian Li. "Beibu Gulf: Emerging Sub-regional Integration between China and ASEAN." S. Rajaratnam School of International Studies (RSIS). *Working Paper* 168, 2009, 16–17. Singapore: RSIS.
73 "Remarks by Assistant Foreign Minister Liu Zhenmin at the Opening Ceremony of the Workshop on Implementing DOC: Maintaining Freedom and Safety of Navigation in the South China Sea." December 19, 2011. http://www.fmprc.gov.cn/mfa_eng/wjdt_665385/zyjh_665391/t888485.shtml.
74 Nazery Khalid. "Sea of Common Destiny: Promoting Economic Cooperation in the South China Sea." Presented at International Workshop on Regional Responses to the Current Situation in the South China Sea. Haikou, Hainan, China, August 31, 2013. http://www.mima.gov.my/mima/wp-content/uploads/Haikou%20(31Aug13).pdf.
75 Ibid.
76 "Speech by Chinese President Xi Jinping to Indonesian Parliament, 2 October 2013, Jakarta, Indonesia." http://www.asean-china-center.org/english/2013-10/03/c_133062675.htm.
77 "Silk Route to Bilateral Growth." *China Daily Asia*, September 19, 2014. http://www.chinadailyasia.com/asiaweekly/2014-09/19/content_15168301.html.
78 The AIIB came into operation in 2015 with 57 founding members.
79 Xinhuanet. "One Belt, One Road Initiatives Key for Building a Safer Asia: Experts." September 25, 2014. http://news.xinhuanet.com/english/china/2014-09/25/c_127030026.htm.
80 "ASEAN Welcomes China's New Maritime Silk Road Initiatives." *China Daily*. August 15, 2014. http://usa.chinadaily.com.cn/business/2014-08/15/content_18322921.htm.

10 The South China Sea conflict, the regional geo-economic order, and ASEAN's institutions

Kheng Swe Lim

The South China Sea dispute fuses issues of great-power politics, intricacies of international law, growing nationalist sentiment, disputed historical narratives, and resource competition. The dispute is a major source of tension in the Sino-Southeast Asian ties, but remains but one aspect of the relationship, which encompasses a range of political, security, and economic aspects. There seems to be a "separation of spheres" between the South China Sea conflict and other areas of the Sino-Southeast Asian relationship, with policymakers unwilling to let the former affect the latter. However, the reverse is not necessarily true, as economic ties between China and its Southeast Asian neighbors do have an indirect impact on the conduct of the South China Sea conflict, due to their effects on Association of Southeast Asian Nations (ASEAN) cohesion. It seems that, going forward, the lack of direct influence of economics on security matters in the South China Sea will continue to hold. However, structural differences in Southeast Asian countries' relations with China, primarily driven by economic interests, may affect the institution's ability to react strongly to crises in the South China Sea, thus providing more space to great-power rivalry. Going forward, the South China Sea disputes could be characterized by a "competition" between structural realist and constructivist ideas, with ASEAN's norms developing when the geopolitical space emerges for them to do so.

This chapter will first survey the development of the South China Sea conflict between 2009 and 2014, and will touch on the dynamics among ASEAN countries in responding to the disputes. It will next detail the broader geo-economic context in which the dispute has developed, and will then briefly survey the state of economic ties between China and Southeast Asia. Next, the chapter will make the case of the "separation of spheres" between China and Southeast Asia with regard to economic ties and the South China Sea dispute. Finally, it will look at how these aspects come together with ASEAN's weak institutional setup, and will touch briefly on the period from 2015 to the present.

For most of this chapter, there is a cut-off point around 2014 in order to gain some form of a "historical lens" on relations between China and Southeast Asia. The period from 2015 onwards is characterized by several events, most notably China's land reclamations in the South China Sea, that are still ongoing as of the time of writing. This means that the current period is still in flux, and the

The South China Sea conflict 145

lack of complete data makes it difficult to pin down the different variables in the South China Sea dispute with certainty. Furthermore, the increasing involvement of the United States in the South China Sea dispute in 2015, particularly given its Freedom of Navigation Operations (FONOPS), adds another actor into the mix, whereas, previously, the United States was primarily involved through the use of rhetoric and arms sales to the Philippines and Vietnam.

However, it would be unfair to exclude the present day altogether, and the final part of this chapter will touch on the period from 2015 onward. However, the speculative nature of the analyses will demonstrate the virtue of focusing the analytical lens on a period slightly removed in time when looking at the South China Sea. If China's land reclamations, the FONOPS by the United States, the election of Rodrigo Duterte, and the UN Convention on the Law of the Sea tribunal's decision on *Philippines v. China* can altogether be taken as turning points in the dispute, it would make sense to look deeper into the period before these turning points came to be in 2015–16. It would then be up to future historians and political scientists to place these two parts together in order to come up with a more detailed analysis of the sea dispute.

The development of the dispute and ASEAN's response to it

From 2009 to 2014, the South China Sea conflict saw an increase in the number of incidents at sea as well as in the sharpness of official and unofficial rhetoric coming from several of the claimant countries. The current phase of the conflict was sparked off by the joint Malaysian–Vietnamese submission to the United Nations Commission on the Continental Shelf. The entry of the United States into the conflict added another layer of complexity to the dispute by superimposing an element of great-power conflict on to what should be a regional sovereignty dispute, as has the use by the Philippines of international arbitration to press its case against China.

The Malaysian and Philippine joint submissions, and the ensuing rhetorical exchanges between the claimant countries, could not be avoided, as the claimant countries were treaty-bound to submit their claims by May 13, 2009. Given that the claims touched on national sovereignty, China had no real choice but to protest their submissions, which staked Malaysia's and Vietnam's claims over a large portion of the South China Sea, to the exclusion of China's claims. In responding to China, though, Malaysia and Vietnam took opposing tactics. The former made efforts to de-escalate tensions by stressing, in a *note verbale* to the commission, that its claims were "without prejudice" to the claims of other countries in the South China Sea.[1] However, Vietnam used its chairmanship of ASEAN to internationalize the dispute by organizing a series of conferences on the topic and bringing the subject up in international forums, including ASEAN-led ones.[2] It was during Vietnam's chairing of ASEAN that Hillary Clinton declared, at the ASEAN Regional Forum in Hanoi, that the freedom of navigation on the high seas and respect for international law in the South China Sea were in the US national interest, drawing an angry reaction from China.[3]

Clinton's statements brought the level of tension over the South China Sea dispute to a new level. Previously, the dispute was mainly a regional one between China and the South China Sea claimant countries, but after the ASEAN Regional Forum meeting, it began to be framed in terms of great-power conflict. Since then, the United States continued to weigh in publicly on the dispute. In 2014, Daniel Russel stressed that the United States deemed China's nine-dashed line to be inconsistent with international law, effectively declaring the line illegal, despite the United States' official stance of not taking any position on the merits of the sovereignty disputes in the South China Sea.[4] This gave the impression of the United States weighing in on the Philippine and Vietnamese side in the sovereignty disputes, contradicting its official policy of neutrality.

The Obama administration's involvement in the South China Sea dispute is part of the larger "pivot to Asia," which inspired a desire to disengage from the Middle East and focus foreign-policy energies on the Asia-Pacific region. Officially, the "pivot" focusses on the Trans-Pacific Partnership as its main pillar, with Mike Froman, the US Trade Representative, calling the deal "central" to the administration's plan.[5] However, the "pivot" has also involved US military outreach to the Vietnam and the Philippines. In 2014, the Philippines drew up a new defense arrangement with the United States, allowing US forces access to Philippine bases for the first time since they were evicted in the 1990s.[6] In the same year, the United States partially lifted its ban on selling weapons to Vietnam, to help boost Vietnam's maritime security.[7] Although the United States views these deals as lending support to its partners in Southeast Asia, in Chinese eyes, these actions look like part of an encirclement strategy. The internationalization of the dispute has therefore had the unintended effect of turning the South China Sea into a stage for great-power rivalry in Asia.

Furthermore, the South China Sea also became more "legalistic" during the period under consideration.[8] In January 2013, the Philippines initiated arbitration proceedings on the legality of the nine-dashed line, prompting China to issue a *note verbale* to the court rejecting the arbitration.[9] In 2014, Vietnam lodged a submission at the Permanent Court of Arbitration, where the proceedings were being heard, requesting that the court give "due regard" to Vietnam's legal rights in the South China Sea while hearing the Philippines' case.[10]

From the point of view of the Philippines, there are three main reasons why it resorted to arbitration. First, the Philippines claimed to have exhausted all other peaceful means of resolving the conflict, resorting to legal arbitration as a last recourse. Second, by taking the case to arbitration, the Philippines would get formal legal judgment to clarify its claims in the South China Sea; for example, there are issues about what consists an "inhabitable island" that are unclear under international law, and the court would be able to clarify these fine points of law and create a reference point for all claimants to agree to. Third, the court's rulings would have a large measure of moral power in the broader international community, and the Philippines believed that it could take the moral high ground over the public discourse over the dispute. Fourth, there is domestic politics:

The South China Sea conflict 147

President Benigno Aquino could demonstrate his resolve over the South China Sea in order to boost popular support for his government, as well as repudiate former president Gloria Arroyo's policy of keeping the South China Sea dispute under wraps.

Nevertheless, the proceedings faced a major problem, namely that China did not, and still does not, recognize them. Although the arbitration case continued without China's presence, in China's view, this fact makes the proceedings inherently illegitimate and one-sided. Furthermore, China viewed the Philippines' arbitration proceedings as a further provocation, given China's insistence that such matters should be handled bilaterally and without the involvement of outside parties.

Meanwhile, crises in the South China Sea continued to play out. In 2010, Chinese vessels cut the cables of a Vietnamese seismic exploration ship in disputed waters in the South China Sea. In 2012, the Scarborough Shoal incident broke out, which saw China seizing effective control of the Scarborough Shoal from the Philippines. In 2014, China tried, and failed, to block the Philippines from restocking the Sierra Madre, beached on the Second Thomas Shoal. The biggest crisis of 2014 was the *Haiyan Shiyou* 981 incident, when the China National Offshore Oil Corporation moved an oilrig into disputed waters between Vietnam and China, near the Paracel Islands. This caused massive popular anger within Vietnam, leading to protests. ASEAN foreign ministers, in a rare move, issued a statement expressing their "serious concerns on the on-going developments in the South China Sea," implying the oilrig incident.[11] China ended up pulling the oilrig out a month early, citing poor weather.

Malaysia had hitherto chosen to take a low profile, believing that, by lying low, it would be able to avoid confrontation with China. However, in 2013, four People's Liberation Army Navy (PLAN) warships sailed to James Shoal, where they conducted an oath-taking ceremony; these ships included the PLAN's most advanced amphibious assault ship, the *Jinggangshan*. In January 2014, Chinese warships again returned to James Shoal and conducted another oath-taking ceremony. The Malaysian authorities played down these incidents, saying that the ships had right of innocent passage through Malaysian waters.[12] Malaysia is building a naval base and Marine Corps base at Bintulu; although ostensibly to guard against piracy and protect Malaysia's oil production, the base is only 60 miles away from James Shoal.[13] However, compared to the Philippines and Vietnam, the Malaysian elites believe that talking about a "China threat" is a self-fulfilling prophecy, and therefore makes a deliberate attempt to not view China as a threat.[14] Meanwhile, among the claimant countries, Brunei has kept the lowest profile, as it occupies no features in the South China Sea and already has ample hydrocarbon resources within its territorial waters.

In all these crises over the South China Sea, ASEAN has kept relatively silent, although the conflict involves four of its ten members. ASEAN does play some role in helping to moderate the conflict; the intensity of the dispute for any particular year can be linked to which country in ASEAN happens to be the chair then. For example, in 2010, Hillary Clinton's comments at the ASEAN Regional

Forum in Hanoi, which caused significant backlash from the Chinese, took place when Vietnam was the chair of ASEAN. In 2012, the ASEAN foreign ministers' meeting in Phnom Penh, for the first time in the grouping's history, was unable to form a consensus on issuing a joint statement. This was because the ASEAN chair, Cambodia, fell out with the Philippines over whether or not to include the Scarborough Shoal in the statement.

In 2013, though, Brunei avoided the controversies that occurred during the 2012 chairmanship, and Noelan Arbis writes that it did so by maintaining a "neutral stance" and using diplomacy with both China and the Philippines to build confidence with both countries.[15] The next year, Myanmar played a balancing act on the South China Sea, including the dispute on the agenda as a "minimum" while being aware that it was "not Myanmar's fight."[16] Furthermore, during the Brunei and Myanmar chairmanships, Thailand acted as the coordinating country for ASEAN–China relations. Thailand played an important role in the negotiations preceding the first code of conduct consultations in 2013.[17] In contrast to Vietnam's attempts to internationalize the dispute, Bangkok chose to work the problem out between ASEAN and China, as opposed to bringing other great powers into the dispute.[18]

A disinterested, capable ASEAN chair could use its position to tone down the rhetoric surrounding the South China Sea disputes, thus helping de-escalation. However, ASEAN's institutions of consensus and dialogue mean that it will be unable to move rapidly to tackle any immediate problems that suddenly emerge, making it unable to react to crises that emerge in the South China Sea. This is because ASEAN consists of ten member countries, each with differing national interests *vis-à-vis* China. For example, Thailand, Laos, and Cambodia have very strong economic ties with China, and are unwilling to do anything that could potentially jeapardize these links; Indonesia is interested in cooperating with China in order to develop its maritime infrastructure; Myanmar is trying hard to balance between opening to the West and keeping civil relations with China; and six out of the ten countries have no national stake in the South China Sea, and are unwilling to make it an issue in their relations.

Finding consensus among all of these parties would mean having to appeal to the lowest common denominator of their interests. Furthermore, China's insistence that the sovereignty disputes are handled bilaterally and not multilaterally means that ASEAN as a whole cannot negotiate on the very heart of the problem. The stresses that the different national interests place on ASEAN's unity will be discussed in the section below.

The South China Sea conflict: the broader regional economic context

As mentioned earlier, the current phase of the South China Sea conflict was sparked off in May 2009, when Malaysia and Vietnam made a joint submission to the Commission on the Limits of the Continental Shelf, under the auspices of the United Nations, thus inviting an assertive Chinese response. However, before the joint submission of 2009, Ralf Emmers wrote that the territorial disputes remained a security issue, but one of a "much less salient nature."[19] He attributed this to a combination of factors, including:

> the lessening of the China threat image, the limited Chinese power projection in the South China Sea, Vietnam joining ASEAN in 1995, the downplaying of nationalist rhetoric, the limited proven oil reserves in the area, and the restrained U.S. involvement in the conflict.[20]

In order to narrow the focus to economic factors, I will focus on the lessening of the "China threat." In 2000, China was still a rapidly developing economy, and needed good relations with its neighbors in Southeast Asia in order to ensure a peaceful international environment, conducive to economic development. In order to do so, China had to build confidence among its neighbors. This was lacking before 2000, for several reasons. Firstly, the 1997 Asian financial crisis had hit the Southeast Asian economies badly, and they were still in the process of economic recovery. At the same time, China entered the World Trade Organization in 2000, causing worries that foreign investment would flow to China instead of Southeast Asia.[21] Second, China's behavior in the South China Sea did not inspire confidence among its neighbors. In 1995, China occupied and built three structures atop the Mischief Reef atoll, also claimed by the Philippines. China completed construction in 1999, which made the Philippines file a diplomatic protest against China.[22] The Philippines, nervous about these actions, ran the rusting BRP *Sierra Madre* aground on the Second Thomas Shoal, not far from Mischief Reef, in order to retain a presence in the area.[23] Furthermore, the 1996 Taiwan Straits crisis and US Navy's intervention in the crisis raised tensions in the region.

China sought to change the situation in order to ensure a friendly geopolitical environment conducive to domestic economic growth by participating more actively in the regional multilateral framework, going on what Emmers calls a "charm offensive" in Southeast Asia and becoming the first non-ASEAN country to sign the Treaty of Amity and Cooperation.[24] Although China had been a dialogue partner of ASEAN since 1996, it moved the relationship up one level by signing a strategic partnership with ASEAN in 2003.[25] China had also bought itself good will in Southeast Asia by not devaluing its currency during the Asian financial crisis.[26] Alice Ba argues that the signing and implementation of the China–ASEAN Free Trade Agreement gave China a chance to ensure that the economies of Southeast Asia remain stable, as a crisis in one could easily spill over into China's economy.[27] In light of these economic priorities, China was therefore more willing to accommodate the needs of its Southeast Asian partners, including over the South China Sea.[28] The countries of ASEAN, meanwhile, also hoped that by interlocking the Chinese and ASEAN economies, relations between the two parties would improve thereafter.[29]

After 2009, though, the balance of economic power between China and the ASEAN countries began to shift. As China's links with Southeast Asian countries have increased and its economy has grown to rival that of the United States, it has become less important for China to continue to de-emphasize the conflict, unlike the previous period when China was still trying to strengthen its ties with ASEAN. These dynamics frame the current phase of the South China Sea conflict as China, now the world's second largest economy and properly integrated into the rest of the world economy, can afford to act in a more assertive manner on matters it deems to be in its national interest. This does not mean that the fluctuations in the balance of economic power between China and the other claimant countries in the South China Sea are the sole reason behind the increase in tensions, but the broader backdrop remains that of China's heightened levels of economic integration with Southeast Asia, including the other claimant countries to the South China Sea.

Despite the controversy over the South China Sea dispute, the economic aspects of the broader Sino-Southeast Asian relationship have generally progressed well. There seems to be a "separation of spheres," by which the South China Sea disputes are relegated to a sphere of their own, with their negative effects not spilling over into other aspects of Sino-Southeast Asian relations. However, the arrow of causality may actually point the other way, and China's strong trade and investment links with Southeast Asian countries could indirectly affect how Southeast Asian countries are able to handle the South China Sea disputes.

China's economic influence is strongest among the countries of mainland Southeast Asia, in particular, Laos, Cambodia, and Thailand. In Laos, for example, China is taking advantage of the government's policy of "turning land into capital," investing heavily in hydroelectric dams, real estate, mining, and retail. Between 1989 and 2014, about 33% of Laos's total foreign direct investment originated from China.[30] China also provides vast amounts of aid to Cambodia, promising US$500–700 billion annually in development loans.[31] China's economic links with Thailand are also deep, and Thai companies such as the Chaoren Pokphand (CP) Group are major investors in China. None of these countries are claimants to the South China Sea, meaning that the dispute does not affect their relations with Beijing. In the case of the countries of maritime Southeast Asia, though, China's economic influence is not as vast as with the countries of mainland Southeast Asia. All three countries are major trading nations, and China is trying to reach out economically to them; for example, Malaysia and China are jointly developing industrial parks in Kuantan, Malaysia, and Qinzhou, China. Nevertheless, these countries are relatively less politically and economically dependent on China than their counterparts in mainland Southeast Asia.

Despite the fact that Vietnam and the Philippines are the main Southeast Asian players in the South China Sea dispute, they maintain economic ties with China. China is Vietnam's second largest trading partner, and China's trade with Vietnam actually increased by 29.8% from 2012 to 2013, while the South China Sea dispute was heating up.[32] This is not to say that Sino-Vietnamese relations are completely insulated from the bad feelings that result from the South China Sea conflict. The riots in Vietnam that damaged several foreign-owned factories were the result of the intense nationalism in Vietnam stoked by the South China Sea conflict.³³ The very fact that China even has such factories in Vietnam, though, is illustrative of the strong investment links between both countries. Le Hong Hiep writes that Vietnam's policy involves building up its military and strengthening its relations with the United States, while at the same time maintaining strong trade and investment links with the Chinese; this is part of a "hedging" strategy which allows these two contradictory strands to coexist.³⁴

The case of the Philippines is a bit different, at least during the period in question. Much of the groundwork for Sino-Philippine economic ties was laid in the early 2000s, when President Joseph Estrada signed a Joint Declaration on the Framework of Bilateral Cooperation in the 21st Century with China. Since the agreement, trade ties between both countries soared, making China the Philippine's third largest trading partner in 2011.³⁵ Philippine exports to China still made up 12% of the country's total exports in 2013, and Philippine Trade Secretary Gregorio Domingo went on record as saying that, "We are separating the commercial relationship from the political and security relationship."³⁶ Nevertheless, the Philippines worries about asymmetrical dependence on China; its trade with China was the lowest among the ASEAN-5 countries in 2011, and its foreign direct investment in China remains small, despite being one of the earliest foreign investors in China.³⁷

To sum up, despite the South China Sea dispute, economic ties between both China and Southeast Asia as a whole remain strong. The case of Malaysia and Vietnam demonstrates that it is possible to maintain strong economic ties despite the territorial disputes in the South China Sea; in fact, Vietnam maintains excellent economic relations with China despite high levels of tensions over maritime affairs. The Philippines breaks with this general pattern, as it does not seem to go out of its way to encourage economic ties with China, but even so, China is still an important trading partner.

The "separation of spheres" and the security–economic nexus in China–Southeast Asia relations

What can we conclude about the interactions between the South China Sea conflict and the region's ASEAN-centered institutional order? Although the Sea dispute is a disturbing factor in the broader Sino-Southeast Asian relationship, it has had little influence on the broader economic relationship between these two regions. Sino-Southeast Asian relations have definitely become tenser, but have not reached the point where the governments of China or the other claimant countries decide to sacrifice the gains from regional economic interactions for the sake of their South China Sea claims. In general, the South China Sea disputes are kept within one sphere, and other aspects of the Sino-Southeast Asian relationship are kept in another, with little interaction between the two. It can be said that, instead of a security–economic "nexus," there is a "compartmentalization"; a "separation of spheres" where the increasing security issues in the South China Sea seem not to have too strong an effect on the everyday conduct of Sino-Southeast Asian economic relations.

However, Sino-Southeast Asian economic ties may have some effect on ASEAN's institutions themselves, which has an indirect impact on the South China Sea dispute. The events during Cambodia's chairmanship of ASEAN showed that Cambodia, which enjoys strong economic ties with China, was not willing to table the South China Sea dispute. Teasing causality out of this correlation is tricky; did Cambodia take this stance because of its economic links with China; because of its strong political links with Beijing; because of a true belief that the South China Sea dispute should not be discussed at an ASEAN forum; or a combination of all of the above? Regardless of the causal links, though, we can say that ASEAN's institutional setup, lacking a strong center, makes it difficult for the institution to stage a firm response to the South China Sea disputes.

It seems that the South China Sea dispute does not square easily with the use of a liberal institutionalist or a constructivist lens. All parties in Southeast Asia ultimately look to "hedge" and preserve the benefits of economic interactions with China while seeking to maximize their own gains in the South China Sea (or, in the case of non-claimant states, to minimize their involvement in the Sea dispute). It could be argued that ASEAN's focus on consensus and non-confrontation represents the construction of a new norm by which to replace the anarchy of the international system. However, the problems created by the South China Sea dispute during the period in question appear to have overridden this norm. Perhaps the situation would have been different if ASEAN was founded with stronger centralized institutions and the ability of the secretariat to override the interests of individual countries, but there is no way for analysts to test whether this scenario would be true.

Possible implications for the future

All this while, the chapter has avoided straying into the more recent period, marked by the land reclamations, the FONOPs of the United States, the Philippine arbitration case, and the election of President Rodrigo Duterte. However, we can make some preliminary extrapolations.

ASEAN's institutions do not seem to be able to respond quickly to crises in the South China Sea, but its norms are often used when the geopolitical space to do so emerges. At the same time, the active presence of the US Navy near the disputed waters and reclaimed areas leads to many potential flashpoints between China and the United States. The dispute, therefore, may come to depend less on diplomatic efforts by ASEAN and more crisis management, diplomacy, and lines of communication between China and the United States, the two great powers in the region. One the one hand, this casts the "great-power" element of the South China Sea dispute into sharper relief. On the other hand, this may, surprisingly, create a more stable status quo in the South China Sea; as the two primary players in the South China Sea emerge and their stances become clearer, it may be easier to draw up a series of expectations and informal rules between them both. This may lead to a new status quo that, while not ideal (as the South China Sea becomes more militarized), would be amenable to professional crisis management between the two great powers. This would place greater emphasis on the balance of power between China and the United States, and less on the power of institutions.

A second stabilizing factor may come from, unexpectedly, the resolution of the Philippine arbitration case and the election of Rodrigo Duterte as Philippine president. The tribunal ruled in favor of the Philippines and against China. However, while the tribunal was still deliberating, the uncertainty that the case presented cast a cloud over South China Sea diplomacy. Now, there is some certainty over how the case has unfolded, making it possible to orchestrate the appropriate reactions.

The ruling itself is less important than how the different parties react, particularly the Philippines and China. Given China's belief in the illegitimacy of the tribunal due to its lack of participation, it has reiterated its non-recognition of the validity of the arbitration ruling. What is interesting is that the new Philippine president has, as of the time of writing, been cautious in his response, warning not to "taunt or flaunt" after the hearing or "put the country in an awkward position."[38] A Sino-Philippine *rapprochement* would remove one major stressor on ASEAN's institutions, namely Sino-Philippine tensions. In the long run, combined with effective Sino-US crisis management and lower regional tensions, ASEAN may be able to yield a framework to manage the South China Sea dispute based on the "ASEAN way." Some signs of this are emerging. China has supported the "dual-track" solution, first suggested by Brunei, of ensuring that disputes are resolved peacefully by parties directly concerned while China and ASEAN would maintain stability in the South China Sea.[39] Meanwhile, the Philippines has proposed establishing a "two-track" system, separating "contentious issues" from broader Sino-Philippine relations.[40]

These facts suggest a growing role for ASEAN's institutions and norms in managing the South China Sea dispute, particularly the use of peaceful negotiations and the non-involvement of ASEAN in immediate bilateral sovereign disputes. While there is room for norm construction, it would require a geopolitical space to develop, some of which may come about by chance (such as the nature of the balance of power between the great powers), and some that can be achieved by careful diplomacy and use of language. Theory-wise, the South China Sea dispute may develop into a "competition" between balance-of-power structural realism and the effort to build a set of ASEAN-centered norms. The question is whether ASEAN and China can use these geopolitical breathing spaces to construct new norms that will ultimately become the new geopolitical reality.

The highly speculative nature of this analysis shows the dangers of extrapolating from the present and the too-recent past. It is too difficult to analyze events that are still unfolding and creating a framework for them without venturing into the realm of crystal ball gazing, which social scientists try to avoid. However, such an exercise can still allow us to see the value of using theoretical frames of analysis in looking at thorny problems in international relations. At the very least, we can conclude that economics, great-power relations, and regional institutions have the potential to combine to act in unexpected but elegant ways in the international relations of Southeast Asia.

Notes

1. The text of Malaysia's *note verbale* to the United Nations Commission can be found at http://www.un.org/depts/los/clcs_new/submissions_files/mysvnm33_09/mys_re_chn_2009re_mys_vnm_e.pdf.
2. Alexander Vuving. "Vietnam, the US and Japan in the South China Sea." *The Diplomat*. November 26, 2014. http://thediplomat.com/2014/11/vietnam-the-us-and-japan-in-the-south-china-sea/.
3. Richard Weitz. "Why US Made Hanoi Move." *The Diplomat*. August 18, 2010. http://thediplomat.com/2010/08/why-us-made-hanoi-move/?allpages=yes.
4. Daniel Russel's full testimony can be found here: http://www.state.gov/p/eap/rls/rm/2014/02/221293.htm.
5. "America's Big Bet." *The Economist*. November 10, 2014. http://www.economist.com/news/special-report/21631797-america-needs-push-free-trade-pact-pacific-more-vigorously-americas-big-bet.
6. Seth Robson. "US Military's Return to the Philippines Sparks Economic Hopes." *Stars and Stripes*. August 21, 2014. http://www.stripes.com/news/us-military-s-return-to-the-philippines-sparks-economic-hopes-1.298937.
7. "US to Partially Lift Vietnam Arms Embargo." *BBC News*. October 2, 2014. http://www.bbc.com/news/world-us-canada-29469719.
8. Li Mingjiang. "Possible Consequences of the Philippines' South China Sea Arbitration Case." Asian Maritime Transparency Initiative. https://amti.csis.org/possible-consequences-of-the-philippines-south-china-sea-arbitration-case/.
9. "The Republic of the Philippines v. The People's Republic of China." *Permanent Court of Arbitration Website*. http://www.pca-cpa.org/showpage.asp?pag_id=1529.
10. Zuraidah Ibrahim and Kristin Kwok. "Beijing Rejects Hanoi's Legal Challenge on Spratly, Paracel Islands Disputes." *South China Morning Post*. December 12, 2014. http://www.scmp.com/news/china/article/1661364/china-rejects-vietnam-claims-arbitration-submission-over-south-china-sea.
11. "ASEAN Foreign Ministers' Statement on the Current Developments in the South China Sea." *ASEAN Secretariat Website*. May 10, 2014. http://www.asean.org/news/asean-statement-communiques/item/asean-foreign-ministers-statement-on-the-current-developments-in-the-south-china-sea.
12. Carl Thayer. "'Speak Softly and Carry a Big Stick': What is Malaysia Playing At?" *The Diplomat*. February 28, 2014. http://thediplomat.com/2014/03/speak-softly-and-carry-a-big-stick-what-is-malaysia-playing-at/.
13. Zachary Keck. "Malaysia to Establish Marine Corps and South China Sea Naval Base." *The Diplomat*. October 19, 2014. http://thediplomat.com/2013/10/malaysia-to-establish-marine-corps-and-south-china-sea-naval-base/.
14. Kuik Cheng-Chwee. "Making Sense of Malaysia's China Policy: Asymmetry, Proximity, and Elite's Domestic Authority." *The Chinese Journal of International Politics*, 6 (2013), 462–3
15. Noelan Arbis. "Brunei's ASEAN Chairmanship Scorecard." *CogitAsia*. November 4, 2014. http://cogitasia.com/bruneis-asean-chairmanship-scorecard/.
16. Yun Sun. "Myanmar's ASEAN Chairmanship." *Great Powers and the Changing Myanmar*, No. 4 (2014), 8. https://www.stimson.org/sites/default/files/file-attachments/Myanmar_Issue_Brief_4.pdf.
17. Kaewkamol Pitakdumrongkit. "Coordinating the South China Sea Issue: Thailand's Roles in The Code of Conduct Development." In *International Relations of the Asia-Pacific* (2015), 20. irap.oxfordjournals.org/content/early/2015/04/02/irap.lcv006.full.pdf+html.
18. Ibid., 22–3.
19. Ralf Emmers. *The De-escalation of the Spratly Dispute in Sino-Southeast Asian Relations*. RSIS Working Paper No. 129 (2007), 1. http://www.rsis.edu.sg/wp-content/uploads/rsis-pubs/WP129.pdf.
20. Emmers, 17.

21 Cheng, Joseph. "The ASEAN–China Free Trade Area: Genesis and Implications." *Australian Journal of International Affairs*, 58, no. 2 (2004), 258.
22 Christopher Joyner. "The Spratly Islands Dispute in the South China Sea: Problems, Policies, and Prospects for Diplomatic Accommodation." In *Investigating Confidence-building Measures in the Asia Pacific Region,* 54, edited by Ranjit Singh. Washington, DC: Henry L. Stimson Center, 1999. http://www.stimson.org/images/uploads/research-pdfs/cbmapspratly.pdf.
23 Tomas Etxzler. "Wrecks, Rats and Roaches: Standoff in the South China Sea." *CNN.com.* http://edition.cnn.com/interactive/2014/07/world/south-china-sea-dispute/.
24 Emmers, 13.
25 "Plan of Action to Implement the Joint Declaration on ASEAN–China Strategic Partnership for Peace and Prosperity." *ASEAN Secretariat Website.* http://www.asean.org/news/item/plan-of-action-to-implement-the-joint-declaration-on-asean-china-strategic-partnership-for-peace-and-prosperity.
26 Gregory Chin and Richard Stubbs. "China, Regional Institution-building and the China–ASEAN Free Trade Area." *Review of International Political Economy*, 18, no. 3 (2011), 281.
27 See Alice Ba. "China–ASEAN Relations: The Significance of a China–ASEAN Free Trade Area." In *China Under Hu Jintao: Opportunities, Dangers and Dilemmas,* 311–48, edited by Tun-jen Cheng, Jacques deLisle, and Deborah Brown. London: World Scientific, 2006.
28 Emmers, 13.
29 Ian Storey. *Southeast Asia and the Rise of China: The Search for Security,* 79–80. Abingdon, Oxon: Routledge, 2011.
30 Figure taken from "Statistics." *Laos Ministry of Planning and Investment Website.* http://www.investlaos.gov.la/index.php/resources/statistics.
31 Chea Vannak. "China to Commit $500 Million Annually to Cambodia." *The Khmer Times.* November 10, 2014. http://www.khmertimeskh.com/news/6130/china-to-commit--500-million-annually-to-cambodia/.
32 John Lee. "Reforms Will Decide Vietnam's Ability to Resist Economic Dominance by China." *ISEAS Perspectives,* No. 34. June 2, 2014), 3–7. http://www.iseas.edu.sg/documents/publication/ISEAS_Perspective_2014_34-Reforms_Will_Decide_Vietnam's_Ability_to_Resist.pdf.
33 For details, see "Vietnam Anti-China Protest: Factories Burnt." *BBC News,* May 14, 2014. http://www.bbc.com/news/world-asia-27403851.
34 Le, Hong Hiep. "Vietnam's Hedging Strategy Against China Since Normalization." *Contemporary Southeast Asia*, 35, No. 3 (2013), 345.
35 Zhao, Hong. "China–Philippines Relations Stunted by the South China Sea Dispute." *ISEAS Perspectives*, no. 17 (2013), 5. http://www.iseas.edu.sg/documents/publication/ISEAS%20Perspective%202013_17.pdf.
36 Karl Lester M. Yap. "Philippines' Domingo Says China May Become Biggest Export Market." *Bloomberg News.* October 7, 2013. http://www.bloomberg.com/news/2013-10-07/philippines-domingo-says-china-may-become-biggest-export-market.html.
37 Zhao, 5.
38 Kathrina Charmaine Alvarez. "Duterte Warns Against Using Tribunal Ruling vs. China to 'Taunt or Flaunt.'" *GMA News Online.* June 30, 2016. http://www.gmanetwork.com/news/story/571930/news/nation/duterte-warns-against-using-tribunal-ruling-vs-china-to-taunt-or-flaunt.
39 "Wang Yi: Stick to "Dual-track Approach" When Dealing with the South China Sea Issue." Ministry of Foreign Affairs of the People's Republic of China. June 24, 2015. http://www.fmprc.gov.cn/mfa_eng/zxxx_662805/t1384511.shtml.
40 "Philippines Eyes 'Two-track' Talks with China: Presidential Envoy Ramos." *The Straits Times.* August 13, 2013. http://www.straitstimes.com/asia/se-asia/philippines-eyes-two-track-talks-with-china-presidential-envoy-ramos.

11 Russia's institutional engagement with the Asia-Pacific

Getting more Asian and less Pacific

Artyom Lukin

Introduction

The chapter provides an overview of Russia's policies toward Asia-Pacific interstate institutions since the late 1980s up to the present. Russia's story of engagement with Asia-Pacific regional institutions dates back to the days of Mikhail Gorbachev, when the Soviet Union showed eagerness to normalize and develop relations with its Asian neighbors. In the 1990s, the post-Soviet Russia was admitted into the ASEAN Regional Forum (ARF) and Asia-Pacific Economic Cooperation (APEC), even though Moscow, distracted and weakened by the domestic mayhem, was not able to make full use of the membership. Since 2000, having finally emerged from the chaos of the Soviet Union collapse, Russia stepped up its policies toward the Asia-Pacific, seeking a larger political and economic role in the region. Moscow secured membership in the Asia-Pacific's major political-security forums (Six-Party Talks (SPT), East Asia Summit (EAS), ASEAN Defense Ministers Meeting + (ADMM+)) and successfully hosted the summit of APEC in Vladivostok in 2012.

From hindsight, 2012 was the high point of Russia's involvement in the Asia-Pacific/East Asian political and economic regionalism. Subsequent deterioration of Russia's relations with the West, particularly in the wake of the Ukraine crisis, led Moscow to prioritize Eurasian continentalism, in which the Russian-led Eurasian Economic Union (EEU) is expected to somehow align with Sino-centric geo-economic initiatives such as the Silk Road Economic Belt, with the Shanghai Cooperation Organization assuming the role of a collective security agent in Eurasia's heartland. The rise of Eurasianism has relegated the Asia-Pacific/East Asian institutions to the back burner in Moscow's list of priorities.

Russia and Asia-Pacific institutions: from high expectations to disillusionment

Despite possessing a Pacific coastline of 16,700 miles, Russia is a latecomer to Asia-Pacific regional institutions. Due to the Cold War, the Soviet Union was shut out of regional cooperation in the Asia-Pacific that was dominated by the United States and its friends, having instead to rely on bilateral ties with few Communist allies such as Vietnam and Mongolia. Overall, the approach to Asia was heavily militarized: the Soviet Pacific Fleet grew rapidly since the late 1960s, while Moscow amassed significant ground forces on the border with China and in Mongolia. This began to change under Gorbachev, who in his July 1986 speech in Vladivostok announced Moscow's intention to shift emphasis from the military buildup to diplomatic and economic engagement with the Asia-Pacific countries. In 1988, the Soviet government set up the National Committee for Pacific Economic Cooperation and the same year the Soviet delegation attended a meeting of the quasi-official Pacific Economic Cooperation Conference, the most prominent Asia-Pacific multilateral body at that time.[1]

Following the end of the bipolar confrontation, Russia joined the region's premier non-governmental forums, Pacific Economic Cooperation Council and Pacific Basin Economic Council, in 1992 and 1994 respectively. Yet acquiring membership to the intergovernmental APEC, which by the early 1990s had established itself as the main vehicle for the region-wide integration, proved much more difficult. For one thing, in the 1990s Russia's share of Asia-Pacific total exports stood at a meager 0.4%. This did not quite square with one of APEC's membership requirements that an applicant country have substantial economic ties to the Asia-Pacific. Another hurdle to Russia's membership was the apprehensions of some of the smaller and middle-sized APEC economies, such as Australia, that the addition of another big country would weaken their positions and raise the risks of great-power domination within the forum.

However, at the 1997 Vancouver summit, Russia's APEC application was finally approved, along with Peru's and Vietnam's. Moscow's bid was supported by the United States, China, and Japan, thus deciding the matter. Not everyone was happy, though. For example, the former Australian Prime Minister Paul Keating lamented the decision as "an act of international vandalism" that risked distracting APEC from its core agenda of promoting economic and political links between East Asia and North America:

> Russia's membership was supported by the United States in part, I believe, to atone for another bad decision – to expand NATO [North Atlantic Treaty Organization] to the borders of the old Soviet Union. This sent a signal to Russia that it wasn't wanted as part of the European system. Instead it was offered APEC membership as a consolation prize in the Asia-Pacific.[2]

In Russia itself admission to APEC was met with a lot of enthusiasm, giving rise to hopes for the country's accelerated engagement with the dynamic Asia-Pacific. In 1994 Russia became a founding member of the ARF and in 1996 it was granted the status of a dialogue partner of ASEAN.[3]

Despite joining APEC and ARF, Russia, due to domestic turmoil, ceased to be a major factor in the Asia-Pacific during the 1990s. However, since 2000, during Putin's and Medvedev's presidential tenures, Russia managed to substantially improve its internal situation, enabling Moscow to embark on more proactive policies in Asia, both on the level of bilateral relations and in multilateral settings. In addition, in the late 2000s the Russian government launched a massive program of state-funded investments in the social and economic development of the country's Far Eastern areas. The objective was not only to upgrade the economy and infrastructure but also to reinforce Russia's political positions in the Asia-Pacific. Russia's more vigorous policy was generally seen in the region as a positive factor: "Russia's pragmatic neomercantilism . . . would do no harm to countries of the region or to the rising Asian regionalism. Properly utilized and implemented, it might actually help facilitate bilateral and multilateral cooperation in Northeast Asia."[4]

In 2003, Russia became one of the co-sponsors of the SPT on the North Korean nuclear issue. From the beginning, Moscow regarded SPT not only as a means of defusing the nuclear problem but also as an incipient multilateral mechanism for general political and security cooperation in Northeast Asia,[5] a concert-like arrangement whose membership would legitimize and solidify Russia's role as a key stakeholder in the region. In 2007, Russia became the chair of one of the five working groups created within the SPT framework – the group on Northeast Asia peace and security mechanism – further raising Moscow's enthusiasm about SPT.

In 2005, Russia sought membership of the EAS at its inaugural meeting in Kuala Lumpur, where President Vladimir Putin attended as a special guest. At that moment, the bid failed to gain consensus approval of the ASEAN+6 forum. Yet, in 2010, Russia, along with the United States, finally secured the invitation to join EAS (effective since 2011). Moscow saw EAS as an umbrella political grouping in the Asia-Pacific that could "integrate regional security agenda in order to promote strategic dialogue."[6]

In 2010 Russia joined ADMM-+, a platform bringing together defense officials from ASEAN and its eight dialogue partners.[7] The same year Russia was admitted into Asia–Europe Meeting (ASEM), although it was designated neither as a "European country" nor an "Asian country," but as a "third category" member, along with Australia and New Zealand.[8]

Thus, by 2011, Russia secured membership of all the Asia-Pacific principal multilateral political and security bodies – SPT, ARF, ADMM-+, EAS, and ASEM. Russia viewed its involvement in the Asia-Pacific diplomatic forums as confirmation of its standing as a major Asia-Pacific power and as a kind of guarantee that its voice would be heard and heeded.

While Russia attained full representation in the Asia-Pacific political institutions, in the economic arena its presence could be characterized as very modest at best. Russia was one of the very few economies in the Asia-Pacific that had no free trade agreements (FTAs) in the region.[9] APEC remained the only regional economic institution Russia had membership in. That was one of the motivations for Moscow to invest considerable efforts and resources in hosting APEC events in 2012, when Russia acted as the forum's chair. The APEC summit in Vladivostok, held in September 2012, was a relative success.[10] One of the major deliverables of the Vladivostok APEC Leaders' Meeting was an environmental goods and services agreement that called for the tariffs on 54 products, like solar panels, to be reduced to 5% or less. From hindsight, the APEC summit in Vladivostok was the high point of Russia's involvement in Asia-Pacific multilateralism.

After 2012, Russia's interest in Asia-Pacific multilateral economic institutions started to wane.[11] Even in APEC, instead of following up on the achievements of the 2012 chairmanship, Russian officials and business leaders significantly scaled down their activities. This was the result of several confluent developments.

First, in the realm of economic integration Moscow decided to concentrate efforts on the promotion of EEU, a Russia-centered single market encompassing the former Soviet republics. As Russian analyst Kirill Muradov argues, "having prioritised its own economic bloc within former Soviet borders, Russia drew a dividing line between itself and the emerging Pacific mega-regionals or even individual state members."[12]

Second, by late 2012, it became exceedingly obvious that APEC would not be the platform for Asia-Pacific trade liberalization and remain at best an OECD-type regional organization for functional cooperation in some niche areas. Instead, two competing integration projects emerged – the United States-led Trans-Pacific Partnership and the Regional Comprehensive Economic Partnership (RCEP) championed by ASEAN and China. Russia was ready to join neither of them: most of its manufacturing industries were (and still are) too uncompetitive to seriously contemplate entering a region-wide FTA with Asia-Pacific economies. Even a "low-quality" FTA, such as RCEP, would be extremely problematic for many sectors of Russia's economy.

Third, drastic deterioration of Russia's relations with the United States over Ukraine had an inevitable impact on their interaction in the Asia-Pacific. Whereas, prior to the Ukraine crisis, Russian–American strategic dialogue and collaboration in the Pacific seemed possible,[13] after the crisis it was out of the question. With the United States imposing sanctions on Russia, and its Pacific allies – Japan and Australia – following suit, Russia obviously could not hope for their support in the Asia-Pacific multilateral bodies.[14]

Having stalled on multilateral regionalism after 2012, Russia's only achievement in institutionalizing its economic links with the Asia-Pacific was the signing, in May 2015, of a bilateral FTA between the EEU and Vietnam, Russia's first in Asia. With a modest volume of bilateral trade and with many tariff lines exempted from liberalization, the FTA, which came into effect in October 2016, is mostly of symbolic and political value. The negotiations on another pilot FTA, with New Zealand, were frozen by Wellington in 2014 in response to Russia's actions in Crimea and eastern Ukraine.

On the political-security front, too, Russia has shown a declining enthusiasm for Asia-Pacific multilateral institutions. SPT – the arrangement in which Moscow had a major interest and certain leverage due to the Korean Peninsula's proximity to Russian borders – has been paralyzed since 2009 because of disagreements between Pyongyang and Washington. EAS, ARF, and ADMM-+ have continued to function, but Russia has kept a low profile in these forums. One indication of Russia's unwillingness to invest much in East Asian institutionalism is Russian presidents' consistent failure to show up at the EAS annual meetings. Ever since Russia was admitted as a full member in 2011, a Russian leader has not once made it to the summit, which is seen as the region's premier security forum,[15] even while Moscow was paying lip service to EAS as the "key element in the construction of the new regional security architecture."[16] Similarly, ADMM-+ was never attended by a Russian minister of defense, who sent his deputies instead.

What are the reasons behind Russia's relative passivity within EAS, ARF, and ADMM-+? For one, all of these bodies are ASEAN-centric and thus focused on Southeast Asia. Unlike Eastern Europe, Central Asia, or the Middle East, this is a region remote from Russia, holding relatively little strategic importance for Moscow, and one where Russia's leverage is limited. Second, EAS, ARF, and ADMM-+ remain toothless and feckless institutions. It is not them but rather the hub-and-spoke system of the US alliances that underpins Asia-Pacific security and will continue to do so in the foreseeable future. Moscow has little motivation to invest its diplomatic resources in institutions whose influence is rather symbolic. Finally, in the last few years the South China Sea sovereignty disputes have emerged as one of the top agenda items for the three forums. Without a direct stake in the South China Sea, Moscow is not interested in tackling this issue or backing any one side in the dispute, especially given the fact that both China and Vietnam – the principal antagonists in the South China Sea – are Russia's strategic partners. If it supported one, it would risk spoiling relations with the other. The wisest course of action, then, is to pursue diplomatic neutrality and eschew commitments to any side of the argument. Thus a lowered level of representation may be the most appropriate.

Despite Moscow's repeated pronouncements about the importance of the relationship with ASEAN, it seems that from the very beginning Russia's involvement in ASEAN-centric political-security forums has been largely determined by prestige considerations – formalizing Russia's status as a great global power and a major Asian player – rather than by the desire to proactively shape international politics in Southeast Asia. The third Russia–ASEAN summit hosted by Putin at Sochi in May 2016 was mostly a ritualistic event with few substantive deliverables.[17]

As Russia's interest in Asia-Pacific multilateralism declines, Moscow shifts emphasis to a different set of institutions – the arrangements that are less "Pacific" and much more "Asian," or "Eurasian," centered on the Moscow–Beijing strategic axis. The following two sections deal with these institutions.

Russo-Chinese strategic partnership: an institutionalized quasi-alliance?

The Russo-Chinese axis began to take shape in the second half of the 1990s when disenchantment with the West induced Moscow to seek closer ties with alternative poles in the international system.[18] Beijing, in turn, was happy to embrace Russia. Aligning with Moscow could help balance America's unipolar predominance that, from Beijing's perspective, had achieved perilous levels.[19]

During Boris Yeltsin's visit to China, in April 1996, the two sides stated their intention to develop "relations of an equal trustworthy partnership aimed at strategic partnership in the 21st century."[20] In April 1997 in Moscow, Yeltsin and Jiang Zemin signed the Declaration on a Multipolar World and Formation of a New International Order which stated their common vision, in clear opposition to US-centered hegemony.[21] This Russian–Chinese strategic partnership pioneered a novel form of alignment in world politics, that was somewhat more institutionalized and broader-based than a coalition, but less formal and involved than an alliance.[22]

Vladimir Putin, who succeeded Yeltsin in 2000, continued to emphasize good relations with China. In July 2001, Putin and Jiang Zemin signed the Treaty of Good Neighborly Friendship and Cooperation, which became the legal foundation for a Sino-Russian strategic partnership. Inter alia, the parties affirmed their respect for joint borders and mutual support for their territorial integrity and national sovereignty.

Moscow–Beijing political interaction is organized around annual bilateral summits, with the Russian president visiting China every other year while the Chinese president reciprocates in alternate years. Besides, in 1997 Russia and China agreed to hold annual meetings at prime ministerial level. In the same year, an intergovernmental commission was established, led by Russian and Chinese deputy prime ministers, with the purpose of preparing the agenda for the regular meetings of heads of governments.[23] In 2012, a separate bilateral commission on energy cooperation was set up, headed by respective deputy prime ministers. There is also a vice prime ministerial commission on cultural and educational collaboration. This adds up to the most extensive intergovernmental dialogue mechanism that Russia maintains with any major country.

The Ukraine crisis, which started to develop in the fall of 2013, further consolidated the Moscow–Beijing axis, turning it into something approaching a quasi-alliance. Beijing refused to join the Washington-led campaign of ostracizing Moscow and displayed benevolent neutrality regarding Russian moves in Crimea and Ukraine. Vladimir Putin's visits to Shanghai (May 2014) and Beijing (September 2015), Xi Jinping's trip to Moscow in May 2015, as well as other multiple Russia–China high-level meetings since the beginning of the Ukraine trouble, underscored the growing closeness between the two great powers. The latest (as of this writing) summit between Putin and Xi took place in June 2016 in Beijing. Although overshadowed in the world media by the shocking outcome of Brexit, this rendezvous was quite remarkable because of the unusually high level of thinly disguised anti-American rhetoric. In their joint communiqué, Russia and China reaffirmed "mutual support on the key issues of sovereignty, security and development."[24] They accused the United States-led West of undermining strategic stability while seeking "the decisive military dominance," and expressed strong opposition to the US missile defense buildup in Europe and Northeast Asia.[25] Putin and Xi also adopted a separate statement on collaboration in cyber space, emphasizing "respect for state sovereignty in the information domain" while setting up a bilateral mechanism to coordinate cyber policies.[26]

In the economic area, in recent years Russia and China have concluded a host of agreements, substantially expanding and deepening bilateral cooperation in energy, finance, high-tech, and other sectors. The biggest among them was a 30-year $400 billion contract to supply natural gas from eastern Russia to northeastern China, signed in May 2014, followed in November by a framework agreement that would allow China to receive gas from Western Siberia. At the same time, China's imports of Russian oil skyrocketed, with Russia challenging Saudi Arabia's long-established position as the top oil exporter to China.[27] The central banks of the two countries signed a currency swap agreement worth 150 billion yuan (around 25 billion dollars), enabling Russia to draw on renminbi in case of need, while Beijing's officials announced China was willing to help the Russian economy.[28]

On the political-military front, Russia and China have been increasing the frequency and scale of their joint drills. In May 2015, in a move fraught with symbolism, they conducted their first naval exercise in the Mediterranean, NATO's maritime backyard, while in September 2016 China and Russia held joint naval drills in the highly contested South China Sea.[29] In May 2016, Russian and Chinese militaries held their first joint exercises of anti-aircraft and anti-missile defense units.[30]

The two countries display close collaboration on the Syrian crisis. In a move apparently coordinated with Moscow, Beijing will be providing assistance to the Assad government's military forces.[31] In June 2016, Chinese and Russian warships sailed simultaneously into the waters off the Senkaku Islands in the East China Sea, whose ownership is a matter of an acute dispute between Tokyo and Beijing, leaving the Japanese government guessing whether it was a coordinated action to put pressure on Japan.[32]

Russia shows increased readiness to sell China its most advanced weapons platforms, such as S-400 surface-to-air missile systems and Su-35 fighter jets. As a sign of growing cooperation in military technology, Moscow and Beijing reached agreement on the joint production of liquid-fuel rocket engines, where Russia has a lot of expertise, and the supply of Chinese avionics for the Russian aerospace industry.[33]

Since its inception in the second half of the 1990s, the Russian–Chinese strategic partnership has received varying assessments. Until recently the dominant view in the West has been that it is "an inherently limited partnership," or "an axis of convenience," which is unbalanced and shaky due to cultural barriers and the two countries' significantly divergent interests that are likely to diverge even more in the future.[34] Any idea of upgrading the partnership to the level of alliance has been rejected as unrealistic.[35]

Yet early on, there was also a dissenting view that saw Russian–Chinese collaboration as something much more durable and having great potential for further development. In 2001, Ariel Cohen characterized it as an "emerging alliance" that would require careful monitoring, predicting that "the degree to which the Sino-Russian alliance may become anti-Western in future depends on how deeply the two Eurasian powers feel that the United States threatens their interests."[36] Tom Wilkins concludes that the Moscow–Beijing partnership is:

a highly efficacious vehicle for coordinating Russo-Chinese-SCO [Shanghai Cooperation Organization] security policy. Those who doubt its capacities and durability may be in for a shock as it increasingly exercises dominance in Central Asia and begins to wield powerful influence on the global stage.[37]

It seems that the latter view, emphasizing the potency of Russian–Chinese collaboration, is borne out by developments in recent years. Since 2012, and especially in the wake of the Ukraine crisis, there has been a steady increase in the depth and scope of the bilateral relationship. It may not be accurate to describe the Russian–Chinese strategic partnership as an alliance yet, but the relationship is certainly growing stronger and stronger. The Russian–Chinese partnership, as it stands today, looks more solid and efficient than some of Washington's "treaty alliances," such as the one with Thailand.

China and Russia see their crucial national interests as mutually non-exclusive at the very least. As Dmitri Trenin observes, the Russia–China bond "is solid, for it is based on fundamental national interests regarding the world order as both the Russian and Chinese governments would prefer to see it."[38] Moscow is not inimical to China's rise as a great power since this creates for Russia economic and political alternatives other than the West. For its part, China sees its security interests as generally compatible with those of Russia.[39] This convergence of basic interests constitutes the foundation for a strategic partnership. The existence of a common foe – the United States – may be transforming the partnership into an entente or perhaps an alliance.[40] References to the Russian–Chinese relationship as a "de facto alliance" are increasingly being used by Russia's leading foreign-policy experts.[41] A joint report by Russian and Chinese scholars sees "elements of a military-political alliance," albeit not legally binding, emerging between the two countries.[42] The report argues that, "if need be, the ties can be converted into an alliance relationship without long preparations."[43]

If an alliance-type relationship between China and Russia eventually arises, its general patterns can already be discerned. This is hardly going to be an alliance of the classical style designed for joint use of military force against other states for defensive or offensive purposes. Russia and China are nuclear-armed powers with formidable conventional armies, which makes them more than capable of independently guaranteeing their national sovereignty and, when necessary, projecting power in their perceived zones of influence. Thus, the strategic value of the alliance will lie primarily in economic and diplomatic dimensions. In the 21st century, economic sanctions and embargos are becoming weapons of choice in the conflicts between major powers. This is what Russia, penalized by the West, has amply experienced in the Ukraine crisis. And this is what China may face, if and when it clashes with the United States. Thus, mutual economic support becomes crucial for Moscow and Beijing. The bond with China will give Russia a considerable degree of economic independence from the sanctions-prone West while China will enjoy secure access to Russia's vast reserves of natural resources so that its voracious economy can continue functioning even in the case of a United States-imposed naval blockade.[44]

In terms of diplomacy, Moscow and Beijing will provide each other support in the geographic areas that they deem their legitimate spheres of influence. Moscow may recognize East Asia as China's domain, but will do so in exchange for Beijing's support of Russian privileged interests in Eastern Europe and the post-Soviet space. That means, for example, that China takes the position of benevolent neutrality regarding Russia's actions on Ukraine, while Moscow looks the other way when Beijing pushes its claims in the South China Sea.[45]

Characterized by converging strategic interests, shared norms (such as the emphasis on the classic Westphalian sovereignty), extensive network of intergovernmental mechanisms and legal agreements, coordination of foreign, and increasingly economic, policies, the Sino-Russian relationship can be viewed as a bilateral institution of consequence for the global and Asian international order.

The rise of Eurasian continentalism

The Sino-Russian strategic partnership serves as the core for an emerging architecture of multilateral institutions in continental Eurasia.[46]

Shanghai Cooperation Organization

The SCO has been the most important institutional element of Eurasian continentalism. It was launched in 2001 and initially included six members – Russia, China, and four Central Asian republics (Kazakhstan, Kyrgyzstan, Tajikistan, and Uzbekistan).[47] As an international institution, SCO can best be defined as a multilateral strategic partnership,[48] modeled in many respects on the Sino-Russian strategic partnership, and one in which Beijing and Moscow play the role of co-leaders. SCO's main areas of activities are regional security (with an emphasis on combating terrorism,[49] extremism, and drug trafficking), economic cooperation, and scientific and cultural exchanges.

So far SCO has mostly acted as a forum for consultation and coordination among Russia, China, and four Central Asian "stans." It has implemented relatively few tangible multilateral projects. For example, SCO has yet to deliver on any substantial economic cooperation, while the SCO University remains more an ambition than a functioning educational institution.[50] However, SCO's most significant contribution has been in maintaining security and stability in Central Asia. SCO has certainly made it easier for Moscow and Beijing to manage Central Asia in a constructive manner while avoiding direct competition and clashes of interest – something that stands in stark contrast to the confrontation of Russia and the West over the post-Soviet space in Eastern Europe. SCO has been a stabilizing factor in an inherently unstable region made up of fragile states under the constant threat of the spread of militant Islamism from the neighboring Afghanistan and the Middle East.

In addition to using SCO as an instrument of maintaining – in collaboration with China – stability in Central Asia, Moscow has seen it mostly as a political institution embodying Russia's ideological preference for a multipolar world order and as an alternative to Western-dominated institutions.[51] This vision is in agreement with China's.[52] As a related and more specific objective, both Moscow and Beijing view SCO as a mechanism to limit what they see as undesirable Western interference in Central Asia.[53]

Since 2001 SCO has developed to go well beyond Sino-Russian co-management of Central Asian security. One crucial indication of the organization's growth is the expansion of its membership from the initial six to eight (with the decision, in July 2015, to add India and Pakistan as full members). SCO also has attracted four observer states (Iran, Afghanistan, Belarus, Mongolia) and six dialogue partners (Azerbaijan, Armenia, Cambodia, Nepal, Turkey, and Sri Lanka). SCO's obvious appeal lies in its role as the only available institutional platform for multilateral interaction in Central Asia and the surrounding areas of continental Eurasia. Given the increasing security and economic interdependence across these parts of Eurasia, SCO is well placed to act as the chief multilateral mechanism there.

Conference on Interaction and Confidence Building Measures in Asia (CICA)

This hitherto obscure forum started in the 1990s as a vanity project of Kazakhstani President Nursultan Nazarbayev. At present CICA brings together 26 participants from different parts of Asia and the Middle East, including Russia, India, South Korea, Iran, Pakistan, Turkey, and Egypt. Of note, the United States and its most loyal Asia-Pacific allies – Japan and Australia – are not among CICA members.

In 2014 China took over the CICA presidency from Turkey and hosted the fourth summit in Shanghai in May 2014. This summit became the group's largest ever, gathering 12 heads of state and government and ten chiefs of international organizations, including presidents of Russia, Iran, and the United Nations Secretary-General. The Shanghai summit marked a notable elevation in CICA's standing.

In his keynote address, Chinese President Xi Jinping spoke of the need for strengthening regional security cooperation and promotion of "common, comprehensive, cooperative and sustainable security in Asia".[54] Xi stated that "it is for people of Asia to run affairs of Asia, solve the problems of Asia and uphold the security of Asia."[55] More than that, he underlined that "it is disadvantageous to the common security of the region if military alliances with third parties are strengthened".[56] Some experts speculate that Beijing's promotion of CICA aims at forming a multilateral security system that covers most countries in Asia but excludes "external forces," above all the United States and its main ally, Japan.[57]

Russia has yet to clarify its strategy toward CICA. On the one hand, Russia is a founding member and has been supportive of CICA. On the other hand, CICA, compared to SCO, is clearly of secondary importance to Moscow. Encompassing countries from the Middle East to Southeast Asia, with members as diverse as Israel and Vietnam, CICA will hardly be able to effectively manage Asian security. Yet it could serve as an umbrella body, connecting Eurasian continentalism to East Asia and the Middle East.

Russia–India–China trilateral

The idea of a tripartite grouping, consisting of Russia, China, and India, was first voiced by Russian Prime Minister Evgeny Primakov in 1998. His vision of a strategic axis of the three largest powers in Eurasia acting as an effective counterbalance to US hegemony has never got off the ground due to Sino-Indian rivalry and Delhi's lack of enthusiasm in associating itself with something that looked like an anti-Western coalition. A more modest version of Primakov's proposal was realized in the form of regular trilateral meetings of foreign ministers, the first of which was convened in Russia's Vladivostok in 2005. The latest (as of this writing) 14th annual meeting of the three countries' foreign ministers, held in Moscow in April 2016, produced quite a substantive communiqué, reiterating their common vision for "a more just and democratic multi-polar international system" as well as rejecting "forced regime change from the outside in any country" and emphasizing the "core principles" of respect for state sovereignty and non-interference in internal affairs of other states. The communiqué's language is in clear opposition to Western liberal hegemony.[58] And, of course, Russia, India, and China form the core of the Brazil, Russia, India, China, and South Africa (BRICS) grouping – the world's most significant non-Western arrangement.

Russia–Mongolia–China trilateral

Another Eurasian trilateral that has been recently taking shape includes Moscow, Beijing, and Ulan Bator. To some extent, Mongolia is being incorporated into the Sino-Russian entente. This was evidenced by the near-simultaneous visits by Xi and Putin to Ulan Bator (the Chinese leader came on August 21–22, 2014; Putin visited on September 5), followed by the first trilateral summit among China, Mongolia, and Russia, held in Dushanbe on September 11, 2014 on the sidelines of the SCO meeting. The three presidents spoke of the "China–Mongolia–Russia economic corridor" and agreed to expand trilateral cooperation.[59] The mechanism of regular meetings at vice ministerial level was put in place. Even though Ulan Bator is still in no hurry to join SCO as a full member and continues with its "third neighbor" policy that seeks to balance its dependence on China and Russia by expanding relations with the West, the new trilateral signals that Mongolia is becoming more accommodating toward its two giant neighbors.

The linking up of Russian and Chinese economic initiatives in Eurasia

The economic foundation of Eurasian continentalism is being formed by China-led multilateral projects, such as the Silk Road Economic Belt (SREB), Asian Infrastructure Investment Bank (AIIB), and Silk Road Fund. Collectively, they add up to a grand plan of creating a single – Sino-centric – economic space in Eurasia.[60]

Russia was initially wary of these Chinese initiatives, fearing that they would compete with its own project of EEU that seeks to (re)integrate the post-Soviet space under Moscow's aegis. However, the conflict with the West and the deteriorating condition of Russia's economy have left Moscow little choice other than bandwagoning with China's Eurasian schemes. In late March 2015, Moscow joined AIIB, and Russia became the third largest AIIB shareholder after China and India.[61] In May 2015, Putin and Xi agreed to coordinate their flagship economic initiatives in Central Asia – Russian-led EEU and China's SREB. In their joint declaration, the parties expressed willingness "to make coordinated efforts toward the integration of constructing EEU and SREB," with SCO serving as the main platform for linking up the two Eurasian initiatives. The document also mentioned "a long-term goal of progressing toward a free trade zone between EEU and China."[62]

In June 2016, speaking at the St Petersburg International Economic Forum, Putin called for the formation of an "extensive Eurasian partnership" that would encompass the EEU and other states in continental Eurasia, such as China, India, Iran, and Pakistan. Putin also announced the start of the EEU–China negotiations on a comprehensive economic cooperation agreement, highlighting the central role Beijing is destined to play in Moscow's project of "Greater Eurasia."[63] However, the EEU–China economic partnership talks that were formally launched during Putin's visit to Beijing in late June 2016 are focused on trade facilitation measures, not a fully fledged FTA. Russian officials recognize that the EEU member states "are not yet in a position for a deep market opening" with China.[64] In addition, the glaring incompatibility in regulations, such as technical, veterinary, and phytosanitary standards, is a major barrier to be overcome if the EEU and China are to achieve any meaningful level of economic integration.[65] Even in its current bilateral format – between the Russian-led EEU and China – the Eurasian partnership negotiations are going to be a difficult and drawn-out process, let alone if this undertaking involves other proposed participants, such as India or Iran.

Conclusion: toward a concert of Eurasia?

In recent years, Russia's approach to regional institutions and regional integration has undergone considerable changes, with the Ukraine crisis serving as the watershed. In 2012, Moscow's paramount goal was to secure economic reintegration of the post-Soviet space under the Russian-led EEU proposed by Vladimir Putin in October 2011. The related priority was close partnership with the European Union. Indeed, according to Putin, the EEU was supposed to become part of "Greater Europe". At the same time, Moscow had an ambitious goal of turning the EEU into a link between Europe and the Asia-Pacific.[66] And the engagement with the Asia-Pacific institutions was Russia's third priority, culminating in the hosting of the APEC summit in Vladivostok in September 2012.

By 2015, in the wake of the Ukraine crisis, the priorities changed. The construction of the EEU remains of paramount importance to Moscow. However, the idea of integrating the EEU with the EU is moot now that Russia finds itself in bitter struggle with the West. Similarly, Russia's engagement with the Asia-Pacific arrangements has been on the wane — partly due to the realization that Russia's economy is not yet ready for comprehensive FTAs with more competitive economies of the Asia-Pacific and partly due to the Ukraine crisis that froze Moscow's collaboration with Washington and its friends in the Pacific. Russia's interest in ASEAN-centric bodies has also declined as Moscow sees little practical value in them and has no desire to get involved in the South China Sea controversies.

Against the backdrop of diminished ties with Europe and the Pacific, Russia has begun to prioritize China and continental Eurasia. Moscow is aiming for the creation of a Eurasian order based on a set of institutions, especially the Sino-Russian strategic partnership and SCO. What Russia seeks is essentially a Eurasian concert of powers – a model that puts a premium on relations among a few major powers.[67] These are Russia itself, China, and India, plus – with some qualifications – Pakistan and Iran. Accounting for the bulk of continental Eurasia's population and landmass, the five big players can collectively manage security and economic affairs of the mega-region, provided, of course, they are capable of restraining elements of competition and conflict in their relationships (especially in China–India and India–Pakistan dyads). Their collective governance will be legitimized via multilateral bodies such as SCO and CICA.

Russia's preference for a new Eurasian order is reflected in its diplomatic activism, such as securing Indian and Pakistani membership in SCO and hosting joint summits of SCO and BRICS in the Russian city of Ufa in July 2015. Kremlin-affiliated pundits are calling for a "Community of Greater Eurasia"[68] and proclaiming a "new Eurasian era" of Russia's foreign policy.[69]

What are Moscow's reasons for pursuing the Eurasian option? First, continental Eurasia is the only region where Russia both retains considerable leverage and maintains good relations with most of the countries. This stands in contrast to Europe and the Asia-Pacific. In Europe, Moscow is locked in confrontation with the European Union and NATO over Ukraine and has been marginalized. In the Asia-Pacific, Russia's influence has always been limited and now this is further compounded by the hostility of the United States. Second, Russia finds much affinity with Eurasian powers in that they are, just like Russia itself, classic Westphalian polities that emphasize state-centric sovereignty and non-interference in internal affairs. All of them, including even democratic India, are uncomfortable with US global hegemony and reject Western promotion of its own values as universal. Third, Russia is interested in collaborating with its Eurasian partners to stem the proliferation of militant Islam. The mounting chaotization of the Middle East and the threat of radicalism metastasizing into Central Asia, Afghanistan, and the Muslim-populated areas of Russia, India, and China are shared concerns for all major Eurasian states. Fourth, a concert of Eurasia will make it possible for Russia to play a balancing game. Moscow seems to have acquiesced to the inevitability of Chinese economic predominance and may accept being subsumed into a Sino-centric *economic* order. However, Moscow wants to countervail China's *political* predominance by engaging other major Eurasian players within the framework of a Eurasian institutional architecture. Russia aspires to be the main security and diplomatic broker in a concert of Eurasia, while leaving China with the role of the economic leader. This division of labor is already emerging in

Central Asia, where, as one Russian expert put it, "China would be the bank and Russia would be the big gun."[70] Such an arrangement might resemble the initial stages of the European Community, when France acted as the political leader while West Germany was the economic engine.

For all Moscow's infatuation with "Greater Eurasia," there are formidable difficulties involved in constructing the new order – from the inherent fragility of many of its future members to fraught relations between some of them. There is also a risk that, even if a Concert of Eurasia takes shape, Russia may be overshadowed by more powerful players such as China and later possibly India. This constitutes one more reason why Russia will still continue to have a stake in European and Asia-Pacific/East Asian institutions. Given Russia's geopolitical position – spanning Europe, Asia, and the Pacific – Moscow's external priorities, and its institutional engagement strategies, will always include these three directions, even though their exact combination may vary at different times.

Notes

1 Daniel Sneider. "Soviets Hanker for Piece of Economic Action in the Pacific." *The Christian Science Monitor.* May 24, 1988. http://www.csmonitor.com/1988/0524/opac.html.
2 Paul J. Keating. "APEC's Sixth Leaders' Summit Meeting: Implications for the Strategic Architecture of the Asian Hemisphere (Speech to 1998 Pacific Rim Forum. Shanghai, September 22, 1998)," *Australian APEC Study Centre Issues Paper 14.* http://www.apec.org.au/docs/iss14.htm.
3 That was upgraded from the status of a "consultative partner" of ASEAN that Moscow received in 1991.
4 Taehwan Kim. "Impassive to Imperial? Russia in Northeast Asia from Yeltsin to Putin." In *Northeast Asia: Ripe for Integration?* edited by Vinod K. Aggarwal, Min Gyo Koo, Seungjoo Lee, and Chung-in Moon, 209. New York: Springer, 2008.
5 Russian officials characterized the SPT's ultimate purpose as "the creation of reliable political and legal guarantees of security in Northeast Asia." See "Remarks on the Developments on the Korean Peninsula and the Prospects for Re-launching of the Six-Party Talks." *Russian Ministry of Foreign Affairs.* February 4, 2011. http://www.mid.ru/bdomp/ns-rasia.nsf/3a0108443c964002432569e7004199c0/432569d80021985fc325782d0057a361!OpenDocument.
6 "Remarks of the Russian Foreign Minister Sergey Lavrov at the Fifth East Summit Meeting (Hanoi, Vietnam)." *Russian Ministry of Foreign Affairs.* October 30, 2010. http://www.mid.ru/bdomp/ns-rasia.nsf/3a0108443c964002432569e7004199c0/bfdfcb19ae127583c32577ce0039e051!OpenDocument.
7 The membership of ADMM-+ exactly corresponds to EAS.
8 "ASEM Member Brief 2014: Russian Federation." *Academia.* http://www.academia.edu/8544396/ASEM_Member_Brief_2014_Russian_Federation (accessed June 30, 2016).
9 This was compounded by Russia's non-participation in the World Trade Organization (WTO). Russian accession to the WTO was not approved until December 2011.
10 Michael F. Martin. *The Asia-Pacific Economic Cooperation (APEC) Meetings in Vladivostok, Russia: Postscript.* Washington, DC: Congressional Research Service. November 19, 2012.
11 Alexander Gabuev. "Russia's Performance in Multilateral Organizations: Pivot to Asia or Just to China?" *Carnegie Moscow Center.* November 6, 2014. http://carnegie.ru/publications/?fa=57144.

12 Kirill Muradov. "Russia's Pivot to Eurasia and the Battle for Ukraine." *East Asia Forum.* September 17, 2013. http://www.eastasiaforum.org/2013/09/17/russias-pivot-to-eurasia-and-the-battle-for-ukraine/.
13 "Japan–Russia–US Trilateral Conference on the Security Challenges in Northeast Asia." Moscow: Institute of World Economy and International Relations, June 16, 2012. http://imemo.ru/en/conf/2012/19062012/19062012_statement_M_EN.pdf.
14 One of the casualties of the Ukraine crisis is Russia's prospective membership in the Asian Development Bank. Long before its present standoff with the West, Moscow applied to join the Asian Development Bank but was denied entry by Japan and the United States, the countries wielding the greatest decision-making power in the multilateral financial institution. Still there remained hope that sooner or later Russia would be admitted. The fallout from the Ukraine mess foreclosed this possibility.
15 In 2011–13, Russia was represented in EAS summit meetings by Foreign Minister Sergey Lavrov, while in November 2014 Prime Minister Dmitri Medvedev attended the summit in Naypyidaw, Myanmar. Incidentally, China's highest representative to EAS has always been the premier (number two) rather than the president (number one). It is telling that Moscow eventually followed Beijing's example in setting its own level of EAS representation.
16 "Commentary of the Russian Ministry of Foreign Affairs in Connection with Foreign Minister Sergey Lavrov's Participation at the East Asia Summit." *Russian Ministry of Foreign Affairs.* October 8, 2013. http://mid.ru/bdomp/ns-rasia.nsf/3a0108443c964002432569e7004199c0/44257b100055e10444257bfe0043ae04!OpenDocument.
17 The previous two summits took place in 2005 in Kuala Lumpur and in 2010 in Hanoi.
18 The list of major Russian grievances included eastern enlargement by NATO, lack of anticipated economic aid from the West, and refusal by the West to grant Moscow its "rightful place" in the international system. Toward the late 1990s, NATO's "humanitarian intervention" in Yugoslavia, Western reaction to the war in Chechnya, and Washington's decision to withdraw from the anti-ballistic missile treaty further exacerbated the frictions.
19 China's sense of vulnerability in the face of the US preponderance grew especially acute as a result of the 1995–6 Taiwan Strait crisis when Washington displayed its military might off Chinese shores in a humiliating warning to Beijing.
20 Alexander Lukin. "The Russian Approach to China Under Gorbachev, Yeltsin, and Putin." In *Russian Strategic Thought Toward Asia*, edited by Gilbert Rozman, 148. New York: Palgrave Macmillan, 2006.
21 "Russian–Chinese Joint Declaration on a Multipolar World and Formation of a New International Order." Adopted in Moscow, April 23, 1997. *Zakony Rossii.* www.lawrussia.ru/texts/legal_743/doc743a830x878.htm (accessed August 31, 2016).
22 Thomas Wilkins. "Russo–Chinese Strategic Partnership: A New Form of Security Cooperation?" *Contemporary Security Policy,* 29, no. 2 (August 2008): 358–83.
23 The commission's activities have expanded over time and now include 11 bilateral subcommittees on trade, energy, nuclear energy, science and technology, transport, telecommunications and information technology, space, finance, environment, civil aviation and civil aircraft building, and customs.
24 "Joint Statement of the Russian Federation and the People's Republic of China." Adopted in Beijing, June 25, 2016. *President of Russia Official Website.* http://kremlin.ru/supplement/5100.
25 "Joint Statement of the President of the Russian Federation and the President of the People's Republic of China on Strengthening Global Strategic Stability." Adopted in Beijing, June 25, 2016. *President of Russia Official Website.* http://kremlin.ru/supplement/5098.
26 "Joint Statement of the President of the Russian Federation and the President of the People's Republic of China on Collaboration in the Area of Development of Information Space." Adopted in Beijing, June 25, 2016. *President of Russia Official Website.* http://kremlin.ru/supplement/5099.

27 Tim Daiss. "Move Over Saudi Arabia, Russia Is Selling More Oil To China Than You." *Forbes.* August 5, 2016. http://www.forbes.com/sites/timdaiss/2016/08/05/move-over-saudi-arabia-russia-is-selling-more-oil-to-china-than-you/print/.
28 "Russia May Seek China Help to Deal with Crisis." *The South China Morning Post.* December 18, 2014. http://www.scmp.com/business/banking-finance/article/1664567/russia-may-seek-china-help-deal-crisis. See also "Beijing Ready to Help Russia's Rattled Economy, Chinese Foreign Minister Says." *The South China Morning Post.* December 22, 2014. http://www.scmp.com/news/china/article/1667633/beijing-ready-help-russias-rattled-economy-chinese-foreign-minister-says.
29 Rowan Callick. "Brothers in Arms: China-Russia Exercise in South China Sea." *The Australian.* August 12, 2016. http://www.theaustralian.com.au/news/inquirer/brothers-in-arms-chinarussia-exercise-in-south-china-sea/news-story/6ff0f51c4dacfcbb48037f1fbf6495c6.
30 "Russia, China Launch First Computer-Enabled Anti-Missile Exercises." *TASS.* May 26, 2016. http://tass.ru/en/defense/878407http://tass.ru/en/defense/878407.
31 "China Says Seeks Closer Military Ties with Syria." *Reuters.* August 16, 2016. http://www.reuters.com/article/us-mideast-crisis-syria-china-idUSKCN10R10R.
32 Robin Harding. "Japan Spooked by Naval Mystery in East China Sea." *The Financial Times.* June 22, 2016. http://www.ft.com/cms/s/0/5ada3fb4-3799-11e6-9a05-82a9b15a8ee7.html#axzz4EQ8VWU2S.
33 Vasily Kashin. "Vladimir Putin's Visit to China: No High Expectations, Concrete Results." *Russian International Affairs Council.* June 30, 2016. http://russiancouncil.ru/en/inner/?id_4=7852#top-content.
34 Bobo Lo. *Axis of Convenience: Moscow, Beijing, and the New Geopolitics.* Washington, DC: Brookings Institution, 2008. See also Stephen Kotkin. "The Unbalanced Triangle." *Foreign Affairs,* 88, no. 5 (September–October 2009): 130–8.
35 See, for example, Natasha Kuhrt. "Russia and China: Strategic Partnership or Asymmetrical Dependence?" In *Russia and East Asia: Informal and Gradual Integration,* edited by Tsuneo Akaha and Anna Vassilieva, 91–107. New York: Routledge, 2014.
36 Ariel Cohen. "The Russia–China Friendship and Cooperation Treaty: A Strategic Shift in Eurasia?" *The Heritage Foundation.* July 18, 2001. www.heritage.org/research/reports/2001/07/the-russia-china-friendship-and-cooperation-treaty.
37 Wilkins, "Russo–Chinese Strategic Partnership: A New Form of Security Cooperation?" 378.
38 Dmitri Trenin. *Russia and the Rise of Asia,* 6. Moscow: Carnegie Moscow Center, November 2013.
39 Rex Li. *A Rising China and Security in East Asia.* New York: Routledge, 2009.
40 Dmitri Trenin. "From Greater Europe to Greater Asia: The Sino-Russian Entente." *Carnegie Moscow Center.* April 9, 2015. http://carnegie.ru/publications/?fa=59728.
41 See, for example, Sergey Karaganov. "*Mezhdunarodny krizis: izbezhat' Afghanistana-2* [International Crisis: Avoiding a Second Afghanistan]." *Vedomosti.* July 28, 2014. www.vedomosti.ru/opinion/news/29501801/izbezhat-afganistana-2.
42 Sergey Luzyanin et al. *Rossiysko-Kitayskiy Dialog: model' 2015* [Russia–China Dialogue: 2015 Model], 6. Moscow: Russian International Affairs Council, 2015.
43 Ibid., 8.
44 Judging from the debate among US security specialists, economic strangulation of China by means of naval blockade may be emerging as the optimal strategy of dealing with China in case of a major conflict. See, for example, Sean Mirski. "Stranglehold: The Context, Conduct and Consequences of an American Naval Blockade of China." *Journal of Strategic Studies,* 36, no. 3 (2013): 10–11. See also T. X. Hammes. "Offshore Control is the Answer." *US Naval Institute.* December 2012. http://www.usni.org/magazines/proceedings/2012-12/offshore-control-answer.

45 For example, Russia's head representative at the 2015 Shangri La Dialogue on Asian security, Deputy Defense Minister Anatoly Antonov, did not even mention the South China Sea controversy. See "Main Points of Speech by Deputy Minister of Defense of the Russian Federation Dr. Anatoly Antonov at the 14th Asia Security Summit 'The Shangri-La Dialogue' (Singapore, May 30, 2015)." *IISS*. http://www.iiss.org/en/events/shangri%20la%20dialogue/archive/shangri-la-dialogue-2015-862b/special-sessions-315c/antonov-da7d.
46 By "continental Eurasia" I mean the area more or less corresponding to Russia, Central Asia, China, Mongolia, South Asia, Afghanistan, and Iran.
47 SCO's precursor had been "The Shanghai Five" (Russia, China, Kazakhstan, Kyrgyzstan, and Tajikistan) which, in 1996 and 1997, signed two multilateral agreements on confidence-building measures and troops reductions in their adjacent border areas.
48 Sergei Luzyanin et al. *Shanghaiskaya Organizatsiya Sotrudnichestva: model 2014–2015* [Shanghai Cooperation Organization: The Model for 2014–2015], 9. Moscow: Russian International Affairs Council, 2015. http://russiancouncil.ru/paper21#top-content.
49 SCO has a dedicated counter-terror arm, Regional Anti-Terror Structure, based in Tashkent, Uzbekistan.
50 SCO University is designed as a consortium of existing universities in member states of SCO to create and administer joint degree programs (see the website of the SCO University, http://uni-sco.com/?lang=EN).
51 Alexander Lukin. "*Shanghaiskaya Organizatsiya Sotrudnichestva: v poiskah novoy roli* [Shanghai Cooperation Organization: In Search of a New Role]." *Russia in Global Affairs*. July 9, 2015. http://www.globalaffairs.ru/valday/Shankhaiskaya-organizatciya-sotrudnichestva-v-poiskakh-novoi-roli-17573.
52 That said, Beijing would also like to enhance an economic integration component in SCO's activities – something that Moscow until recently was reluctant to do due to fears of losing Central Asia economically to China.
53 For example, in 2005 Russia and China initiated an SCO collective decision to call on the United States to withdraw its military forces from Central Asia.
54 "President Xi Addresses CICA Summit." *Xinhua News*. May 21, 2014. http://www.chinausfocus.com/china-news/president-xi-addresses-cica-summit.
55 Xi Jinping. "Remarks at the Fourth Summit of the Conference on Interaction and Confidence Building Measures in Asia." *China Internet Information Center.* May 28, 2014. http://www.china.org.cn/world/2014-05/28/content_32511846.htm.
56 Ibid.
57 Mu Chunshan. "What is CICA (and Why Does China Care About It)?" *The Diplomat.* May 17, 2014. http://thediplomat.com/2014/05/what-is-cica-and-why-does-china-care-about-it/.
58 "Joint Communiqué of the 14th Meeting of the Foreign Ministers of the Russian Federation, the Republic of India and the People's Republic of China." Adopted in Moscow, April 18, 2016. Ministry of External Affairs, Government of India. http://mea.gov.in/bilateral-documents.htm?dtl/26628/Joint_Communiqu_of_the_14th_Meeting_of_the_Foreign_Ministers_of_the_Russian_Federation_the_Republic_of_India_and_the_Peoples_Republic_of_China.
59 Alicia Campi. "Transforming Mongolia–Russia–China Relations: The Dushanbe Trilateral Summit." *The Asia-Pacific Journal.* November 10, 2014. http://www.japanfocus.org/-Alicia-Campi/4210/article.html.
60 "Vision and Actions on Jointly Building Silk Road Economic Belt and 21st-Century Maritime Silk Road." *National Development and Reform Commission (People's Republic of China)*. March 28, 2015. http://en.ndrc.gov.cn/newsrelease/201503/t20150330_669367.html.

61 "Graphics: AIIB Voting Stakes." *Caixin Online.* July 3, 2015. http://english.caixin.com/2015-07-03/100825189.html.
62 "Joint Declaration by the Russian Federation and the People's Republic of China on the Coordination of the Construction of the Eurasian Economic Union and the Silk Road Economic Belt." *President of Russia Official Website.* May 8, 2015. http://kremlin.ru/supplement/4971.
63 Vladimir Putin. "Transcript of the Speech at the Plenary session of St Petersburg International Economic Forum." *President of Russia Official Website.* June 17, 2016. http://en.kremlin.ru/events/president/news/52178.
64 Gleb Fedorov. "Interview with the Eurasian Economic Union's Minister of Trade Veronika Nikishina." *RBTH.* August 8, 2016. http://rbth.com/business/2016/08/08/russian-automobiles-to-have-free-access-to-asean-via-vietnam-eaeu-minister_619053.
65 Ibid.
66 Vladimir Putin. "*Noviy Integratsionniy Proekt dlya Evrazii* [A New Integration Project for Eurasia]." *The Website of the Head of Government of Russia.* October 4, 2011. http://premier.gov.ru/events/news/16622/.
67 Hugh White defines a concert of powers as "an agreement among a group of great powers not to try to dominate one another, but to accept one another as great powers and work to resolve differences by negotiation." See Hugh White. *The China Choice: Why America Should Share Power*, 137. Collingwood: Black, 2012. According to Muthiah Alagappa, concert is joint management of international affairs by great powers on the basis of certain common goals, values, and interests. See Muthiah Alagappa. "The Study of International Order." In *Asian Security Order*, edited by Muthiah Alagappa, 55. Stanford, CA: Stanford University Press, 2003.
68 Sergey Karaganov. "*Evroaziatskiy Vyhod iz Evropeyskogo Krizisa* [Euro-Asian Solution to the European Crisis]." *Russia in Global Affairs.* June 19, 2015. http://www.globalaffairs.ru/pubcol/Evroaziatskii-vykhod-iz-evropeiskogo-krizisa-17541.
69 Timofey Bordachev. "*Novaya Povestka dlya Rossii i Evrazii* [New Agenda for Russia and Eurasia]." *Izvestiya.* June 29, 2015. http://izvestia.ru/news/588257.
70 Reid Standish. "China and Russia Lay Foundation for Massive Economic Cooperation." *Foreign Policy.* July 10, 2015. http://foreignpolicy.com/2015/07/10/china-russia-sco-ufa-summit-putin-xi-jinping-eurasian-union-silk-road/.

12 The Indian Ocean matters for East Asia

Emerging Indo-Pacific interests in East Asian affairs

Michael R. Porter

Of contemporary importance

The Indian Ocean region today stands as a microcosm of the contemporary global condition. Worldwide economic and political trends suggest that this region will not only mirror, but significantly influence, the larger budding confrontation playing out between the rising economic and political giants of the developing world and the contemporary international economic and security structures that have taken hold throughout the last seven decades of American ascendency. The momentum behind Asia's ongoing economic growth potential has, in fractional but profound ways, encouraged a gradual distribution of economic and political orientations that will likely promote a relative and measured decline in US influence in the coming years should this trajectory continue. The "rise of the rest," as one public commentator put it, will almost certainly come to define this significant and transitional period in world history.[1]

Stretching from the east African coast, across the Arabian Peninsula, and through the Indian subcontinent into East Asia, the resources and transportation corridors of the greater Indian Ocean region support the ever-growing appetite of today's newest, largest, and fastest-growing global economic and political powers. As both a geographic backdrop to the most significant development advances in recent history, as well as the cradle of many of today's most destabilizing transnational concerns, this maritime region is once again becoming center stage to some of the world's most critical geopolitical maneuvering. Realizing the growing influence and relevancy of the Indian Ocean to global affairs, this chapter explores the ways in which traditional East Asian economic and political interests are being increasingly linked to interests in the greater Indian Ocean region. As a way of introducing this notion, the chapter spends considerable effort in setting a context by first defining the terms and space of the geographic scope under consideration. The discussion then goes on to assess the relevancy and strategic implications of this space to East Asian affairs, with a focus on the region's major players.

In late 2011, the Obama administration began articulating a long-term strategic vision for enhancing US engagement in the Asia-Pacific.[2] In an effort to secure its relevance and prosperity in the "Asia-Pacific century" the US government set out repackaging existing initiatives with a series of new diplomatic, military, and economic agendas aimed at creating an integrated strategy that "rebalances" US foreign-policy priorities towards the Asia-Pacific. While the merits of such a strategy, and discussions over its implementation and efficacy, will be debated for some time, this chapter explores the important ways in which, in an era of Asian ascendency, it is becoming increasingly clear that a truly comprehensive "Asia" strategy (whether under the current "rebalance" or any future initiative) is neither sufficient nor sustainable if the Indian Ocean region – as Asia's next fully exploited commercial and geopolitical theater beyond the Western Pacific – were to be strategically isolated from America's "Western Pacific" or "East Asian" priorities. Asia's rising powers themselves – most notably India and non-littoral China – have begun to pursue with more purpose maritime-oriented agendas that include long-term investments (i.e., financing port infrastructure, energy projects, and military expenditures) throughout the broader Indian Ocean region as their own economic and security interests expand. Such investments incentivize further commercial activities that in turn promote new security rationales for safeguarding both the initial investments and the economic dependencies that develop through the maturation of an investment's subsequent returns. Without a comprehensive appreciation of the Indian Ocean region's growing East Asian footprint – as the resources and energy rich countries of Africa and the Middle-East enter into more interdependent relationships with the enormous and vibrant markets of the Indian subcontinent and East and Southeast Asia – countries that strategically adhere to the strict regional demarcations of the last half-century will find themselves increasingly undercut economically and politically in the adjoining Asia-Pacific.

American efforts to forge closer diplomatic, economic, and security ties with Southeast Asia, for example (through an embrace of its multilateral forums; the conclusion of a comprehensive Asia-Pacific free trade deal (Trans-Pacific Partnership Agreement); and the strengthening of security partnerships) find much of their strategic capital in the subregion's standing as the fourth largest overall trading partner of the United States, but also because of its geographic importance in facilitating nearly a third of all international commerce – including the transshipment of energy and other natural resource commodities to Northeast Asian markets from as far afield as the Middle East and Africa. To reiterate a few commonly referenced numbers, we see the Indian Ocean playing host to roughly half of the world's total container traffic, which within that includes around 80% of China's crude oil imports, 60% of Japan's energy supplies, two-thirds of South Korea's energy supplies, and 75% of India's energy supplies.[3] Thus, any "East Asian" engagement strategy, such as the American rebalance, is bound to an Indian Ocean strategy that fully comprehends how Southeast Asia's own contemporary strategic relevance is tied to its geographical proximity to the Bay of Bengal and the greater Indian Ocean. More specifically, such strategies must comprehend the range of transnational economic and security opportunities (and challenges) that now link the Indian Ocean increasingly closer to the South China Sea and the greater Asia-Pacific. This is reminiscent of a time when the

Asia-Pacific as a defined economic and political space had not yet existed, and when Southeast Asian trade, culture, and politics faced more naturally towards the civilizations of the Indian Ocean region.

Tangible examples of Northeast and Southeast Asia's current economic, military, and diplomatic reach towards the far corners of the Indian Ocean region show that the natural links that existed across the Indian Ocean are very much intact in the contemporary world. While ambitious infrastructure projects throughout the Indian Ocean have received most of the mainstream publicity, a number of commercial partnerships and investment deals akin to one completed in 2013 – which saw Singapore's Concord Energy sell a 50% stake in its Fujairah Oil Terminals storage facilities project to Sinomart KTS Development of China (a wholly owned subsidiary of Sinopec Kantons Holdings, which falls directly under the ownership of state-run China Petroleum and Chemical Corporation – Sinopec) have become increasingly commonplace.[4]

Hardly surprising in today's economic environment is a Singaporean–Chinese–United Arab Emirates "partnership" that leverages the strengths and meets the needs of each of these three countries, and in doing so orients each toward an emerging worldview that is increasingly defined and made possible by the Indian Ocean maritime corridor. The Arab port city is itself gaining strategic importance as East Asian countries deepen their investments in this only emirate that openly faces the Gulf of Oman and the greater Indian Ocean, thereby bypassing the crowded and politically sensitive Strait of Hormuz.

Militarily, East Asia's presence in the far reaches of the Indian Ocean is evident in the rapidly modernizing Chinese Navy, which has now proved that it can, at least minimally, operate with effect in a permissive environment in the greater Indian Ocean through its emerging regional blue-water naval capabilities. Specifically, China has been deliberately open in discussing its growing nuclear attack submarine capabilities, and had in December 2013 made its first announced trip through the Malacca Straits into the Indian Ocean, initially surfacing in Sri Lankan waters before making its way further west into the Persian Gulf.[5] This came on the heels of Beijing's inclusion in late 2008 in counter-piracy campaigns in the Gulf of Aden,[6] which established the first sustained Chinese naval contingency in the western Indian Ocean alongside a cast of other East Asian and Pacific navies vying for a more permanent naval presence in the region. The other countries included Japan, South Korea, and Australia.

Diplomatically, the Chinese have begun wading into high-profile conflict areas by stepping-up their involvement in Afghanistan – an important diversification of their presence in Southwest Asia which piggy-backs on their established relationships in Pakistan at the very same time American and European support draws down after 13 years of military engagement.

Due to a long and disruptive relationship with its Uighur minority population, Beijing continues to be highly sensitive to the spread of militant groups crossing into the Xinjiang region from bordering Pakistan and Afghanistan. A public statement by the Chinese special representative for Afghanistan and Pakistan soon after Afghan President Ashraf Ghani's first symbolic trip overseas to Beijing in

November 2014 stated succinctly (when speaking about China's peacemaking role in Afghanistan) that "we are ready to do more, we want to play a bigger role"; a role that currently has Beijing playing facilitator to several forums addressing reconciliation within and between Afghanistan and its neighbors.[7]

Economic and geopolitical expansion

Robert D. Kaplan's book *Monsoon: The Indian Ocean and the Future of American Power* provides a compelling rethink of the Indian Ocean region which reorients the Indian Ocean discourse away from a Cold War phenomenon where an "artificial dichotomy on area studies" had developed that effectively severed the "single organic unit" that was – from the precolonial period until the early 20th century – an inherent trait of this broader maritime region.[8] Contextualizing today's world through this historical and geographic perspective, it should not be surprising that, as the legacy of the Cold War's artificial boundaries continues to wane – both physically and mentally – and as the liberal international economic order continues to promote growth and prosperity in Asia, countries (facilitated by the appetites of their economic agents) will continue to re-institute and further expand linkages throughout the Indian Ocean in order to grow the economic space needed to sustain their expanding growth strategies. This view, coupled with the simple fact that there exist "more economic players in the planet than we had in the 20th century, with power and with a sense of independence,"[9] indicates that a natural progression of purposeful Asian expansion and diversification in the Indian Ocean for the foreseeable future in both economic and geopolitical terms is highly certain – barring political instability in Asia's dominant economies and/or playing host to an economic shock or reversal similar in scope to the one experienced globally in 2008. What is currently playing out is a critical period of economic expansion that is taking Asian economies and their national interests far beyond the economic and political domains of the recent past. With sea-borne trade and rising transnational investments underwriting Asia's growing prosperity and influence, national governments have begun to adjust their single "obsession with controlling land frontiers" to include ambitious naval and other maritime expansion programs to independently ensure these new interests are protected in the increasingly significant Indian Ocean geo-strategic arena.[10]

The Indo-Pacific: a strategic coupling

Due in large part to complementary strategic priorities, there has been a growing, albeit measured, acceptance of the term "Indo-Pacific" in contemporary strategic discussions. This measured acceptance speaks to the concept's infancy, but also to a natural hesitation to ensure that the term is constructed in a way that best reflects an individual actor's own interests. While a mutual definition is yet to be recognized, broader "Asia" policies that include within their scope the whole of the Indian Ocean maritime region find common ground with concepts that posit the greater Indo-Pacific area as a distinct political space.

The Australian vision of an emerging "Indo-Pacific system," through its 2013 Defence White Paper, has been the first to describe such a space in clear policy-oriented terms. From the Australian perspective, as India emerges as both an economic and political power, and as trade and investment across the region reinforce economic and security interdependence throughout Asia, "a new Indo-Pacific strategic arc is beginning to emerge, connecting the Indian and Pacific Oceans through Southeast Asia."[11] While the Australian construct does not itself include predetermined political space beyond India, and is an attempt to position Australia as a geographic center of a burgeoning and strategically relevant Indo-Pacific region,[12] it does acknowledge for the first time that the growing levels of integration that now exist between the Indian and Pacific Oceans are worthy of high-level policy considerations. Complicating this integration is the simultaneous rise of new influential regional actors that will most certainly escalate the stakes of state-to-state cooperation and/or competition in the broader Indo-Pacific region in the coming decades. As the policy construct of a regional power, the Australian perspective does not represent the full story for a country like the United States as a global power; however, it does reflect a more contemporary view of the basic environment in which the United States, India, China, and other actors must operate as they continue to project themselves economically, diplomatically, and militarily from the Western Pacific across the Indian Ocean and into the Middle East.

In addition to the concept's utility as a deliberate policymaking principle, there have been a number of key public endorsements favoring a strategic coupling of the Indian and Pacific Oceans from both East and South Asia, as Indian strategist C. Raja Mohan has pointed out. While the use of the precise term "Indo-Pacific" is found to be most frequently propagated and adopted from Australian commentators to date, strong lip service that draws on the same principles has been publicly delivered by both Japanese Prime Minister Shinzo Abe in his speech to the Indian Parliament in 2007 and former Indian Foreign Secretary Shyam Saran in an opinion piece published in 2011.[13] C. Raja Mohan himself positions his broader discussion on the budding Sino-Indian rivalry within the context of a unitary Indo-Pacific space. While the term "Asia-Pacific" still dominates the broader Asia foreign-policy discourse in the United States, high-level public statements from both the current and former secretaries of state and military commanders within the Obama administration have promoted the terms "Indo-Pacific" or "Indo-Asia-Pacific" where suitable, as Rory Medcalf[14] of the Australian Lowy Institute has noted. As Medcalf rightly states, "words matter," and such words describe with more accuracy the positioning of contemporary economic and political orientations.

It is necessary at this point to acknowledge that the conceptual coupling of the Indian and Pacific Ocean regions has emerged in step with a meaningful expansion of East Asian capital and other ensuing East Asian interests into the Indian Ocean. Therefore, while large Indian Ocean littoral countries like India do have "Pacific" ambitions, the emergence of a recognized "Indo-Pacific" space is more in response to East Asian capital and influence projecting westward into the Indian Ocean rather than the admittedly weaker Indian Ocean regional states projecting eastward into the Pacific. Commentators have gone so far as to blame the region's overt weaknesses for keeping geopolitical discourses from acknowledging the Indian Ocean region as a proper geopolitical area in its own right.[15] It is thus important to recognize that scholars have settled around five possible scenarios for the future look of East Asia's strategic order over the next several decades. "A Sino-centric order, a division between democratic and authoritarian states, Sino-US cohegemeny, a regional concert of powers, and the continuation of American preponderance."[16] With the relative weaknesses of Indian Ocean regional states continuing for some time, the futures of both East Asia and the increasingly connected Indian Ocean are thus hugely dependent upon how East Asia and the Western Pacific come to organize themselves.

Diversity and contested definitions

In order to reorient perceptions more accurately towards today's regional realities, the basic argument of this chapter has thus far advanced the idea that the greater Indian Ocean region – as a cohesive entity in its own right – is emerging as one part of a larger and increasingly influential Indo-Pacific economic and political space. Without losing sight of this critically fundamental perspective, it is worth acknowledging the varieties of identities that make up the broader Indian Ocean region. Mindful of the emerging trend toward more overt Indo-Pacific geopolitical and economic alignments, it would be helpful to consider the diversities and the contested definitions of the Indian Ocean maritime region for a couple of key reasons. First, an understanding of Indian Ocean regional relations requires an appreciation of how the region's various ethnic, social, and religious traditions project themselves on to equally diverse sets of political and economic orientations and arrangements. Second, the applicability of such an understanding is susceptible to overtly simplistic generalizations without such an acknowledgment.

Taking from Bouchard's[17] assessment of the emerging geopolitical order in what he terms the "Indianoceanic" region, there can be said to exist nine distinct "sub-regional systems" that make up the larger regional landscape, namely: Southern Africa, Eastern Africa, the South-West Indian Ocean Islands, the Horn of Africa, the Persian Gulf, Central Asia, South Asia, Southeast Asia, and the Austral Islands. These subsystems in turn operate within an organization of larger "peripheral" regional systems that are drawn from the African Union, the Middle East, the Asia Pacific, and finally the South Pacific (Oceania). What makes these distinctions important, Bouchard argues, is the fact that Indianoceanic states tend to be relatively weak in exerting influence beyond their immediate localities, forcing any analysis of relations to be initially undertaken at the subregional level. As Bouchard explains, "It is at this level that the main power relations are established, that the significant geopolitical equilibrium is formed as well as that the operative economic and political integration processes are organized".[18] This basic framework provides a valuable perspective for understanding the contemporary regional environment and describes succinctly the relative strength and influence, or lack thereof, of the region's individual states. Mindful of the region's economic, political, and sociocultural diversities, and the various ways in which extraregional influences must be absorbed as a more purposeful and integrated Indo-Pacific system develops, there is little doubt that the political and economic diversities found within and between the subregional systems will remain critical variables in the development of foreign-policy approaches toward the Indian Ocean maritime region in the years to come.

In the contemporary nation-state environment, it is implicitly understood that interaction beyond a nation's own political domain requires that such "inter-national" interaction be undertaken between seemingly equal and autonomous political institutions and structures. With this in mind, it is no small matter that a significant number of states (spanning five continents) make up the Indian Ocean region; a fact made substantially more complicated by the diversity seen between each state's internal political structures and varying levels of development and overall stability.

In defining the scope of the aforementioned "Indianoceanic" region, the author adopts as his determining factors a state's orientation towards, and its level of dependency on, the Indian Ocean and its natural extensions for trade and logistics. Simply stated, for a state to be included in the Indianoceanic region, the Indian Ocean must be the "unique maritime connection or one of their maritime connections to the rest of the world".[19] This take consequentially goes beyond a strict interpretation of the mere 28 littoral states by identifying a total of 56 littoral and adjoining (inland) states, including the countries of Zimbabwe and Malawi in Africa with their dependencies on the East African coast, Israel and Jordan in the Middle East with their dependencies on the Red Sea, and Afghanistan, Bhutan, and Nepal in South and Southwest Asia. Expand the scope to include the broader Indo-Pacific space and the number of countries climbs to well over 60. Regional groupings are therefore no more than geographically justified political and economic associations that serve the purpose of those who choose to ascribe to them. If a comprehensive and inclusive definition were not to be assumed for this study, we run the risk of falling prey to special-interest exclusions that take us no further away from the "artificial dichotomy" that existed during and after the Cold War period. While this inquiry does not take an indepth look into every one of these states, it does consciously acknowledge the immense scope that this grouping represents, particularly in geostrategic terms, as new political, economic, and security realities emerge within a developing Indo-Pacific. The high number and wide distribution of states that make up the region reinforce the importance of the region's political heterogeneity as a critical component for directing foreign-policy initiatives aimed at safeguarding the various national interests, littoral or otherwise, in the region.

Security issues of the Indian Ocean region

A unique concentration of flashpoints and security issues endemic to the greater Indian Ocean region has swayed the calculations of the largest and smallest of contemporary regional actors. Many of the world's major pressure points find residence or touch in some way the territorial spaces of the greater Indian Ocean region. Therefore, not only is the region a microcosm of the current global condition, it is in fact contributing a great deal to the persistent push and pull of political and economic forces that are common in today's decentralizing international environment. In adopting the list of regional security concerns outlined by Michael J. Green and Andrew Shearer,[20] we see a host of traditional and non-traditional security issues that require both immediate crisis management intervention and long-term geostrategic planning considerations. The transport of oil supplies between the Persian Gulf and East Asia; arms proliferation; the threat of piracy and terrorist acts; and the trafficking of persons and drugs across the region are all examples of the more immediate concerns that are today drawing actors in. In the mid term regional actors must address the large proportion of fragile and failing states along the ocean's littoral; sea-level rise and other effects of climate change on low-lying islands and coastal areas; and conflicts between India and its neighbors over exclusive economic zone claims. Looking toward the horizon is the looming threat of "sea denial" posed by an increasingly crowded and complex regional environment; the increasing competition over seabed resources; and the potential for great-power rivalry – particularly between India and China.

The most critical long-term security challenges facing the Indian Ocean maritime region tend to center around the possible repercussions of an increasingly crowded and complex regional environment. Shared legacies of global trade show a fundamental link between security and commerce. Therefore, history suggests that, as the need to protect growing economic interests throughout the Indian Ocean creates increasingly complex geostrategic security priorities, a greater level of responsiveness to the challenges (and opportunities) in the often volatile areas of Africa, the Middle East, and South/Southwest Asia will be required of China, India, and possibly Japan (when taking into account the broader effects of natural disasters such as Japan's growing dependency on Middle East oil after the Fukushima nuclear disaster in 2011).

Crucially for the region's security environment, issues may very well arise as more countries are pulled further into the Indian Ocean, crowding the existing space with more actors that feel equally compelled to protect their own domestic interests.[21] A particularly sensitive outlook is if this heightened sense of concern were to then be coupled with a premature rush to fill a perceived power vacuum if the United States were to ever indicate a substantial retreat of its forward positions in and around the Indian Ocean – an event that does not lie far outside the scope of the contentious and arbitrary nature of national budget negotiations in the US Congress. The cyclical nature of such negotiations ensures that future budget talks will play hostage to the type of political maneuvering that led to what was commonly referred to as the budget "sequestration" following the January 2013 budget negotiation deadlines. The critical aspect of this maneuvering was that it sought to impose automatic and largely indiscriminate spending cuts on the US's federal government that would have impacted the U.S. Department of Defense, among others.

Lacking any sort of effective multilateral security structures in the Indian Ocean that might institutionalize state–state interaction during a time of rising military force capabilities (in this already highly militarized part of the world), such overcrowding would require a sustained and complex diplomatic presence where individual geopolitical maneuvering will be the sole guarantor or obstacle to regional stability. Already a topic of diplomatic banter, this concern had in 2010 compelled the Indian Minister of State for Defense to go so far as to state how "happy" he was to offer Indian naval protection to Beijing to secure the Indian Ocean shipping corridors that China so heavily relies on in transporting energy supplies from the Middle East.[22] The addition of new players into the region would force a measure of accommodation that will yield to a cooperative and/or competitive environment that would, for the first time in a substantial way, span the combined physical and political spaces of the Indian and Pacific Oceans.

As East Asian countries' dependency on the Indian Ocean steadily increases, America's own interests in the Indian Ocean will be tied increasingly and more directly to its interests in the Western Pacific. A proper US strategy towards Asia in the coming decades would thus include the appropriation of events from as far away as Africa, the Middle East, and Southwest Asia into a broader Asian context just as easily as it would a North American, Middle East, or African regional context. This wider interpretation of a US "Asia" strategy would in the process satisfy the concerns reflected in the media and in anxious diplomatic statements that portray the ongoing "rebalance" to the Asia-Pacific as nothing more than a rhetorical promotion held hostage to the continuing unrest in the Middle East and surrounding hot-spot areas. A sustained American engagement with Asia may very well find its evolving legitimacy in the Indian Ocean maritime context.

Maritime commerce of the Indian Ocean region

International trade embodies the economic environment of the Indian Ocean maritime region. A convergence of unique geographical dependencies and commercial opportunities has for centuries shaped the region's reliance on trade as a crucial lifeline for sustaining its most prosperous and influential population centers. Much in line with this tradition, today's commercial activities are by far the most frequent and well-established sources of contact between countries and peoples within the Indo-Pacific and with the rest of the world. As a critically important component of today's global economy, commentators are right to have focused most extensively on the maritime trade aspects of the Indian Ocean when discussing the region's significance. When analyzed in purely commercial terms, the topic is on its own an enormously complex enterprise. Added to this, we are now entering an era that appears ripe for new strategic competition as the balance of power in the Indian Ocean adjusts to the economic and political posturing of the Indo-Pacific's increasingly influential national economies.

As a result, new economic and political variables are now being woven into the existing fabric of Indian Ocean maritime commercial activities in ways that mirror evolving economic dependencies and shifting power balances. Implications of this reach far beyond the shores of the Indian Ocean as economies on every continent are in varying degrees dependent upon Indian Ocean maritime trade – primarily through its role in connecting large portions of the global supply and value chains between the world's largest resource, manufacturing, and consumer markets. The United States, despite its Pacific Ocean trade route with East Asia, finds much of its economic dependency on the Indian Ocean via East Asia's dependency on resources and raw materials from Africa, the Middle East, South Asia, and Australia, linking the consumer in rural America much more closely to the waters of the Indian Ocean in today's integrated global economy than one might initially expect. Knowing that link in turn emphasizes the growing significance of intra-Asia trade to the global economy in ways that would not have been acknowledged just a few decades ago.

With Asian markets serving as a key driver of global trade growth, developing countries' economies share of total world trade in exports and imports of goods and commercial services have risen to 41% and 39% respectively in 2012.[23] These numbers are made all the more noteworthy when considering that this rise has materialized through a surge in "South–South" trade, with increases in Asia continuing at a faster yearly rate than world trade averages. International seaborne trade has itself benefited from intra-Asia and South–South trade by outpacing global merchandise trade in volume during this same period – with seaborne trade increasing by an estimated 4.3%, in contrast to a global trade growth of just 1.8% in 2012.[24] In step with such trade developments, rising flows of investment and transnational labor mobility are expanding and strengthening these South–South linkages, much of which is facilitated by the physical and symbolic corridors of the Indian Ocean. As the developing world contributes larger shares to global economic output, and as key developing economies such as China continue to rely in significant ways on extensive growth strategies[25] to grow those shares, the sheer volume, substance, and destinations of seaborne trade that traverse the Indian Ocean make this region poised to gain even more significance in the years to come.

For all the benefits the Indian Ocean region provides to international trade and commerce, there exists a unique set of geographical dependencies that come in the form of maritime "chokepoints" to which trade through the Indian Ocean is so heavily dependent. Despite being the world's third largest ocean, it is for all practical purposes a land-locked body of water that is most conveniently accessed through a series of strategic and commercially important channels, canals, and straits that line its eastern and western perimeters. The seven key chokepoints, from the western perimeter of Africa over to Southeast Asia in the east, are the Mozambique Channel, the Bab el Mandeb, the Suez Canal, the Strait of Hormuz, the Malacca Straits, the Sunda Strait, and the Lombok Strait. The high volumes of seaborne trade that must traverse these chokepoints are further complicated by the geopolitical and security realities of their surrounding environments. The Strait of Hormuz, for example, which lies between Iran and Oman, serves as the critical link between the oil-rich countries of the Persian Gulf and the open corridors of the Arabian Sea and the greater Indian Ocean, and continues to be by far the world's most important energy chokepoint, with an estimated 17 million barrels of oil a day traversing its waters in 2013. Regulating this sheer volume is a massive logistical undertaking on its own, made significantly more complicated by the ongoing hostilities between littoral and non-littoral powers (namely the United States and its regional partners) and Iran. With 85% of Persian Gulf oil bound for Asian markets – primarily to those in India, China, Japan, and South Korea[26] – it is patently clear how linked East Asia, and consequently the global economy, is to the far reaches of the greater Indian Ocean region.

Prosperity and the emerging geopolitics of the Indo-Pacific

After decades in which economic interests seemed to have been a mutually beneficial end in and of itself, we are witnessing a rapid reemergence of geopolitical concerns in the region. In light of Asia's expanding economic reach, commentators are increasingly voicing their concerns that the economic prosperity that had been gained through the deliberate integration of national economies is now being tapped by independent national actors as a means of achieving zero-sum geopolitical ends at the expense of those to whom they are economically linked. The last several decades have seen the region benefit greatly from the positive-sum gains made through the expansion of economic and commercial interests over long-simmering zero-sum geopolitical urges. However, prosperity has brought with it actors who are increasingly adept and willing to pursue their own interests in a way that now tests the resolve of the existing regional status quo.

In the wake of the 2008 global financial crisis, as America's global leadership capabilities were being severely questioned, opportunistic inclinations born out of years of reflection and economic and political "preparation" were quickly leveraged in an environment of perceived transitional instability. For China, this meant that the growing influence it had acquired (and the promise of even greater influence in the years to come) over its "smaller" neighbors could potentially be exploited to unilaterally alter in its favor the balance of power in the Western Pacific, thereby testing the resolve of the current regional status quo that has been largely underwritten by American security assurances and force projection in East Asia.

For the "smaller" states in the region, this period of transitional instability in turn supported both an overall preference for multilateral approaches for pursuing national interests and, within that paradigm, a renewed embrace of a more engaged United States which for the first time has found practical legitimacy in engaging new partners and participating in the region's multilateral institutions. This while the United States continues to position itself independently as the regional hegemon through its "rebalancing" initiatives, and in doing so has thus far accommodated the rise of a more prosperous and confident China within the East Asian political space.

From the perspective of China's immediate neighbors, however, the threat of a more assertive China appears more imminent and there have thus been quick and vocal criticisms of Chinese political and strategic actions in the East and South

China Seas that stem from competing territorial designs. China, for its part, in countering such perceptions and strategic maneuvering, has vocalized an "Asia for Asians" agenda in a rhetorical show of Asian unity while preferring to engage with its neighbors bilaterally on the political front (where it is argued that China most often has the upper hand) and by pursuing parallel bilateral and multilateral approaches on the economic front; this through direct financing of major infrastructure projects and other investments while successfully launching the Asian Infrastructure Investment Bank.

In the aggregate, however, latent but deep-seated suspicions stemming from long histories of accumulated grievances have quickly gained renewed vigor under these conditions with the same confrontational patterns that come with competing historical interpretations of territorial demarcations and past war reparations. Despite these hostilities, relations with China remain a critical concern for all Asian states, and because of that, confrontation and/or engagement with China must be weighed carefully as such interaction will directly impact relations with other states as well. As China emerges as an influential actor capable of asserting national economic and political interests in the region – and as domestic populations in the region's developing countries stake their prosperity on Chinese markets and a newly emerging regional environment – a delicate balancing act between economic engagement and security risk has now become the dominant driver of international relations in Asia.

While the merits and/or the faults of China's growing confidence and assertiveness should be seen through a complex lens that reflects the true intricacies of the country's economic, political, and security interests, the mere fact that China has chosen to unilaterally assert itself in meaningful ways, both regionally and globally, has given license to forecasters to project a certain level of Chinese unilateral action as it enters, with more purpose, the Indian Ocean.[27] However long-viewed these projections may be, a delicate balancing act between economic engagement and military threat is now the dominant driver of international relations in Asia and, with increasing frequency, the broader Indo-Pacific. Within this context, ensuring that the strategic chokepoints and important sea lines of communication remain free and open to a broad range of commercial activities is at the heart of both regional and global prosperity (under the current liberal international economic order) and an impending test of the measured accommodation that will be required as increasingly influential actors, with long-standing historical rivalries, crowd the Indian Ocean's physical, political, and economic spaces.

Traditional interests, evolving priorities

The relevancy of discussing contemporary national interests in the Indian Ocean comes not from a fundamental shift in geostrategic interests, but rather in the evolving context by which traditional interests must now be ensured. Navigating the nexus between economics and security has long guided the direction of US foreign policy in Asia and around the world. During the Cold War, the overall risk of ceding relative power to increasingly prosperous and economically interdependent allies and partners had been outweighed by America's primary security interest in confronting Soviet expansion. Optimistic about its ability to sustain its competitive economic advantages, the United States bet on open-market access, with particular success in East Asia. Under this confidence, the United States and its partners found strategic capital in an engaged and prosperous China which had itself already begun a process of national economic and strategic reflection. While America's initial engagement with China came as an international shock (particularly to its Japanese allies), countries like Japan – with its own history of sensitive and at times hostile relations with China – would soon join and benefit immensely alongside the United States as China became increasingly open for business. This approach would eventually prove to be geostrategically successful in combating Soviet expansion, while simultaneously expanding the "economic pie" in America's likeness, providing the United States and likeminded partners with a larger pool to both access and shape as they in turn expanded their own established economic and security levers.

In the aftermath of the Cold War, the early economic liberalization that had laid the groundwork for increasingly lucrative commercial gains continued to reinforce greater economic collaboration and interdependence. Within this environment, a proliferation of both sovereign and private economic agents effectively solidified links between the emerging markets in the East and the mature and technically more advanced economies in the West. Without the security threat posed by great-power rivalries, post Cold War thinking increasingly favored economic factors in international relations, with remarkable success for the now mutually dependent economies of the Asia-Pacific. The economic and security interests of the United States, Japan, and other like-minded partners had largely won out in the last 30 years, resulting in a relatively stable regional environment that has sought to integrate a new and growing cast of commercially minded participants. Even China, in an effort to reverse the disastrous policies of its Cultural Revolution, found itself transforming its once-planned socialist economy into one that is today fully dependent upon the liberal international economic system.

As this largely American-led liberal economic model adopts new and diverse identities and becomes the standard playing field for global economic activity (as the broader economic sphere incorporates more equally the cultural and social identities of a growing pool of economic players), the need to overtly link economic and security interests is increasingly the new norm for more and more countries around the world. This has become particularly true as governments have felt compelled to stake their political survival on their abilities to corner their fair share of the world's growing prosperity (whether driven by the personal appetites of those in power or as a response to the collective desires of national constituents; with most cases being a combination of the two).

A new cast of economic actors from all over the world are learning, and by-and-large excelling in, the competitive transnational economic environment that US economic and security structures have facilitated and where economics and foreign relations are quite simply "indivisible".[28] Indeterminate of political structure or ideology, the world now competes, grows, and even contracts within the same global competitive market-based system on a more equal footing than ever before. While extremely compelling economically, such variables can complicate the relationship between national security priorities and the often transnational and decentralized economic objectives that come with the adoption of a liberal economic system – a system where security and economic priorities have been shown to both indiscriminately compete and complement each other in ways that can complicate a nation's efforts at delineating a set of constant strategic priorities.

As the "rise of the rest" embroils the larger Indo-Pacific in an environment of transitional uncertainty, the United States finds itself in a situation where Washington continues to champion and safeguard a liberal international economic system that has facilitated enormous wealth and prosperity, but has in its wake fueled a potentially volatile geopolitical environment. Policymakers and economic agents alike must now consider with more concern the potential effects of their actions in a global economic landscape that is becoming increasingly flattened.

While still largely in the driver's seat when viewed from a macro level, the advantages that America's economic agents have long enjoyed have been on the relative decline as countries from around the world engage with more autonomy, and thus by different interpretations of rules, with today's global competitive markets. This includes, among other things, new interpretations of what constitutes market fairness and a level playing field – concepts that the United States has consequently pushed hard to enshrine in the Trans-Pacific Partnership Agreement under its own interpretation, ensuring that American economic agents continue to maintain their competitive advantages. "Fair" market advocates in the United States have thus begun to replace the long-time champions of "open" markets. Symbolic of this are recent developments in the traditionally American-dominated international airline industry, where a shift by American air carriers – which now face stiff competition from a new generation of global airlines (with new business models and domestic subsidy arrangements) – now oppose the "open-skies" agreements they long advocated and benefitted from.[29] Hence, the global order the United States had so adamantly propagated and so heavily invested in to protect its own interests and prosperity has now given rise to influential actors with new and often competing agendas.

China, as both an economic and political entity, is by far the most significant example of this emerging story. While no one doubts China's hand in orchestrating its own impressive rise, it is also understood that it has done so by embracing the liberal international economic order that had been forged through American leadership and safeguarded by American military assurances. A consequence of this has been the creation of new, vibrant markets around the world that look singularly to Asia and that have in part led to a growing sense of autonomy and confidence in Asian capitals.

Current US involvement in Asia underscores a continuing belief by American policymakers that, if managed properly, opportunities in Asia still provide the United States with enormous long-term economic benefits and security assurances. Thus, the Obama administration's "rebalancing" strategy is at its core a reinvestment in the same theater that the United States has already found so much success from in the past. Again, the new lease here comes not from a shift in geostrategic interests, but rather in response to contextual changes that require renewed levels of investment that will ensure that the region remains prosperous and stable within a framework that continues to be open and favorable to American economic and security interests. The United States' embrace of the Trans-Pacific Partnership free trade agreement is an overt example of such an initiative, where the US government has been "extremely bullish"[30] in its attempt to instill in the region economic structures that promote "fairness" by upholding American ideals of international commerce, investment, intellectual property rights, and legal norms (ideals that America will continue to argue to be universally advantageous).

While the United States is compelled into a leadership role in the Western Pacific through its "in-network" security structure, the Indian Ocean necessitates a somewhat different approach, which Green and Shearer[31] do well to discuss. With key allies such as Japan and South Korea dependent upon America's presence in East Asia, stability and the balance of power in the Western Pacific hinge on US engagement – largely through its continuing ability to maintain a loosely coordinated "hub-and-spoke" arrangement. While American preeminence in Northeast Asia has largely been a welcome mainstay over the last 70 years, no such hegemonic legacy in the Indian Ocean exists during this same period. In fact, any such condition would immediately invoke unwelcomed comparisons to the region's colonial past. This detail, in concert with the region's tremendous social and political heterogeneity and the overt weaknesses of its member states, makes any attempt to organize the region by either the United States or any individual regional actor untenable, regardless of their hegemonic ambition.

Indigenous efforts at establishing broad regional geopolitical and economic structures have been attempted through the establishment of the South Asian Association for Regional Cooperation and the Indian Ocean Rim Association. However, these structures have yielded relatively little in the way of political and economic cooperation, with their merits coming more in the symbolism of their inception rather than in their ability to create a real cohesion that facilitates stability and prosperity through greater regional political and/or economic cooperation.

Precisely because such structures have been shown to hold very little sway in such a diverse region, the safeguarding of United States interests in the Indian Ocean will not come from a region-wide architectural solution.[32] What is more feasible, given the region's diversity and its high concentration of pressure points, is a mix of independent issue-specific structures (coalitions, partnerships, task forces, etc.) that converge around specific topics that, as a collection, cut across sectors to address a portfolio of issues – from security and economic development to social and environmental. The multinational counter-piracy operations in the Gulf of Aden and the Western Indian Ocean under Combined Task Force 151, NATO's Operation Ocean Shield, and the European Union's Operation Atalanta are examples of such an approach. These structures serve individual national interests (in this case to safeguard commercial investments while providing logistical and operational training and sea-time experience to national navies) while also facilitating a level of naval coordination between potential adversaries over topics of mutual interest.

Conveniently, broader American interests in the Indian Ocean are largely mutually beneficial. Safeguarding the Indian Ocean as a free and open corridor for international commerce and trade is the United States' most critical immediate interest and one that spans the interests of a number of influential countries in the Indo-Pacific and around the world which are today fully invested in the contemporary transnational economic environment. It is particularly important that these corridors continue to facilitate trade between the oil- and resource-rich countries of the Western Indian Ocean and the vibrant markets of East Asia, as such trade provides the means through which much of the world's manufacturing and production is now powered.

Energy and resources are thus symbolic and tantamount to a continued trajectory of rising global prosperity. While the United States has itself pursued a path towards energy independence (dramatically reducing its own direct dependency on Middle East oil), the trend has been precisely the opposite for America's largest trading partners and allies in East Asia. China's unquenchable thirst for energy has made it the number-one net importer of oil in the world at the same time as Japan has increased its own oil imports in the aftermath of the 2011 Fukushima nuclear disaster, and while South Korea continues to import nearly all of its energy needs. Certain predictions have Chinese oil imports making up about 75% of overall Chinese demand by 2035, where the majority of it – more than 85% – will be transported via the Indian Ocean through the Strait of Malacca.[33] Thus, it is largely through today's global economic interdependencies that Indo-Pacific nations' stake in the Indian Ocean continues to materialize. As a result, economic interests are today the overriding priority that is keeping a relative check on the significant geopolitical and security concerns emerging in the Indo-Pacific.

Conclusion

The importance of East Asia to the global economy cannot be overstated. However, just as important is the fact that the region, even in its aggregated diversity, is not self-sustaining due to the current economic and social demands of its member countries. With increased global economic connectivity and greater transnational dependencies (sanctioned by a need to support the insatiable appetite and growing demands of an increasingly prosperous regional and global population), it is clearer now, more than ever, that all national interests and subsequent strategic maneuvering that seek to harness the East Asian economic engine must now incorporate, more deliberately, Indian Ocean economic and political variables. Not only is the region geographically expansive, it is becoming commercially expansive, encompassing all stages of contemporary transnational supply and value-added chains (with greater potential yet to be tapped).

The Indo-Pacific, as a defined political and economic space, is crucial today in supporting global economic growth and prosperity by providing the corridor between resource acquisition (which supports East Asia's manufacturing industries) and the transfer and sale of those manufactured goods to consumers around the world. Because of the region's growing strategic importance, we are now witnessing a convergence of complementary and competing national interests, specifically in the maritime arena. As Asia's next fully exploited commercial and geopolitical theater beyond the Western Pacific, security concerns will continue to be heightened in the Indian Ocean, where the subregion's own stability will play a decisive role in the stability and prosperity of the broader Indo-Pacific, pulling littoral and non-littoral powers alike into this important theater.

Notes

1 Fareed Zakaria. *The Post-American World.* New York: W. W. Norton, 2009.
2 The Obama administration coordinated a series of op-eds and speeches in the fall of 2011 by then Secretary of State Hillary Clinton, National Security Advisor Tom Donilon, and President Barack Obama to publicize its strategic *pivot* or *rebalance* towards the Asia-Pacific. See Hillary Clinton. "America's Pacific Century." *Foreign Policy.* October 11, 2011. http://www.foreignpolicy.com/articles/2011/10/11/americas_pacific_century (accessed September 9, 2014); Tom Donilon. "America is Back in the Pacific and will Uphold the Rules." *Financial Times.* November 27, 2011. http://www.ft.com/cms/s/0/4f3febac-1761-11e1-b00e-00144feabdc0.html#axzz1lvbgzfyEc (accessed September 9, 2014); Barack Obama. "Remarks by President Obama to the Australian Parliament." November 17, 2011. http://www.whitehouse.gov/the-press-office/2011/11/17/remarks-president-obama-australian-parliament (accessed September 1, 2014).
3 Rani D. Mullen and Cody Poplin. "The New Great Game: A Battle for Access and Influence in the Indo-Pacific." *Foreign Affairs.* September 29, 2015. https://www.foreignaffairs.com/articles/china/2015-09-29/new-great-game (accessed August 25, 2016).
4 Concord Energy. "Completion of Sale of 50% interest in Fujairah Oil Terminals." January 2013. http://concordenergygroup.com/january-2013-completion-of-sale-of-50-interest-in-fujairah-oil-terminals/ (accessed October 14, 2013); Sinopec Kantons Holdings. "Fujairah Oil Terminal FZC." 2013. http://www.sinopec.com.hk/en/getNewsDetailAction.do?target=GuandeNews&key=0CDEE9FE69E0EC4E69D7613CA42B9B4B (accessed October 12, 2014).
5 Jeremy Page. "Deep Threat: China's Submarines Add Nuclear-Strike Capability, Altering Strategic Balance." *Wall Street Journal.* October 24, 2014. http://online.wsj.com/articles/chinas-submarine-fleet-adds-nuclear-strike-capability-altering-strategic-balance-undersea-1414164738 (accessed November 11, 2014).
6 C. Raja Mohan. *Samudra Manthan: Sino-Indian Rivalry in the Indo-Pacific.* Washington, DC: Carnegie Endowment for International Peace, 2012.
7 Ahmed Rashid. "Viewpoint: Can China Bring Peace to Afghanistan?" *BBC News.* December 1, 2014. http://www.bbc.com/news/world-asia-30273431 (accessed December 14, 2014).
8 Robert D. Kaplan. *Monsoon: The Indian Ocean and the Future of American Power,* 13. New York: Random House, 2010.
9 John Kerry. "Remarks: U.S. Vision for Asia-Pacific Engagement." East-West Center, Honolulu, Hawaii. August 13, 2014. http://www.state.gov/secretary/remarks/2014/08/230597.htm (accessed September 15, 2014).
10 Mohan. *Samudra Manthan: Sino-Indian Rivalry in the Indo-Pacific,* 12.

11 Department of Defence. *Defence White Paper 2013*. Canberra: Commonwealth of Australia http://www.defence.gov.au/whitepaper2013/docs/WP_2013_web.pdf (accessed September 10, 2014).
12 Chengxin Pan. "The 'Indo-Pacific' and geopolitical anxieties about China's rise in the Asian regional order." *Australian Journal of International Affairs*, 68, no. 4 (2014), 453–69. http://www.tandfonline.com/doi/pdf/10.1080/10357718.2014.8840 54, 459 (accessed September 10, 2014).
13 Mohan. *Samudra Manthan: Sino-Indian Rivalry in the Indo-Pacific*, 12.
14 Rory Medcalf. "The Indo-Pacific: What's in a Name?" *The American Interest*. October 10, 2013. http://www.the-american-interest.com/2013/10/10/the-indo-pacific-whats-in-a-name/ (accessed November 20, 2014).
15 Christian Bouchard. "Emergence of a New Political Era in the Indian Ocean: Characteristics, Issues and Limitations of the Indianoceanic Order." In *Geopolitical Orientations, Regionalism and Security in the Indian Ocean*, edited by Dennis Rumley and Sanjay Chaturvedi, 84–109. New Delhi: South Asian Publishers, 2004.
16 Mingjiang Li and Dongmin Lee, eds. *China and East Asian Strategic Dynamics*, xi. Lanham, MD: Lexington Books, 2011.
17 Bouchard, in *Geopolitical Orientations, Regionalism and Security in the Indian Ocean*, 92–3.
18 Ibid., 92.
19 Ibid., 88.
20 Michael J. Green and Andrew Shearer. "Defining U.S. Indian Ocean Strategy." *Washington Quarterly*, 35, no. 2 (2012), 175–89. http://csis.org/files/publication/twq12springgreenshearer.pdf, 176 (accessed September 9, 2014).
21 Ibid., 182.
22 James Lamont and Geoff Dyer. "India to Help China Protect Oil Interests." *Financial Times*. February 18, 2010. http://find.galegroup.com/ftha/infomark.do?&source=gale&prodId=FTHA&userGroupName=apu&tabID=T003&docPage=article&docId=HS230 7374650&type=multipage&contentSet=LTO&version=1.0 (accessed October 1, 2014).
23 World Trade Organization. Committee on Trade and Development. "Participation of Developing Economies in the Global Trading System." *Note by the Secretariat*, WT/COMTD/W/201. October 14, 2013. https://docs.wto.org/dol2fe/Pages/FE_Search/FE_S_S006.aspx?Query=(%20@Symbol=%20wt/comtd/w/*%20and%20@Title=%20 (participation%20and%20developing%20economies%20in%20the%20global%20 trading%20system))&Language=ENGLISH&Context=FomerScriptedSearch&languageUIChanged=true# (accessed September 29, 2014).
24 United Nations Conference on Trade and Development. "Review of Maritime Transport 2013." *Report by the UNCTAD Secretariat*. UNCTAD/RMT/2013. 2013. http://unctad.org/en/PublicationsLibrary/rmt2013_en.pdf (accessed September 12, 2014).
25 "Extensive growth" is an economic term that refers to a reliance on expanding resources in order to maintain growth, where inputs must be continually increased in order to increase the quantity of outputs, thereby encouraging growth.
26 U.S. Energy Information Administration. "Analysis Brief: World Oil Transit Chokepoints." November 10, 2014. http://www.eia.gov/countries/analysisbriefs/World_Oil_Transit_Chokepoints/wotc.pdf (accessed December 1, 2014).
27 While it is important to acknowledge China's successes in modernizing its military capabilities, it is broadly accepted that the strategic and logistical dimensions of unilateral action in the Indian Ocean by a non-littoral state would require a much more robust and coordinated projection of military and diplomatic force than China is capable of committing at the moment, particularly as it safeguards its core interests in the Western Pacific – namely Taiwan and its territorial claims in the South China Sea.
28 Stated by Hillary Clinton. "Remarks: Economic Statecraft." Economic Club of New York, New York City. October 14, 2011 http://www.state.gov/secretary/20092013 clinton/rm/2011/10/175552.htm (accessed April 14, 2015); for an in-depth look into

the convergence of contemporary economic and geopolitical concerns, see also Robert D. Blackwill and Jennifer M. Harris. *War by Other Means: Geoeconomics and Statecraft.* Cambridge, MA: Belknap Press, 2016.
29 Jad Mouawad. "United States Airlines Are Challenging Open-Skies Agreements." *The New York Times.* February 6, 2015. http://www.nytimes.com/2015/02/07/business/us-airlines-challenge-open-skies-agreements.html?action=click&contentCollection=Asia%20Pacific&region=Footer&module=MoreInSection&pgtype=article (accessed February 6, 2015).
30 Kurt M. Campbell. "U.S. Foreign Policy in the Asia-Pacific Region." New York Foreign Press Center Briefing with Assistant Secretary for East Asia and Pacific Kurt M. Campbell. The New York Foreign Press Center. September 28, 2012. http://fpc.state.gov/198185.htm (accessed December 11, 2014).
31 Green and Shearer. "Defining U.S. Indian Ocean Strategy."
32 Ibid.
33 Charles L. Glaser. "How Oil Influences U.S. National Security." *International Security,* 38, no. 2 (2013): 112–46.

13 Conclusions

Interests and strategies in Asian regional institutional development

Steven B. Rothman

This project set out to understand changes in institutions and state interests and strategies in the Asia-Pacific region considering the context of global and regional changes in power. In particular, we asked questions about how states might (re)define their interests in the region due to the changes in institutions and power, how states strategically engage in forming new institutions or changing existing institutions, and the role of these new institutional structures for future state behavior.

The book presents several empirical arguments showing state use of institutions to achieve the strategic goals in the Asia region. This perspective somewhat contrasts with the liberal institutionalist perspective, where scholars focus on the importance of peaceful means to provide governance to the ungoverned realm of international politics and the cooperative power of international institutions. We can see in this volume, however, institutions becoming part of regional or global struggles for power and strategic advantages, just as the acquisition of military resources and territory has done historically.

The work in this volume presents a mixed prognosis for future cooperation in Asia with a potential trajectory for further deepening and broadening or a trajectory toward fracturing. Regionally, and globally, we are witnessing a transition, and states struggle and compete for influence during this transition period. Without a clear regional hegemon and no strong developed regional institutional governing structures, the situation permits greater strategic play, unlike areas in Europe or the Americas. Due to the nature of the transition and the dynamics among regional actors through institutional reforms and creating new institutions, the future of the region remains uncertain. The direction largely depends on China's involvement and the response to Chinese leadership among other nations in the region.

Although the book organizes chapters based on national perspective and interest, this conclusion cuts across the discussions and examines the ideas presented through theoretical and practical factors: the origins of national interest, state use and interest in international institutions, the future policy trajectories, and theoretical impact of the conclusions presented.

International interests

In this volume, several authors argue that state interests vary and change with changes based on collective interpretations and constructed identities, contrary to much of the conclusions from traditionally realist theories. For realist theories, international interests reflect the importance of state security and the acquisition of power to achieve greater security. Some realist theories suggest that balance of power prevents states from acquiring too much power,[1] while other theories suggest power acquisition comes to those with particular strategic advantages and characteristics.[2] Despite these differences in the ability to acquire power, state interest does not generally change from state to state.

Beyond realism, other theories postulate the importance of varied interests in international politics among states. In particular, under some conditions of hegemonic rule, for example, when another state provides security, interests may move away from security concerns toward economics, environment, or human rights.[3] Under these conditions, cooperation becomes more likely, though states continue to act as rational decision makers and attempt to acquire the greatest benefits for themselves. Constructivist theories, on the other hand, suggest that states do not have any particular inherent self-interest and do not necessarily adhere to a rational decision-making model. Under the constructionist model of interest formation, identity, norms, and ideas contribute to the formation of state interest, which may vary widely among different states.[4]

In particular, Robichaud suggests that China altered its international interests with influences from Western international relations theories and a strong identity based on China as the center of the world. Robichaud states that China's adherence to a Marxist–Leninist perspective in the past, which China used as a tool to structure its society and its relations with other, limited its interest in international affairs. Originally eschewing Western thought, China did not begin to consider Western international relations theories until after normalization, which created an internal conflict to separate China's own practices from those of the West.[5] This separation allowed China to reconnect to its imperial past, suggesting a change from China's traditional role as a passive rising state to a more engaged and "realist" state seeking great-power status.[6] Ba and Vyas also note China's changing interest in establishing itself in a more active and regional role in Asia. Either by creating institutions like the Asian Infrastructure Investment Bank[7] or dominating the international currency market,[8] China continues to work toward establishing itself at the center of a new era of international relations, becoming a great power and more influential in world affairs, reflective of its historical identity.

Yoshimatsu and Trinidad suggest, in contrast to other states, that Japan remains concerned over balancing power, in a realist fashion, readying for further pressure from China as it grows. Japan's interest, Yoshimatsu and Trinidad suggest, remains largely in the balance of power of the region against a rising China power. In order to accomplish this goal, Kaseda shows how Japan engages in both domestic and international political changes, such as altering its constitutional interpretation, strengthening its alliance with the United States, improving military capabilities, and building alliances with other Asian nations. At one point, as von Solms notes, Japan attempted to place itself at the center of international finance by proposing the Asian Monetary Fund to again balance against Chinese influence. Although the early efforts were difficult, Japan tried to open institutional cooperation through the East Asia Summit, increasing membership to both India and Australia to counterbalance China's influence.[9] Despite Japan's concern over the balance of power in the region, Kaseda concludes that the relationship with China is vital for the region, and to open dialogue about the island dispute further may be productive to reducing conflict.

India's identity, Chotani argues in this volume, presented a reluctant power and a laggard in the region, and guided its lack of involvement in the Asia region despite maintaining desire to engage in multilateral institutions. A rivalry between the United States and China would push other regional nations out of the institution-building process. This would limit Indian influence to promote a stable security regime in the region; therefore, India used more aggressive policies for entry into Asian institutions, described by Chotani in this volume. This more aggressive push also works to change the Indian identity toward a more involved state in the region.[10]

Likewise, Chen states that Taiwanese interests in the region are partially determined by their dual identity, belonging to the Western ideologies and the *Chineseness*. Taiwan's identity crisis, which allows it to see itself as China and sometimes as the "other," contradicts the general policy toward building "One China," which generates tension and conflict in the region, Chen suggests. This conflict is brought by not only its own identity as "China," but also the perception of other nations that see Taiwan as a proxy for Chinese policy in the region.[11]

The chapters in this book argue the importance of identity and perception in constructing state interests in the region. In some cases, such as the Japanese case, the interests remain relatively stable across time, though influenced by ideology nonetheless. Other states, such as China and India, change their interests based on constructed identities, which are also changing based on their behavior. These case studies, together, illustrate the driving forces of identity and international perceptions on international policy interest, and the mutual constitutiveness between identity and interest.

Strategies of engagement

Often when we look at strategy in international relations, research takes us in one of two directions: discussions of grand strategy or discussions of foreign policy. Defining grand strategy is generally illusive, but primarily involves the use of power for particular goals, reflecting higher, global, and a long-term perspective.[12] Foreign-policy studies mostly involve discussions of the determinants of foreign policy and the interaction among domestic and international forces that push the state in one direction or another.[13] These scholarly discussions of strategy and foreign policy both generally neglect the narrower field of strategic foreign policy, while practitioners and scholars of domestic political systems often center rhetorical strategy,[14] institutional manipulations,[15] and voting manipulations[16] within institutional structures.

The chapters in this volume document state strategies for engaging relations with other states through institutions. In all the cases discussed in the volume, states use or build multilateral institutions as an important part of their strategic involvement in the region. This illustrates a shift in international politics since the Cold War, where Western ideology dominated international institutions following World War II. In recent years, states have gained openings within the international system or within institutions to challenge the previously dominant Western views, which may help these challengers gain strategic advantages. The strategies used by states described in this series of case studies vary between the development of new institutions and working within existing international institutions.

The United States and allies created a number of international institutions after World War II to push forward Western ideology and a new Western-based world order.[17] The dominant ideological powers, led by the United States, continue to surpass previous efforts as well, by creating institutions such as the Transatlantic Trade and Investment Partnership, the Trans-Pacific Partnership, and a Trade in Services Agreement, which bypass current institutions and reject involvement from challengers. These institutional rules lock states into narrower policy tracks, which have an impact on future policy making during decision making.[18] Given the importance of institutions as constraints on states, some Asian states create new usurping institutions with different rules instituting an altered international order. For example, Ba suggests that China, the leading actor in the region, creates a new institutional order and locks in states to new norms and rules through the Asian Infrastructure Investment Bank to lead the region in a positive direction. Vyas also discusses Japan's attempt to generate new institutional framework by creating the Asian Monetary Fund, which never actually materialized. It is not yet possible to determine the extent to which these institutions will constrain member state behavior in a new set of institutional rules and norms differing from other international financial institutions.

Framing and agenda setting are also important ways to influence institutional rules and norms without generating new institutions. This strategy, well described by Schattschneider, discusses how changing the number of actors interested in an issue through framing or rhetoric can dictate the outcome of policy debates.[19] Japan, India, and China engage in varying degrees of institutional or norm manipulation in order to extract greater benefits from the structure of the global institutional framework. Von Solms discusses Japan's attempts to increase the membership of additional countries in Asian institutions to change dynamics within the institution and balance power. Chotani also discusses that India, likewise, influences the membership of Asian institutions by changing the way it frames itself in the Asian context. By changing the makeup of international institutions, states may change the policy outcomes produced by those institutions when decision-making rules rely on some type of voting mechanism. For consensus-based institutions, as most international institutions process decisions, other factors, such as framing and issue linkages, become more important influential factors.

Future of Asian cooperation

Recent events in Europe and the British national vote to leave the European Union placed the future of regional and eventual global cooperation in doubt. Likewise, the prognosis for cooperation in the Asia region is mixed. Some scholars point to the importance of the lack of a single hegemon historically in the Asian region as the primary, but not complete, explanation for lack of institutional framework in Asia.[20] Other scholars argue that cultural differences and lack of binding identity stemming from historical animosity between Asian nations prevent deepening of cooperative efforts among the states.[21] Concerns over the lack of hegemon in the region may diminish as China gains strength and takes an increasingly active role in institutional and norm development as well as maintaining regional security. However, a new hegemon creates concerns over the international ideological perspective of the state and whether the state pursues revisionist policy goals.

Current efforts in Asia to generate cooperative institutions involve clear competition and strategy. Von Solms suggests that Japan desires more inclusive arrangements to counter Chinese influence, while Ba and Vyas suggest that China creates new institutions to pull states away from dominant institutions. China's attempts to create bilateral relationships with many of the Association of Southeast Asian Nations (ASEAN) nations specifically undermine the effectiveness of many institutions currently in place. In contrast to China's policy to undermine the strength of the existing (United States-led) institutions in the region, Chotani discusses that India is more likely to increase its involvement in the region, while Porter points to the increasing importance of the Indian Ocean among regional states. Because Japan also seeks to expand the definition of Asia to include a greater number of actors, institutions and nations lack a current definition of the region and the actors that should participate in regional institutions. Conflicting strategies to increase membership and decrease membership will play out to determine the exact makeup of dominant construction of the region and eventual dominant institutions in the region.

Although the bulk of this volume focuses on the questions of relations through institutions in Asia, we must address the fundamental question about institutional influence over states in the region. Realist theory suggests prominently that institutions lack influence over member states in international politics due to the anarchical system and no monitoring and enforcement above state power. The realist perspective is somewhat echoed in this volume, at least in respect to security and conflict over strategic resources and waterways in the South China Sea.

Lim argues in this volume that these institutional arrangements in Asia may have little effect on conflict in the South China Sea. China's policies attempt to isolate the issues in the South China Sea from regional institutional agreements, especially trade agreements. Examining the counterfactual, the regional conflicts may be worse without such trade agreements in place, but the fundamental conflicts are unlikely to diminish due to the presence of such agreements.[22] Thus, as realist theory suggests, when conflict is deep enough and focuses on conditions of survival or security, regional agreements and institutions have a lesser effect on state policy. As argued by Lim, China may also make use of these institutions to influence states and pressure them to adhere to Chinese roles and demands during disputes in the South China Sea, taking strategic advantage of its position within the regional economic institutions. Contrastingly, Kaseda implies the importance of institutional norms and historical decisions affecting the relationship between Japan and China, suggesting that these institutions have important influences over state behavior.

The volume also argues that Russia may take a lesser role in the Asian institutional arena, though recent developments have demonstrated increased cooperation between Russia and China.[23] Russia, for its part, desires a prominently central position in the Eurasia new order, as originally proposed under Putin and, yet, put on hold due to the current conflicts with the West and the Middle East, beginning with the Ukraine crisis, Lukin argues in this volume. Furthermore, Lukin suggests that Russian development of the European–Asian order has many risks, including being overshadowed by other actors such as China; therefore, Russia will always have a primary focus toward Europe.

Theoretical impact

Much of neo-liberal tradition involves the benefits of cooperation and interdependence on state welfare and peace.[24] This interdependence and institutional design, however, allow states to use their relationships strategically to gain advantages over others. Yoshimatsu and Trinidad demonstrate this clearly, describing the efforts of both China and Japan in utilizing their institutional relationships and their trade and financial relationships with Southeast Asian states to improve their regional position in maritime disputes. This is an important description of international events to combine both realist goals with neo-liberal institutional means.

This book contributes to the discussion of utilizing theory for understanding current issues in foreign policy and institutional design and development. In particular, it highlights the necessity to use more than one theoretical paradigm to understand actors' interests and actions within the context of global strategy. Throughout the chapters, authors individually made use of constructivist theories to understand the preferences and interests of actors, particularly the changing Chinese interests in international relations. Interaction and design, for the most part, are governed by our understanding of geostrategy and politics with particular desires for gaining strength and power through changes in or developing new institutions.

There is little doubt that constructivist theory is important in understanding national identity formation and change in China as well as the perception of those changes by surrounding nations. In particular, Robichaud, Ba, and Vyas, in their respective discussions, all point to the importance of Chinese identity in its desire to make China great again and remove the stigma of previous domination by Western nations. In addition, the nature of Chinese emergence as a great power placing itself at the center of institutions, such as finance, global currency, and global banking institutions, changes the perceptions of other actors. The response of those other actors – acceptance or rejection of China as an important central great state – reflects on the identity of those states and their perceptions of China in the context of world politics.

State acceptance, rejection, and alteration of institutions partially determine the future of institutional dominance in Asia, making the future prospects uncertain. As Ba suggests in her chapter, the future of China's new role as center of the regional and global institutions depends largely on acceptance of China's role by other regional and global actors, considering that China's involvement is contentious.

Chen also uses realist and constructivist-based theories in pointing out that Taiwanese policies are determined partly by the structural power distribution and changes occurring in the region coupled with their own identity crisis with China, "estranged-self turned Other," and leadership perceptions of their "One China" conflicting with the emergence of their own nation as Taiwanese. This "Chineseness" also leads Taiwan toward conflicts with neighboring states, regardless of being a relatively smaller power, because the "Chineseness" identity provides a larger sense of itself, leading to greater conflict with some Southeast Asian states interpreting Taiwan as a Chinese proxy.

Summary

The book examines the creation and use of international institutions within the context of the Asia-Pacific region (broadly conceived). Examining how nations use and create institutions in the Asian region is important for theory development, which too often focuses on Western interests and Western design of international institutions. The examination illustrates the geostrategic and realist perspective in the way nations in Asia create and use institutions, diverging from the popular description of institutions as a cooperative building enterprise, within the liberal institutionalist perspective. In other words, the work in this book suggests that national interest and strategy do not stop at the proverbial door of international institutions. National interests and strategies are present in both the creation of international institutions and the way states operate within the institutions.

Notes

1 Robert Jervis. "Hypotheses on Misperception." *World Politics,* 20, no. 3 (1968): 454–79; Kenneth Neal Waltz. "Anarchic Orders and Balances of Power." In *Neorealism and Its Critics*, edited by Robert O. Keohane, 70–130. New York: Columbia University Press, 1986.
2 See John J. Mearsheimer. *The Tragedy of Great Power Politics.* New York: Norton, 2001; Colin Elman. "Extending Offensive Realism: The Louisiana Purchase and America's Rise to Regional Hegemony." *American Political Science Review,* 98, no. 4 (2004): 563–76.
3 Robert O. Keohane. *After Hegemony: Cooperation and Discord in the World Political Economy.* Princeton, NJ: Princeton University Press, 1984.
4 See Alexander Wendt. *Social Theory of International Politics. Cambridge Studies in International Relations, 67.* Cambridge: Cambridge University Press, 1999.

5 See Robichaud in this volume.
6 Ibid.
7 See Ba in this volume.
8 See Vyas in this volume.
9 See von Solms in this volume.
10 See Chotani in this volume.
11 See Chen in this volume.
12 See Timothy Andrews Sayle. "Defining and Teaching Grand Strategy" 4, January (2011): 1–11.
13 Walter Carlsnaes. "Foreign Policy." In *Handbook of International Relations*, edited by Walter Carlsnaes, Thomas Risse, and Beth A. Simmons, 331–49. London: SAGE Publications, 2002.
14 William H. Riker, Randall L. Calvert, John E. Mueller, and Rick K. Wilson. *The Strategy of Rhetoric: Campaigning for the American Constitution.* New Haven, CT: Yale University Press, 1996; Brian F. Schaffner and Patrick J. Sellers. *Winning with Words: The Origins and Impact of Political Framing.* New York: Routledge, 2010.
15 Marc L. Busch. "Overlapping Institutions, Forum Shopping, and Dispute Settlement in International Trade." *International Organization,* 61, Fall (2007): 735–61; Thomas A. Birkland. "Focusing Events, Mobilization, and Agenda Setting." *Journal of Public Policy,* 18, no. 1 (1998): 53–74; Jutta M. Joachim, *Agenda Setting, the UN, and NGOs: Gender Violence and Reproductive Rights.* Washington, DC: Georgetown University Press, 2007. http://www.loc.gov/catdir/toc/ecip0711/2007007012.html.
16 Kenneth Joseph Arrow. *Social Choice and Individual Values,* 2nd ed. New York: Wiley, 1963; Dennis C. Mueller. *Public Choice III.* Cambridge: Cambridge University Press, 2003; James M. Buchanan and Gordon Tullock. *The Calculus of Consent, Logical Foundations of Constitutional Democracy.* Ann Arbor, MI: University of Michigan Press, 1962.
17 G. John Ikenberry. *After Victory: Institutions, Strategic Restraint, and the Rebuilding of Order after Major Wars. Princeton Studies in International History and Politics.* Princeton, NJ: Princeton University Press, 2001.
18 Paul Pierson. *Politics in Time: History, Institutions, and Social Analysis.* Princeton, NJ: Princeton University Press, 2004; Alex Mintz. "How Do Leaders Make Decisions? A Poliheuristic Perspective." *Journal of Conflict Resolution,* 48, no. 1 (2004): 3–13.
19 E. E. Schattschneider. *The Semisovereign People: A Realist's View of Democracy in America.* Hinsdale, MA: Dryden Press, 1975.
20 Vinod K. Aggarwal. "Comparing Regional Cooperation Efforts in the Asia-Pacific and North America." In *Pacific Cooperation: Building Economic and Security Regimes in the Asia Pacific Region,* edited by Andrew Mack and John Ravenhill 40–65. Boulder, CO: Westview, 1995.
21 Barry Buzan. "The Post-Cold War Asia-Pacific Security Order – Conflict or Cooperation?" In *Pacific Cooperation: Building Economic and Security Regimes in the Asia-Pacific Region,* edited by Andrew Mack and John Ravenhill, 130–51. Boulder, CO: Westview Press, 1995.
22 See Lim in this volume.
23 In April 2016, Chinese and Russian defense ministers agreed to increase joint military exercises, the largest of which involves a joint Russia–Chinese naval drill in the South China Sea. This event (Joint Sea 2016), took place from September 12 to 19, following closely behind Chinese military exercises denounced by many countries in Asia after an international tribunal ruled against Chinese ownership claims of disputed areas.
24 Robert O. Keohane and Joseph S. Nye. *Power and Interdependence. Scott, Foresman/ Little, Brown Series in Political Science,* 2nd ed. Glenview, IL: Scott, Foresman, 1989.

Bibliography

14th Summit Conference of Heads of State or Government of the Non-Aligned Movement, Havana, Cuba, September 2006. http://cns.miis.edu/nam/documents/Official_Document/14NAMSummit-Havana-Compiled.pdf.

"17th Japan–ASEAN Summit Meeting, MOFA." http://www.mofa.go.jp/a_o/rp/page3e_000260.html.

Acharya, Amitav. "Don't Let Superpowers Run the Show: How Regional Institutions can Stabilize Southeast Asia." Interview by Claudia K. Huber and Priya Shankar. *Global Policy Journal,* March 1, 2013.

Acharya, Amitav, and Evelyn Goh, eds. *Reassessing Security Cooperation in the Asia-Pacific: Competition, Congruence, and Transformation.* Cambridge, MA: MIT, 2007.

"ADB Lowers Projection Over China Tensions." *Japan Times,* December 8, 2012.

ADB. *Asian Economic Monitor.* Asian Development Bank. March 2013. http://www.adb.org/publications/asian-economic-integration-monitor-march-2013 (accessed June 1, 2015).

"After Numerous Delays, Park to Visit US in October for Talks with Obama." *Korea Times,* August 12, 2015.

Aggarwal, Vinod K. "Comparing Regional Cooperation Efforts in the Asia-Pacific and North America." In *Pacific Cooperation: Building Economic and Security Regimes in the Asia Pacific Region,* edited by Andrew Mack and John Ravenhill, 40–65. Boulder, CO: Westview Press, 1995.

"AIIB, ADB Sign Memorandum to Co-Finance Projects." *AFP,* May 2, 2016.

Alagappa, Muthiah. "The Study of International Order." In *Asian Security Order,* edited by Muthiah Alagappa, 33–69. Stanford, CA: Stanford University Press, 2003.

Alesina, Alberto and David Dollar. "Who Gives Foreign Aid to Whom and Why?" *Journal of Economic Growth,* 5, no. 1 (2000): 33–63.

Alvarez, Kathrina Charmaine. "Duterte Warns Against Using Tribunal Ruling vs. China to 'Taunt or Flaunt'." *GMA News Online.* June 30, 2016. http://www.gmanetwork.com/news/story/571930/news/nation/duterte-warns-against-using-tribunal-ruling-vs-china-to-taunt-or-flaunt.

"America's Big Bet." *The Economist.* November 10, 2014. http://www.economist.com/news/special-report/21631797-america-needs-push-free-trade-pact-pacific-more-vigorously-americas-big-bet.

"An Asian Infrastructure Bank." *Economist,* October 4, 2013.

Anderlini, Jamil. "China Debt Tops 250% of National Income." *Financial Times.* July 21, 2014. http://www.ft.com/intl/cms/s/0/895604ac-10d8-11e4-812b-00144feabdc0.html (accessed July 23, 2014).

———. "Surprise China Devaluation Marks Escalation of Currency War." *Financial Times,* August 11, 2015. http://on.ft.com/1WeWi2K (accessed August 11, 2015).

Angell, Norman. *The Great Illusion, 1933*. New York: G.P. Putnam's sons, 1913. http://archive.org/details/cu31924014535888.

Arbis, Noelan. "Brunei's ASEAN Chairmanship Scorecard." *CogitAsia*. November 4, 2014. http://cogitasia.com/bruneis-asean-chairmanship-scorecard/.

Arrow, Kenneth Joseph. *Social Choice and Individual Values*, 2nd ed. New York: Wiley, 1963.

"The ASEAN Community: Unblocking the Roadblocks." *ASEAN Studies Centre*. Singapore: ISEAS Publishing, 2008.

"ASEAN Fails to Agree on East Asian Summit Plan." *Japan Economic Newswire*, November 27, 2004. LexisNexis.

"ASEAN Foreign Ministers' Statement on the Current Developments in the South China Sea." *ASEAN Secretariat Website*. May 10, 2014. http://www.asean.org/news/asean-statement-communiques/item/asean-foreign-ministers-statement-on-the-current-developments-in-the-south-china-sea.

ASEAN Regional Forum. *Concept Paper of ARF*. Jakarta: ASEAN Secretariat, 1995.

ASEAN. "Hanoi Plan of Action to Implement the ASEAN Regional Forum Vision Statement." Hanoi: ASEAN Secretariat, 2010.

ASEAN Regional Forum. *Preventive Diplomacy Work Plan*, 2010. http://aseanregionalforum.asean.org/files/Archive/18th/5th%20ARF%20EEPs,%20Dili,%2027-28Jan2011/Annex%2012%20-%20ARF%20Preventive%20Diplomacy%20Work%20Plan.pdf.

"ASEAN Welcomes China's New Maritime Silk Road Initiatives." *China Daily*. August 15, 2014. http://usa.chinadaily.com.cn/business/2014-08/15/content_18322921.htm.

"ASEAN+3 Foreign Ministers Meeting (Summary)." *Ministry of Foreign Affairs of Japan*. July 28, 2005. http://www.mofa.go.jp/region/asia-paci/asean/conference/asean3/summary0507.html.

"ASEM Member Brief 2014: Russian Federation." *Academia*. http://www.academia.edu/8544396/ASEM_Member_Brief_2014_Russian_Federation (accessed June 30, 2016).

Asian Development Bank. *Annual Report 2014*. Manila: Asian Development Bank, 2014. http://www.adb.org/sites/default/files/institutional-document/158032/oi-appendix1.pdf.

"Asian Sell-Off Accelerates on Weak China PMI." *Financial Times*, August 21, 2015. http://www.ft.com/fastft/2015/08/21/post-379741/ (accessed August 21, 2015).

Australia Department of Foreign Affairs and Trade. http://dfat.gov.au/trade/resources/trade-at-a-glance/pages/html/two-way-trading-partners.aspx.

"Australia to Sign Southeast Asian Non Aggression Pact." *AM*. ABC Local Radio. Sydney, NSW: 2BL, December 10, 2005.

Awai, Yasuo. "Chinese Yuan Coming Up in the World." *Nikkei Asian Review*, July 31, 2014. http://asia.nikkei.com/magazine/20140731-Enter-Alibaba/Markets/Chinese-yuan-coming-up-in-the-world (accessed January 15, 2015).

Axelrod, Robert, and Robert O. Keohane. "Achieving Cooperation Under Anarchy: Strategies and Institutions." In *Neorealism and Neoliberalism*, edited by David A. Baldwin, 85–115. New York: Columbia University Press, 1993.

Ba, Alice, "China–ASEAN Relations: The Significance of a China–ASEAN Free Trade Area." In *China Under Hu Jintao: Opportunities, Dangers and Dilemmas*, 311–48, edited by Tun-jen Cheng, Jacques deLisle, and Deborah Brown. London: World Scientific, 2006.

Baba, Yōzō. "*Reaāsu mondai no seiri*" [A Summary of the Rear Earth Issue]. *Kinzoku Shigen Repōto* [Metal Resources Report], September 2014, 71.

Bibliography 203

"Background Briefing on Obama Meetings at ASEAN, East Asia Summit." *U.S. Department of State*. November 19, 2011. http://iipdigital.usembassy.gov/st/english/texttrans/2011/11/20111119142035su0.1164907.html#axzz3OAEEsk5k.

Bader, Jeffrey A., *Obama and China's Rise: An Insider's Account of America's Asia Strategy*. Washington, DC: Brookings Institution Press, 2013.

———. "The U.S. and China's Nine-Dash Line: Ending the Ambiguity." Opinion, Brookings Institution, February 6, 2014.

Baldwin, David A. *Economic Statecraft*. Princeton, NJ: Princeton University Press, 1985.

Ball, Desmond. "Multilateral Security Cooperation in the Asia-Pacific Region." In *The Security Environment in the Asia-Pacific*, edited by Hung-mao and Tun-jen Cheng Tien, 129–53. Armonk: ME Sharpe, 2000.

Ball, Desmond, Anthony Milner, and Brendan Taylor. "Track 2 Security Dialogue in the Asia-Pacific: Reflections and Future Directions. *Asian Security*, 2, no. 3 (2006): 174–88.

Bank of England. "Announcement of Renminbi Clearing Bank in London." http://www.bankofengland.co.uk/publications/Pages/news/2014/091.aspx (accessed August 6, 2014).

Bateman, Sam. "India and Regional Maritime Security." In *India's Naval Strategy and Asian Security*, edited by Anit Mukherjee and C. Raja Mohan. Abingdon, Oxon: Routledge, 2016.

Bayly, Christopher, and Tim Harper. *Forgotten Wars: The End of Britain's Asian Empire*. London: Allen Lane, 2007.

Beeson, Mark. *Institutions of the Asia-Pacific: ASEAN, APEC, and Beyond*. London: Routledge, 2009.

Beeson, Mark. "Developmental States in East Asia: A Comparison of the Japanese and Chinese Experiences. *Asian Perspective*, 33, no. 2 (2009): 5–39.

"Beijing Faces up to its Monetary Trilemma." *Financial Times*, September 7, 2015. http://on.ft.com/1QkvIB2 (accessed May 10, 2016).

"Beijing Ready to Help Russia's Rattled Economy, Chinese Foreign Minister Says." *The South China Morning Post*. December 22, 2014. http://www.scmp.com/news/china/article/1667633/beijing-ready-help-russias-rattled-economy-chinese-foreign-minister-says.

Birkland, Thomas A. "Focusing Events, Mobilization, and Agenda Setting." *Journal of Public Policy*, 18, no. 1 (1998): 53–74.

Blackwill, Robert D. and Jennifer M. Harris. *War by Other Means: Geoeconomics and Statecraft*. Cambridge, MA: Belknap Press, 2016.

Blanchard, Jean-Marc F. "China's Grand Strategy and Money Muscle: The Potentialities and Pratfalls of China's Sovereign Wealth Fund and Renminbi Policies. *The Chinese Journal of International Politics*, 4, no. 1 (2011): 31–53.

Boltho, Andrea, and Maria Weber. "Did China Follow the East Asian Development Model? *The European Journal of Comparative Economics*, 6, no. 2 (2009): 267–86.

Bordachev, Timofey. "*Novaya Povestka dlya Rossii i Evrazii* [New Agenda for Russia and Eurasia]." *Izvestiya*, June 29, 2015. http://izvestia.ru/news/588257.

Bouchard, Christian. "Emergence of a New Political Era in the Indian Ocean: Characteristics, Issues and Limitations of the Indianoceanic Order". In *Geopolitical Orientations, Regionalism and Security in the Indian Ocean*, edited by Dennis Rumley and Sanjay Chaturvedi, 84–109. New Delhi: South Asian Publishers, 2004.

Bowring, Philip. "Taiwan's Reaction to Killing of Fisherman is out of Proportion." *South China Morning Post*, May 19, 2013.

Brant, Philippa. "Australia and the AIIB: A Lost Opportunity." *Lowy Interpreter*, October 31, 2014.

Brautigam, Deborah. "Aid with Chinese Characteristics: Chinese Foreign Aid and Development Finance meet the OECD-DAC Aid Regime." *Journal of International Development*, 23, no. 5 (2011): 752–64. DOI: 10.1002/jid.1798.

"Brunei to Sign on to Asian Infrastructure Investment Bank." *Brunei Times*, November 10, 2014.

Bryce, James. "The Relations of Political Science to History and to Practice: Presidential Address, Fifth Annual Meeting of the American Political Science Association." *The American Political Science Review*, 3, no. 1 (1909): 1–19. http://archive.org/details/jstor-1945905.

Buchanan, James M., and Gordon Tullock. *The Calculus of Consent, Logical Foundations of Constitutional Democracy*. Ann Arbor, MI: University of Michigan Press, 1962.

Bui, Truong Giang. "ASEAN and China Relations: Seeking for Economic Cooperation." In *Making New Partnership: A Rising China and Its Neighbors*, edited by Zhang Yunling, 153–76. UK: Paths International Ltd. And Beijing: Social Sciences Academic Press, 2011.

Busch, Marc L. "Overlapping Institutions, Forum Shopping, and Dispute Settlement in International Trade." *International Organization*, 61, Fall (2007): 735–61.

Bush, Richard C. *Uncharted Strait: The Future of China–Taiwan Relations*. Washington, DC: Brookings Institution Press, 2013.

Buzan, Barry. "The Post-Cold War Asia-Pacific Security Order – Conflict or Cooperation?" In *Pacific Cooperation: Building Economic and Security Regimes in the Asia-Pacific Region*, edited by Andrew Mack and John Ravenhill, 130–51. Boulder, CO: Westview Press, 1995.

———. *From International to World Society? English School Theory and the Social Structure of Globalisation*. Cambridge, UK: Cambridge University Press, 2004.

"Cabinet Decision on the Development Cooperation Charter." February 10, 2015. http://www.mofa.go.jp/files/000067701.pdf.

Cain, Peter. "Capitalism, War and Internationalism in the Thought of Richard Cobden." *British Journal of International Studies*, 5, no. 3 (1979): 229–47.

Calder, Kent E. "China and Japan's Simmering Rivalry." *Foreign Affairs*, 85, no. 2 (2006): 129–39.

Callahan, William A. *China: The Pessoptimist Nation*. Oxford: Oxford University Press, 2010.

———. *China Dreams: 20 Visions of the Future*. Oxford: Oxford University Press, 2013.

Callick, Rowan. "Brothers in Arms: China–Russia Exercise in South China Sea." *The Australian*. August 12, 2016.

Campbell, Kurt M. "U.S Foreign Policy in the Asia-Pacific Region". New York Foreign Press Center Briefing with Assistant Secretary for East Asia and Pacific Kurt M. Campbell. The New York Foreign Press Center. September 28, 2012. http://fpc.state.gov/198185.htm (accessed December 11, 2014).

Campi, Alicia. "Transforming Mongolia–Russia–China Relations: The Dushanbe Trilateral Summit." *The Asia-Pacific Journal*. November 10, 2014. http://www.japanfocus.org/-Alicia-Campi/4210/article.html.

Cao, Belinda, and Judy Chen. "China's Premier Wen 'Worried' on Safety of Treasuries." *Bloomberg*, 2009. http://www.bloomberg.com/apps/news?pid=email_en&sid=aXW9G UdIySss (accessed June 15, 2015).

Capannelli, Giovanni, Jong-Wha Lee, and Peter Petri. *Developing Indicators for Regional Economic Integration and Cooperation*. Asian Development Bank. 2009. http://www.adb.org/publications/developing-indicators-regional-economic-integration-and-cooperation (accessed June 1, 2015).

Carlsnaes, Walter. "Foreign Policy." In *Handbook of International Relations*, edited by Walter Carlsnaes, Thomas Risse, and Beth A. Simmons, 331–49. London: SAGE Publications, 2002.

Carr, Andrew. "Will a Turnbull Government Mean a New Foreign Policy for Australia?" *East Asia Forum,* November 3, 2015.

Cha, Victor. *Alignment Despite Antagonism: The United States–Korea–Japan Security Triangle.* Stanford, CA: Stanford University Press, 2000.

"Chairman's Press Release on the Asian Bond Markets Initiative." *Ministry of Finance Japan.* August 7, 2003. http://www.mof.go.jp/english/international_policy/convention/asean_plus_3/20030807_02.htm (accessed December 3, 2016).

"Chairman's Statement at the 11th ASEAN–India Summit." October 10, 2013. http://asean.org/wp-content/uploads/images/archive/23rdASEANSummit/chairmans%20statement%20asean-india.pdf (accessed December 3, 2016).

"Chairman's Statement at the 13th ASEAN–India Summit." November 21, 2015. http://asean.org/chairmans-statement-of-the-13th-asean-india-summit/.

"Chairman's Statement of the 10th East Asia Summit." ASEAN: November 22, 2015. http://asean.org/chairmans-statement-of-the-10th-east-asia-summit/.

"Chairman's Statement of the 17th ASEAN–Japan Summit. November 12, 2014, Nay Pyi Taw, Myanmar," 2. http://www.mofa.go.jp/files/000059372.pdf.

"Chairman's Statement of the 23rd ASEAN Regional Forum." July 2016. http://asean.org/storage/2016/07/Chairmans-Statement-of-the-23rd-ASEAN-Regional-Forum_FINAL.pdf.

"Chairman's Statement of the 8th East Asia Summit." October 10, 2013. http://www.asean.org/storage/images/archive/23rdASEANSummit/chairmans%20statement%20-%208th%20east%20asia%20summit%20-%20final.pdf のHTMLバージョンです。

Chairman's Statement on the PMC 10+1 Sessions, August 9–10, 2014. Nay Pyi Taw, Myanmar.

Chan, Gabrielle. "Australia Won't Join Asian Infrastructure Bank 'Until Rules Change'." *The Guardian,* October 31, 2014.

Chan, Thul Prak. "Hu Wants Cambodia Help on China Sea Dispute, Pledges Aid." *Reuters.* April 1, 2012. http://www.reuters.com/article/us-cambodia-china-idUSBRE82U04Y20120331.

Chang, Rachel. "Singapore, China Looking at Possible Third Projects." *Straits Times,* July 29, 2014.

Chang, Rich. "Strengthen Taiping Defense: Lawmakers." *Taipei Times,* May 3, 2012.

Chang-am, Ko (of the Korea Railway Association). "Asian Infrastructure Investment Bank and Korea's Position." *Korea Times,* August 4, 2014.

Chen, Ching-Chang. "The Weakest Link? Explaining Taiwan's Response to the US Rebalancing Strategy." In *United States Engagement in the Asia Pacific: Perspectives from Asia,* edited by Yoichiro Sato and See Seng Tan, 89–114. New York: Cambria Press, 2015.

Chen, Fielding, and Tom Orlik. "Something in Reserve? Assessing China's FX Buffer." *Bloomberg Intelligence,* May 10, 2016. http://www.bloomberg.com/professional/blog/something-in-reserve-assessing-chinas-fx-buffer/ (accessed June 1, 2016).

Chen, Michelle. "Yuan Suffers Biggest Weekly Loss as PBOC Punishes Speculators." *Reuters,* February 28, 2014. http://www.reuters.com/article/2014/02/28/us-markets-china-yuan-close-idUSBREA1R0FK20140228 (accessed January 16, 2015).

Cheng, Joseph. "The ASEAN–China Free Trade Area: Genesis and Implications." *Australian Journal of International Affairs,* 58, no. 2 (2004), 258.

Chin, Gregory and Richard Stubbs. "China, Regional Institution-building and the China–ASEAN Free Trade Area." *Review of International Political Economy*, 18, no. 3 (2011), 281.

"China Adding School to Outpost Island in Disputed Waters." *Taipei Times*, June 16, 2014.

"China has Done a Lot in Regional Economic Integration: Philippine Official." *Xinhua*, November 5, 2014.

"China Invites Korea to Join Asian Infrastructure Investment Bank." *Korea Herald*, July 3, 2014.

"The China–Philippine Banana War." *Asia Sentinel*. June 6, 2012. http://www.asiasentinel.com/society/the-china-philippine-banana-war/.

"China Says Abe No Longer Welcome after Yasukuni Visit." *Japan Times*, January 1, 2014.

"China Says Seeks Closer Military Ties with Syria." *Reuters*. August 16, 2016. http://www.reuters.com/article/us-mideast-crisis-syria-china-idUSKCN10R10R.

"China Starts Work on $50 bln Asia Infrastructure Bank." *Reuters*, March 7, 2014.

"China Travel Agencies Suspend Philippine Tours." *BBC*, May 10, 2012.

"China Warns on Sovereignty at Island Talks with Japan." *BBC*, September 25, 2012, http://www.bbc.com/news/world-asia-19709355 (accessed August 29, 2016).

"China's $50 Billion Asia Bank Snubs Japan, India." *Bloomberg*, May 12, 2014.

"China's Financial System: The Coming Debt Bust." *The Economist*, May 7, 2016. http://www.economist.com/news/leaders/21698240-it-question-when-not-if-real-trouble-will-hit-china-coming-debt-bust (accessed June 15, 2016).

"Chinese Activists Reach Senkaku." *BBC News*, March 24, 2004. http://news.bbc.co.uk/2/hi/asia-pacific/3563777.stm.

"Chinese Premier Advocates Peace, Economic Integration at East Asia Summit." *People's Daily Online*. November 14, 2014. http://en.people.cn/n/2014/1114/c90883-8808772.html.

"*Chugoku, Senkaku wa 'kakushin-teki rieki' to hajimete meigen* [The Senkakus, Referred to as China's 'Core Interests' for the First Time]." *Nihon Keizai Shimbun*, April 26, 2013.

"*Chugokujin sencho, shobun horyu de kaiho Naha chiken 'Nicchu kankei o koryo*' [Chinese Captain Released with Punishment Pending. Naha District Public Prosecutors Office: '[We] Take Japan–China Relations into Account']." *Kyodo*, September 25, 2010.

Chung, Chien-Peng. "China and Japan in 'ASEAN Plus' Multilateral Arrangements." *Asian Survey*, 53, no. 5 (2013): 801–24.

Clinton, Hillary. "America's Pacific Century." *Foreign Policy*. October 11, 2011. http://www.foreignpolicy.com/articles/2011/10/11/americas_pacific_century (accessed September 9, 2014).

———. "Remarks: Economic Statecraft." Economic Club of New York, New York City. October 14, 2011. http://www.state.gov/secretary/20092013clinton/rm/2011/10/175552.htm (accessed April 14, 2015).

Cohen, Ariel. "The Russia–China Friendship and Cooperation Treaty: A Strategic Shift in Eurasia?" *The Heritage Foundation*. July 18, 2001. www.heritage.org/research/reports/2001/07/the-russia-china-friendship-and-cooperation-treaty.

Cole, Michael J. "How Taiwan Bungled the Philippine Crisis." *The Diplomat*, May 21, 2013.

"Commentary of the Russian Ministry of Foreign Affairs in Connection with Foreign Minister Sergey Lavrov's Participation at the East Asia Summit." *Russian Ministry of Foreign Affairs*. October 8, 2013. http://mid.ru/bdomp/ns-rasia.nsf/3a0108443c964002432569e7004199c0/44257b100055e10444257bfe0043ae04!OpenDocument.

Comte, Auguste. *The Positive Philosophy of Auguste Comte*. Translated by Harriet Martineau. Vol. 1. 3 vols. London: George Bell, 1896. http://archive.org/details/positive philosop01comt.
Concord Energy. "Completion of Sale of 50% Interest in Fujairah Oil Terminals." January 2013. http://concordenergygroup.com/january-2013-completion-of-sale-of-50-interest-in-fujairah-oil-terminals/ (accessed October 14, 2013).
Cookson, Robert. "China Eases Corporate Rules on Renminbi." *Financial Times*, January 13, 2011. http://on.ft.com/1Jnd5eo (accessed June 1, 2016).
Coorey, Phillip. "Australia Offered Top Role in China's $57b Infrastructure Bank." *Australian Financial Review*, November 3, 2014.
Council for the Development of Cambodia (CDC). *The Cambodia Aid Effectiveness Report 2010*. Phnom Penh: The Cambodian Rehabilitation and Development Board of the CDC, Royal Government of Cambodia, 2010. http://www.cdc-crdb.gov.kh/cdc/third_cdcf/aer_2010_en.pdf.
———. "Investment Trend." 2016. http://www.cambodiainvestment.gov.kh/investment-enviroment/investment-trend.html.
Cunningham-Cross, Lindsey. "Narrating a Discipline: The Search for Innovation in Chinese International Relations." In *Chinese Politics and International Relations: Innovation and Invention*, edited by Nicola Horsburgh, Astrid Nordin, and Shaun Breslin. Warwick Studies in Globalisation. London: Routledge, 2014.
Daiss, Tim. "Move Over Saudi Arabia, Russia Is Selling More Oil To China Than You." *Forbes*. August 5, 2016. http://www.forbes.com/sites/timdaiss/2016/08/05/move-over-saudi-arabia-russia-is-selling-more-oil-to-china-than-you/print/.
"Dangerous Shoals." *The Economist*, January 19, 2013. http://www.economist.com/news/leaders/21569740-risks-clash-between-china-and-japan-are-risingand-consequences-could-be.
"Defense Ministry Rules Out Deploying Missiles in S. China Sea." *China Post*, May 4, 2012.
Dent, Christopher (ed.). *China, Japan, and Regional Leadership in East Asia*. Cheltenham: Edward Elgar, 2008.
———. *East Asian Regionalism*. Abingdon: Routledge, 2008.
Department of Defence. *Defence White Paper 2013*. Canberra: Commonwealth of Australia. http://www.defence.gov.au/whitepaper2013/docs/WP_2013_web.pdf (accessed September 10, 2014).
Department of National Defense (DND). "Philippines and Japan Ink Defence Cooperation Agreement." Manila: DND, 2015. http://www.dndph.org/2015-updates/philippines-and-japan-ink-defense-cooperation-agreement.
Depasupil, William. "Japan to Defend PH from China." *The Manila Times*, June 27, 2013. http://www.manilatimes.net/japan-to-defend-ph-from-china/13666/.
Dewey, John. "Austin's Theory of Sovereignty." *Political Science Quarterly*, 9 (1894): 31–52. http://archive.org/details/jstor-2139902.
Di, Dongsheng. "The Renminbi's Rise and Chinese Politics." In *The Power of Currencies and the Currency of Power*, edited by Alan Wheatley, 115–26. Abingdon: Routledge/IISS, 2013.
———. Personal Interview. Beijing, August 13, 2013.
Dillon, Michael. *China: A Modern History*. New paperback edition. London: I.B. Tauris, 2012.
"The Dodgiest Duo in the Suspect Six." *The Economist*, November 8, 2014. http://www.economist.com/news/finance-and-economics/21631134-emerging-economies-hit-hard-times-brazil-and-russia-look-particularly-weak (accessed August 21, 2015).

Donilon, Tom. "America is Back in the Pacific and will Uphold the Rules." *Financial Times.* November 27, 2011. http://www.ft.com/cms/s/0/4f3febac-1761-11e1-b00e-00144feabdc0.html#axzz11vbgzfyEc (accessed September 9, 2014).

Dou, Eva and Richard Paddock. "Behind Vietnam's Anti-China Riots, A Tinderbox of Wider Grievance." *The Wall Street Journal,* June 17, 2014.

Du Mei. "HISTORY – Chinese Academy of Social Sciences." *Chinese Academy of Social Sciences*, September 18, 2015. http://casseng.cssn.cn/about/about_history/.

"East Asia Summit: In the Shadow of Sharp Divisions." *People's Daily Online.* December 7, 2005. http://en.people.cn/200512/07/eng20051207_226350.html.

East Asia Vision Group. *Towards an East Asian Community: Region of Peace, Prosperity and Stability.* Ministry of Foreign Affairs of Japan, 2001. http://www.mofa.go.jp/region/asia-paci/report2001.pdf.

——. *Report of the East Asia Vision Group II.* Ministry of Foreign Affairs of the Kingdom of Thailand. 2013. http://www.mfa.go.th/asean/contents/files/asean-media-center-20130312-112418-758604.pdf.

Eichengreen, Barry J. *Exorbitant Privilege: The Rise and Fall of the Dollar and the Future of the International Monetary System.* New York: Oxford University Press, 2011.

——. "Number One Country, Number One Currency? *World Economy,* 36, no. 4 (2013): 363–74.

"The Eighth East Asia Summit." http://www.mofa.go.jp/mofaj/area/page3_000488.html.

Ek, Chanboreth and Hach Sok. "Aid Effectiveness in Cambodia." *Working Paper* 7. Washington, D.C.: Wolfensohn Center for Development at Brookings, 2008.

Elek, Andrew. "Welcoming China's Asian Infrastructure Investment Bank Initiative." *East Asia Forum.* September 21, 2014.

Elleman, Bruce A. *International Competition in China, 1899–1991: The Rise, Fall, and Eventual Success of the Open Door Policy.* Routledge Studies in the Modern History of Asia 106. New York: Routledge, 2015.

Elman, Colin. "Extending Offensive Realism: The Louisiana Purchase and America's Rise to Regional Hegemony." *American Political Science Review,* 98, no. 4 (2004): 563–76.

Emmers, Ralf. *The De-escalation of the Spratly Dispute in Sino-Southeast Asian Relations.* RSIS Working Paper No. 129 (2007), 1. http://www.rsis.edu.sg/wp-content/uploads/rsis-pubs/WP129.pdf.

——. *ASEAN and the Institutionalization of East Asia.* Routledge Security in Asia Pacific Series. New York: Routledge, 2012.

——. "ASEAN's Search for Neutrality in the South China Sea." *Asian Journal of Peacebuilding* 2, no. 1 (2014): 61–77.

Etxzler, Tomas. "Wrecks, Rats and Roaches: Standoff in the South China Sea." *CNN.com.* http://edition.cnn.com/interactive/2014/07/world/south-china-sea-dispute/.

"Exercise Force 18 Takes India's Act East Policy to the Next Level." *Rediff,* March 8, 2016. http://www.rediff.com/news/column/exercise-force-18-takes-indias-act-east-policy-to-the-next-level/20160308.htm.

Fackler, Martin. "Japan Said to Have Tentative Deal to Buy 3 Disputed Islands From Private Owners." *New York Times*, September 6, 2012.

——. "Japan Ends Decades-long Ban on Export of Weapons." *The New York Times.* April 1, 2014. http://www.nytimes.com/2014/04/02/world/asia/japan-ends-half-century-ban-on-weapons-exports.html?_r=1.

Fedorov, Gleb. "Interview with the the Eurasian Economic Union's Minister of Trade Veronika Nikishina." *RBTH.* August 8, 2016. http://rbth.com/business/2016/08/08/russian-automobiles-to-have-free-access-to-asean-via-vietnam-eaeu-minister_619053.

Fravel, M. Taylor. "China's Strategy in the South China Sea." *Contemporary Southeast Asia*, 33, no. 3 (2011): 292–319.

Fravel, M. Taylor, and Alastair Iain Johnston. "Chinese Signaling in the East China Sea?" *Washington Post*, April 12, 2014.

Fray, Keith. "China's Leap Forward: Overtaking the US as the World's Biggest Economy." *Financial Times*, October 8, 2014. http://blogs.ft.com/ftdata/2014/10/08/chinas-leap-forward-overtaking-the-us-as-worlds-biggest-economy/ (accessed January 12, 2015).

Furceri, Davide, and Annabelle Mourougane. *The Effect of Financial Crises on Potential Output: New Empirical Evidence from OECD Countries*. OECD Economics Department Working Paper No. 699. OECD, 2009. http://dx.doi.org/10.1787/224126122024 (accessed June 1, 2016).

Gabuev, Alexander. "Russia's Performance in Multilateral Organizations: Pivot to Asia or Just to China?" *Carnegie Moscow Center*. November 6, 2014. http://carnegie.ru/publications/?fa=57144.

"*Gaikōbu: Nihon no gōiihan ga kinchō wo maneita* [Foreign Ministry: Japan's Breach of Agreement Caused Tension]." *Record China*, June 5, 2013, http://j.people.com.cn/94474/8271617.html (accessed August 30, 2016).

Gettell, Raymond Garfield. *Introduction to Political Science*. Boston, MA: Ginn, 1910. http://archive.org/details/introductiontop00gett.

———. "Nature and Scope of Present Political Theory." *Proceedings of the American Political Science Association*, 10 (1913): 47–60. http://archive.org/details/jstor-3038416.

Gill, Bates and Tom Switzer. "The New Special Relationship." *Foreign Affairs*, February 19, 2015.

Glaser, Bonnie. "A Role for Taiwan in Promoting Peace in the South China Sea." Commentary, CSIS, April 15, 2014.

Glaser, Bonnie, and Jacqueline Vitello. "Taiwan's Marginalized Role in International Security: Paying a Price." Report of the Center for Strategic and International Studies (CSIS Freeman Chair in China Studies). Washington, DC: Center for Strategic and International Studies, 2015.

Glaser, Charles L. "Realists as Optimists: Cooperation as Self-help." *International Security*, 19, no. 3 (1994/95): 50–90.

———. "How Oil Influences U.S. National Security." *International Security*, 38, no. 2 (2013): 112–46.

Goertz, Gary. *Social Science Concepts: A User's Guide*. Princeton, NJ: Princeton University Press, 2005.

Goh, Evelyn. *The Struggle for Order: Hegemony, Hierarchy, and Transition in Post-Cold War East Asia*. Oxford: Oxford University Press, 2013.

Gold, Michael. "Taiwan Considers Permanent Armed Ships for Disputed South China Sea Island." *Reuters*, October 16, 2014.

Goldstein, Avery and Edward D. Mansfield (eds.) *The Nexus of Economics, Security, and International Relations in East Asia*. Stanford, CA: Stanford University Press, 2012.

Gomez, Jim. "Indonesia Scrambles to End ASEAN Rift Over Sea." Associated Press, July 18, 2012.

Government of India. *History and Evolution of Non-Alignment*. New Delhi: Ministry of External Affairs, 2012.

———. *Indian Ocean Rim Association for Regional Co-operation (IOR-ARC)*. New Delhi: Ministry of External Affairs, 2012. http://mea.gov.in/in-focus-article.htm?20707/Indian+Ocean+Rim+Association+for+Regional+Cooperation+IORARC.

———. *Presentation of Credentials by H.E. Mr. Suresh K. Reddy as Ambassador of India to ASEAN*. Press release. New Delhi: Ministry of External Affairs, 2015.

———. *About East Asia Summit*, February 2016. New Delhi: Ministry of External Affairs. http://mea.gov.in/aseanindia/about-eas.htm.

———. *ASEAN Regional Forum (ARF)*, May 2016. New Delhi: Ministry of External Affairs. https://www.mea.gov.in/Portal/ForeignRelation/ARF_May_2016.pdf.

"Govt Leaders Flinch at China Intimidation." *Daily Yomiuri*, September 26, 2010.

"Graphics: AIIB Voting Stakes." *Caixin Online*. July 3, 2015. http://english.caixin.com/2015-07-03/100825189.html.

Green, Michael J., and Andrew Shearer. "Defining U.S. Indian Ocean Strategy." *Washington Quarterly*, 35, no. 2 (2012), 175–89. http://csis.org/files/publication/twq12springgreenshearer.pdf (accessed September 9, 2014).

Grieco, Joseph M. "Anarchy and the Limits of Cooperation: A Realist Critique of the Newest Liberal Institutionalism." In *Neorealism and Neoliberalism: The Contemporary Debate*, edited by David A. Baldwin. New York: Columbia University Press, 1988.

Gu, Bin. "Mineral Export Restraints and Sustainable Development—Are Rare Earths Testing the WTO's Loopholes?" *Journal of International Economic Law* (2011): 1–42.

Gu, Xiaosong and Mingjian Li. "Beibu Gulf: Emerging Sub-regional Integration between China and ASEAN." S. Rajaratnam School of International Studies. *Working Paper* 168, 2009. Singapore: RSIS.

Gustafsson, Karl. "Routinised Recognition and Anxiety: Understanding the Deterioration in Sino-Japanese Relations." *Review of International Studies* (2016), doi:10.1017/S0260210515000546 (accessed September 6, 2016).

Haddick, Robert. "Salami Slicing in the South China Sea." *Foreign Policy*, August 3, 2012.

Haggard, Stephan. "Liberal Pessimism: International Relations Theory and the Emerging Powers." *Asia and Pacific Policy Studies*, 1, no. 1 (2014): 1–17.

Hagström, Linus. "'Power Shift' in East Asia? A Critical Reappraisal of Narratives on the Diaoyu/Senkaku Islands Incident in 2010." *The Chinese Journal of International Politics*, 5, no. 3 (2012): 267–97.

Hagström, Linus, and Björn Jerdén. "East Asia's Power Shift: The Flaws and Hazards of the Debate and How to Avoid Them." *Asian Perspective*, 38, no. 3 (2014): 337–62.

Hamada, Koichi, and Yasushi Okada. "Monetary and International Factors Behind Japan's Lost Decade." *Journal of the Japanese and International Economies*, 23, no. 2 (2009): 200–19.

Hammes, T. X. "Offshore Control is the Answer." *US Naval Institute*. December 2012. http://www.usni.org/magazines/proceedings/2012-12/offshore-control-answer.

Haokip, Thongkholal. "India's Look East Policy: Its Evolution and Approach." *South Asian Survey*, 18 (2011): 239–57.

Harding, Robin. "Japan Spooked by Naval Mystery in East China Sea." *The Financial Times*. June 22, 2016. http://www.ft.com/cms/s/0/5ada3fb4-3799-11e6-9a05-82a9b15a8ee7.html#axzz4EQ8VWU2S.

Hasenclever, Andreas, Peter Mayer, and Volker Rittberger. "Interests, Power, Knowledge: The Study of International Regimes." *Mershon International Studies Review*, 40, no. 2 (1996): 177–228.

Hayton, Bill. *The South China Sea: The Struggle for Power in Asia*. New Haven, CT: Yale University Press, 2014.

Hearn, Mark. "Australia Must Adjust to a Shifting Center of Gravity." *Sydney Morning Herald*, November 3, 2014.

Heng, Peakdey. "Chinese Investment and Aid in Cambodia: A Controversial Affair." *East Asia Forum*. July 16, 2013. http://www.eastasiaforum.org/2013/07/16/chinese-investment-and-aid-in-cambodia-a-controversial-affair/.

"Higashi ajia samitto, 12 gatsu 14 nichi, 16 kakoku de – ASEAN+3, gaishoukaigi de goui" ["East Asia Summit, December 14th, 16 participating countries – Agreement at ASEAN+3 Foreign Ministers' Meeting"]. *Nihon Keizai Shimbun*, July 28, 2005.

Higgott, Richard. "The Asian Economic Crisis: A Study in the Politics of Resentment." *New Political Economy*, 3, no. 3 (1998): 333–56.

Hideki, Nagayama. "*Fukuda shushō ga shazai wo mōshide?* [Did PM Fukuda Offer an Apology?]" *Taiwan wa nihon no seimeisen [Taiwan is the Lifeline of Japan]* (personal blog), June 21, 2008, http://mamoretaiwan.blog100.fc2.com/blog-entry-410.html (accessed August 29, 2016).

Hiroshima, Atsushi. "Abe Administration Seeks to Revise ODA Charter to Assist Militaries." *The Asahi Shimbun*, April 1, 2014. http://ajw.asahi.com/article/behind_news/politics/AJ201404010044.

Hirschman, Albert O. *National Power and the Structure of Foreign Trade*. Berkeley, CA: University of California Press, 1980.

Ho, Benjamin. "ASEAN's Centrality in Rising Asia." *RSIS Working Paper*, 249 (2012).

Hobbes, Thomas. *Leviathan*. University Press, 1904. http://archive.org/details/leviathan00hobbgoog.

Hodge, Amanda. "Kevin Rudd Heads Push for India to Join APEC." *The Australian*, September 3, 2015. http://www.theaustralian.com.au/business/kevin-rudd-heads-push-for-india-to-join-apec/news-story/b5ba9d0f5ca93ce9f8b40590b197aa47.

Hodgson, Geoffrey M. "What Are Institutions?" *Journal of Economic Issues*, XL, no. 1 (2006): 1–25. doi: 10.1080/00213624.2006.11506879.

Holbig, Heike, and Bruce Gilley. "Reclaiming Legitimacy in China. *Politics and Policy*, 38, no. 3 (2010): 395–422. http://dx.doi.org/10.1111/j.1747-1346.2010.00241.x.

Hollingworth, William. "Japan, China had Agreement to Maintain Senkaku Status Quo, Suzuki-Thatcher Files Show." *The Japan Times*, December 31, 2014. http://www.japantimes.co.jp/news/2014/12/31/national/history/japan-china-agreement-maintain-senkaku-status-quo-82-suzuki-thatcher-files/#.V8jbrFuLTcs (accessed July 20, 2016).

Hookway, James. "Philippines Warns China in Naval Crisis." *Wall Street Journal*, April 11, 2012.

Hooley, John. "Bringing Down the Great Wall? Global Implications of Capital Account Liberalisation in China." *Bank of England Quarterly Bulletin*, 53, no. 4 (2013): 304–15. http://www.bankofengland.co.uk/publications/Documents/quarterlybulletin/2013/qb1304prereleasechina.pdf (accessed August 29, 2016).

Hosokawa, Daisuke. "*Betonamu no keizai to anzen hosho* [Vietnam's Economy and Security]." *Kokusai Mondai*, 634 (2014): 25–36.

Hsiung, James C. "A Re-Appraisal of Abrahamic Values and Neorealist IR Theory: From a Confucian-Asian Perspective." In *China and International Relations: The Chinese View and the Contribution of Wang Gungwu*, edited by Zheng Yongnian, 17–41. China Policy Series. London: Routledge, 2010.

Hsu, Stacy. "Taiwan, Philippines Sign Fishing Treaty." *Taipei Times*, November 20, 2015.

"Hu Wants Cambodia Help on China Sea Dispute, Pledges Aid." *The Asahi Shimbun*, April 1, 2012. http://ajw.asahi.com/article/asia/china/AJ201204010010.

Huang Hua. *Huang Hua Memoirs*. Beijing: Foreign Languages Press, 2008.

Huang, Yasheng. *Capitalism with Chinese Characteristics*. New York: Cambridge University Press, 2008.

Huang, Yiping. "From Crisis to Crisis: Changing Capital Flows and Foreign Exchange Reserves in Asia." In *Asian Regionalism in the World Economy: Engine for Dynamism and Stability*, 279–308, edited by Masahiro Kawai, Jong-Wha Lee, and Peter A. Petri. Cheltenham, UK: Edward Elgar, 2010.

Huang, Yukon. "Beijing's Drive to Make the Renminbi a Global Currency is Misguided." *Financial Times*, August 26, 2015. http://on.ft.com/1fBzYyD (accessed August 26, 2015).

Hwang, Jaeho. "The ROK's China Policy Under Park Geun-hye." Washington, DC: The Brookings Institution, August 2014.

Ibrahim, Zuraidah and Kristin Kwok. "Beijing Rejects Hanoi's Legal Challenge on Spratly, Paracel Islands Disputes." *South China Morning Post*, December 12, 2014. http://www.scmp.com/news/china/article/1661364/china-rejects-vietnam-claims-arbitration-submission-over-south-china-sea.

Ikawa, Motomichi. "Reform of the International Monetary System Based on Special Drawing Rights and its Implications for Asia. *Pacific Economic Review*, 14, no. 5 (2009): 668–81. http://dx.doi.org/10.1111/j.1468-0106.2009.00481.x.

Ikenberry, G. John. *After Victory: Institutions, Strategic Restraint, and the Rebuilding of Order after Major Wars. Princeton Studies in International History and Politics.* Princeton, NJ: Princeton University Press, 2001.

"India Calls For Early Conclusion of South China Sea Code of Conduct." *Indian Express*, November 5, 2015. Available at: http://indianexpress.com/article/india/india-news-india/india-calls-for-early-conclusion-of-south-china-sea-code-of-conduct/.

"India for Strong International Legal Regime to Deal with Terrorism-Related Cases." *Indian Express*, July 25, 2016. Available at: http://indianexpress.com/article/india/india-news-india/india-for-strong-international-legal-regime-to-deal-with-terrorism-related-cases-2935245/.

"Indonesia Raises Questions About Planned East Asia Summit." *Deutsche Presse Agentur*, November 30, 2004. LexisNexis.

Information Office of the State Council of the People's Republic of China (PRC). *China's Foreign Aid*. Beijing, PRC: Information Office, 2014. http://english.gov.cn/archive/white_paper/2014/08/23/content_281474982986592.htm.

Inoguchi, Takashi, G. John Ikenberry, and Yoichiro Sato, editors. *The U.S.–Japan Security Alliance: Regional Multilateralism.* New York: Palgrave Macmillan, 2011.

Irrawaddy. "Burma–China Strategic Alliance Threatens ASEAN Unity." May 30, 2011. http://www2.irrawaddy.org/article.php?art_id=21390.

Ishikane, Kimihiro. "After the Closing of ASEAN Plus Three and East Asia Summit. A Report at the 48th Policy Plenary Meeting." December 19. Tokyo: The Council on East Asia Community, 2011.

Jafferlot, Christopher. "India's Look East Policy: An Asianist Strategy in Perspective." *India Review*, 2, no. 2 (2003): 35–68.

"Japan, China Clash over Senkaku." *BBC News*, January 16, 2004. http://news.bbc.co.uk/2/hi/asia-pacific/3402077.stm.

"Japan–China Joint Declaration on Building a Partnership of Friendship and Cooperation for Peace and Development." *Ministry of Foreign Affairs of Japan.* November 26, 1998. http://www.mofa.go.jp/region/asia-paci/china/visit98/joint.html.

"Japan, Philippines to Finalize New Military Aircraft Deal for Five TC-90s." *The Diplomat*, May 4, 2016.

"Japan Reluctant to Join China-led Investment Bank." *Japan Times,* July 5, 2014.

"Japan–Russia–US Trilateral Conference on the Security Challenges in Northeast Asia." Moscow: Institute of World Economy and International Relations. June 16, 2012. http://imemo.ru/en/conf/2012/19062012/19062012_statement_M_EN.pdf.

Jervis, Robert. "Hypotheses on Misperception." *World Politics,* 20, no. 3 (1968): 454–79.

———. "Realism, Neoliberalism, and Cooperation: Understanding the Debate." In *Progress in International Relations Theory: Appraising the Field*, edited by C. Elman and M. F. Elman, 277–310. Cambridge, MA: MIT Press, 2003.

Jiang Zemin. *Selected Works of Jiang Zemin, Vol. I*. Beijing: Foreign Languages Press, 2009. http://book.theorychina.org/upload/9912d625-487c-4b71-bc52-c514d6037af2/flipviewerxpress.html?pn=38.
Jiang, Yang. "Response and Responsibility: China in East Asian Financial Cooperation." *Pacific Review*, 23, no. 5 (2010): 603–23.
J. M. F., and L. P. "Crowning the Dragon." *The Economist*, April 30, 2014. http://www.economist.com/blogs/graphicdetail/2014/04/daily-chart-19.
Joachim, Jutta M. *Agenda Setting, the UN, and NGOs: Gender Violence and Reproductive Rights*. Washington, DC: Georgetown University Press, 2007. http://www.loc.gov/catdir/toc/ecip0711/2007007012.html.
Johnson, Chalmers. *MITI and the Japanese Miracle: The Growth of Industrial Policy*. Stanford, CA: Stanford University Press, 1982.
Johnston, Alastair Iain. "Cultural Realism and Strategy in Maoist China." In *The Culture of National Security: Norms and Identity in World Politics*, edited by Peter J. Katzenstein, 216–68. New York: Columbia University Press, 1996.
"Joining the Dashes." *The Economist*, October 4, 2014.
"Joint Communiqué of the 14th Meeting of the Foreign Ministers of the Russian Federation, the Republic of India and the People's Republic of China." Adopted in Moscow, April 18, 2016. Ministry of External Affairs, Government of India. http://mea.gov.in/bilateral-documents.htm?dtl/26628/Joint_Communiqu_of_the_14th_Meeting_of_the_Foreign_Ministers_of_the_Russian_Federation_the_Republic_of_India_and_the_Peoples_Republic_of_China.
"Joint Declaration by the Russian Federation and the People's Republic of China on the Coordination of the Construction of the Eurasian Economic Union and the Silk Road Economic Belt." *President of Russia Official Website*. May 8, 2015. http://kremlin.ru/supplement/4971.
"Joint Statement of the President of the Russian Federation and the President of the People's Republic of China on Collaboration in the Area of Development of Information Space." Adopted in Beijing, June 25, 2016. *President of Russia Official Website*. http://kremlin.ru/supplement/5099.
"Joint Statement of the President of the Russian Federation and the President of the People's Republic of China on Strengthening Global Strategic Stability." Adopted in Beijing, June 25, 2016. *President of Russia Official Website*. http://kremlin.ru/supplement/5098.
"Joint Statement of the Russian Federation and the People's Republic of China." Adopted in Beijing, June 25, 2016. *President of Russia Official Website*. http://kremlin.ru/supplement/5100.
"Joint Statement on East Asia Cooperation 28 November 1999." *Association of Southeast Asian Nations*. November 8, 1999. http://www.asean.org/news/item/joint-statement-on-east-asia-cooperation-28-november-1999.
Joyner, Christopher. "The Spratly Islands Dispute in the South China Sea: Problems, Policies, and Prospects for Diplomatic Accommodation." In *Investigating Confidence-building Measures in the Asia Pacific Region*, edited by Ranjit Singh. Washington, DC: Henry L. Stimson Center, 1999. http://www.stimson.org/images/uploads/research-pdfs/cbmapspratly.pdf.
"*Jyunshisen to yūgyosen, ryōsenchō shoruisōken* [The Papers of the Captains of the Patrol Ship and the Sport Fishing Ship Sent to the Prosecutor's Office]." *Asahi Shimbun*, June 15, 2008, 37.
Kaijyō Hoanchō [Japan Coast Guard]. *Heisei 10 nenban Kaijyō Hoan Hakusho [JCG White Paper 1998]*. Tokyo: Ōkurasho Insatsukyoku, 1998, II-1-I-1-(2). http://www.kaiho.mlit.go.jp/info/books/h10haku/2-1.htm (accessed August 20, 2016).

―――. *Heisei 11 nendoban Kaijyō Hoan Repōto [JCG White Paper 1999]*. Tokyo: Ōkurasho Insatsukyoku, 1999, 2-1-3. http://www.kaiho.mlit.go.jp/info/books/h11haku/1-1.htm (accessed August 21, 2016).

―――. *Heisei 9 nenban Kaijyō Hoan Hakusho [JCG White Paper 1997]*. Tokyo: Ōkurashō Insatsukyoku, 1997, II-1-I-1-(2). http://www.kaiho.mlit.go.jp/info/books/h9haku/2-1-1.htm (accessed August 20, 2016).

―――. *Kaijyō Hoan Repōto 2004 [JCG White Paper 2004]*. Tokyo: Kokuritsu Insatsukyoku, 1998, Topics 7. http://www.kaiho.mlit.go.jp/info/books/report2004/honpen/hp02010700.html (accessed August 21, 2016).

―――. *Kaijyō Hoan Repōto 2005 [JCG White Paper 2005]*. Tokyo: Kokuritsu Insatsukyoku, 1999, Tokushū 1-1-(1). http://www.kaiho.mlit.go.jp/info/books/report2005/tokushu/p018.html (accessed August 21, 2016).

Kan, Shirley A. "Taiwan: Major U.S. Arms Sales Since 1990." *CRS Report for Congress* RL 30957. August 29, 2014.

Kang, Jen-chun. "*Qiang kaizhan! Su Ching-chuan: Feilubin zhe xiao hunhun, sadao women toushang!* [Declare War! Su Ching-chuan: The Philippines is a Little Scoundrel Riding on Us!]" *NOWnews.com*, May 10, 2013.

Kant, Immanuel. *Perpetual Peace: A Philosophical Essay*. Translated by Mary Campbell Smith. London: G. Allen & Unwin, 1917. http://archive.org/details/perpetualpeaceph00kantuoft.

Kaplan, Robert D. *Monsoon: The Indian Ocean and the Future of American Power*. New York: Random House, 2010.

Karaganov, Sergey. "*Mezhdunarodny krizis: izbezhat' Afghanistana-2* [International Crisis: Avoiding a Second Afghanistan]." *Vedomosti*. July 28, 2014. www.vedomosti.ru/opinion/news/29501801/izbezhat-afganistana-2.

―――. "*Evroaziatskiy Vyhod iz Evropeyskogo Krizisa* [Euro-Asian Solution to the European Crisis]." *Russia in Global Affairs*. June 19, 2015. http://www.globalaffairs.ru/pubcol/Evroaziatskii-vykhod-iz-evropeiskogo-krizisa-17541.

Kashin, Vasily. "Vladimir Putin's Visit to China: No High Expectations, Concrete Results." *Russian International Affairs Council*. June 30, 2016. http://russiancouncil.ru/en/inner/?id_4=7852#top-content.

Kawamura, Noriyuki. "*Nicchu reisen wo ikani kaihi suruka* [How to Avoid a Cold War Between Japan and China]." *Diamond Online*, October 22, 2013. http://diamond.jp/articles/-/43305 (accessed August 7, 2016).

Keating, Paul J. "APEC's Sixth Leaders' Summit Meeting: Implications for the Strategic Architecture of the Asian Hemisphere (Speech to 1998 Pacific Rim Forum. Shanghai, September 22, 1998)." *Australian APEC Study Centre Issues Paper 14*. http://www.apec.org.au/docs/iss14.htm.

Keck, Zachary. "Malaysia to Establish Marine Corps and South China Sea Naval Base." *The Diplomat*. October 19, 2014. http://thediplomat.com/2013/10/malaysia-to-establish-marine-corps-and-south-china-sea-naval-base/.

Kelly, Paul. "Strategy Fears Sank China Deal." *Australian*, October 31, 2014.

Kelly, Tim and Nobuhiro Kubo. "Testing Beijing, Japan Eyes Growing Role in South China Sea Security." *Reuters*. March 10, 2015. http://www.reuters.com/article/2015/03/11/us-japan-southchinasea-idUSKBN0M62B920150311.

Keohane, Robert O. "The Demand for International Regimes." In *International Regimes*, edited by Stephen D. Krasner, 141–72. Ithaca, NY: Cornell University Press, 1983.

―――. *After Hegemony: Cooperation and Discord in the World Political Economy*. Princeton, NJ: Princeton University Press, 1984.

———. "International Institutions: Two Approaches." *International Studies Quarterly*, 32, no. 4 (1988): 379–96.
Keohane, Robert O., and Joseph S. Nye. *Power and Interdependence*. Scott, Foresman/ Little, Brown Series in Political Science. 2nd ed. Glenview, IL: Scott, Foresman, 1989.
Keohane, Robert O., and Lisa L. Martin. "The Promise of Institutionalist Theory." *International Security* 20, no. 1, Summer (1995): 39–51.
Kerry, John. "Remarks: U.S. Vision for Asia-Pacific Engagement". East-West Center, Honolulu, Hawaii. August 13, 2014. http://www.state.gov/secretary/remarks/2014/08/230597.htm (accessed September 15, 2014).
"Kerry Renews U.S. Pledge to Japan Security, Including East China Sea Islets." *Reuters*, April 27, 2015.
Kesavan, K. V. "The Role of Regional Institutions in India's Look East Policy." In *South and Southeast Asia, Responding to Changing Geo-Political and Security Challenges*, edited by K. V. Kesavan and Daljit Singh. New Delhi: K. W. Publishers, 2010.
Khalid, Nazery. "Sea of Common Destiny: Promoting Economic Cooperation in the South China Sea." Presented at International Workshop on Regional Responses to the Current Situation in the South China Sea. Haikou, Hainan, China, August 31, 2013. http://www.mima.gov.my/mima/wp-content/uploads/Haikou%20(31Aug13).pdf.
Kijvasun, Sarun and Suphanee Pootpisut. "Thailand to Help Launch Investment Bank for Asia." *The Nation (Thailand)*, July 17, 2014.
Kim, Taehwan. "Impassive to Imperial? Russia in Northeast Asia from Yeltsin to Putin." In *Northeast Asia: Ripe for Integration?* edited by Vinod K. Aggarwal, Min Gyo Koo, Seungjoo Lee, and Chung-in Moon, 179–212. New York: Springer, 2008.
King, Michael R. "Who Triggered the Asian Financial Crisis?" *Review of International Political Economy*, 8, no. 3 (2001): 438–66.
Kishimoto, Masato. *Nihon no Gaikōryoku [Japan's Diplomatic Capability]*. Tokyo: Mainichi Shimbun-sha, 2013.
Kitano, Naohiro and Yukinori Harada. "Estimating China's Foreign Aid 2001–2013." *Working Paper* No. 78, June 2014. Tokyo: Japan International Cooperation Agency (JICA) Research Institute (RI), 2014.
Koo, Min Gyo. *Island Disputes and Maritime Regime Building in East Asia: Between a Rock and a Hard Place*. Dordrecht: Springer, 2009.
Kotkin, Stephen. "The Unbalanced Triangle." *Foreign Affairs*, 88, no. 5 (September–October 2009): 130–8.
Krasner, Stephen D. *Sovereignty: Organized Hypocrisy*. Princeton, NJ: Princeton University Press, 1999.
"Kuala Lumpur Declaration on the East Asia Summit." *Ministry of Foreign Affairs of Japan*. December 14, 2005. http://www.mofa.go.jp/region/asia-paci/eas/joint0512.html.
Kuhrt, Natasha. "Russia and China: Strategic Partnership or Asymmetrical Dependence?" In *Russia and East Asia: Informal and Gradual Integration*, edited by Tsuneo Akaha and Anna Vassilieva, 91–107. New York: Routledge, 2014.
Kuik Cheng-Chwee. "Making Sense of Malaysia's China Policy: Asymmetry, Proximity, and Elite's Domestic Authority." *The Chinese Journal of International Politics*, 6 (2013): 462–3.
Kuo, Adam Tyrsett. "Taipei–Tokyo Fishery Pact a Good Start for Further Progress: Ma." *China Post*, April 23, 2013.
Kuok, Lynn. "Tides of Change: Taiwan's Evolving Position in the South China Sea and Why Other Actors Should Take Note." *East Asia Policy Paper*, 5 (The Brookings Institution), (May 2015): 8–9.

Kuik, Cheng-Chwee. "Making Sense of Malaysia's China Policy: Asymmetry, Proximity, and Elite's Domestic Authority." *The Chinese Journal of International Politics*, 6 (2013), 462–3.

Kurlantzick, Joshua. *Charm Offensive: How China's Soft Power is transforming the World.* New Haven, CT: Yale University Press, 2007.

Kynge, James, and Josh Noble. "China: Turning Away From the Dollar." *Financial Times*, December 9, 2014. http://www.ft.com/cms/s/0/4ee67336-7edf-11e4-b83e-00144feabdc0.html (accessed January 7, 2015).

Lam, Willy. "The Maoist Revival and the Conservative Turn in Chinese Politics. *China Perspectives,* no. 2 (2012): 5–15.

Lamont, James, and Geoff Dyer. "India to Help China Protect Oil Interests." *Financial Times.* February 18, 2010. http://find.galegroup.com/ftha/infomark.do?&source=gale&prodId=FTHA&userGroupName=apu&tabID=T003&docPage=article&docId=HS2307374650&type=multipage&contentSet=LTO&version=1.0 (accessed October 1, 2014).

Larano, Chris. "Obama Vows 'Ironclad' U.S. Defense of Philippines." *Wall Street Journal*, April 29, 2014.

Larkin, Stuart. "The Conflicted Role of the AIIB in Southeast Asia." *ISEAS Perspective,* 23, May 8 (2015).

Le, Hong Hiep, "Vietnam's Hedging Strategy against China since Normalization." *Contemporary Southeast Asia*, 35, no. 3 (2013), 345.

Leacock, Stephen. *Elements of Political Science.* Boston: Houghton, Mifflin, 1906. http://archive.org/details/elementspolitic00leacgoog.

Lee, John. "Reforms Will Decide Vietnam's Ability to Resist Economic Dominance by China." *ISEAS Perspectives*, no. 34. June 2, 2014. http://www.iseas.edu.sg/documents/publication/ISEAS_Perspective_2014_34-Reforms_Will_Decide_Vietnam's_Ability_to_Resist.pdf.

Lee, Youkyung. "AIIB Chief Says Door Open for America, Japan." *The China Post,* September 10, 2015.

Levine, Steven. "Perception and Ideology in Chinese Foreign Policy." In *Chinese Foreign Policy: Theory and Practice*, edited by Thomas W. Robinson and David Shambaugh, 30–46. Studies on Contemporary China. Oxford: Clarendon Press, 1998.

Levy, Marc A. "Is the Environment a National Security Issue?" *International Security,* 20, no. 2 (1995): 35–62.

Leyco, Chino. "PH Still Keen on AIIB—DOF." *Manila Times,* June 29, 2015.

Li, Mingjiang. "Possible Consequences of the Philippines' South China Sea Arbitration Case." Asian Maritime Transparency Initiative. https://amti.csis.org/possible-consequences-of-the-philippines-south-china-sea-arbitration-case/.

Li, Mingjiang and Dongmin Lee, eds. *China and East Asian Strategic Dynamics.* Lanham, MD: Lexington Books, 2011.

Li, Rex. *A Rising China and Security in East Asia: Identity Construction and Security Discourse.* Abingdon: Routledge, 2009.

Lieber, Francis. *Manual of Political Ethics.* Edited by Theodore Dwight Woolsey. Philadelphia, PA: J. B. Lippincott, 1911. http://archive.org/details/manualofpolitic01lieb.

Liu Wei. *China in the United Nations.* Hackensack, NJ: World Century, 2014.

Lo, Bobo. *Axis of Convenience: Moscow, Beijing, and the New Geopolitics.* Washington, DC: Brookings Institution, 2008.

Locke, John. *Two Treatises of Government*. London: Whitmore and Fenn and C. Brown, 1821. http://archive.org/details/twotreatisesofg00lockuoft.
Lowther, William. "US Tries to Avoid Taiwan in S China Sea Dispute." *Taipei Times*, December 18, 2013.
———. "Washington 'Disappointed' with Ma's Decision." *Taipei Times*, January 29, 2016.
———. "US Navy Aircraft Carrier, Escorts Arrive in South China Sea for 'Show of Force'." *Taipei Times*, March 6, 2016.
Lu Dingyi. *Education Must Be Combined with Productive Labour*. Peking: Foreign Languages Press, 1958, 3–4.
Lu, Jianren. "East Asia Summit: In the Shadow of Sharp Divisions." *People's Daily Online*. December 14, 2005. http://en.people.cn/200512/07/eng20051207_226350.html.
Lu Ning. *The Dynamics of Foreign-Policy Decisionmaking in China*. 2nd ed. Boulder, CO: Westview Press, 2000.
Luhilima, C. P. F. "Superimposition of China's 'Silk Road' and Indonesia's Maritime Fulcrum." *Jakarta Post,* December 13, 2014.
Lukin, Alexander. "The Russian Approach to China Under Gorbachev, Yeltsin, and Putin." In *Russian Strategic Thought Toward Asia*, edited by Gilbert Rozman, 139–65. New York: Palgrave Macmillan, 2006.
———. "Shanghaiskaya Organizatsiya Sotrudnichestva: v poiskah novoy roli [Shanghai Cooperation Organization: In Search of a New Role]." *Russia in Global Affairs*. July 9, 2015. http://www.globalaffairs.ru/valday/Shankhaiskaya-organizatciya-sotrudnichestva-v-poiskakh-novoi-roli-17573.
Luzyanin, Sergey et al. *Rossiysko-Kitayskiy Dialog: model' 2015 [Russia–China Dialogue: 2015 Model]*. Moscow: Russian International Affairs Council, 2015. http://russian council.ru/inner/?id_4=5614#top-content.
———. *Shanghaiskaya Organizatsiya Sotrudnichestva: model 2014–2015 [Shanghai Cooperation Organization: The Model for 2014–2015]*. Moscow: Russian International Affairs Council, 2015. http://russiancouncil.ru/paper21#top-content.
"Ma sōtō to nihon seifu ni rūto? [A Route Between Japan and President Ma?]" *Naruhodo za Taiwan, Narutai News*, June 23, 2008. http://www.naruhodo.com.tw/news/index.php?page_num=1302&key= (accessed: August 30, 2016).
Ma, Ying-jeou. "A Plan for Peace in the South China Sea." *Wall Street Journal*, June 12, 2015.
Magosaki, Ukeru, ed. *Kenshō Senkaku Mondai [Examination of the Senkaku Issue]*, 117–50. Tokyo: Iwanami-shoten, 2012.
Magosaki, Ukeru. *Shōsetsu Gaimushō [A Novel: Foreign Ministry]*. Tokyo: Gendai Shokan, 2014.
Magtulis, Prinz. "Phl to Participate in AIIB Crafting of By-Laws, Lending Rules." *Philippine Star,* September 7, 2015.
"Main Points of Speech by Deputy Minister of Defense of the Russian Federation Dr. Anatoly Antonov at the 14th Asia Security Summit 'The Shangri-La Dialogue' (Singapore, May 30, 2015)." *IISS*. http://www.iiss.org/en/events/shangri%20la% 20dialogue/archive/shangri-la-dialogue-2015-862b/special-sessions-315c/ antonov-da7d.
Manyin, Mark E., et al.. "Pivot to the Pacific? The Obama Administration's 'Rebalancing' Toward Asia." *CRS Report for Congress,* 28 March 2012.
Mao Tse-tung. *Selected Works of Mao Tse-Tung*. Vol. 1. 5 vols. Beijing: Foreign Languages Press, 1965 (295–309). http://archive.org/details/SelectedWorksOfMaoTse-tungVol.I.

"Marines Conduct a Drill on Spratly Islands: Lawmaker." *Central News Agency*, April 29, 2014.

Martin, Michael F. *The Asia-Pacific Economic Cooperation (APEC) Meetings in Vladivostok, Russia: Postscript.* Washington, DC: Congressional Research Service. November 19, 2012.

Maslow, Sebastian. "A Blueprint for a Strong Japan? Abe Shinzō and Japan's Evolving Security System." *Asian Survey*, 55, no. 4 (2015): 739–65.

Mastanduno, Michael. "Economics and Security in Statecraft and Scholarship." *International Organization*, 52, no. 4 (1998): 825–54.

——. "Economics Statecraft." In *Foreign Policy: Theories, Actors, Cases*, edited by S. Smith, A. Hadfield, and T. Dunne. Oxford: Oxford University Press, 2008.

Mauro, Paolo. "Why America Should Join the AIIB." *Project Syndicate*, June 12, 2015.

Mazza, Michael. "To Fix the South China Sea, Look to Taiwan." *The National Interest*, February 1, 2016.

McDevitt, Michael. "The South China Sea and U.S. Policy Options." *American Foreign Policy Interests*, 35 (2013): 175–87.

McKinlay, Robert D. and R. Little. "A Foreign Policy Model of U.S. Bilateral Aid Allocation." *World Politics*, 30, no. 1 (1977): 58–86.

McMillan, Susan M. "Interdependence and Conflict." *Mershon International Studies Review*, 41, no. 1 (1997): 33–58.

Mearsheimer, John J. "The False Promise of International Institutions." *International Security*, 19, no. 3, Winter (1994): 5–49.

——. *The Tragedy of Great Power Politics*. New York: Norton, 2001.

Medcalf, Rory. "The Indo-Pacific: What's in a Name?" *The American Interest*. October 10, 2013. http://www.the-american-interest.com/2013/10/10/the-indo-pacific-whats-in-a-name/ (accessed November 20, 2014).

"*Mentsu tsubusare ikari*' ['Angered for Being Disgraced']." *Sankei News*, September 28, 2012, http://sankei.jp.msn.com/world/news/120928/chn12092801060002-n1.htm (accessed November 17, 2012).

Michel, David and Russell Sticklor, eds. *Indian Ocean Rising: Maritime Security and Policy Challenges*. Washington, DC: Stimson, 2012. http://www.stimson.org/images/uploads/research-pdfs/Book_IOR_2.pdf (accessed September 12, 2014).

Midford, Paul. "Sino–Japanese Conflict and Reconciliation in the East China Sea." In *The China–Japan Border Dispute: Islands of Contention in Multidisciplinary Perspective*, edited by Tim F. Liao, Kimie Hara, and Krista Wiega, 177–97. Surrey: Ashgate, 2015.

Mikoyan, Anastas Ivanovich, and Zhou Enlai. "Memorandum of Conversation between Anastas Mikoyan and Zhou Enlai." February 1, 1949. APRF: F. 39, Op. 1, D. 39, Ll. 17–24. Reprinted in Andrei Ledovskii, Raisa Mirovitskaia, and Vladimir Miasnikov. *Sovetsko-Kitaiskie Otnosheniia*, Vol. 5, Book 2, 1946–February 1950. Moscow: Pamiatniki Istoricheskoi Mysli, 2005, pp. 43–8. Translated by Sergey Radchenko. History and Public Policy Program Digital Archive. http://digitalarchive.wilsoncenter.org/document/110003.

Ministry of Foreign Affairs of Japan. *Japan's Official Development Assistance White Paper 2006*. Tokyo: MOFA, 2006. http://www.mofa.go.jp/policy/oda/white/2006/ODA2006/html/honpen/index.htm.

——. *Situation of the Senkaku Islands*, April 4, 2014. http://www.mofa.go.jp/a_o/c_m1/senkaku/page1we_000010.html (accessed August 29, 2016).

———. *Senkaku Islands Q&A*, April 13, 2016. http://www.mofa.go.jp/region/asia-paci/senkaku/qa_1010.html (accessed August 29, 2016).

Ministry of Foreign Affairs of the People's Republic of China. "Wang Yi: Stick to 'Dual-track Approach' When Dealing with the South China Sea Issue." Ministry of Foreign Affairs of the People's Republic of China. June 24, 2015. http://www.fmprc.gov.cn/mfa_eng/zxxx_662805/t1384511.shtml.

Mintz, Alex. "How Do Leaders Make Decisions? A Polihueristic Perspective." *Journal of Conflict Resolution*, 48, no. 1 (2004): 3–13.

Mirski, Sean. "Stranglehold: The Context, Conduct and Consequences of an American Naval Blockade of China." *Journal of Strategic Studies*, 36, no. 3 (2013): 385–421.

Mitchell, Ronald B. "International Environmental Agreements: A Survey of Their Features, Formation, and Effects." *Annual Review of Environmental Resources*, 28 (2003): 429–61.

Mohan, C. Raja. *Samudra Manthan: Sino-Indian Rivalry in the Indo-Pacific*. Washington, DC: Carnegie Endowment for International Peace, 2012.

———. "India and ASEAN: Toward Maritime Security Cooperation." In *Enhancing India–ASEAN Connectivity*, edited by Ted Osius and C. Raja Mohan. Lanham, MD: Centre for Strategic and International Studies (CSIS), 2013.

———. "How India Can and Must Shape Asia's Future Political Order." *Observer Research Foundation*, March 2016.

———. "Making India a Leading Power." *Live Mint*, April 6, 2016. http://www.livemint.com/Opinion/Xiw11wTk3zMHLbUw80ayWP/Making-India-a-leading-power.html.

Morris, Scott and Mamoru Higashikokubaru. "Doing the Math on AIIB Governance." Center for Global Development, last modified July 2, 2015. http://www.cgdev.org/blog/doing-math-aiib-governance.

Morrison, Charles E. "Track 1/Track 2 Symbiosis in Asia-Pacific Regionalism." *Pacific Review*, 17, no. 4 (2004): 547–65.

Moss, Trefor. "China Says Philippines is Part of Trade Plan." *Wall Street Journal*, 14 November 14, 2014.

Mouawad, Jad. "United States Airlines Are Challenging Open-Skies Agreements." *The New York Times*. February 6, 2015. http://www.nytimes.com/2015/02/07/business/us-airlines-challenge-open-skies-agreements.html?action=click&contentCollection=Asia%20Pacific&region=Footer&module=MoreInSection&pgtype=article (accessed February 6, 2015).

Mu Chunshan. "What is CICA (and Why Does China Care About It)?" *The Diplomat*. May 17, 2014. http://thediplomat.com/2014/05/what-is-cica-and-why-does-china-care-about-it/.

Mueller, Dennis C. *Public Choice III*. Cambridge: Cambridge University Press, 2003.

Mukherjee, Anit. "ADMM Plus Talk Shop or Key to Asia Pacific Security." *The Diplomat*, August 22, 2013. Available at: http://thediplomat.com/2013/08/admm-plus-talk-shop-or-key-to-asia-pacific-security/1/.

Mullany, Gerry, and David Barboza. "Vietnam Squares Off With China in Disputed Seas." *New York Times*, May 7, 2014.

Mullen, Rani D. and Cody Poplin. "The New Great Game: A Battle for Access and Influence in the Indo-Pacific". *Foreign Affairs*. September 29, 2015. https://www.foreignaffairs.com/articles/china/2015-09-29/new-great-game (accessed August 25, 2016).

Mun, Chak. *India's Strategic Interests in Southeast Asia and Singapore*. New Delhi: Macmillan, 2009.

Muni, S. D. "East Asia Summit and India." *Institute of South Asian Studies*, Working Paper No. 13, 2006.
Muni, S. D., and See Chak Mun. "ASEAN–India Relations: Future Directions." *ISAS Special Reports* (2012): 1–17.
Muradov, Kirill. "Russia's Pivot to Eurasia and the Battle for Ukraine." *East Asia Forum*. September 17, 2013. http://www.eastasiaforum.org/2013/09/17/russias-pivot-to-eurasia-and-the-battle-for-ukraine/.
Naidu, G. V. C. "Whither the Look East Policy: India and Southeast Asia." *Strategic Analysis*, 28, 2 (2004): 331–46.
———. "India and the East Asian Summit." *Strategic Analysis*, 29, no. 4 (2005): 716.
Naikaku Kanbō [Cabinet Secretariat]. *Senkakushotō no shutoku ni kansuru kankei kakuryō mōshiawase [A Mutual Consent Among the Relevant Ministers on Acquisition of Senkaku Islands]*, Kaijyo Hoancho [Japan Coast Guard], September 10, 2012. www.kaiho.mlit.go.jp/info/kouhou/h24/k20120910/k120910-2.pdf.
Nanda, Prakash. *Rediscovering Asia: Evolution of India's Look East Policy*. New Delhi: Lancer Publishers, 2003.
Nanto, Dick K., James K. Jackson, Wayne M. Morrison, and Lawrence Kumins. *China and the CNOOC Bid for Unocal: Issues for Congress*. No. 24/10/07. Congressional Research Service. 2005. http://research.policyarchive.org/2571.pdf (accessed August 1, 2016).
National Economic and Development Authority (NEDA). *ODA Portfolio Review 2014*. Pasig City, Philippines: Monitoring and Evaluation Staff, NEDA, 2015.
National Institute for Defence Studies (NIDS). *East Asian Strategic Review 2014*, 144–5. Tokyo: NIDS, 2014.
Natsuda, Kaoru, and John Thoburn. "Industrial Policy and the Development of the Automotive Industry in Thailand." *Journal of the Asia Pacific Economy*, 18, no. 3 (2012): 413–37. http://dx.doi.org/10.1080/13547860.2012.742690 (accessed August 20, 2015).
Naughton, Barry. *The Chinese Economy: Transitions and Growth*. Cambridge, MA: MIT Press, 2007.
Network of East Asian Think Tanks. "Financing Infrastructure Connectivity in East Asia: Challenges and Solutions." Draft Report of NEAT Working Group on Connectivity Cooperation in East Asia, Beijing, China, June 2013.
Ng, Teddy. "China to Push for More Trade Pacts to Strengthen Global Economic Influence." *South China Morning Post*, December 19, 2013. http://www.scmp.com/news/china/article/1384923/china-push-regional-trade-pacts-despite-territorial-disputes-analysts (accessed December 19, 2013).
Nguyen, Hung Son. "ASEAN–Japan Strategic Partnership in Southeast Asia: Maritime Security and Cooperation." Tokyo: Japan Center for International Exchange, 2013. http://www.jcie.or.jp/books/abstracts/A/asean-japan-partnership.html.
Ni, Zhimin. "*Chōgyotō (Senkakushotō) ryōyūken mondai nikansuru chūnichikan no 'tanaagegōi' no shiteki keii* [Diaoyu Islands Historical Developments of the 'Shelving Agreement' Between China and Japan over the Diaoyu Island (Senkaku Islands) Territorial Dispute]." *Shakaikagaku Kenkyū Nenpo [Social Science Research Yearbook]*, 43 (2012): 83–94.
"*Nicchū kankei wo sogaisenuyō taisho*' [Responding so as not to Obstruct the Japan–China Relations]."*Asahi Shimbun*, March 25, 2004, http://www.asahi.com/special/senkaku/TKY200403250206.html (accessed August 17, 2016).
"*Nicchū ryōseifu, reiseina taiō wo kyōchō* [The Japanese and Chinese Governments Both Stress Calm Response]." *Asahi Shimbun*, March 24, 2004, http://www.asahi.com/special/senkaku/TKY200403240321.html (accessed July 25, 2016).

"Nichibei kyoudou yoron chousa." ["Japan–U.S. Joint Survey of Public Opinions"]. *Yomiuri Shimbun*. December 16, 2004. Tokyo ed.

Nihon Seinen-sha Sōhonbu [Nihon Seinen-sha Headquarters]. *Mainichi Shimbun-sha yori kaitō todoku! [Arrival of a Reply from the Mainichi Shimbun Corporation]*. March 9, 2002. http://www.seinensya.org/topic/mein/020309mainichi.htm (accessed August 19, 2016).

Nihon Seinen-sha ga torikumu Senkakushoto jikkōshihai [Effective Control Over the Senkaku Islands Attempted by Nihon Seinen-sha]. June 17, 2003. http://www.seinensya.org/undo/ryodo/senkakushoto/030616ayumi.htm (accessed August 19, 2016).

———. *Senkakushotō 25nen no ayumi [Steps Over 25 Years Regarding the Senkaku Islands]*. June 17, 2003. http://www.seinensya.org/ (accessed August 10, 2016).

———. *Senkakushotō Uotsurijimatodai Kokkaijyō madeno Keii to sonogono dōkō [The Developments Leading to the Ownership Transfer of the Lighthouse on Uotsuri Island to the Government and the Developments Thereafter]*. March 15, 2005. http://www.seinensya.org/ (accessed August 19, 2016).

———. *Senkaku shotō no rekishi gaiyō [A Historical Overview of the Senkaku Islands]*. April 26, 2007. http://www.seinensya.org (accessed August 28, 2016).

———. *Tokubetsukikaku: Nihon Seinen-sha no mokuteki to sono katsudō wo kataru zadankai (4) [Special Event: A Round-Table Talk on Nihon Seinen-sha's Objectives and Activities (4)]*, n.d. http://www.seinensya.org/series/zadankai_sp/04.html (accessed August 19, 2016).

North, Douglass C. *Institutions, Institutional Change and Economic Performance*. Cambridge: Cambridge University Press, 1990.

Note Verbale of the Permanent Mission of Malaysia to the United Nations to the Secretary General of the United Nations. 20 May, 2009. http://www.un.org/depts/los/clcs_new/submissions_files/mysvnm33_09/mys_re_chn_2009re_mys_vnm_e.pdf.

Nye, Joseph S. Jr. *Soft Power: The Means to Success in World Politics*. New York: Public Affairs, 2004.

Nye, Joseph, and Kevin Rudd. "How to Navigate the East China Sea Dispute Between Japan and China." *The Washington Post*, April 18, 2014. https://www.washingtonpost.com/opinions/how-to-navigate-the-east-china-sea-dispute-between-japan-and-china/2014/04/18/953731a8-c67b-11e3-9f37-7ce307c56815_story.html?utm_term=.037bda7b6af4 (accessed August 30, 2016).

Obama, Barack. "Remarks by President Obama to the Australian Parliament." November 17, 2011. http://www.whitehouse.gov/the-press-office/2011/11/17/remarks-president-obama-australian-parliament (accessed September 1, 2014).

Odell, John S. "The US and the Emergence of Flexible Exchange Rates: An Analysis of Foreign Policy Change." *International Organization*, 33, no. 01 (1979): 57–81.

OECD. *OECD Benchmark Definition of Foreign Direct Investment (4th ed.)*. OECD, 2008. http://www.oecd.org/document/33/0,3343,en_2649_33763_33742497_1_1_1_1,00.html (accessed March 12, 2012).

Office of the President, Republic of China (Taiwan). "Safeguarding Sovereignty, Shelving Disputes, Pursuing Peace and Reciprocity, and Promoting Joint Exploration and Development." September 1, 2014. http://english.president.gov.tw/Default.aspx?tabid=1124&itemid=33217&rmid=3048 (accessed May 7, 2016).

———. "President Ma's Remarks at International Press Conference Regarding Taiping Island in Nansha Islands." March 23, 2016. http://english.president.gov.tw/Default.aspx?tabid=491&itemid=36980&rmid=2355 (accessed May 7, 2016).

O'Hanlon, Michael. "A Six Point Plan to Solve the Senkaku Island Dispute." *The National Interest*, December 29, 2014, http://nationalinterest.org/feature/six-point-plan-solve-the-senkaku-island-dispute-11925 (accessed August 30, 2016).

Okada, Takashi. "*Kokuyūka to tanaage wa kinkō suruka?* [Will There be an Equilibrium Between Nationalization and Shelving?]" *Kaikyō Ryōganron [Discussions on Both Sides of Strait]*, 33, September 20, 2012. http://www.21ccs.jp/ryougan_okada/ryougan_35.html (accessed August 29, 2016).

Oros, Andrew. *Normalizing Japan: Politics, Identity, and the Evolution of Security Practice*. Stanford, CA: Stanford University Press, 2009.

Osiander, Andreas. "Rereading Early Twentieth-Century IR Theory: Idealism Revisited." *International Studies Quarterly*, 42, no. 3 (1998): 409–32.

——. "History and International Relations Theory." In *War, Peace, and World Orders in European History*, edited by Anja Hartmann and Beatrice Heuser, 14–24. The New International Relations. London: Routledge, 2001.

——. *Before the State: Systemic Political Change in the West from the Greeks to the French Revolution*. Oxford: Oxford University Press, 2007.

Page, Jeremy. "Deep Threat: China's Submarines Add Nuclear-Strike Capability, Altering Strategic Balance". *Wall Street Journal*. October 24, 2014. http://online.wsj.com/articles/chinas-submarine-fleet-adds-nuclear-strike-capability-altering-strategic-balance-undersea-1414164738 (accessed November 11, 2014).

——. "Taiwan Cultivates an Argument for China's Spratlys Claim." *Wall Street Journal*, March 23, 2016.

Pan, Chengxin. "The 'Indo-Pacific' and Geopolitical Anxieties About China's Rise in the Asian Regional Order." *Australian Journal of International Affairs*, 68, no. 4 (2014): 453–69. http://www.tandfonline.com/doi/pdf/10.1080/10357718.2014.884054 (accessed September 10, 2014).

Pan, Jason. "Itu Aba Military Outpost Not Under Threat by Vietnam: Defense Minister." *Taipei Times*, December 30, 2014.

Pan, Jason, and Tien-pin Lo. "Threat to Spratlys Outposts 'Growing.'" *Taipei Times*, December 26, 2014.

Pan, Jennifer, and Yiqing Xu. *China's Ideological Spectrum*. MIT Political Science Department Research Papers. Paper No. 2015-6. http://papers.ssrn.com/sol3/papers.cfm?abstract_id=2593377 (accessed August 1, 2016).

Panda, Ankit. "Is India's APEC Membership on the Table at This Year's Summit?" *The Diplomat*, September 8, 2015. Available at: http://thediplomat.com/2015/09/is-indias-apec-membership-on-the-table-at-this-years-summit/.

Panikkar, K. M. *The Future of South-East Asia, An Indian View*. New York: Macmillan, 1943.

Parameswaran, Prashanth. "Vietnam a Growing Threat to Taiwan's South China Sea Claims: Report." *The Diplomat*, December 31, 2014.

——. "Japan, Philippines to Finalize New Military Aircraft Deal for Five TC-90s." *The Diplomat*, May 4, 2016.

Park, Jinsoo. "Political Rivals and Regional Leaders: Dual Identities and Sino-Japanese Relations within East Asian Cooperation." *Chinese Journal of International Politics*, 6 (2013): 85–107.

The PCIJ Blog. "U.P. Study Finds North Rail Contract Illegal, Disadvantageous to Government." 2005. http://pcij.org/blog/2005/09/29/up-study-finds-north-rail-contract-illegal-diadvantageous-to-government.

People's Republic of China State Department Press Office. *Diaoyudao shi Zhongguo de guyou lingtu [Diaoyu Islands are China's Inherent Territory]*. 2012. http://www.scio.gov.cn/zfbps/ndhf/2012/Document/1225272/1225272.htm (accessed May 7, 2016).

Perkowski, Jack. "China's Debt: How Serious is it?" *Forbes*, January 21, 2014. http://www.forbes.com/sites/jackperkowski/2014/01/21/chinas-debt-how-serious-is-it/ (accessed September 12, 2015).

Perlez, Jane. "Australia to Join Regional Development Bank Led by China." *New York Times*, March 28, 2015.

Permanent Court of Arbitration. "In the Matter of the South China Sea Arbitration Before an Arbitral Tribunal Constituted Under Annex VII to the United Nations Convention on the Law of the Sea Between the Republic of the Philippines and the People's Republic of China: Award." *PCA Case N° 2013-19*, July 12, 2016.

Philippine Statistics Authority (PSA). *Foreign Trade*. Manila: PSA, 2014. http://www.nscb.gov.ph/secstat/d_trade.asp.

———. *Philippine Major Trading Partners: First Semester 2015*. 2016. https://psa.gov.ph/sites/default/files/attachments/itsd/specialrelease/TABLE%204%20%20Philippine%20Major%20Trading%20Partners%20%20First%20Semester%202015.pdf.

"Philippines Eyes 'Two-Track' Talks with China: Presidential Envoy Ramos." *The Straits Times*. August 13, 2013. http://www.straitstimes.com/asia/se-asia/philippines-eyes-two-track-talks-with-china-presidential-envoy-ramos.

"Philippines Gives Praise to China." *Xinhua*, November 7, 2014.

Pierson, Paul. *Politics in Time: History, Institutions, and Social Analysis*. Princeton, NJ: Princeton University Press, 2004.

Pitakdumrongkit, Kaewkamol, "Coordinating the South China Sea Issue: Thailand's Roles in The Code of Conduct Development." In *International Relations of the Asia-Pacific* (2015), 20. irap.oxfordjournals.org/content/early/2015/04/02/irap.lcv006.full.pdf+html.

"Plan of Action to Implement the Joint Declaration on ASEAN–China Strategic Partnership for Peace and Prosperity." *ASEAN Secretariat Website*. http://www.asean.org/news/item/plan-of-action-to-implement-the-joint-declaration-on-asean-china-strategic-partnership-for-peace-and-prosperity.

Pollack, Mark A. "Delegation, Agency, and Agenda Setting in the European Community." *International Organization*, 51, no. 1 (1997): 99–134.

Pomfret, John. "U.S. Takes a Tougher Tone with China." *Washington Post*, July 30, 2010.

"President Xi Addresses CICA Summit." *Xinhua News*. May 21, 2014. http://www.chinausfocus.com/china-news/president-xi-addresses-cica-summit.

"Press Conference by Foreign Minister Taro Aso." *Ministry of Foreign Affairs of Japan*. December 22, 2005. http://www.mofa.go.jp/announce/fm_press/2011/3/0304_01.html.

Public Television Service (Taiwan). "*Shen Ssu-Tsun baogao Tai Ri Guanxi hanwei zhuquan* [Shen Ssu-Tsun on Taiwan–Japan Relations, Defend Sovereignty]." September 13, 2012. https://tw.news.yahoo.com/沈斯淳報告台日關係-捍衛主權-120000258.html (accessed May 8, 2016).

Putin, Vladimir. "*Noviy Integratsionniy Proekt dlya Evrazii* [A New Integration Project for Eurasia]." *The Website of the Head of Government of Russia*. October 4, 2011. http://premier.gov.ru/events/news/16622/.

———. "Transcript of the Speech at the Plenary session of St Petersburg International Economic Forum." *President of Russia Official Website*. June 17, 2016. http://en.kremlin.ru/events/president/news/52178.

Ram, A. N. "India-ASEAN Relations: Evolving Convergences." In *India and South East Asia: Strategic Convergences in the Twenty First Century*, edited by T. Nirmala Devi and Adluri Subramanyam Raju. New Delhi: Manohar, 2012.

Rana, Pradumna B., and Chia Wai-Mun. "Strengthening Economic Linkages between South Asia and East Asia: The Case for a Second Round of 'Look East' Policies." *RSIS Working Paper* 253: 2013.

Rashid, Ahmed. "Viewpoint: Can China Bring Peace to Afghanistan?" *BBC News*. December 1, 2014. http://www.bbc.com/news/world-asia-30273431 (accessed December 14, 2014).

Reardon-Anderson, James. *Yenan and the Great Powers: The Origins of Chinese Communist Foreign Policy, 1944–1946*. Studies of the East Asian Institute, Columbia University. New York: Columbia University Press, 1980.

Reddy, Y. Yagama. "India and ASEAN: Towards an Integrated Regional Cooperation." In *India and South East Asia: Strategic Convergences in the Twenty First Century*, edited by T. Nirmala Devi and Adluri Subramanyam Raju. New Delhi: Manohar, 2012.

Reeves, Jeffrey. "China's Unraveling Engagement Strategy." *Washington Quarterly*, 36, no. 4 (2013): 139–49.

Reilly, James. "China's Economic Statecraft: Turning Wealth into Power." *Analysis*. Sydney, NSW: Lowy Institute for International Policy, November, 2013.

Reinsch, Paul Samuel. *World Politics at the End of the Nineteenth Century as Influenced by the Oriental Situation*. New York: The Macmillan Company, 1900. http://archive.org/details/worldpoliticsate01rein.

"Remarks of the Russian Foreign Minister Sergey Lavrov at the Fifth East Summit Meeting (Hanoi, Vietnam)." *Russian Ministry of Foreign Affairs*. October 30, 2010. http://www.mid.ru/bdomp/ns-rasia.nsf/3a0108443c964002432569e7004199c0/bfdfcb19ae127583c32577ce0039e051!OpenDocument.

"Remarks on the Developments on the Korean Peninsula and the Prospects for Re-launching of the Six-Party Talks." *Russian Ministry of Foreign Affairs*. February 4, 2011. http://www.mid.ru/bdomp/ns-rasia.nsf/3a0108443c964002432569e7004199c0/432569d80021985fc325782d0057a361!OpenDocument.

Republic of China Ministry of Foreign Affairs. "*Waijiao bu yanzheng chongshen Diaoyutai wei woguo guyou lingtu* [MOFA Solemnly Reaffirms Diaoyutai Islands as Our Country's Inherent Territory]." Press release, September 13, 2010.

——. "*Guanyu jinri Diaoyutai lie yu fujin haiyu dongtai, zhengfu chixu baochi gaodu guanzhu ji shiqie yinying* [Government Continues to Monitor Recent Situation in Waters near Diaoyutai Islands]." Press release, September 13, 2010.

——. "*Xinwen shuoming hui jiyao* [News Briefing Summary]." Taipei: Republic of China Ministry of Foreign Affairs, September 14, 2010.

——. "*Diaoyutai lie yu shi Zhonghua Minguo de guyou lingtu* [Diaoyutai Islands are the Republic of China's Inherent Territory]." 2012. http://www.mofa.gov.tw/News_Content.aspx?n=AA60A1A7FEC4086B&sms=66ECE8A8F0DB165D&s=26CF6ADBA824644B (accessed May 7, 2016).

——. "The Ministry of Foreign Affairs of the Republic of China (Taiwan) Reiterates its Position on the Huangyan Island and its Surrounding Waters." Press release, April 20, 2012.

——. "*Xinwen shuoming hui jiyao* [News Briefing Summary]." August 16, 2012.

——. "The Government of the Republic of China (Taiwan) Proposes the East China Sea Peace Initiative." August 5, 2012. http://www.mofa.gov.tw/News_Content.aspx?n=9FB1B5F1C76243EE&sms=20EB7F887746D351&s=4D897496805D198C (accessed May 7, 2016).

——. "*Zai Diaoyutai lieyu zhengduan, woguo bu yu Zhongguo dalu hezuo zhi lichang* [Why Our Country Does Not Cooperate with Mainland China over the Diaoyutai Islands Dispute]."

February 8, 2013. http://www.mofa.gov.tw/News_Content.aspx?n=AA60A1A7FEC4086B&sms=66ECE8A8F0DB165D&s=68C9A7761280E9E6 (accessed May 7, 2016).

———. "MOFA Expresses Grave Concern and Reiterates Government's Position Regarding Recent Maritime Confrontation near Shisha Islands." Press release, May 9, 2014.

Republic of the Philippines. "Notification and Statement of Claim on West Philippine Sea." No. 13-0211. January 22, 2013. http://docslide.us/documents/notification-and-statement-of-claim-on-west-philipphil-sea.html (accessed May 7, 2016).

"The Republic of the Philippines v. The People's Republic of China." *Permanent Court of Arbitration Website*. http://www.pca-cpa.org/showpage.asp?pag_id=1529.

"Remarks by Assistant Foreign Minister Liu Zhenmin at the Opening Ceremony of the Workshop on Implementing DOC: Maintaining Freedom and Safety of Navigation in the South China Sea." December 19, 2011. http://www.fmprc.gov.cn/mfa_eng/wjdt_665385/zyjh_665391/t888485.shtml.

"Resolution Adopted by Conference on Indonesia Held in New Delhi." *International Organization*, 3 (1949): 389–91.

Riker, William H. *The Art of Political Manipulation*. New Haven, CT: Yale University Press, 1986.

Riker, William H., Randall L. Calvert, John E. Mueller, and Rick K. Wilson. *The Strategy of Rhetoric: Campaigning for the American Constitution*. New Haven, CT: Yale University Press, 1996.

Robson, Seth. "US Military's Return to the Philippines Sparks Economic Hopes." *Stars and Stripes*. August 21, 2014. http://www.stripes.com/news/us-military-s-return-to-the-philippines-sparks-economic-hopes-1.298937.

Roochma, Malia. "Banking on Infrastructure (Opinion)." *Jakarta Post*, December 17, 2014.

Rosen, Mark E. "Fixing the Senkaku/Diaoyu Problem Once and For All." *The Diplomat*, December 19, 2014. http://thediplomat.com/2014/12/fixing-the-senkakudiaoyu-problem-once-and-for-all/ (accessed August 30, 2016).

Rousseau, Jean-Jacques. *The Social Contract and Discourses*. Translated by G. D. H. (George Douglas Howard) Cole. London: J.M. Dent & Sons, 1923. http://archive.org/details/therepublicofpla00rousuoft.

Rowley, Anthony. "China's Global Financing Goals Face Pushback from Development Banks." *Institutional Investor*, December 19, 2014.

"Russia May Seek China Help to Deal with Crisis." *The South China Morning Post*. December 18, 2014. http://www.scmp.com/business/banking-finance/article/1664567/russia-may-seek-china-help-deal-crisis.

"Russia, China Launch First Computer-Enabled Anti-Missile Exercises." *TASS*. May 26, 2016. http://tass.ru/en/defense/878407http://tass.ru/en/defense/878407.

"Russian–Chinese Joint Declaration on a Multipolar World and Formation of a New International Order." (Adopted in Moscow, April 23, 1997.) *Zakony Rossii*. www.law russia.ru/texts/legal_743/doc743a830x878.htm (accessed August 31, 2016).

Russel, Daniel, "Maritime Disputes in East Asia." *U.S. Department of State Website*. http://www.state.gov/p/eap/rls/rm/2014/02/221293.htm.

SAFE. "Official Reserve Assets." http://www.safe.gov.cn/wps/portal/english/Data (accessed September 1, 2016).

Saitō, Shinji. "*Senkakushotō Tōdai Kōbō Monogatari* [A Story of the Struggle Over the Lighthouses on the Senkaku Islands]." In *Wareware Nihonjin ga Senkaku wo Mamoru [We the Japanese Protect the Senkaku]*, edited by Kase Hideaki. Tokyo: Takagi Shobou, 2012, pp. 33–66.

Santos, Lean Alfred. "ADB Open to Asia Pacific Infrastructure Development Bank." *Development Newswire,* February 21, 2014. https://www.devex.com/news/adb-open-to-asia-pacific-infrastructure-development-bank-82902.

——. "Exclusive Details: China's Plans for a New Asian Infrastructure Investment Bank." *Development Newswire,* June 2, 2014. https://www.devex.com/news/adb-open-to-asia-pacific-infrastructure-development-bank-82902.

Saran, Shyam. "Mapping the Indo-Pacific". *The Indian Express,* October 29, 2011. http://archive.indianexpress.com/news/mapping-the-indopacific/867004/0 (accessed November 12, 2014).

Satake, Minoru. "Thailand, Other Holdouts Could Still Join AIIB This Year." *Nikkei Asian Review,* June 30, 2015.

Sato, Masaru. "*Gaimusō wa naze yarubeki shigoto wo shinainoka* [Why Doesn't Foreign Ministry do What it Should Do?]." *Gendai Business,* August 19, 2012. http://gendai.ismedia.jp/articles/-/33307 (accessed August 25, 2016).

Sato, Yoichiro. "The Senkaku Dispute and US–Japan Security Treaty." PacNet No. 57, *Pacific Forum CSIS,* September 10, 2012.

Sato, Yoichiro, and See Seng Tan, eds. *United States Engagement in the Asia Pacific: Perspectives from Asia.* New York: Cambria Press, 2015.

Sayle, Timothy Andrews. "Defining and Teaching Grand Strategy" 4, January (2011): 1–11.

Schaffner, Brian F., and Patrick J. Sellers. *Winning with Words : The Origins and Impact of Political Framing.* New York: Routledge, 2010.

Schattschneider, E.E. *The Semisovereign People: A Realist's View of Democracy in America.* Hinsdale, MA: Dryden Press, 1975.

Schmidt, Brian C. *The Political Discourse of Anarchy: A Disciplinary History of International Relations.* SUNY Series in Global Politics. Albany, NY: State University of New York Press, 1998.

"Scholars Call for Cross-Strait S. China Sea Cooperation." *Central News Agency (Taiwan),* June 20, 2013.

Scott, David. "India's Role in the South China Sea: Geopolitics and Geoeconomics in Play." *India Review,* 12, no. 2 (2013): 51–69.

"*Seifu senkaku seibi niwa tadachini ōjizu* [Government, Not Promptly Agreeing to Develop the Senkaku Islands]." *NHK,* September 1, 2012, http://www3.nhk.or.jp/news/html/20120901/k10014702731000.html (accessed November 20, 2012).

Sen, Rahul, Mukul G. Asher, and Rakishen S. Rajan, "ASEAN–India Economic Relations: Current Status and Future Prospects." *RIS Discussion Paper,* 73. New Delhi: Research and Information Systems for the Non Aligned and Other Developing Countries, 2004.

"*Sengoku kike! Inochigake taihogeki* [Listen, (Chief Cabinet Secretary) Sengoku, A Life-risking Arrest Operation]." *Zakzak,* November 19, 2010. http://web.archive.org/web/20101121225603/http://www.zakzak.co.jp/society/politics/news/20101119/plt1011191617006-n1.htm (accessed August 18, 2016).

"*Senkaku mondai no shinjitsu* (4/4) [The Truth of the Senkaku Issue]." *Record China,* March 6, 2015. http://www.recordchina.co.jp/a103430.html (accessed August 20, 2016).

"*Senkaku taiō 'gokuhi manyuaru* ['A Secret Manual' for Handing the Senkaku]." *AERA,* September 10, 2012, 10.

"*Senkaku' giron fukairi sezu* [Not Extensively Discussing 'the Senkaku']." *Asahi Shimbun,* October 2, 1972, 1.

"*Senkaku' ni tanai dantai ga todai* [A Political Group in Tokyo, a Lighthouse in 'Senkaku']." *Yomiuri Shimbun*, July 18, 1996, 2.

Severino, Rodolfo C. "East Asian Regionalism and India's Possible Role in it." New Delhi: K W Publishers, 2010.

Shalal, Andrea, and David Brunnstrom. "U.S. Navy Destroyer Nears Islands Built by China in South China Sea." *Reuters*, October 26, 2015.

Shambaugh, David L. "China's National Security Research Bureaucracy." *The China Quarterly*, 110 (1987): 276–304.

———. "International Relations Studies in China: History, Trends, and Prospects." *International Relations of the Asia-Pacific*, 11, no. 3 (September 1, 2011): 339–72. doi:10.1093/irap/lcr013.

Shambaugh, David L., and Wang Jisi. "Research on International Studies in the People's Republic of China." *PS* 17, no. 4 (1984): 758. doi:10.2307/418762.

Shao Binhong, ed. *The World in 2020 According to China: Chinese Foreign Policy Elites Discuss Emerging Trends in International Politics*. Vol. 2. China in the World : A Survey of Chinese Perspectives on International Politics and Economics. Leiden: Brill, 2014.

"*Sheping: Wei Taiwan de Nansha Taiping dao jun yan guzhang* [Editorial: Applaud Taiwan's Military Drill in Nansha's Taiping Island]." *Global Times*, September 3, 2012.

Sheridan, Greg. *The Partnership: The Inside Story of the US–Australian Alliance Under Howard and Bush*. Sydney: University of New South Wales, 2006.

Shih, Chih-yu. "Constituting Taiwanese Statehood: The World Timing of Un-Chinese Consciousness." *Journal of Contemporary China*, 16 (53) (2007): 699–716.

Shih, Chih-yu, ed. *Re-producing Chineseness in Southeast Asia: Scholarship and Identity in Comparative Perspectives*. London: Routledge, 2015.

Shih, Chih-yu, and Ching-Chang Chen. "How Can They Theorize? Strategic Insensitivity towards Nascent Chinese International Relations Thinking in Taiwan." In *Asian Thought on China's Changing International Relations*, edited by Niv Horesh and Emilian Kavalski, 205–9. Basingstoke: Palgrave Macmillan, 2014.

Shih, Hsiu-chuan. "Japan Stole the Diaoyutais, MOFA Says." *Taipei Times*, August 19, 2012.

———. "Taiwan, Japan Ink Fisheries Agreement." *Taipei Times*, April 11, 2013.

———. "S China Sea Claims in Line with Law: Ma." *Taipei Times*, May 28, 2015.

Shimoyachi, Nao. "Chinese Submarine Intrusion Considered an Act of Provocation." *The Japan Times,* November 13, 2004. http://www.japantimes.co.jp/news/2004/11/13/national/chinese-submarine-intrusion-considered-an-act-of-provocation.

"Silk Route to Bilateral Growth." *China Daily Asia*, September 19, 2014. http://www.chinadailyasia.com/asiaweekly/2014-09/19/content_15168301.html.

Sinopec Kantons Holdings. "Fujairah Oil Terminal FZC". 2013. http://www.sinopec.com.hk/en/getNewsDetailAction.do?target=GuandeNews&key=0CDEE9FE69E0EC4E69D7613CA42B9B4B (accessed October 12, 2014).

"The Sixth Japan–ASEAN Defence Vice-Ministerial Meeting." http://www.mod.go.jp/j/approach/exchange/dialogue/asia_tokyoseminar/06a.html.

Sneider, Daniel. "Soviets Hanker for Piece of Economic Action in the Pacific." *The Christian Science Monitor*. May 24, 1988. http://www.csmonitor.com/1988/0524/opac.html.

Snidal, Duncan. "Relative Gains and the Pattern of International Cooperation." *American Political Science Review*, 85, September (1991): 701–26.

Snyder, Jack L. "The Security Dilemma in Alliance Politics." *World Politics*, 36, no. 4, July (1984): 461–95.

Snyder, Scott, editor. *The US–South Korea Alliance: Meeting New Security Challenges.* Boulder, CO: Lynne Rienner, 2012.

Solingen, Etel. "East Asian Regional Institutions: Characteristics, Sources, Distinctiveness." In *Remapping East Asia: The Construction of a Region*, edited by T. J. Pempel, 31–53. New York: Cornell University Press, 2005.

Song Xinning, and Gerald Chan. "International Relations Theory in China." In *China's International Relations in the 21st Century Dynamics of Paradigm Shifts*, edited by Hu Weixing, Gerald Chan, and Daojiong Zha, 15–40. Lanham, MD: University Press of America, 2000.

Song, Yann-Huei. "Taiwan's Development Work on Taiping Island." *Asia Maritime Transparency Initiative*, February 18, 2015. http://amti.csis.org/taiwans-development-work-on-taiping-island/ (accessed May 7, 2016).

Spandler, Kilian. "The Political International Society: Change in Primary and Secondary Institutions." *Review of International Studies,* 41, no. 03 (2015): 601–22.

"Speech by Chinese President Xi Jinping to Indonesian Parliament, 2 October 2013, Jakarta, Indonesia." http://www.asean-china-center.org/english/2013-10/03/c_133062675.htm.

Spence, Jonathan D. *The Search for Modern China.* New York: Norton, 1990.

Srivastava, Shruti. "India Signs FTA in Services and Investments with ASEAN." *Indian Express,* September 9, 2014. Available at: http://indianexpress.com/article/business/business-others/india-signs-fta-in-services-investments-with-asean/.

Standish, Reid. "China and Russia Lay Foundation for Massive Economic Cooperation." *Foreign Policy.* July 10, 2015. http://foreignpolicy.com/2015/07/10/china-russia-sco-ufa-summit-putin-xi-jinping-eurasian-union-silk-road/.

Stanton, William A. "The U.S. Pivot to Asia and Taiwan's Role." World United Formosans for Independence. http://www.wufi.org.tw/the-u-s-pivot-to-asia-and-taiwans-role/ (accessed May 7, 2016).

"Statistics." *Laos Ministry of Planning and Investment Website.* http://www.investlaos.gov.la/index.php/resources/statistics.

Stein, Arthur R. "Governments, Economic Interdependence, and International Cooperation." In *Behavior, Society and International Conflict, vol. 3*, edited by P. Tetlock, et al., 241–324. New York: Oxford University Press, 1993.

Stockholm International Peace Research Institute. *SIPRI Yearbook 2015 Armaments, Disarmament and International Security.* Oxford: Oxford University Press, 2015, 384–5.

Storey, Ian. *Southeast Asia and the Rise of China: The Search for Security.* Abingdon, Oxon: Routledge, 2011.

———. "Japan Steps Up to the South China Sea Plate: Tokyo is Confronting Beijing and Increasing Defence Ties with ASEAN Members to Protect Maritime Trade." *Wall Street Journal* July 9, 2012. http://search.proquest.com/docview.1024132884/131979D7E21C.

———. "Japan's Maritime Security Interests in Southeast Asia and the South China Sea Dispute." *Political Science,* 65, no. 2 (2013): 135–56.

Storey, Ian and Cheng-Yi Lin, eds. *The South China Sea Dispute: Navigating Diplomatic and Strategic Tensions.* Singapore: ISEAS – Yusof Ishak Institute, 2016.

Stubbs, Richard. "ASEAN Plus Three: Emerging East Asian Regionalism?" *Asian Survey,* 42, no. 3 (2002): 440–55.

Subramanian, Arvind. *Eclipse: Living in the Shadow of China's Economic Dominance.* Washington, DC: Peterson Institute for International Economics, 2011.

Sumsky, Victor. "The Enlargement of the East Asia Summit: The Reasons and Implications of Bringing Russia in." In *ASEAN-Russia: Foundations and Future Prospects*, edited by Victor Sumsky, Mark Hong, and Amy Lugg, 70–9. Singapore: ISEAS Publications, 2012.
Yun Sun. "Myanmar's ASEAN Chairmanship." *Great Powers and the Changing Myanmar*, No. 4 (2014), 8. https://www.stimson.org/sites/default/files/file-attachments/Myanmar_Issue_Brief_4.pdf.
Sunohara, Tsuyoshi. *Antō Senkaku Kokuyūka* [*The Secret Strife behind the Senkaku Nationalization*]. Tokyo: Shinchō-sha, 2015.
Sutter, Robert. "China's Regional Strategy and Why it May Not Be Good for America." In *Power Shift: China and Asia's New Dynamics*, edited by David Shambaugh, 289–305. Berkeley, CA: University of California Press, 2006.
"*Taiwan chūnichi daihyō ga jii* [The Taiwan Representative in Japan Intends to Resign]." *Asahi Shimbun*, June 17, 2008, 8.
"*Taiwan jyunshisen ga 'ryōkai shinpan'* ['Territorial Incursion' by Taiwanese Patrol Ships]". *47NEWS*, July 28, 2005. http://www.47news.jp/CN/200507/CN200507 2801002551.html (accessed April 23, 2013).
"*Taiwan no chinbotsusen senchō ni nihongawa ga shazai* [The Japanese Side Apologizes to the Captain of the Sunken Taiwanese Ship]." *Asahi Shimbun*, June 21, 2008, 11.
"Taiwan Sends Equipment to Build S. China Sea Island Pier." *China Post*, June 18, 2014.
"Taiwan Won't Accept Court Ruling on Islands Disputes." *China Post*, February 18, 2016.
"*Taiwan, chinbotsu ni kōgi* [Taiwan, Protest Against Shipwreck]." *Asashi Shimbun*, June 13, 2008, 39.
"*Taiwan, nihon he taido kōka* [Taiwan Stiffened its Attitude toward Japan]." *Asahi Shimbun*, June 16, 2008, 4.
"*Taiwan: Gangao Bao-Diao renshì fangqi chuhai dasuan* [Taiwan: Hong Kong and Macao Bao-Diao Activists Gave up Plan to Board]." *BBC Zhongwen*, September 13, 2010.
"*Taiwansen, jyunshisen to shōtotsu* [A Taiwanese Ship, Collision with a Patrol Ship]." *Asahi Shimbun* (evening edition), June 10, 2008, 1.
Tanaka, Sakai. "*Nicchū tairitsu no sainen* [Resurfacing of the Japan–China Confrontation]." *Tanaka Sakai no kokusai nyūsu kaisetsu* [Tanaka Sakai's News Analyses], September 17, 2010. http://www.tanakanews.com/100917senkaku.htm (accessed July 31, 2016).
Teo, Eric Chu Cheow, "E. Asia Summit's Birthing Pains." *Straits Times*, February 22, 2005. LexisNexis.
Terada, Takashi. "Constructing an 'East Asian' Concept and Growing Regional Identity: From EAEC to ASEAN+3." *The Pacific Review*, 16, no. 2 (2003): 251–77.
Thayer, Carl. "'Speak Softly and Carry a Big Stick': What is Malaysia Playing At?" *The Diplomat*. February 28, 2014. http://thediplomat.com/2014/03/speak-softly-and-carry-a-big-stick-what-is-malaysia-playing-at/.
"The Holding of the First Japan–Philippines Dialogue on Maritime and Oceanic Affairs." September 9, 2011. http://www.mofa.go.jp/mofaj/press/release/23/9/0909_09.html.
Thul, Prak Chan. "Hu Wants Cambodia Help on China Sea Dispute, Pledges Aid." *Reuters*. April 1, 2012. http://www.reuters.com/article/us-cambodia-china-idUSBRE82U04Y20120331.
Tobin, Damian. "Renminbi Internationalisation: Precedents and Implications." *Journal of Chinese Economic and Business Studies*, 11, no. 2 (2013): 81–99. http://dx.doi.org/10.1080/14765284.2013.789677 (accessed April 12, 2014).
Tow, William, Mark Thomson, Yoshinobu Yamamoto, and Satu Limaye, editors. *Asia-Pacific Security: US, Australia and Japan and the New Security Triangle*. London: Routledge, 2007.

Trajano, Julius Cesar I. "Japan–Philippine Relations: New Dynamics in Strategic Partnership." *RSIS Commentaries*, 037 (2013). February 28, 2013. https://dr.ntu.edu.sg/bitstream/handle/10220/13333/RSIS0372013.pdf?sequence=1.

"Transcript of New York Times Interview With President Ma Ying-jeou of Taiwan." *New York Times*, October 31, 2014.

Trenin, Dmitri. *Russia and the Rise of Asia*. Moscow: Carnegie Moscow Center, November 2013.

———. "From Greater Europe to Greater Asia: The Sino–Russian Entente." *Carnegie Moscow Center*. April 9, 2015. http://carnegie.ru/publications/?fa=59728.

Trinidad, Dennis D. *China and Japan's Economic Cooperation with the Southeast Asian Region: The Foreign Aid of a Rising and a Mature Asian Power*. Tokyo: The Japan Institute of International Affairs (JIIA), 2013.

Twining, Daniel. "Daniel Twining's Testimony Before the House Ways and Means Committee's Trade Subcommittee About Indian Trade Protectionism." *German Marshall Fund of the United States*, March 13, 2013. Available at: http://www.gmfus.org/publications/daniel-twinings-testimony-house-ways-and-means-committee%E2%80%99s-trade-subcommittee-about.

UNIDO. *The Global Financial Crisis and the Developing World: Transmission Channels and Fall-Outs for Industrial Development*. Research and Statistics Branch Working Papers. United Nations Industrial Development Organization. June 2009. https://http://www.unido.org/fileadmin/user_media/Publications/RSF_DPR/WP062009_Ebook.pdf (accessed August 21, 2015).

United Nations Conference on Trade and Development. "Review of Maritime Transport 2013." *Report by the UNCTAD Secretariat*. UNCTAD/RMT/2013. 2013. http://unctad.org/en/PublicationsLibrary/rmt2013_en.pdf (accessed September 12, 2014).

"*Uotsurijima ni jyōriku, hinomaru kakagaru* [Landing on the Uotsuri Island, Hoisting the Hinomaru]." *Asahi Shimbun*, May 18 (1972) 23.

U.S. Energy Information Administration. "Analysis Brief: World Oil Transit Chokepoints." November 10, 2014. http://www.eia.gov/countries/analysisbriefs/World_Oil_Transit_Chokepoints/wotc.pdf (accessed December 1, 2014).

U.S. Department of State, Bureau of Oceans and International Environmental and Scientific Affairs. *Limits in the Seas No. 143; China: Maritime Claims in the South China Sea*, December 5, 2014. http://www.state.gov/documents/organization/234936.pdf (accessed May 7, 2016).

"US to Partially Lift Vietnam Arms Embargo." *BBC News*. October 2, 2014. http://www.bbc.com/news/world-us-canada-29469719.

"US–Philippine War Games Begin as China Warns US." *Taipei Times*, April 5, 2016.

"*Uyoku dantai reinen yori 2kagetsu hayaku Uotsurijima jyōriku keikaku* [A Right-Wing Group Plans Landing on Uotsuri Island 2 Months Earlier Than in the Past Years]."*Mainichi Shimbun*, March 6 (2002), 29.

Vannak, Chea. "China to Commit $500 Million Annually to Cambodia." *The Khmer Times*. November 10, 2014. http://www.khmertimeskh.com/news/6130/china-to-commit--500-million-annually-to-cambodia/.

Venzon, Cliff. "Philippines Gives China's Regional Bank Benefit of the Doubt." *Nikkei Asian Review*, December 11, 2014.

Vestergaard, Jakob and Robert H. Wade. "Out of the Woods: Gridlock in the IMF, and the World Bank Puts Multilateralism at Risk." Danish Institute of International Studies (DIIS) Report 2014:06.

"Vietnam Anti-China Protest: Factories Burnt." *BBC News*, May 14, 2014. http://www.bbc.com/news/world-asia-27403851.

Vietnam Ministry of Foreign Affairs. "Remarks by MOFA Spokesperson Le Hai Binh on the South China Sea Arbitration Case." December 11, 2014. http://www.vietnamembassy-seoul.org/en/vnemb.vn/tinkhac/ns141217145309 (accessed May 7, 2016).

"Vision and Actions on Jointly Building Silk Road Economic Belt and 21st-Century Maritime Silk Road." *National Development and Reform Commission (People's Republic of China).* March 28, 2015. http://en.ndrc.gov.cn/newsrelease/201503/t20150330_669367.html.

"Vision Statement, ASEAN India Commemorative Summit." December 20, 2012. Available at: http://en.vietnamplus.vn/vision-statement-of-aseanindia-commemorativesummit/41008.vnp.

Volz, Ulrich. "All Politics is Local: The Renminbi's Prospects as a Future Global Currency." In *Financial Statecraft of Emerging Powers*, edited by Leslie Armijo and Saori Katada, 103–37. Houndmills, Basingstoke: Palgrave Macmillan, 2014.

Vuving, Alexander. "Vietnam, the US and Japan in the South China Sea." *The Diplomat*, November 26, 2014, http://thediplomat.com/2014/11/vietnam-the-us-and-japan-in-the-south-china-sea/.

Wakatsuki, Hidekazu. "*Heiwayūkō jyōyaku teiketsu kōshō kara taichū enshakkan no kyōyo he* [From Negotiations of Conclusion of a Peace and Friendship Treaty to Provision of Yen Loans to China]." In *Nicchū Kankeishi 1972–2012, I. Seiji [History of the Japan–China Relations: 1972–2012, I. Politics]*, 99–132, edited by Takahara Akio and Hattori Ryuji. Tokyo: Tokyo Diagaku Shuppankai, 2012.

Waltz, Kenneth Neal. "Anarchic Orders and Balances of Power." In *Neorealism and Its Critics*, edited by Robert O. Keohane, 70–130. New York: Columbia University Press, 1986.

Wang, Chao-kun. "*Nanhai wenti Xia Liyan: Jue bu yu Dalu lianshou* [On South China Sea Issue, Hsia: Never Join Forces with the Mainland]." *Radio Taiwan International*, May 27, 2015.

Wang, Hongfei. "*Renminbi Guojihua de Xianzhuang, Yingxiang ji Weilai Huobi Zhengce Quxiang* [Status Quo and Impact of RMB Internationalisation, and Orientation of the Future Monetary Policy]. *Kexue Juece (Scientific Decision Making)*, 2 (2013): 56–70.

Wang, Yu-chung, and Hui-ping Chen. "*Nanhai yiti jiaofeng: Cai pan liaojie guanfang dangan* [South China Sea Issue Confrontation: Tsai Hopes to Understand Official Archives]." *Liberty Times* (Taiwan), March 31, 2016.

Wang, Zheng. "National Humiliation, History Education, and the Politics of Historical Memory: Patriotic Education Campaign in China." *International Studies Quarterly*, 52, no. 4 (2008): 783–806.

Weitz, Richard. "Why US Made Hanoi Move." *The Diplomat.* August 18, 2010. http://thediplomat.com/2010/08/why-us-made-hanoi-move/?allpages=yes.

Wendt, Alexander. *Social Theory of International Politics. Cambridge Studies in International Relations, 67.* Cambridge: Cambridge University Press, 1999.

Whaley, Floyd. "Charges Urged in Filipino Raid on Taiwanese Boat." *New York Times*, June 13, 2013.

Wheatley, Alan. "The Origins and Use of Currency Power." In *The Power of Currencies and the Currencies of Power*, edited by Alan Wheatley, 17–43. Abingdon: Routledge/IISS, 2013.

White, Hugh. *The China Choice: Why America Should Share Power.* Collingwood: Black, 2012.

———. "Power Shift." *Quarterly Essay*, 39, December 2010.

"Why PH is Not Yet Joining the China-Led Infra Bank." *Rappler.com*, June 15, 2015.

Wildau, Gabriel. "China Knocks on Door of Reserve Currency Club." *Financial Times*, May 5, 2015. http://on.ft.com/1GZv6N4 (accessed June 1, 2015).

———. "China to Allow Individuals to Buy Overseas Financial Assets." *Financial Times*, May 29, 2015. http://on.ft.com/1FGUwyM (accessed June 1, 2015).

Wildau, Gabriel, and Tom Mitchell. "China Spent $470bn to Maintain Confidence in Renminbi." *Financial Times*, June 13, 2016. http://on.ft.com/1WLepiV (accessed June 13, 2016).

Wilkins, Thomas. "Russo–Chinese Strategic Partnership: A New Form of Security Cooperation?" *Contemporary Security Policy*, 29, no. 2 (August 2008): 358–83.

Woo-Cumings, Meredith, ed. *The Developmental State*. Ithaca, NY: Cornell University Press, 1999.

Woolsey, Theodore Dwight. *Introduction to the Study of International Law, Designed as an Aid in Teaching, and in Historical Studies*. New York: Charles Scribner, 1864. http://archive.org/details/introductiontos02woolgoog.

World Bank. *GDP Ranking, PPP Based*. World Bank. 1 July 2015. http://data.worldbank.org/data-catalog/GDP-PPP-based-table (accessed August 21, 2015).

World Trade Organization. Committee on Trade and Development. "Participation of Developing Economies in the Global Trading System". *Note by the Secretariat*, WT/COMTD/W/201. October 14, 2013. https://docs.wto.org/dol2fe/Pages/FE_Search/FE_S_S006.aspx?Query=(%20@Symbol=%20wt/comtd/w/*%20and%20@Title=%20(participation%20and%20developing%20economies%20in%20the%20global%20trading%20system))&Language=ENGLISH&Context=FomerScriptedSearch&languageUIChanged=true# (accessed September 29, 2014).

———. "Participation of Developing Economies in the Global Trading System". *Note by the Secretariat*, WT/COMTD/W/201. October 14, 2013. https://docs.wto.org/dol2fe/Pages/FE_Search/FE_S_S006.aspx?Query=(%20@Symbol=%20wt/comtd/w/*%20and%20@Title=%20(participation%20and%20developing%20economies%20in%20the%20global%20trading%20system))&Language=ENGLISH&Context=FomerScriptedSearch&languageUIChanged=true# (accessed September 29, 2014).

———. "Trade Profiles: Cambodia." 2014. http://stat.wto.org/CountryProfile/WSDBCountryPFView.aspx?Language=E&Country=KH.

———. "Trade Profiles." http://stat.wto.org/CountryProfile/WSDBCountryPFHome.aspx?Language=E (accessed August 1, 2015).

Wu, Liming. "Commentary: Harassing East Asia Summit with Islands Disputes Was 11/21/c_131989588.htm.

Wu Shicun, *Solving Disputes for Regional Cooperation and Development in the South China Sea: A Chinese Perspective*. Oxford: Chandos Publishing, 2013.

Wu, Wendy. "AIIB and World Bank Reach Deal on Joint Projects, as China-Led Lender Prepares to Approve US$1.2 Billion of Funds This Year." *South China Morning Post*, April 14, 2016.

Xi Jinping. "Remarks at the Fourth Summit of the Conference on Interaction and Confidence Building Measures in Asia." *China Internet Information Center*. May 28, 2014. http://www.china.org.cn/world/2014-05/28/content_32511846.htm.

Xiao Ren. "Traditional Chinese Theory and Practice of Foreign Relations: A Reassessment." In *China and International Relations: The Chinese View and the Contribution of Wang Gungwu*, edited by Yongnian Zheng, 102–16. China Policy Series. London: Routledge, 2010.

Xinhua. "President Vows to Bring Benefits to People in Realizing 'Chinese Dream'." *Xinhua News*, March 3, 2013. http://news.xinhuanet.com/english/china/2013-03/17/c_132240052.htm (accessed January 8, 2015).

Xinhuanet. "'One Belt, One Road' Initiatives Key for Building a Safer Asia: Experts." September 25, 2014. Available from http://news.xinhuanet.com/english/china/2014-09/25/c_127030026.htm.

Xue, Litai. "The Role That US Plays in Asia." *China Daily.* November 24, 2011. http://www.chinadaily.com.cn/cndy/2011-11/24/content_14151382.htm.

Yahuda, Michael. "China's New Assertiveness in the South China Sea." *Journal of Contemporary China,* 22, no. 81 (2013): 446–59.

Yang Rui, Lesley Vidovich, and Jan Currie. "'Dancing in a Cage': Changing Autonomy in Chinese Higher Education." *Higher Education,* 54, no. 4 (August 28, 2007): 575–92. doi:10.1007/s10734-006-9009-5.

Yang, Wenchang. "My Views About 'Tao Guang Yang Hui'. *Waijiao Liqi [Foreign Affairs Journal],* 102, Winter (2011). http://cpifa.org/en/q/listQuarterlyArticle.do?articleId=214 (accessed December 18, 2014).

Yap, Karl Lester M. "Philippines' Domingo Says China May Become Biggest Export Market." *Bloomberg News.* October 7, 2013. http://www.bloomberg.com/news/2013-10-07/philippines-domingo-says-china-may-become-biggest-export-market.html.

Yardley, Jim. "In Soccer Loss, a Glimpse of China's Rising Ire at Japan." *The New York Times.* August 9, 2004. http://www.nytimes.com/2004/08/09/international/asia/09china.html.

Yee, Tan Hui. "South China Sea Dispute: Asean Voice Drowned Out as Big Powers Pipe Up." *The Straits Times.* July 29, 2016. http://www.straitstimes.com/asia/se-asia/asean-voice-drowned-out-as-big-powers-pipe-up.

Yeh, Joseph. "Tokyo's Fishery Talks Calls Show 'Good Will': Minister." *China Post,* September 15, 2012.

———. "Ma Taiping Visit Could Cause Tension: Former US Official." *China Post,* December 18, 2015.

Yoshida, Reiji. "Beijing Says Tech Glitch Led to Sub Intrusion." *The Japan Times.* November 17, 2004. http://www.japantimes.co.jp/news/2004/11/17/national/beijing-says-tech-glitch-led-to-sub-intrusion.

Yuan, Jingdong. "Emerging Maritime Rivalry in the South China Sea: Territorial Disputes, Sea-lane Security, and the Pursuit of Power." Paper prepared for the International Security Research and Outreach Programme, International Security and Intelligence Bureau, 2012.

Yu Du, Roger. "China Expands Asian Infrastructure Investment Bank Proposal." *Global Risk Insights,* July 13, 2014. http://globalriskinsights.com/2014/07/chinas-asian-infrastructure-investment-bank-throwing-carrots/.

Zakaria, Fareed. *The Post-American World.* New York: W. W. Norton, 2009.

Zhang Feng. "Rethinking the 'Tribute System': Broadening the Conceptual Horizon of Historical East Asian Politics." In *China and International Relations: The Chinese View and the Contribution of Wang Gungwu,* edited by Zheng Yongnian, 75–101. China Policy Series. London: Routledge, 2010.

Zhang, Tuosheng. "Disputes over Territories and Maritime Rights and Interests: Their Political Economic Implications." In *The Nexus of Economics, Security, and International Relations in East Asia,* edited by A. Goldstein and E. D. Mansfield, 120–143. Stanford, CA: Stanford University Press, 2012.

Zhao, Bo, and Xueyi Xu. "General Secretary Xi Jinping Meets with Taiwan Peaceful Reunification Groups." *Xinhuanet,* September 26, 2014. http://news.xinhuanet.com/politics/2014-09/26/c_1112641354.htm (accessed May 7, 2016).

Zhao, Hong. "China–Philippines Relations Stunted by the South China Sea Dispute." *ISEAS Perspectives*, No. 17 (2013). http://www.iseas.edu.sg/documents/publication/ISEAS%20Perspective%202013_17.pdf.

——. "The South China Sea Dispute and China–ASEAN Relations." *Asian Affairs*, 44, no. 1 (2013): 27–43.

Zhao, Xiaochuan. *Reform the International Monetary System.* People's Bank of China. March 23, 2009. http://www.pbc.gov.cn/publish/english/956/2009/20091229104425550619706/20091229104425550619706_.html (accessed January 15, 2015).

Zheng Yongnian, ed. *China and International Relations: The Chinese View and the Contribution of Wang Gungwu.* China Policy Series. London: Routledge, 2010.

Zhong, Yang. *Political Culture and Participation in Rural China.* London: Routledge, 2012.

Zhou Fangyin. "China's Rise, the Transformation of East Asian Regional Structure, and Development Direction of the East Asian Order." In *The World in 2020 According to China: Chinese Foreign Policy Elites Discuss Emerging Trends in International Politics*, edited by Shao Binhong, vol. 2: 157–82. China in the World : A Survey of Chinese Perspectives on International Politics and Economics. Leiden: Brill, 2014.

Index

Act East Policy 67–71
ASEAN Defense Ministers Meeting + (ADMM+) 69
ASEAN Regional Forum (ARF) 67–8
ASEAN+3 113–15
Asia-Europe Meeting (ASEM) 158
Asia-Pacific 1, 3, 6, 8, 146, 156–60
Asia-Pacific Economic Cooperation (APEC) 64, 71, 157–9
Asian Development Bank (ADB) 38–40
Asian Infrastructure Investment Bank (AIIB) 27–30, 39–40, 167
Association of Southeast Asian Nations (ASEAN) 7, 31–3, 64, 122–3, 144, 147–8

bilateralism 63

China 8, 11–12, 27, 46, 75, 93, 127, 144, 185
Chinese Communist Party (CCP) 13, 15, 20, 46–7
Code of Conduct (COC) in the South China Sea 134
commerce 181–3
currency: national currency 46, 48; international currency 48–50; renminbi reserve 54

debt 48–9, 54–5
developmentalism 47
dollar 48–9

East Asia 6–7
East Asia Summit (EAS) 69–70
East China Sea 38, 115, 130
economic relations 35–6, 151
economic statecraft 128

Eurasian continentalism 156, 164–6
Eurasian Economic Union 156
Eurasianism 156
Exclusive Economic Zone (EEZ) 96–7, 115, 136

financial system 48, 54

geopolitics 21–2, 27, 184
global economic crisis 52

heresthetics 5

India 59–72, 166
Indian Ocean 174–83
Indo-Pacific 177–80
Infrastructure 28–9, 31–5, 39–40
institutions (defined) 3
international currency 48–50
international relations (IR) 11–17
investment 28, 46, 53–4, 149–51

Japan 1, 38–40, 55, 93, 101–5, 115, 129–33

liberalization 54–5, 159, 186
Look East Policy 62–3, 66–8

maritime disputes 76–7, 83, 130
maritime security 68–9, 122, 128–9, 132–3, 146
Maritime Silk Road 33–4, 137–8
Mikhail Gorbachev 156
multilateral regional institutions 63
multilateralism 60, 72, 158
multinational development banks (MDBs) 27, 39

nation-building 47
national identity 47–9
neo-liberal institutionalist 4
new Development Cooperation Charter 131
Non-Aligned Movement 59

One Belt, One Road (OBOR) 28, 138
"One China" institution 76, 83, 136
open regionalism 117, 119, 138

People's Bank of China (PBOC) 49–51, 54
People's Republic of China (PRC) 12, 17, 22, 47, 75–6, 80–2, 93, 100
Permanent Court of Arbitration (PCA) 83, 146
Philippines 31–4, 123, 134, 136, 146
protests 77, 81–2, 96–8, 100, 116, 121–2

realism (realist) 19–20, 22, 83, 128, 153, 194, 197–9
regional cooperation 113, 117–18
regional institutions 38, 51, 60, 63–4, 156
regionalism 113–14, 117–18, 158–9
renminbi reserve 54
Russia 156, 160, 166

sea lines of communications (SLOCs) 127
security 7–8, 59–60, 68–9, 75, 84–5, 104–6, 130–31

security relationship 151
Senkaku/Diaoyutai Islands 75–9, 93–4, 96, 98, 101–2, 105
Shanghai Cooperation Organization 164
Silk Road Economic Belt 156, 166
Sino-Japanese relations 77, 123
Six-Party Talks (SPT) 158–9
South China Sea 75, 80–5, 122, 129–30, 134–8
South China Sea arbitration 76, 84
South Korea 34, 36–7, 188
Southeast Asia 127–38
Soviet Union 6, 62, 156
Spratly Islands 75, 80, 133
Strategy (strategic) 85–6, 124, 146, 151, 175

Taiping/Itu Aba 80, 82–3
Taiwan 76–85, 95–8, 101
territorial disputes 79, 81, 84, 122, 130, 134, 149
trade 6, 35–6, 46, 48–52, 66, 71, 119, 135–8, 150–51, 167, 175–8, 180–83

United States 6–8, 11, 13, 15, 30, 52, 93, 145–6, 151, 159, 188–9

Vladimir Putin 161

yen 52